# Nationalists,
# Cosmopolitans,
# and Popular Music
# in Zimbabwe

Thomas Turino

# Nationalists, Cosmopolitans, and Popular Music in Zimbabwe

THE UNIVERSITY OF CHICAGO PRESS

CHICAGO AND LONDON

Thomas Turino is professor of musicology and anthro-
pology at the University of Illinois at Urbana-Champaign.
He is the author of *Moving Away from Silence: The
Music of the Peruvian Altiplano and the Experience
of Urban Migration* (1993), also published by the
University of Chicago Press.

The University of Chicago Press, Chicago 60637
The University of Chicago Press, Ltd., London
© 2000 by The University of Chicago
All rights reserved. Published 2000
Printed in the United States of America
10  09  08  07  06  05  04  03  02  01      5  4  3  2  1

ISBN (cloth): 0-226-81701-6
ISBN (paper): 0-226-81702-4

Library of Congress Cataloging-in-Publication Data

Turino, Thomas.
    Nationalists, cosmopolitans, and popular music in
Zimbabwe / Thomas Turino.
        p.   cm.—(Chicago studies in ethnomusicology)
    Includes bibliographical references, discographies, and
index.
    ISBN 0-226-81701-6 (cloth)—ISBN 0-226-81702-4
(paper)
    1. Popular music—Zimbabwe—History and criticism.
2. Music—Social aspects—Zimbabwe.   I. Title.
II. Series.
ML3503.Z55 T87   2000
781.63'096891—dc21
                                                    00-008067

*This book is dedicated to my beautiful children,
Cristina and Matthew Turino,
who have so brightened my days.*

# Contents

Acknowledgments                                                                              ix

**Part One**  **Critical Foundations**
            Introduction                                                                     3
One         Social Identities and Indigenous Musical Practices                               31

**Part Two**  **Colonialism and the Rise of Urban Popular Music**
Two         Indigenous Music and Dance in Mbare
            Township, 1930–1960                                                              63
Three       The Settler-State and Indigenous Music during
            the Federation Years                                                             93
Four        The African Middle Class: Concerts, Cultural
            Discourse, and All That Jazz                                                     119

**Part Three**  **Musical Nationalism**
Five        Music, Emotion, and Cultural Nationalism,
            1958–1963                                                                        161
Six         Musical Nationalism and Chimurenga Songs
            of the 1970s                                                                     190

**Part Four**  **Guitar Bands and Cosmopolitan Youth Culture**
Seven       On the Margins of Nationalism: Acoustic Guitarists
            and Guitar Bands of the 1960s                                                    223
Eight       Stars of the Seventies: The Rise of Indigenous-Based
            Guitar Bands                                                                     262

**Part Five**  **Globalization Begins at Home**
Nine        Nationalism, Cosmopolitanism, and Popular Music
            after 1980                                                                       311
            Notes                                                                            355

References and Bibliography                      377

Discography                                     391

Index                                           393

A gallery of photographs follows page 158

# Acknowledgments

My fieldwork was conducted in Harare and northeastern Zimbabwe in the summer of 1991, from September 1992 to August 1993, and in the summer of 1996. The first and last trips were funded by University of Illinois Research Board, a Tinker Fellowship, and a University Scholar Award from the University of Illinois. The year-long stay was supported by a Fulbright Fellowship. Research assistance throughout the process of preparing this book was provided by the University of Illinois Research Board. I gratefully acknowledge this support and the wonderful help of my graduate assistants, Stephen Hill, Tammy Livingston, and Lise Waxer, who transcribed interviews, organized and indexed the data, and offered helpful criticism along the way.

Phil Bohlman, Veit Erlmann, Paul Berliner, and James Lea read the entire book in an earlier form and provided extremely detailed and helpful criticism. I lived with their commentaries while preparing this final draft and cannot thank them enough for their time, energy, and friendship. My ideas about nationalism and cosmopolitanism owe much to discussions with my colleagues Donna Buchanan, Charles Capwell, Bruno Nettl, and Isabel Wong at the University of Illinois. Joanna Bosse and Chris Scales read portions of an earlier draft and provided useful feedback. I am grateful to these and many other colleagues, students, and friends who continue to engage with the ideas presented here.

Jon Zilberg helped me get established on my first visit to Zimbabwe; the ease of my subsequent work there was aided by that smooth beginning. I would particularly like to thank my primary friends, teachers, and consultants in Zimbabwe whose ideas, experiences, and opinions fill the following pages: Chris Mhlanga, Tute Chigamba, Irene and Henry Chigamba; Chartwell Dutiro and the Blacks Unlimited; Mondrek Muchena; Patrick Nyandoro, Reason Muskwe, Mr. Shumba, Nicholas Kambiriri, and all the members of the Murehwa Jerusarema Club and Burial Society; Noah Mapfumo; Thomas Mapfumo; Joshua Dube Hlomayi, Jonah Mukona and the members of Shangara; Jonah Sithole; Kenneth Mattaka; Stephen Chifunyise; Jackson Phiri; Zexie and Stella Manatsa; Oliver M'tukudzi; I. Simango and sons; Mr. Mbofana; Steve Raskilly; Henry Maposa; George Natonga; Emmanuel Vori;

Piyo Murugweni; the Mudzimu Uripo Ngororombe Club; Dave Smith and Victor Tangweni of Music Express; Jacob Mhungu, Frank Gomba; the staff at the National Archives; and many others. Thank you for your graciousness, hospitality, and help.

# Part One

# Critical Foundations

# Introduction

"We moderns believe in a great cosmopolitan civilisation, one which shall include all the talents of all the absorbed peoples—"

"The Señor will forgive me," said the President. "May I ask the Señor how, under ordinary circumstances, he catches a wild horse?"

"I never catch a wild horse," replied Barker, with dignity.

"Precisely," said the other; "and there ends your absorption of the talents. That is what I complain of your cosmopolitanism. When you say you want all peoples to unite, you really mean that you want all peoples to unite to learn the tricks of your people. If the Bedouin Arab does not know how to read, some English missionary or schoolmaster must be sent to teach him to read, but no one ever says, 'This schoolmaster does not know how to ride on a camel; let us pay a Bedouin to teach him.' You say your civilisation will include all talents. Will it? Do you really mean to say that at the moment when the Esquimaux has learnt to vote for a County Council, you will have learnt to spear a walrus?

"I recur to the example I gave. In Nicaragua we had a way of catching wild horses—by lassoing the fore feet—which was supposed to be the best in South America. If you are going to include all the talents, go and do it. If not, permit me to say what I have always said, that something went from the world when Nicaragua was civilised."

—G. K. Chesterton, 1904[1]

Globalization begins at home. The question is, whose home? How many homes have to be involved with a computer, Michael Jackson, or an indigenous African instrument like the *mbira* before people begin to speak of them as "global?" How do people understand this term in relation to "the local?" Where is value placed? What ideological work does this terminology accomplish in the press, on the street, in the boardroom, and when elaborated and legitimated by academics? How is the conceptualization of the global and the local related to earlier descriptive categories such as "modern" and "traditional," "Western" and "non-Western?" What are the concrete conduits that bring localized, indigenous musics into national and transnational markets, and what happens to the music and musicians in the process?

3

The interaction of local cultural practices and "global" processes—
the dynamics of cultural heterogenization and homogenization (Appadurai 1996: 32; Erlmann 1993: 5)—have become central concerns in
ethnomusicology, anthropology, cultural studies, and other disciplines.
This book addresses these dynamics through a social and style history
of urban-popular music in Harare, Zimbabwe, from the 1930s to the
mid-1990s. It offers concrete case studies of how "cultural globalization" happens through colonialism, nationalism, and postcolonial state
policy.

In the chapters that follow, I trace the trajectories of black, middle-
class, "concert" performers who imitated the Mills Brothers, Carmen
Miranda, and Elvis (chapter 4), and itinerant acoustic guitarists playing
everything from Jimmie Rodgers to indigenous Shona music in bottleneck guitar style (chapter 7). I am particularly interested in the development of several urban-popular genres such as *jit* and "mbira-guitar"
music that are unique to Zimbabwe. As performed by Thomas Mapfumo, Stella Chiweshe, the Bhundu Boys, and others, these genres em-
body the processes of transnational-indigenous encounter, and for this
very reason became linked to Zimbabwean nationalism in the 1970s
and to transnational "worldbeat" markets in the 1980s (chapters 7–9).
I also follow the trajectory by which indigenous Shona music and dances
became organized and professionalized by the colonial and, later, black-
nationalist states for urban stage performance and, ultimately, for international consumption (chapters 2, 5, and 9). The processes of musical
nationalism receive special attention in chapters 5 and 6.

My main theoretical goal is to clarify the continuities and parallel
cultural effects of colonialism, nationalism, and cosmopolitanism—
three phenomena often understood in opposition to each other. The
Zimbabwe case suggests that the oppositions are, in important ways,
ephemeral and that the linkages underwrite the accelerated neocolonial
expansion of modernist-capitalist economics and ethics—what is eu-
phemistically referred to as "global culture." From the point of view of
people in Zimbabwe who maintain a different ethos, or people like myself who view capitalism as a negative force in relation to ecological and
social health, it is important to look at how globalization progresses at
the levels of values and lifeways. As a particularly direct medium of
value, identity, and social relations, music making provides a useful
window to the problem.

* * *

As recently as the mid-1950s, very few black Zimbabweans conceived of musical activities as a full-time professional career—as acoustic labor within the stream of market forces (Araujo 1992). For indigenous people, music and dance were aspects of participatory occasions that were part of sociability and spirituality itself (see chapter 1). As colonial subjects, people still thought of themselves primarily in terms of their specific communities, regions, and sometimes religious affiliations, or as 'African'[2] when interacting with white people; most had not yet considered the abstract possibility of belonging to a nation. While the radio constantly filled them in on happenings in London, Paris, and Washington, these names too were abstractions. Probably few Shona peasants seriously entertained the idea of ever visiting such places or thought of distant events there as having much bearing on their daily lives.

By 1995 things were quite different. Zimbabwe had been a nation-state for fifteen years; a broad spectrum of people were at least aware of the international ranking of the national football team, the impact of government subsidies, and the words 'national culture.' By the mid-1990s the ranks of full-time professional musicians and dancers had swelled considerably, and competition among them was, to quote a Zimbabwean arts administrator, "cutthroat." Although there was not enough work to support them at home, township and peasant youth dreamed of touring Europe, the United States, and Japan with their bands or dance groups. Professional aspirations brought them into direct relations with international markets, and thus aesthetics, in powerful new ways. Following on the heels of successful touring artists like Thomas Mapfumo, Stella Chiweshe, and the Bhundu Boys, or state-sponsored groups like the National Dance Company, foreign cities no longer seemed so distant and out of reach. In a country as small as Zimbabwe, many people knew, or knew somebody who knew, people who 'had gone out'; local, face-to-face contacts took on new significance as windows to transnational travel, experience, taste, and desires.

This is a familiar story which could be retold in many places throughout the postcolonial world, but it is no less dramatic for that. The Zimbabwean case is particularly striking both because of the historical proximity and the rapid pace of these processes. How *do* you get people who did not use money or think of music making as acoustic labor one hundred years ago to shape their aesthetics, music, and dance so as to compete more effectively in mass-national and transnational markets? Early in the colonial period the hut tax was a concrete device for forcing subsistence farmers into the wage labor system. What

complex of forces brings people to shape their musical styles and practices for cosmopolitan consumption?

Within the last fifty years, nationalism, musical professionalism,
and other cosmopolitan perspectives have been added to deep-seated,
radically different indigenous notions of self, of social relations and
identity, of subsistence, and of the meaning of artistic practice. For ever-
increasing numbers within the peasant majority and working class, this
represents nothing short of a cultural revolution, and like all revolu-
tions it must be born in and diffused to real neighborhoods and villages—at home.

## The Global and the Modern: Of Space and Time

In what follows, I reserve the term *global* to describe phenomena such
as the contemporary state system that literally or very nearly encom-
pass the totality of the earth. Other phenomena, such as a modernist-
capitalist ethos or the use of computers, may be widespread but have
not been incorporated by substantial portions of the populations even
in capitalist countries like Peru or Zimbabwe. In my terms it is inaccurate to describe such phenomena as global. More important, the totalizing character of the term is part of a discourse that contributes to the
*globalization* (processes that contribute to making something global) of
the phenomena it is used to describe.[3]

The contemporary language of globalism rhetorically and ideologi-
cally links a particular cultural aggregate (modernist capitalism) to the
totalized space of the globe, leaving people with alternative lifeways
no place to be and no place to go. I believe that this spatially based
discourse may well operate in a manner parallel to, and may ultimately have effects similar to, the totalizing, temporally based discourse
of modernity with its concomitant "traditional/modern" dichotomy
and central ideas of progress, rationalism, and objectification (Weber
1958). As the Comaroffs suggest, modernity is not an analytical category. Rather it is a continuation of evolutionary discourse that posits
European and American post-Enlightenment ethics and economics as
the apex of universal development through the rhetorical hijacking of
contemporary time; it is an "ideology-in-the-making" (Comaroff and
Comaroff 1993: xii).

Drawing on earlier social-evolutionist theory which defined the
"modern" industrialized countries (civilization) as the present and "traditional" societies (the savage and barbarian stages) as the past, the discourse of modernity defines *itself* as the all-encompassing present and

future, and all alternatives ("the traditional") as an outmoded past (Fabian 1983). The discourse of globalism operates from similar premises and, although using space rather than time, similarly argues for the naturalness of the modernist-capitalist formation by equating it with the all-encompassing space of the globe.

The Zimbabwean situation strongly suggests that the modern-traditional dichotomy, used and diffused by the white settlers as well as by members of the black middle class, had real cultural effects on the ground (chapters 4 and 5). Modernist ideology militated against the so-called traditional—that is, the various indigenous alternatives to modernity and capitalism—precisely by redundantly projecting them as a primitive past. I prefer not to use the discourse of globalism because I believe it may well have similar effects in the future. If we have learned anything from recent social theory, we should be able to begin to identify such dangers in our own terminology *before* we help legitimate and generalize a discourse that furthers the very processes we are seeking to critique.

## Cosmopolitanism

In place of the term *global,* which is often used in an unrestricted way nowadays, I use the term *cosmopolitan* to refer to objects, ideas, and cultural positions that are widely diffused throughout the world and yet are specific only to certain portions of the populations within given countries. My usage is based on a common meaning of the word, "of the world": to be cosmopolitan, given ideas and features must be widely diffused among *particular* social groups in dispersed locales. Cosmopolitanism is a specific *type* of cultural formation and constitution of habitus that is translocal in purview. Because cosmopolitanism involves practices, material technologies, and conceptual frameworks, however, it has to be realized in specific locations and in the lives of actual people. It is thus always localized (Robbins 1992), and will be shaped by and somewhat distinct in each locale. Cosmopolitan cultural formations are therefore always simultaneously local and translocal.

Cosmopolitan formations are largely like other cultural complexes in that they comprise aggregates of tendencies and resources for living and conceptualizing the world which are used variably by people engaged with that formation ("the culture group") to inform thought and practice. Cosmopolitanism, however, differs from other types of cultural formations in one important respect. Particular cosmopolitan lifeways, ideas, and technologies are not specific to a single or a few neighboring locales, but are situated in many sites which are not necessarily

in geographical proximity; rather, they are connected by different forms
of media, contact, and interchanges (what I call "cosmopolitan loops").
Most important, cosmopolitan groups are connected across space by a
similar constitution of habitus itself, which creates the foundation for
social communication, alliances, and competition.

At the same time, cosmopolitanism is different from other types of
transnational cultural formations, such as diasporas or overseas immigrant communities, because it lacks the specific grounding (actual or
symbolic) around a single homeland or place of origin. As they emerge
and mature, cosmopolitan cultural formations draw on and comprise
diffuse sources from an increasing number of local sites. This feature
is crucial to understanding the workings of cosmopolitanism. Local
branches of a given cosmopolitan formation will have their own distinct
features and unique slants because of specific conditions and histories
in particular locales.

Cosmopolitan cultural formations are composites of multiple sites
and their contributions. Yet cosmopolitan formations are also usually
more heavily influenced by certain particularly powerful sites—England and various European countries in the nineteenth century, the
United States, Japan, Russia, and China in the twentieth—through processes such as colonialism and neocolonial economic controls. Cosmopolitanism lacks the discourse of a center or of a "homeland," and in
fact is often linked with universalism, but it will have power centers
nonetheless (Brennan 1997).

## Cosmopolitanism and
## Socialization

Central to my use of the term, the concept of cosmopolitanism must
fully take into account the issue of *time* in relation to processes of socialization.[4] In colonial situations such as that of Zimbabwe, ideas and
cultural practices were initially imported from Europe and North America and were gradually taught to black Zimbabweans in mission schools
and in many other ways. In the initial stages of this process, these cultural features were indeed 'foreign' and 'European,' rather than being
cosmopolitan per se, in the black Zimbabwean context. Discussions of
westernization and colonialism have told us this much.

Within my framework, however, the major break comes when local
people deeply internalize foreign ideas and practices and make them
their own; that is, foreign dispositions become deeply constitutive of
local habitus. This was most common in Zimbabwe among people
socialized within particularly potent spheres of colonial influence—

among people living on mission station land or in African purchase areas as opposed to, say, peasants in non-missionized regions. It is crucial to understand that once thus socialized, such individuals are not simply imitating foreign activities and thinking foreign thoughts when they go ballroom dancing, take part in nationalist movements, or contemplate Jesus. Rather they are acting and thinking from their own cultural position—*this is part of who they are*. Meanwhile in various places, new choreographic accents and genres are added to ballroom dancing, new shades of meaning attached to Jesus, and new strategies added to nationalism. The key difference for the concept of cosmopolitanism is between imitation and internalization; the latter allows for internally generated cultural creativity, practices, and identities.

As a matter of course, people involved in this process socialize their own children, students, and neighbors from the basis of their own emerging cosmopolitan habitus. At this point they join with the colonizers in the creation of a locally generated branch of a translocal cultural complex. It is at this point that 'native' cosmopolitans begin to emerge as a distinctive cultural group in their own right, relative to other indigenous groups in the same locale. It is at this point that they begin to be more firmly connected to cosmopolitans elsewhere—through a similar habitus, social style and connections, communication styles, systems of knowledge, access to translocal communication technologies, and travel.

It is also at this point that binary conceptions of African/European, insider/outsider, and local/global identities need to be refined. Zimbabwean cosmopolitans are Africans and locals, but of a particular type. It is commonly local cosmopolitans in places like Zimbabwe who get the scholarships to study abroad, get government and NGO jobs, and who are relied on to represent other local groups to the "outside world," precisely because they have already become relatively socialized to that world. The formation of similar local, yet translocal, cultural groups, *from within the groups themselves,* both defines cosmopolitanism and explains its continuing expansion.

## Multiple Cosmopolitan Formations

As suggested by recent writers, cosmopolitanism is not uniform across different places, and it is not a unitary phenomenon. James Clifford's idea of discrepant cosmopolitanisms certainly points in this direction (1992). Different cosmopolitan formations of varied size and global influence and power may coexist, and many forces for cosmopolitanism have existed historically (e.g., Roman or Inca imperialism). Presently we might identify various cosmopolitan formations—the "modernist-capitalist," the "modernist-socialist," and the "fundamentalist-Islamic." Some ideas and practices may be shared across different cosmopolitan formations because of a similar translocal purview—what we might call general cosmopolitanism: the political validity of the nation-state, the use of money, industrial production.

Formations also differ in basic structural features that influence practice and belief. Katherine Verdery illustrates how the socialist system favors personal patronage networks for social advancement and power over the more direct forms of personal accumulation favored in the capitalist formation (1991). The idea that "music" can and should be objectified (on stage and in scores, recordings, and videos) to enhance value articulates with modernist-capitalist ethos in specific ways, whereas musical value may well be conceptualized according to different principles within fundamentalist Islamic circles (Nelson 1985). Certain features will pertain to cosmopolitanism in general (across formations), while others should be analyzed in relation to specific cosmopolitan cultural complexes.

Although modernist capitalism is currently the dominant cosmopolitan formation, it is analytically important to distinguish between the predominance of a particular, historically contingent, cosmopolitan complex and cosmopolitanism as a general type of phenomenon. For the Zimbabwean situation, we are most concerned with modernist-capitalist cosmopolitanism, but the modernist-socialist formation offered an important alternative for the Patriotic Front nationalists in the 1970s. Given the leadership's own cultural position, it is significant that they naturally turned to a 'modern' cosmopolitan alternative for strategy and ideology rather than to indigenous models or one of their own making (chapter 5). The conceptualization of distinct, coexisting, cosmopolitan formations is key for analyzing this and other conjunctures.

### Cosmopolitanism, Individualism, and Elites

The term *cosmopolitan* often carries connotations of elite status and sophistication. Although not necessarily so by definition, cosmopolitans generally have tended to be of the economic and/or educated elites of any given society or social group. Such was the case among black Zimbabweans during the colonial period. In that context, however, the connection is circular, since African class status was largely defined by the inculcation of cosmopolitan lifeways and perspectives according to the white colonialists' system of values, which in turn determined the limited avenues of advancement.

Extending this example theoretically beyond colonial situations, we might discover such circularity elsewhere. The general association of cosmopolitanism with sophistication and elite status—functioning cultural capital—is an idea diffused by cosmopolitans themselves (e.g., intellectuals, government officials), who frequently influence mainstream hierarchies of cultural value. Many cultural groups will define their lifeways and social styles as superior and as "natural," and will propagate these ideas, often unreflexively, when they have the power to do so. Cosmopolitans are no different. The proposed link between universalism and particular brands of cosmopolitanism (Anderson 1998) is part of the intellectual apparatus that functions to "universalize" or naturalize a particular cultural position in ways parallel to other universalizing terminology such as "modern" and "global" (Brennan 1997).

The universalist and individualist notions commonly associated with the concept of cosmopolitanism—"citizen of the world" or "member of an undifferentiated humanity"—places it in opposition to specific local and national identities. This fails to recognize that given locations will include other like-minded individuals who will be drawn to each other because of, and will raise their children with, a similar cultural orientation (e.g., see Cheah 1998; Appiah 1998; Anderson 1998). Such is the basis of all local identity-group formation; cosmopolitans are no different. Cosmopolitan groups differ from other local groups, however, in the degree of translocal features that constitute the habitus, and thus they are more firmly linked to other similar groups elsewhere. These linkages often provide a basis of social power in given locales (e.g., connections with NGOs and other international granting agencies).

The universalist idea that cosmopolitans individualistically supersede actual local or national identities and affiliations is, in my view, an inaccurate part of their ideology about themselves. Throughout this study we will see that in Zimbabwe, cosmopolitanism became a central basis for a corporate, black, middle-class identity and for nationalism itself. Moreover, shared cosmopolitan habitus facilitated alliances between members of this class and white liberals, missionaries, foreign government and NGO officials, and other 'foreign experts' such as ethnomusicologists. Sharing similar modes of thinking, styles of communication, and systems of value (e.g., regarding types of credentials), cosmopolitans will gravitate toward each other as do the members of most cultural groups; the cultural effects of cosmopolitan alliances are abundantly illustrated throughout this book. Coupled with the greater prestige of modernist cosmopolitan aesthetics, practices, and forms among the more politically powerful cosmopolitans themselves, such alliances were critical to the continuing expansion of capitalist ethos into different parts of the Zimbabwean population.

## Nationalism

Current emphasis on globalization has led writers such as Arjun Appadurai (1990) to view cosmopolitan cultural flows as being in competition with, or superseding, "national culture" (see Brennan 1997: 25; Toloylan 1996). Others argue that the nation-state is becoming less relevant for cultural analysis (see Cheah 1998: 31–35). Deborah Pacini Hernandez, for one, suggests that "National boundaries are becoming increasingly irrelevant as commodities of all sorts—including music— are being produced and consumed in multiple international contexts rather than one culturally specific location. One of the most prominent musical indicators of these new conditions is the phenomenon known as 'world beat'" (1993: 48). I conclude this book with an analysis of Zimbabwe's contribution to worldbeat, especially through the career of Thomas Mapfumo. What is striking in this instance is that Mapfumo was actually marketed to worldbeat audiences on the strength of his localist and nationalist imagery.

Events in Zimbabwe strongly suggest that nationalism is neither increasingly irrelevant for cultural analysis nor at odds with cosmopolitanism and globalization. In fact, in the twentieth century, nationalism is a key cosmopolitan doctrine, and it emanates from modernist cosmopolitanism which is its prerequisite (Chatterjee 1986). Like other aspects of cosmopolitanism, the original idea of nationalism was diffused in Africa through colonialism, and especially mission education (see chapter 5). As in so many places, the nationalist leadership emerged from the cosmopolitan middle class, members of which directed masscultural nationalism beginning around 1960, led the political and military Liberation War effort of the 1970s, and directed state cultural policy after independence in 1980.

Regardless of the European and American origins of nationalism as an idea, nationalists in Zimbabwe learned special slants on this doctrine and distinctive nationalist techniques from China, Russia, Tanzania, and Ghana, as well as through European and American mission education at home and higher education abroad (see chapters 5 and 6). By the time mass nationalism emerged in Zimbabwe in the late 1950s, it was no longer simply a "Western" model, but had become truly cosmopolitan in the sense of emanating from and being shaped in multiple locales, including Zimbabwe. Locating nationalism within the broader dynamics of cosmopolitanism supports Chatterjee's (1986) and Herzfeld's (1997: 6) call for understanding nationalism in all its local particularity and adds weight to their criticism of overly modular, uniform analyses by scholars like Gellner and Anderson.

Nationalism emerges out of cosmopolitanism and, in turn, it functions to diffuse cosmopolitan ethics and practices among culturally distinct groups within the state's territory. This is because the nationalists who come to power are cosmopolitans themselves and operate from this basis as a matter of common sense. Along with the mass media, nationalist cultural programs in Zimbabwe provide the most concrete conduits between indigenous arts, cosmopolitan aesthetics, and transnational markets—much as colonial programs did formerly (chapters 2, 3, 9). Cosmopolitanism begets more cosmopolitanism, in this case through nationalist subsidiaries, and in this way is linked to processes of globalizing that particular formation.

## Nationalism as an Idea

Drawing on the work of Gellner (1983), Smith (1971), Anderson (1991), Seton-Watson (1977), Chatterjee (1986), and others, I use the widely accepted concept of *nationalism* to denote a political movement or ideology that bases the idea of legitimate sovereignty on a coterminous relationship between a "nation" and a state. In this study, *nation* refers to an identity unit that, circularly, depends on the post-1789 idea of the nation-state and nationalism; it is a group of people who recognize or come to accept common bonds of some type as the basis of a social unit labeled 'nation' and deemed legitimately entitled to its own state.[5] For my analytical purposes, this specific meaning is preferable to vaguer usages where *nation* has come to connote almost any type of identity unit. Nationalism as a concept is also distinguished from *national sentiment,* which Smith (1971) has discussed as the more general feelings of belonging to a nation, and which other writers like Anderson and Appadurai refer to as *patriotism.*

Finally, unlike the standard musicological usage where *musical nationalism* is assumed when local "folk" elements are incorporated into elite or cosmopolitan styles, or national sentiment is somehow evoked, I use this term to refer specifically to musical styles, activities, and discourses that are explicitly part of nationalist political movements and programs. I have found this conceptual specificity of great use for sorting out different types of motivations underlying musical styles and practices that hitherto simply had been considered nationalist.

Nationalism, as a political movement, has taken a variety of forms. In some cases a preexisting social unit defines itself as a nation and then endeavors to secure its own state. It also commonly happens in colonial situations, however, that a small local vanguard—typically a "middle group" between the colonial elite and the masses—is faced with the twin tasks of creating a nation out of formerly distinct social groups in order to underpin their legitimacy for taking the state.[6] A third basic type of nationalism occurs when a small leading group secures the state and then engages a posteriori in processes of nation-building. Actually, the Zimbabwean case combines the latter two types of nationalism at different historical stages, and nationalism typically requires ongoing processes of nation-building or maintenance.

### Nationalism and
### Cultural Analysis

"Nation-building"—the forging of national sentiment—largely involves cultural and artistic domains, with language, music-dance, sports, food, religion, and clothing style often being central. The use of art and other cultural practices to develop or maintain national sentiment for political purposes is termed *cultural nationalism*. Zimbabwean political leaders felt that music and dance had a special type of efficacy in the project of nation-building, and in subsequent chapters I introduce the semiotic theories of C. S. Peirce to analyze why this might be so.

To understand processes of nation-building, it is crucial to keep the concept of national sentiment distinct from that of nationalism. Creating or maintaining national sentiment is a necessary goal of nationalist movements, but it is only one of two fundamental goals, the other being the military or political maneuvering to secure and maintain control of a coterminous state. To blur the concepts of national sentiment and nationalism, as some musicologists have, is to confuse the part for the whole, and to confuse two very different types of goals and operations.

Analysis of the musical and cultural effects of nationalism requires understanding the twin goals of nation-building and securing the state in relation to each other at particular historical moments and from the vantage point of specific political positions. Thus in the late 1970s, Mugabe's Shona-associated Zimbabwe African National Union-Patriotic Front (ZANU-PF) party undertook a complex process of nation-building that included the Ndebele and other minority groups while simultaneously emphasizing Shona emblems implicitly as the core of the national culture in preparation for taking the state. Whether consciously or not, Shona-centered nationalism was maintained through the first half of the 1980s as ZANU-PF, the ruling party, continued to fortify its position in relation to the Ndebele-associated Zimbabwe African People's Union (ZAPU) party of Joshua Nkomo. This began to shift around 1987 as the Unity Accord between ZANU and ZAPU was being negotiated and ratified. Such background is essential for comprehending the Shona-centered quality of ZANU's cultural programs (e.g., the National Dance Company) and discourses in the 1970s and in the 1980s prior to the Unity Accord.

### The Twin Paradoxes of Nationalism and Cultural Reformism

Like any unit of identity, nations require other units of the same type for their very existence; nations can only understand themselves as such in relation to other nations that are relatively similar in character. Hence, new nation-states require cosmopolitan institutions, roles, and emblems (diplomats, finance and foreign ministers, airports, national sports teams and dance companies, flags, anthems) homologous with those of the other members of the global family of nations so as to be recognizably like them. Moreover, nationalism is itself a modernist-cosmopolitan idea diffused as a part of this cultural formation. A basic paradox of nationalism is that nation-states are dependent on cosmopolitanism, but are simultaneously threatened by it: unless nation-states maintain their unique identity, they will disappear as distinct, and thus operative, units on the international scene.

Distinguishing emblems and discourses (e.g., of "national character") are thus required to circumscribe nations. When available, indigenous or "folk" arts and practices are often key emblems because they offer the sharpest contrast to cosmopolitan forms. Distinctly local indigenous practices and emblems are also crucial as indices of actual affective identities and bonds which can help imbue the rather abstract concept of the nation with sentiment.

A second paradox of nationalism is that nation-states celebrate and are dependent on local distinctiveness, but they are simultaneously threatened by it. A core doctrine of nationalism is that distinctive cultural groups ("nations") should be in possession of their own states. Nationalists' need to celebrate local distinctiveness carries its own dangers since culturally distinct groups within the state's territory could potentially claim a separate national status by the orthodox logic of nationalism itself. Nationalist discourse thus creates potential rivals within its own territory (Herzfeld 1997).

For their very existence, nation-states must balance the needs and threats inherent in both localism and cosmopolitanism—that is, within the twin paradoxes of nationalism. This balancing act is accomplished in a variety of ways. International forums like the Olympics and arts exchanges emphasize national difference upon the very foundations of parity and similarity—an understanding of the cosmopolitan rules of the games as well as cosmopolitan artistic and concert conventions. In relation to the local, states foster concepts like "ethnicity" and "tribe" to get groups within their territories to conceptualize themselves "below" the level of nation—thereby diffusing their emergence as possible rivals while maintaining the idea of internal cultural differences.[7]

A key way of balancing the needs and threats within the twin paradoxes is through the process of *modernist reformism*. Modernist reformism refers to projects based on the idea that 'a new culture,' or new genres, styles, and practices, should be forged as a synthesis of the 'best' or 'most valuable' aspects of local 'traditional' culture and 'the best' of foreign 'modern' lifeways and technologies. Although theoretically "reform" could go either way, what typically happens is that distinctive local arts and lifeways are reformed, or 'developed,' in light of cosmopolitan ethics, aesthetics, and worldview because of the cultural positions of the reformers.

Put more directly, reformism typically objectifies, recontextualizes, and alters indigenous *forms* for emblematic purposes in light of cosmopolitan dispositions and social contexts and programs. The meanings, ethics, and practices that originally infused indigenous forms are typically not transferred into the reformist mix—that is, they are not considered part of the 'most valuable' features of indigenous lifeways, or are not even recognized, by those directing reformist programs. Through this process, diverse local forms are incorporated and homogenized within the same cosmopolitan frame while maintaining surface (emblematic) differences in relation to the cosmopolitan. In short, reformism both uses and diffuses local difference and uses and contributes to modernist cosmopolitanism, thereby balancing the needs and threats within the twin paradoxes.

While cultural nationalism is typically reformist in character, reformism is not limited to nationalist movements; it is rather an aspect of various types of encounters between localized indigenous societies and modernist cosmopolitanism. As we shall see for Zimbabwe, modernist reformism characterized colonial music education and missionary music policies in and after the 1950s, cultural nationalism in and after the 1960s, and the transnational worldbeat phenomenon in the 1980s. In terms of similar artistic results, the concept of modernist reformism is central to understanding the continuities between colonial, nationalist, and postcolonial cultural projects.

## The Local

I began this project with the assumption that to understand the complex social field of music making in Harare I would have to talk with, interview, and get to know as many different types of people as possible. This included white music teachers, farmer's wives, and suburbanites; music-business executives, producers, and managers; professionals of the black middle class; Shona peasants of different age groups in the rural northeast; members of regional, working-class, dance-drumming clubs in the townships around Harare (I joined and performed with the Murehwa Jerusarema Club and Burial Society of Mbare township); a number of mbira players dedicated to indigenous Shona practices and knowledge (several of whom became my teachers, especially Chris Mhlanga, Tute Chigamba, and the late Mondrek Muchena); members of professional "folkloric" dance groups; state cultural officials and workers; my black, middle-class neighbors in Mabelreign suburb where I lived with my family; and a broad spectrum of popular guitar-band musicians.

As we trace the rise of Zimbabwean popular music and musical professionalism, I discuss artists like Kenneth Mattaka, Jackson Phiri, Zexie Manatsa, Thomas Mapfumo, Oliver M'tukudzi, and Comrade Chinx, among many others who were kind enough to talk with me. Other teachers, friends, acquaintances, and interviewees who represent a variety of cultural positions and relations to musical practice in Harare are also woven through the narrative to provide alternative views. I offer my heartfelt thanks to all those who took the time to help me and who go named and unnamed in these pages.

All of these people represent different positions within and versions of "the local" and local histories. A basic theme of this book is that there is not a single local "history of music" in Zimbabwe but rather multiple histories that depend on the subject positions and varied experiences of the actors involved. As suggested above, cosmopolitans are as much a facet of local life in Zimbabwe as Shona peasants are. For me, *local* simply indicates a place where face-to-face interchanges are common, likely, or at least possible. In this sense most nation-states are not "local," just as many large cities are not. My use of the word does not necessarily indicate cultural distinction or a binary opposition in relation to cosmopolitanism (as in "local-global").

Nonetheless, there are people in Zimbabwe, especially among the African peasantry and lower working classes, who remain culturally distinct from modernist cosmopolitanism. For lack of a better term I will use the word *indigenous* to refer to people and lifeways that are part of cultural trajectories with roots predating the colonial period or that, in terms of ethos and practice, provide local alternatives to cosmopolitanism.

### Tribal Fantasy and
### Indigenous Realities

Based on the premise of realism, a current academic orthodoxy holds that everyone is implicated within "the global." There is a growing tendency to pronounce radically distinctive indigenous lifeways, or autonomous cultural spheres, to be dying, already dead, or only fantasy anyway in the face of ubiquitous translocal interchange. As in my own work (1993), attention to translocal relations initially was seen as a corrective to overly static, romantic portrayals of isolated indigenous communities. Such was the impetus behind James Clifford's idea of *discrepant cosmopolitanisms:*

> In this emphasis we avoid, at least, the excessive localism of particularist cultural relativism, as well as the overly global vision of a capitalist or technocratic monoculture. And in this perspective the notion that certain classes of people are cosmopolitan (travelers) while the rest are local (natives) appears as the ideology of one (very powerful) traveling culture. (1992: 108)

In spite of Clifford's warning about overly global perspectives, however, at times the pendulum has moved too far. Appiah describes as *tribal fantasy:* "an ideal—which is to say imaginary—type of a small-scale, technologically uncomplicated, face-to-face society, in which one conducts most interactions with people one knows, that we usually call *traditional*" (1998: 99). I have lived in or visited places that fit Appiah's description; they seemed real enough to me and to the people living there. I am troubled that writers involved with globalist discourse take such pains to argue alternative cultural spaces into the realm of the imaginary, thereby implying that cosmopolitan spheres define a total-ized reality.

At the same time, I do not want to tie indigenous cultural alterna-tives to certain types of places—the most typical conception being iso-lated rural as opposed to urban settings. In Zimbabwe, people move and live between rural and urban homes, and these different types of places do not necessarily define cultural orientation; class and religious beliefs are the more important variables within the black population. More to the point are studies of the myriad creative responses to colonialism and modernity: "Thus new political cultures were born from countless couplings of "local" and "global" worlds, from intersecting histories that refocused European values and intentions—thus rerouting, if not reversing, the march of modernity" (Comaroff and Comaroff 1993: xii; see Erlmann 1993: 5).

While people in Zimbabwe commonly use the traditional/modern, rural/urban, and African/European dichotomies to distinguish major cultural tendencies, they also recognize that almost everyone incorpo-rates many different beliefs, practices, and technologies into their lives. What defines distinctive indigenous Shona perspectives, however, are the radically different impetuses and criteria for practice and incorpo-ration (see chapter 1). My main point is simply that substantial portions of the population in places like Zimbabwe continue to operate from premises that are fundamentally distinct to the various brands of con-temporary cosmopolitanism, and that these alternative lifeways should not be written off as imaginary.

Because the discourse of globalism downplays alternative indige-nous spaces, its proponents frequently relocate cultural difference and homogenization-heterogenization dialectics *within* cosmopolitan spheres rather than in contrast to them (e.g., Hall 1991; Appadurai 1990). Increasingly, ethnomusicological attention is turned to local uses and meanings of electric guitars, syncretic urban musical styles, T-shirts, and cassette technology—the new authenticity—with atti-tudes ranging from the critical to the ironic to the celebratory. In a sense my focus on the emergence of urban popular music and the commodi-fication of indigenous dance is open to the same charge. My goal, how-ever, is to look at such processes while bearing in mind that they repre-sent a contrast, and in many ways a challenge, to distinctive and vibrant contemporary indigenous musical practices.

In reaction against earlier styles of ethnomusicology that mainly recognized indigenous music as valid, David Coplan (1985: 3) suggests and Veit Erlmann (1991: 2) applauds the idea that urban performing arts "represent not the disintegration but the creation of a culture." In his article "The Astonished Ethnomuse," David McAllester (1979) had already presaged the celebration of the myriad fusions that would come to define local popular musics and worldbeat in reaction against the greyout doomsayers. This was a necessary corrective phase vis-à-vis static or preservationist treatments of indigenous lifeways. Yet it may be time to look at the processes of capitalist expansion and modernist-cosmopolitan creativity anew. The truism that societies are always changing in creative ways does not imply that change is ethically neutral, nor that the power of nationalist states and transnational capital will not erode existing alternative indigenous ethics and aesthetics.

## A Brief Historical Overview

Various musical and social trajectories are woven through the chapters of this book. The overall organization is largely chronological because later historical conjunctures include aspects of, and thus are only intelligible in relation to, earlier ones. A brief overview of major historical developments in Zimbabwe will help contextualize the discussions that follow.

In Zimbabwe, British colonialism began in the 1890s. The region became a British Protectorate in 1891 and was named Rhodesia in 1895. The following year, violent Shona and Ndebele uprisings against the invaders (the 'First Chimurenga') failed, and the region became a British colony with internal, white self-government in 1923 under the name Southern Rhodesia.

Pass-laws were instituted in 1902, and an apartheidlike segregationist system was firmly in place by 1930 when the Land Apportionment Act formerly divided the country into 'African' and 'European' areas. For decades, the cities were legislated as white areas, as was the best agricultural land, taken from indigenous communities. Black Zimbabweans were compressed into African areas, and the surplus population became laborers at white farms and mines, as well as in the growing urban industrial sector, which expanded rapidly around World War II. Africans also found employment in white households as domestic servants.

Racism was, and among some white Zimbabweans still is, pronounced. Although colonial discourse tended to lump all 'natives' into one category based on color,[8] class distinctions among Africans had already emerged by the 1930s and became more pronounced in the following decades. European education, largely supplied by various missionary groups, was the primary avenue to higher class standing within the black population. European education was a means to slightly better employment (as teachers, clerks, foremen), although the economic basis for class distinctions was never particularly great. Perhaps more important, education carried prestige in itself, as did the concomitant adoption of 'European' social and cultural style. Within a colonialist discourse of 'equal rights for all civilized men' initiated by Rhodes himself, some Africans believed for a time that the attainment of European culture ('civilization') was a means to political and economic rights. This attitude was fundamental to the direction of early urban-popular music in Harare (1930–60).

During the 1953–63 period, Southern Rhodesia formed a Federation with Nyasaland (Malawi) and Northern Rhodesia (Zambia). The proposal for federation was initially blocked by the British government because of harsh racist policies in Southern Rhodesia. In response, the settler government made a public display of liberalism through the discourse of 'racial partnership.' During the Federation, indigenous African cultural practices and arts were revalued within colonial state programs, and political alliances were formed between the emergent black middle class and white liberals. Also during this conjuncture, various mission groups began to 'indigenize' African church music, and the colonial state supported the teaching of African music in schools and recorded African music for radio broadcast, among other programs (see chapter 3).

Frustration over the failure of 'racial partnership' to secure real political and economic rights inspired the black middle class and certain working-class leaders to initiate mass nationalism between 1958 and 1963. This period marks the beginning of Zimbabwean cultural nationalism, guided by the hand of a young Robert Mugabe—Publicity Secretary of the National Democratic Party in 1960 and of its replacement party, ZAPU, in 1961. The ZANU nationalist party split off from ZAPU in 1963 over issues of leadership and tactics.

In 1965, the white Rhodesian government, led by Ian Smith, declared a Unilateral Declaration of Independence (UDI) from Britain. The British government had intimated that legal independence would not be granted until black majority rule was established. The white Rhodesian government rejected this prospect. Smith declared independence and widespread sanctions were brought against Rhodesia. Around this time, the two major nationalist parties, ZAPU and ZANU, initiated the guerrilla war with the Smith regime.

The war heated up during the 1970s, with ZANU's ZANLA army

(Zimbabwe African National Liberation Army) being the most effective force. ZANLA largely worked out of Mozambique; schooled in Maoist tactics, it's primary objective was to win the Zimbabwean peasantry over to its cause. In this objective, ZANLA guerrillas used music— "Chimurenga songs"—at all-night *pungwe* gatherings and on the radio to politicize the peasantry. At this time, ZANU expounded a socialist program and played down class divisions within the black population in the name of national unity; it used a largely Shona-centric cultural nationalism as a primary means of winning "the hearts and minds" of the peasantry. Meanwhile, in 1978 and 1979, Ian Smith continued to negotiate with various 'moderate' African leaders, and in 1979 Abel Muzorewa became titular prime minister of Zimbabwe-Rhodesia. This settlement was not recognized by the two guerrilla forces representing ZANU (ZANLA) and ZAPU (the Zimbabwe People's Revolutionary Army, ZIPRA). They continued to fight in what had become an increasingly brutal conflict; the peasant population, caught between Rhodesian and guerrilla forces, suffered much violence, hardship, and insecurity.

In 1979 the war, at a stalemate, was resolved at the Lancaster House negotiating tables in England, where majority rule was established. The ZANU-ZAPU Patriotic Front, however, also made major concessions. The new constitution protected the property and businesses of the white minority for ten years. Against most predictions in Zimbabwe and abroad, ZANU-PF, led by Robert Mugabe, won the election. On 18 April 1980, Zimbabwe became an independent nation-state; Mugabe was sworn in as prime minister and Canaan Banana as president. Mugabe and ZANU-PF were at first dedicated to a socialist program. Mugabe remained in power in the late 1990s, but the party's political position shifted in the course of the 1980s.

Soon after independence, the state initiated a number of cultural nationalist programs, including the National Dance Company, a plan to establish Culture Houses throughout the country, and the stationing of cultural officers (often ex-combatants or loyal party members) in districts throughout the country. Between 1982 and 1987 violent conflicts between the Ndebele-associated ZAPU party and Shona-associated ZANU-PF took place, ending in the Unity Accord between the two parties in 1987. State cultural nationalism remained strongly Shona-centered in the first half of the 1980s, with indigenous village dance and music receiving special attention. By the time the Unity Accord was ratified in 1988, the emphasis on indigenous music and dance within state cultural nationalism was beginning to decline.

At independence, Mugabe immediately surprised the world by insti-
tuting a Policy of Reconciliation with white Zimbabweans. He included
several prominent whites in his cabinet and combined the Rhodesian
and guerrilla armies, at first under a white commander! Given the bru-
tality of the war and enmity between the different forces, this was a bold
stroke. Reconciliation helped reduce "white flight" and the draining of
capital, resources, and expertise from the new country, as had occurred
in so many African states after independence.

The Policy of Reconciliation marks the beginning of an alliance between the white economic elite and the black political elite of Zimbabwe. Thus, in spite of ZANU's socialist stance, which continued
through the 1990s, and its initiation of major education and health reforms in the 1980s (major land reforms were not instituted), the position of national and international capital was secured within the country. The government changed hands from whites to blacks, but the
economy remained largely under white control; the populist promises
of economic equality for the masses, made during the war, remained
largely unfulfilled. The black elite, however, benefited economically
from this arrangement.

The watershed of ZANU's abandonment of a socialist program
came in the early 1990s when the government accepted an Economic
Structural Adjustment Program (ESAP) designed by the International
Monetary Fund (IMF) and the World Bank. The measures of this program (ending subsidies, diminishing protectionism, deflating the currency, "downsizing" government social and economic programs) favored transnational companies and the economic and political elites
of Zimbabwe (aid and loans were contingent on accepting ESAP) at
the great expense of the poorer segments of the population. By the
time ESAP had been instituted, state cultural nationalism using Shona
emblems had declined substantially. ESAP required government belt-
tightening, and cultural projects like the National Dance Company
were discontinued. In keeping with the openly capitalist spirit of ESAP,
during the first half of the 1990s the Ministry of Culture began to
place particular emphasis on the professionalization of indigenous and
"folkloric" dance and music groups so that they could become self-
sustaining, income-generating entities.

By the early 1990s, the honeymoon of the independence period
between the masses and the state had been over for several years. The
effects of droughts in the early 1990s and the effects of ESAP and other
events led to major economic recession and hardship for the

majority of Zimbabweans. During my visits in 1992–93 and 1996, faith in the political leadership and in the state seemed at a low ebb. This issue, however, is somewhat separate from Zimbabweans' continuing concern with their own cultural identities and future cultural directions. The reality of being a member of the nation-state sometimes defines the outer boundaries of peoples' self-definitions, but people are just as likely to frame discourses of identity in racial, ethnic, regional, religious, or class terms, as well as in relation to rural or urban residence.

## Rural and Urban Residence
## and Cultural Orientation

Zimbabweans often discuss cultural identity in rather essentialist terms using stereotypic dichotomies—African/European, traditional/ modern, rural/urban (see chapter 1). As I have suggested in previous work (1993: 13, 1996), essentialism is often important to people's self-definitions, and as Herzfeld notes: "Distrust of essentialism in social theory should not blur our awareness of its equally pervasive presence in social life" (1997: 27). Zimbabweans constantly evoke rural or urban residence as an essential determination of cultural orientation. I view it more as a symbol paradigmatically related to the other standard dichotomies.

Many of the distinctive features of Zimbabwean lifeways *are* rooted in village practices that existed before the building of contemporary colonial cities such as Harare and Bulawayo at the end of the nineteenth century. Moreover, a more profound adherence to indigenous conceptions and practices is probably more common statistically in villages in rural communal areas. But in other, perhaps more important, ways the rural/urban cultural dichotomy is a trope within the problematic discourse of modernity itself, and in Zimbabwe it may obscure more than it illuminates (Stopforth 1972).[9]

Throughout much of this century, there has been a tremendous amount of movement between rural and urban places in Zimbabwe, and between different regions in southern Africa more broadly. Most people that I met currently living in the rural areas had spent some time studying or working outside their home region, and had usually lived for a time in a city or large town.

Most working-class people living in the townships of Harare that I know have two residences, one in the city and one in the countryside, and they move between them constantly. Even people who live most of the time in an urban township consider their rural *musha* their primary "home." *Musha* means "home," but it signifies more than residence.

*Musha* is also one's spiritual home; it is the land that a person is tied to because her or his ancestors are buried there.

According to some people, the spiritual connections implied by the concept of *musha* require a family's residence in a place over at least two generations. For example, one friend who lived most of the time in a Harare township acquired a relatively new rural homestead. While he called his rural residence "home" and intended to retire there, he told me that the rural home was not *his musha* because his parents were not buried there. He said, however, that if he died and was buried there, it would be his children's *musha*.

During the colonial period, peasants were continually being moved from their ancestral homes to augment white landholdings (e.g., see Moyana 1984; Ranger 1985). This was, of course, extremely painful in relation to subsistence as well as for spiritual and social reasons. The African nationalists' promise of returning land to displaced Africans was *the* most important plank of their program for gaining peasant support, a promise that largely remained unfulfilled in the late 1990s. Within the indigenous Shona perspective, the concept of *musha* hinders thinking about land as a commodity—simply in terms of exchange value—and it represents a major point of conflict with colonial and modernist-capitalist conceptions of land.

Many township dwellers have a primary identification with their rural *musha,* and they frequently move back and forth between their rural and urban residences, which indicates a basic problem with using the categories of rural and urban for thinking about or defining distinct lifeways and social identities. While people may alter their dress and other activities somewhat, they do not become fundamentally different people with contrasting cultural orientations and identities when in the city and at 'home.'

There are people who live much of the time in a township but think and act largely in terms of an indigenous Shona ethos and practice (see chapter 1). There are also people in rural areas who have deeply inculcated Christian and cosmopolitan-capitalist ethos and practices. Throughout the colonial period, missions were particularly active in the rural areas; displaced people dependent on mission land came under particularly strong Christian influence. In addition to segregating white and black areas, the 1930 Land Apportionment Act created sixty-six small African purchase areas (only 3.8 per cent of Zimbabwe). These areas attracted black Zimbabweans who operated from a modernist-capitalist cultural position and who were already of a higher class standing—indicated by the fact that they had enough capital to buy land. Such people represented a break from indigenous Shona economic practices, in which family networks required a continual redistribution of wealth, thus hindering personal accumulation. In her study of the Msengezi purchase area in central Zimbabwe, Angela Cheater comments,

> Individual innovators in old societies tend to cluster around particular religious ideologies [e.g., Christianity] which justify ignoring pressures towards redistribution of wealth, as well as offering social and psychological support for these innovators in a potentially hostile society. However, in Msengezi, which is a new society, such religious justification for accumulation is largely unnecessary, again because farmers bought their land in order to accumulate free from the constraints of old-established redistributive economies. (1984: xvii)

Nonetheless, Cheater states that over 90 per cent of Msengezi's population is Christian and that "Western life-styles and techniques of production are widely accepted" (1984: xiii). In this case, Christianity may not have been necessary to justify modern-capitalist practices in the rural Msengezi purchase area. The crucial connection is that mission education facilitated the capital accumulation necessary to become an African purchase farmer in the first place—both by serving as a gateway to better jobs that could underwrite the purchase, and by fostering an ideological position that made personal accumulation desirable and ethically possible.

In rural Zimbabwe, the African communal areas (formerly called Tribal Trust Lands, TTLs) were, and still are, the places where indigenous Shona lifeways remain strongest. Even in modernist rural Msengezi, however, "modified 'traditional' rituals are held occasionally, usually by the younger generation in response to stress in the wider society (ancestral spirits may be consulted in cases of continued unemployment, for example)" (Cheater 1984: xiv). Hence, as Zimbabweans commonly recognize, there is probably a mainstay of both township and rural dwellers who combine indigenous ethos and practices with modernist-cosmopolitan thinking to different degrees and in variable ways, especially in times of crisis.

Likewise, in his study of Highfield Township outside Harare, Stopforth shows how different types of cosmopolitan and indigenous-based attitudes and models for action come to the fore depending on the given problem or domain of life in question. He concludes that "a new, emergent social entity, i.e., urban African society, has come into being in Rhodesia" (Stopforth 1972: 56; 1971: 36). I would add that rural Zimbabwean situations are emergent as well, but that it is not ruralness or urbanness that is at issue. Rather, *class* is the crucial variable, as the Msengezi case illustrates. African residence patterns in and around the city of Harare are likewise based on class, and they correlate with variations in cultural orientation within the urban environment itself.

## An Introduction to Harare
## and Surrounding Townships

Harare, known as Salisbury before majority rule in 1980, is the capital and the largest city of Zimbabwe. According to the national census it had 849,235 inhabitants in 1982, and 1,478,810 in 1992. It is located in Mashonaland East province to the north and east of the center of the country, in the region inhabited by the Zezuru Shona subgroup. Established by white settlers, Fort Salisbury was granted municipal status in 1897, and became the capital of the colony in 1902. The city expanded rapidly after World War II; there was an influx of settlers from overseas and black laborers from the rural areas in response to growing industry. Salisbury served as the capital of the Federation with Northern Rhodesia and Nyasaland between 1953 and 1963 (Sayce 1987: 172). It has been and is still the hub of communications, government, transportation, and, after World War II, many industries in Zimbabwe.

Before 1980, private and business real estate in the attractive metropolitan center and spacious northern suburbs was reserved for whites. The Land Apportionment Act legislated strict segregation of African and white-settler land ownership. This act and the Natives (Urban Areas) Act of 1946 ensured that within cities, defined as white, Africans "could only live, or occupy any sort of business or professional premises, in areas designated by the European town councils as "African locations" (Davies 1975: 294). As a major exception, a large number of African domestic servants did reside in quarters in white areas.[10]

Because of the need for black labor in the city and continuing urban migration, African locations, or townships, were established and multiplied, especially on the southern and southwestern outskirts of the city. Ideally, they were placed where people would not be too far from work and yet far enough away from white areas so as not to "bring down property values" (Cormack 1983: 80–81). After 1980, middle-class and elite black Zimbabweans began to move into the former exclusively white "lower density" suburbs and into apartments near the center, but the vast majority of working- and lower-class blacks still reside in the townships (now known as "high-density" suburbs).

## The Townships

The oldest township connected to the capital is Mbare (known as Harare in the pre-1980 period). It was established in 1907 and separated from the city center on the south side of the railway line. The Native Locations Ordinance of 1906 stipulated that anyone living in the

> location must be employed in the area and gave broad powers to the Salisbury City Council over Blacks in the area. The Council built the 50 huts, constructed from corrugated iron tanks with thatched roofs, and a brick barrack of four rooms, thus providing housing for a total of 328 natives. (Patel and Adams 1981: 5)

For a long time Mbare has been the poorest, most densely inhabited, liveliest, but also the roughest of the townships.[11] According to Zimbabwean journalist Lawrence Vambe, the poorest members of the African working class were housed "either at the factory premises under very primitive conditions or in Mbare, usually in huge prison-like hostels, where bedbugs, fleas, and cockroaches were a part of [their] daily existence" (1976: 197).

Along with the hostels and row houses, Mbare has a large market and commercial area, and a number of recreational facilities, including Rufaro stadium, Stodart Hall, and a variety of beerhalls. It also has a major bus terminal for traveling to the rural areas, accounting for even more of the human traffic in the central market area. During my stay, the main streets around the market and depot buzzed with people at most times, day or night, and Mbare is especially active on weekends.

Among the former "African locations," Marimba Park, located some twelve kilometers southwest of the city center, is at the opposite end of the economic spectrum from Mbare.

> [Marimba Park] was established in 1961 to cater for the demand for low-density, high-cost housing by Africans in the higher income brackets. In its early days only two-acre plots were available, but this was followed by a scheme for one-acre plots with a building clause of $10,000 and later by smaller plots, all with building clauses. The houses in Marimba Park are as well-built, spacious and well-kept as houses in the better-class European suburbs of Salisbury. As Marimba Park is a proclaimed African township, the land is available for freehold tenure. (Davies 1975: 299)

A variety of townships fall between Mbare and Marimba Park in regard to quality of housing, "density," and incomes required to live there. Surrounding Marimba Park are the more modest Kambuzuma, started (circa 1964) with a government-controlled home-ownership arrangement, and the working-class Mufakose township.[12] Lawrence

Vambe makes the case that the white settlers did not recognize class distinctions among Africans and "lumped us together as 'natives.'" He goes on to say that "so far as the Rhodesian Government's native policy and its supporting laws were concerned, we were a classless race of people. No distinctions were made" (1976: 197). In some realms, such as the law prohibiting Africans from drinking European liquor, Vambe's comment is accurate. The establishment of the different types of townships, however, points to an official recognition of class stratification among Africans by the 1960s.

The home-ownership plans in the middle- and upper-strata townships also point to a changing conception of black urban residence as more permanent, especially in contrast to the hostels of Mbare, although only since the 1960s "has it been public policy to regard the Black urban worker as anything but a temporary visitor to the urban areas" (Patel and Adams 1981: 10).

Moving further southwest from Mbare on Beatrice Road, one comes to one of the most famous of the capital's 'high-density suburbs': Highfield. The government proposed to create this native settlement in 1935 in order to control squatters on private land (Patel and Adams 1981: 5). It represented the first attempt for an improved African residence community around Harare; occupants began arriving in 1936. Michael West writes,

> The two- and three-room cottages had fairly large kitchens, plus washing places outside. Each house was built on an individual plot of land, which was much bigger than anything found in the municipal townships. As in the townships, however, water had to be obtained from standpipes in the streets, and, unlike most townships, electricity was not available. All in all, these were not exactly the suburban dream houses of the emerging African middle class.
>
> Nevertheless, as the new village represented a general improvement over the municipal township [Mbare], elite Africans in Salisbury apparently moved in without delay. (1990: 159–60)

Although still considered high-density, and generally inhabited by lower-income families relative to Kambuzuma and Marimba Park, Highfield has sections with medium-sized single-family houses and more space as compared to Mbare. Highfield is a large area with various commercial centers, markets, and recreational facilities such as Cyril Jennings Hall, beerhalls, and (more recently) hotels and nightclubs.

Highfield's fame is tied partially to the fact that many of the important nationalists of the 1960s lived there; it is often considered the "cradle of Zimbabwean nationalism":

> To the colonialists, [Highfield] represented a dangerous hotbed of Af-
> rican nationalism which gave them nightmares, but to the black ma-
> jority it was the kick-off point of the long road to freedom.
>     To this day, Harare's Highfield high-density suburb is still re-
> vered, and the house of Enos Nkala where the ruling Zanu-PF party
> was formed, is regarded as a national heritage.
>     Such illustrious persons as President Robert Mugabe and Vice-
> President Joshua Nkomo own houses in the suburb, while nationalist
> stalwarts such as the late Herbert Chitepo, . . . James Chikerema,
> George Nyandoro, . . . among others all lived there in the heyday of
> African nationalism. (*Sunday Mail,* 4 April 1993, 9)

Also, many of the important nationalist rallies of the early 1960s were
held in Highfield.

Although by now there are dance groups and musicians in many of
the working-class townships surrounding Harare, Mbare and Highfield
have long been primary centers of African music and dance performance in the capital area. Activities ranged from the performance of
indigenous dances and music in open areas of Mbare to the formal concerts of tuxedoed vocal quartets in Stodart Hall. Many of the musicians
I worked with lived either in Mbare or Highfield, and the burial society
I danced with, Murehwa Jerusarema Club and Burial Society (MJCBS),
was located and most frequently performed in the Vito Beerhall in
Mbare. In later chapters we go to Mbare where urban groups performing indigenous music and dance first appeared in the early decades of
this century, and to Highfield, the cradle of Zimbabwean nationalism.

# Chapter One

# Social Identities and Indigenous
# Musical Practices

Colonial domination creates a particularly acute identity crisis that nationalists and postindependence states must take on. The heart of it lies in the active thinking—plans, worries, pride, shame, joys—of normal people as well as in the most unreflexive moments of daily life. For some Zimbabweans, especially middle-aged or older peasants and members of the urban working class, pronounced sensitivity to issues of cultural identity and practice might involve a strong attachment to parents and ancestors. It might involve attachment to indigenous ways of living that have required effort to maintain in the face of prejudice, or to lifeways that are simply considered common sense. It also might involve worries about the future and about their children—if the ancestors are forgotten and ceremonies not held, drought and other catastrophes will surely come.

For other people, especially members of the black middle and elite classes, sensitivity about cultural identity might involve their own complexly constituted upbringing. It might surface through tensions with relatives expecting financial support—expectations based in indigenous ethics but which hinder goals of personal advancement in the 'modern' world. It might come to the fore through a tension between faith in scientific method and having witnessed the results of divination or witchcraft. Internal conflicts might involve the ambiguous lessons learned through cultural nationalism which celebrated the very indigenous lifeways that were not a major part of their own lives. Depending on the period and individuals in question, middle-class attitudes might also include a categorical rejection of 'the old ways' and 'superstitions'

in the name of progress, righteousness, or hipness—at least most of
the time.

Along with gender roles and religious orientation, musical practices
and styles have long been central points for articulating cultural position and identity in Zimbabwe. In this chapter I consider how different
Zimbabweans discussed local subjectivities and identities during my period of fieldwork. I also begin sketching contrasts between indigenous
and cosmopolitan cultural perspectives and musical practices, with the
understanding that each partakes of the other to varying degrees.

## Discourses of Identity

Regardless of class, when Shona speakers in Zimbabwe discuss 'our culture,' or 'our customs,' the vast majority point to rural village life, just
as images of 'the modern' are usually connected to cities. In addition to
the rural/urban divide, Zimbabweans also paradigmatically use the
categories 'African,' 'indigenous,' and 'traditional' in contrast to 'European,' 'Western,' and 'modern' to distinguish what they regard as distinctive Shona practices and ideas from foreign contributions. These
concepts are rooted in local experience, but part of this experience is the
discourse of modernity itself—diffused by white colonists, missionaries,
black nationalists, black and white school teachers, visiting scholars,
journalists, and the mass media. As used currently, the terms 'culture,'
'nation,' 'modern,' and 'traditional' are not of indigenous origin; they
were adopted from cosmopolitan discourse to make sense of new local
conditions created by colonialism and later nationalism.

### Dichotomies of Identity and the
### Decline of Indigenous Culture

Frequently, Zimbabweans discussed cultural identity and orientation
with me using stark dichotomies. For example, mbira player and maker
Mr. Chris Mhlanga noted,

> We have got two groups here in Zimbabwe. I think in Africa each
> country is divided into two: those who like much Western culture,
> who want their own culture to be abolished, and those who stay with
> their own culture who don't want their culture to be abolished.
> (Zim96-1: 4)[1]

Many Zimbabweans spoke and wrote in these categorical, combative
terms for the obvious reason that they have felt under attack. Music
writer and University of Zimbabwe faculty member Fred Zindi ex-
presses a viewpoint similar to Mhlanga's:

Cultural values were either neglected or dropped altogether by those Africans who saw Western civilisation as the way forward. Traditional clothes, food, musical tastes, languages, and attitudes began to change from what they were to those preferred by the colonial masters. . . .

Because of changes in attitudes, especially by the Africans living in urban areas, traditional African instruments were abandoned, and preference was given to the Western versions. (1993: 11)

These sentiments echo official ZANU cultural nationalist discourse of the 1970s. Nathan Shamuyarira, Director of ZANU's Zimbabwe Institute, an educational and cultural arm of the ZANU party, paraphrased an official party document when he wrote,

The imperialists have diluted our rich cultural heritage by way of films, literature, mass media, schools and Church and doctrinaire. They have plunged our people into a morass of emotional and spiritual confusion. Most of our people are now at crossroads. They believe the Western culture is right and that ours is wrong and uncivilized. This is a mental process that has taken years of intense cultural aggression, and which has resulted in *the loss of our cultural heritage.* (1978: 61, my emphasis)

The theme of the decline of indigenous culture under the pressure of colonialism was also common in scholarly writings about Zimbabwean music and, as in ZANU and ZAPU statements, it was often coupled with the idea of a nationalist-generated cultural revival. Paul Berliner, for example writes,

As a result of the hostile, anti-traditionalist pressure that followed the European invasion of Zimbabwe, mbira music suffered a decline in popularity in certain parts of the country, as the biographical sketches show. . . .

In recent years the mbira has enjoyed a resurgence of popularity and has become a major force within the complex contemporary Shona music world. . . . This trend, which seems likely to continue, is the result of a number of interrelated factors, not the least of which is the growth of African nationalism and black pride in the late 1950s and 1960s. (1978: 240–41)

Berliner goes on to mention the various factors, including the mass media and shifts in church and state education policy, topics I later take up in detail. He concludes by highlighting the nationalists' role in the indigenous cultural renaissance:

Rebirth of interest among the Shona in mbira music is explained as the result of a number of interrelated factors ranging from the

> African nationalist movement to the upsurge of cultural nationalism with its particular emphasis on traditional Shona religious practice. The subsequent renewal of African concern for classic Shona music has helped to mitigate the influence of those factors which, for a period of Shona history, were antithetical to the survival of the mbira, and has led to what might well be called an mbira renaissance in contemporary Zimbabwe. (1978: 245)

The themes of cultural decline and nationalist renaissance have become generalized in various writings about Zimbabwean music. Summarizing some of these in his account, Bender writes,

> The traditional music of Southern Rhodesia [Zimbabwe] has disappeared to an alarming degree. Christian missionaries, recognizing the close relationship between heathen religion and music, ensured a fast decline in traditional culture. . . . Only emerging nationalism during the 1960s . . . and world-wide recognition of black culture, including the Black Power movement in the United States, led to a reconsideration of their own traditions. (1991: 154–55)

I pursue the theme of indigenous-cultural decline and revival at various points in my narrative and add detail to the complex interrelation of factors that Berliner has identified as being involved (1978: 240–44). At this point, I simply want to note that this view of Zimbabwean musical and cultural history is widely held both inside and outside the country, and that it was generated both from local experience and from nationalist and other cosmopolitan (e.g., ethnomusicological) quarters.

The position I will develop is that the colonial-decline/nationalist-revival trajectory is certainly valid for some Zimbabweans but does not fit the experiences of others, and it should not be generalized for black Zimbabweans as a whole. I also suggest two reasons why this particular historical view became predominant over other equally valid histories. First, the people who became most acutely aware of their own distance from indigenous lifeways because of nationalist discourse ('decline and revival') were missionized Africans and especially members of the middle class. Such people were more likely to have access to print media where their views could be aired and where official histories are made (e.g., Professor Zindi). Second, the decline/revival view fit with and received validation from prevailing cosmopolitan visions of the general decline of 'traditional' cultures in the face of modernity, an idea diffused in Zimbabwe by white liberal educators and media personnel, black nationalists and intellectuals, and foreign anthropologists and ethnomusicologists. It also fit with the prevalent view of African nationalism as a uniform populist movement that defended indigenous

culture—a view made official after 1980 in Zimbabwe by the nationalists themselves. In short, this valid but partial version of Zimbabwean
history was itself the result of the interaction of certain local cosmopolitan experiences and discourses, and thus will be a subject for further
investigation.

### Identity, Practice, and
### Religious Orientation

Among all the variables affecting broader patterns of cultural practice
and identity, Zimbabweans often emphasize religious orientation as the
most influential (e.g., Maraire 1990). Mr. Tute Chigamba, an mbira
player and maker who, like Mhlanga, lives most of the time in Highfield
township, underlines the importance of religion as an arbitrator of cultural identity:

> I think one thing going to destroy our culture is Christianity, because
> most of youth, they are flocking to the churches and doing Christian-
> ity, they don't want our culture now. But people in rural areas, those
> are the people who are still keeping our culture. You can go into the
> rural areas, you see them brew beer, they brew beer for our culture,
> and they make ceremonies from brewing beer. But here in city cen-
> ters, you know, ah, some can brew beer, but they are no more brew-
> ing beer. They buy beer from the pubs, they bring and they do their
> ceremony with beer from the pubs which is not of our culture now.
> So, we would say in city centers they are no more doing the real cul-
> ture we used to do here before.
>
> So here [in Highfield Township], with my family, yes, when we
> want to do a ceremony we have to brew beer, and do what we do at
> home in the rural areas. We do exactly the ceremony. And if we find
> that the beer is not enough, then we have to go [to] the pub. We buy
> the beer for people who want to drink, but it will be in the next morn-
> ing, not the whole night. The whole night, we have to use the beer
> which we brew here. (Zim96-1: 1)

Indigenous Shona religion broadly defines the ethics of living and the
meaning of practice in relation to the ancestors—owners of the land
and concrete representatives of the past. The beer served at ceremonies
must be produced in the old way if the meaning and function of the
ceremony are to be realized. For people like Mhlanga, Chigamba, and
others who define themselves largely in terms of indigenous lifeways,
ancestral spirits are also considered in the decisions affecting daily life.

Indigenous Shona ethics involve maintaining relationships with
family ancestors (usually up to two or three generations back) as well as
with older spirits who have influence over larger regions and greater

numbers of people (e.g., clan spirits). These relationships are maintained through ceremonies *(bira)* involving spirit possession and indigenous drum and mbira music (see Berliner 1978), as well as through other means such as diviners. But for indigenous people, the presence and influence of ancestors is fairly ubiquitous and is not restricted to ceremonial occasions.

In the conversation just quoted, Chigamba uses the beer which is brewed for seven days by a family before a *bira* as an index for the indigenous religion and cultural ways. Among people who hold indigenous beliefs, maintaining practices such as brewing beer for a *bira* is not merely an emblematic act, nor is it an end in itself. Rather, if these ceremonies are to be successful—that is, if the required spirit is to be enticed to come into her medium—things have to be done in ways recognized and appreciated by that spirit when she was alive in generations past.

Cultural conservatism is thus *instrumental* to the primary goal of these ceremonies that are so central to contemporary indigenous religious, social, and musical life. This type of conservatism is also an impetus for maintaining older styles and repertories of drum and mbira music played in ceremonies. Specific pieces and styles known to and particularly enjoyed by the spirit when she was alive are key inducements to come to the ceremony, as are 'seven-day beer' and snuff. Mr. Chigamba, a composer of mbira music, once remarked that he could occasionally play his new compositions at ceremonies, but not too often because the spirits would not recognize them and thus would not be attracted by them. My other mbira teachers, such as Chris Mhlanga and Mondrek Muchena, likewise downplayed the importance of new compositions and innovations in performance style for the same reason. Thus indigenous religious beliefs perpetuate cultural conservatism as a basic tenet and mode of practice for maintaining a good relationship with the ancestors.

The instrumentality of conservatism, however, is balanced by cultural flexibility involving the individual dispositions and attitudes of particular spirits—attitudes developed when they were living. For example, when attending my first ceremony in 1991, I was instructed not to smoke and to take my watch and shoes off, because many spirits are offended by unfamiliar practices and things. During the ceremony, after the medium had become possessed, however, he lit up a cigarette. Mhlanga, who took me to the ceremony (and who had not been well acquainted with the particular spirit), then turned to me and said, "It's OK, you can smoke." This ancestor had evidently enjoyed smoking while he was alive, and thus it was perfectly acceptable to do so in his presence in spite of the general orthodoxy that spirits don't like European habits like smoking.

This same type of flexibility also affects musical practice. Certain repertories of drum and mbira music are closely associated with spirit possession and 'inside the house' activities (where possession typically takes place). Other genres, like the militaristic *muchongoyo* or the playful *jerusarema* dance-drumming genres, are specifically defined as being unrelated to possession and are 'outside the house' activities.[2] In discussions about their musical practices and styles, Zimbabweans were often adamant about a classificatory distinction hinging on possession. As explained to me, genres were either associated with spirit possession or they weren't, giving the impression that this distinction was set in stone. Nonetheless, in 1993 I attended a ceremony where the principal spirit for whom the ceremony was being held came from the southern Zimbabwe region where the muchongoyo dance is particularly popular. In the ceremony, mbira music failed to bring the spirit; after a while some of the participants began to drum muchongoyo, and the ancestor rapidly appeared. This surprised me because I had been taught specifically that muchongoyo was unrelated to spirit possession; other participants simply explained that this particular ancestor liked muchongoyo and thought no more about it.

Paul Berliner (1978: 235) describes "the law of mbira"—a series of tenets about how and where mbira can be played and how the instrument should be treated. Several of my mbira teachers (who had not worked with Paul) repeated many of these same tenets. Chigamba, for example, told me that mbira should not be played in bars. Months later, he and his family got a contract and played mbira in a bar. I asked Chigamba about this, and he replied that he had consulted with his spirits and they had agreed that the family needed income and so would allow such performance. Like loving (although also sometimes stern) parents and grandparents, family ancestors are concerned with the well-being of their children and so may exhibit flexibility in what they will allow.

Both the conservatism and flexibility of particular spirits affect the definitions of identity and cultural practices of the present generations since, for those Zimbabweans grounded in indigenous lifeways, one's ancestors are important arbitrators and guides for practice. Yet there is also room for dynamism across generations. The music and practices popular with people currently living will be the things needed to bring them back after they pass on. Although my more conservative musician friends scoffed at the idea that electric-band versions of mbira music could bring about possession, several conceded that guitar-band music might have this function in the future when fans of the music died and became spirits.

## 'Cultural Mixing' and Identity

In the interviews quoted above, both Mhlanga and Chigamba were rather categorical about cultural orientation: There are Zimbabweans who adopt 'Western' culture, and there are those who maintain indigenous culture. Like older people in many societies, Chigamba identified the youth as being most likely to abandon indigenous lifeways. Like so many Zimbabweans, Chigamba also expressed the idea that rural or urban residence indicates a fundamental cultural divide. Yet Chigamba and Mhlanga both live most of the time in an urban township but remain strongly conscious of, and committed to, indigenous lifeways, thus belying a strict rural/urban cultural dichotomy. In my experience, many people in the working-class townships are similar in this regard. So, too, Chigamba's children are involved with indigenous lifeways, as are other young people in both the townships and rural areas. The rural/urban dichotomy and age thus do not work well categorically for understanding the cultural orientation of specific individuals.

As in classic ethnographies (see Rosaldo 1989), the sharp distinctions made by Mhlanga and Chigamba point to general tendencies as well as to stereotypic orthodoxies. Although they are valid at a certain level of description, additional depth is necessary for understanding the complexity of individual cultural positions, as Mhlanga and Chigamba themselves are aware.

In the same interviews, both Mhlanga and Chigamba indicated that most Zimbabweans, themselves included, incorporated some combination of indigenous and 'Western' ideas and practices. For example, Chigamba stated that he sometimes buys pub beer as well as brews it for ceremonies held in the township, but his family draws the line at serving pub beer during the actual ceremony, and serves it only in the morning after the ceremony proper is over. Other families in the townships draw the line at different places in relation to the beer they serve, but they are still holding ceremonies for their ancestors. It is crucial to understand that from an indigenous perspective the balancing of indigenous and cosmopolitan lifeways is not always a matter of one's own choice and dispositions—the spirits themselves take a hand in guiding decision making and practice.

## Spirit Guides of Cultural Practice

Mhlanga emphasized that an individual's relationship to the spirits determined his or her cultural orientation. A spirit medium, for example, would have to eschew most 'Western' things if his spirit required it because of the particularly close relationship between medium and ancestor. Mhlanga felt that, like most Zimbabweans, he 'was in the middle.' He was quite conscious of the role of his ancestors in his life; for example, an ancestor guided him to become an mbira maker by profession in the early 1960s. At the same time he is very fond of using electric grinders and other cosmopolitan tools for making mbira. Having a relation with his spirit, he is bound to Shona lifeways, but not being so deeply involved as a medium might be, he also has the freedom to adopt different ways and technologies if they do not conflict with his spirits' wishes.

Mhlanga told me that even upper-class Africans and Christians who wanted to become, or presented themselves as, totally 'Western' could not completely escape indigenous ways:

MHLANGA: I don't believe someone telling me that 'I'm a Christian, I've forgotten all this of your culture, I am not a person who goes for my [spirit] guide.' Because in the night, those people go to *n'anga* [indigenous healer and diviner]. They do it privately. . . .

Partly there is a change; that's why I said most of the people here are all *on the middle part,* which means they have changed, but they have not entirely changed. They know the change is needed, but some are forced not to change.

TURINO: By the spirits?

MHLANGA: By the spirits. You know? Those who are *in the middle* are not very much restricted. They can do the Western life, they can do the spiritual life, so they stay *in the middle.* Some who believe they are staying in the Western style, of course, they stay in the Western style because they are in good houses [i.e., members of higher classes], everything is good, but when it comes to spiritual life now, there is a bar [constraint], a little bar, that will never take them completely to the Western. (Zim96-1: 10)

Chigamba at times stated a positive view of adopting cosmopolitan cultural ways and technologies: "We have to take our culture as from the ground and combine it with your culture, and hey, everything will be okay. And we will have a good, you know, improvement, in our country" (Zim96-1: 6). Chigamba goes on to say, however, that even material well-being may be tied to the ancestors:

CHIGAMBA: But now let's say, we are taking this culture, eh, Western culture, as more popular than our culture, and so we are

> destroying our culture, and our culture will go down,
> down, down, and we keep on learning it from you.
> TURINO: You mean you become more like us?
> CHIGAMBA: Yes, that's it.
> TURINO: And would that be bad?
> CHIGAMBA: Yeah, it will be bad. You see, we have here lots and lots of
> minerals. . . . What we do here in our culture, there are an-
> cestors who were miners, and there are ancestors who were
> agricultural[ists] . . . we have to look for those spirits and
> ask them how are we going to do with this mining aspect,
> and they will tell us what to do. . . . Even in the mines, if
> you go there, they subscribe [hold ceremonies] every year
> to the ancestors so that they don't get any of these disasters,
> you know. Otherwise we may find a mine somewhere there,
> if we don't pay this subscription to the spirits, then you will
> find that the mine is full of water, and then you can't drain
> water, and you can't finish it. So you stop the mine.
> (Zim96-1: 6)

Mhlanga offers a similar viewpoint but with a more personal example:

> Although I may pretend that I don't like this Zimbabwean life, I can
> [ignore] it for two or three years, but there will be something very
> distracting which comes through a spirit in my family which would
> turn me to go to spiritual life again, because, for instance, if this kid
> is ill, then I go to a *n'anga* [indigenous healer] or a doctor. A doctor
> can't heal him, so I go to a *n'anga*. The *n'anga* does the whole
> thing. . . . He will be telling you that this father [ancestor] wants this
> kid to have your father's name, you must name this kid the name of
> your father. Then, that will lead [to] my own culture. I divert from
> the Western culture to this culture again. That is why I say it's diffi-
> cult. No one of our culture will just surrender forever from our cul-
> ture, because there are some other forces. (Zim96-1: 6)

Like people everywhere, especially at times of crisis, Zimbabweans
approach problems by drawing on the variety of resources at hand—a
doctor, a *n'anga*; a pump to rid a mine of water, a ceremony for miner
ancestors—to see what works. What differs place to place, and among
different groups in the same place, are the nature of the resources, of the
constraints, and of the dispositions toward one type of solution over
another. A pump and Western medicine are, by now, cosmopolitan resources; the manner in which ancestors intervene in decision making is
specific to Zimbabwe and to other African societies outside cosmopolitan spheres.

As Mhlanga says, sometimes spirits will take a hand in guiding
people's future directions even when they have rejected indigenous

beliefs and, I would add, are not apparently in crisis. The story of Noah Mapfumo is a case in point. Mapfumo maintained a home in rural Murehwa but lived most of the time in a township outside Harare. He worked for a tobacco company in town, had very little interest in going to his rural home, and had no interest in indigenous Shona rituals or practices such as music and dance. He described himself as being dedicated to 'modern' life, and his wife and children were strict Christians who eschewed indigenous ritual.

One day while drinking in a store during a visit to his rural home, Noah was knocked off a chair unconscious. He showed me the scar on his face resulting from the fall. Not knowing what had happened and being frightened, he consulted a diviner who told him that he had been chosen as medium by a particular ancestor. He now attends ceremonies regularly and has become an enthusiastic *dandanda* dancer (the dance tradition used in his village for spirit possession; see chapter 2). Noah told me that his life changed because of this experience and his continuing role as medium. Like Mhlanga, he points out that there are spiritual forces that may constrain or redirect an individual's way of living, tempering ideas about individual choice and control. Noah's experience is not uncommon. Even dedicated churchgoers may be chosen as medium by an ancestor, and consequently undergo radical changes in cultural orientation (see Maraire 1990).

### "Global Fantasy" and Indigenous Alternatives

Indigenous beliefs remain powerful in urban, working-class townships as well as in rural areas. This was dramatically demonstrated during my first visit to Zimbabwe in 1991. Tute Chigamba's son Henry, a young man in his twenties, was taking me to their rural home in Mount Darwin. We were to meet some distance from the bus station in the Mbare township market area, and Henry repeatedly warned me to be very careful in Mbare because of the thieves and roughnecks who congregated there.

Henry arrived late, and I saw him running towards me up the street. When he arrived I asked him where his things for the trip were. He told me that he had left his belongings by the side of the road near the bus station. I asked who was looking after them, and he replied, "No one, but I left my mbira on top of my bag so no one will touch it." He explained that mbira are associated with ancestors, and so people would be afraid to bother his belongings. Henry turned out to be right, but given his previous warnings about thieves in Mbare I was surprised that his faith was so strong—a faith that everyone else in Mbare, even thieves, shared his views about mbira and the ancestors.

When I insist that distinctive indigenous lifeways remain vital among certain contemporary Zimbabweans, I am not romanticizing some imaginary cultural difference or "tribal fantasy." It is not that Henry doesn't take buses, but that he makes decisions en route by very different criteria from my own cosmopolitan mode of operating. Even now I would not leave my bag unattended in Mbare, mbira or no mbira, and neither, I am certain, would many of my black middle-class neighbors in Mabelreign suburb were I lived. Although I now know, intellectually, about the spiritual power of mbira for indigenous Zimbabweans, the full ramifications of this are not deeply ingrained in me, and hence I cannot share Henry's level of confidence and comfort in leaving a bag unattended. Underlying his decision is a very different sense of reality.

### Contemporary Middle-Class Discourses of Identity

Like Chigamba and Mhlanga, members of the numerically small African middle class described Zimbabwean cultural identity as some blend or balance of indigenous and foreign elements.[3] Black, middle-class Zimbabweans also recognized forces that constrain and shape people's cultural practices and identities. What differed from indigenous perspectives was the nature of those forces.

Many middle-class Zimbabweans viewed economic goals and constraints as particularly important determiners of cultural practice and orientation. Regardless of class, dedicated churchgoers might be particularly conscious of the Lord's will. Middle-class Zimbabweans and orthodox Christians, however, typically did not articulate the importance of the ancestors as determinants in decision making and cultural orientation. This has broad ramifications.

Not only would my middle-class acquaintances be unlikely to trust that an mbira would protect their belongings in Mbare, their sense of basic things like home and family are closer to mine than to those of indigenous Zimbabweans. For example, among colleagues that I got to know at the University of Zimbabwe, the idea of *musha* as a spiritual home seemed greatly diminished, and extended family ties appeared to be weakening. Unlike my working-class friends in the high-density townships, my middle-class friends regarded their urban residence as their permanent home. They often avoided visiting the rural home, or visits from extended family, because of inconvenience, expense, and expectations that they should give gifts to, or support, less fortunate family members. One young colleague expressed outrage that his country kin thought they could just drop in and stay at his downtown apartment any time day or night! While I, too, might feel this way, small lower- and working-class homes in the townships are often crowded with extended kin, who sometimes stay on a semipermanent basis. In indigenous Shona homes, the sense of family, as well as the sense of personal space, differs from mine and that of my middle-class colleagues.

Like capitalist cosmopolitans elsewhere, middle-class acquaintances in Zimbabwe were concerned with saving for the security of their nuclear families—for investment, for college, for better material well-being in the form of houses, cars, and appliances. These values certainly felt familiar to me, and this familiarity—across national boundaries and geographical distance—is precisely what cosmopolitanism is all about.

Deputy Secretary of Culture Stephen Chifunyise discussed his conception of forces shaping Zimbabwean culture from a pronounced cosmopolitan perspective:

> What is Zimbabwean is a difficult thing to describe. Many times when I [define] Zimbabwean music, Zimbabwean theatre, Zimbabwean dance, I use two premises. First of all, I start from an understanding that an indigenous, a national person, has the world heritage at his disposal. He has his own, or she has her own, national heritage. And then there is a world heritage. Anyone who has the capacity to use the world heritage to further sharpen the national heritage does so with two things at risk. One risk is that the national heritage will be diluted. The second risk is the national heritage will be secondary, the international heritage will be first. The basic sensitivity to the world heritage is a plus for the individual. The minus is not on the individual in some cases, the minus is on the society that has not valued the national heritage.
>
> The economic dilemma is trying to make a living using the national heritage—I may love the national heritage, but what is there for me to survive? So in actual fact, the individual fails to survive. There are a number of our musicians who really are fantastic indigenous ones, but they cannot get grants, they cannot get scholarships, they cannot get commissions, they cannot get even private company support. Now, that is for me, the cause, much more than anything else. (Zim93-55: 21)

As the deputy secretary of culture,[4] as a professional playwright, and as a university-based scholar of indigenous dance, Chifunyise exemplifies the pronounced cosmopolitan orientation of the new black elite of Zimbabwe. He does not think in terms of rural/urban or African/

European dichotomies within Zimbabwe, but rather hinges his analysis on a distinction between 'world' and 'national' cultures. He is, thus, particularly conscious of cosmopolitanism (world heritage) as a cultural formation, and it is also significant that he conceptualizes local indigenous practices as synonymous with the 'national.' As a cosmopolitan, his units of analysis are much broader in scope as compared to, say, those of Mhlanga or Chigamba—he thinks about the development of the nation on a world stage.

Even more important, for Chifunyise professional goals and economic considerations, not the spirits, are primary forces constraining cultural choices and directions. Speaking as an arts administrator and as a professional artist, he indicates that being "too indigenous" is a hindrance to getting grants, scholarships, commissions, and company support. These types of resources are, themselves, cosmopolitan. Economics as a central concern certainly differs from the concerns of people who still think of music and dance primarily as a special type of sociability, as recreation, or as a means of attracting ancestors into a ceremony. He notes that adopting cosmopolitan aesthetics ("sensitivity to the world heritage") is an economic advantage for the individual, although it may not be good for the society since it will dilute the 'national heritage.' Nonetheless, in the 1990s, the Ministry of Culture undertook various programs precisely to further the professionalization of indigenous arts (see chapter 9), a decision that makes sense if, from your particular cultural vantage point, individual economic considerations are major criteria for practice.

## Class and Cultural Tendencies

I agree with the general consensus in Zimbabwe that religious orientation is a central variable for determining cultural orientation. But Christianity is closely tied to higher-class positions, although it is not restricted to them, because mission education and the status attached to education was the primary engine for class mobility during the colonial period. Hence, class, religion, and cultural orientation are mutually dependent variables.

While Mhlanga recognizes class as a variable influencing individuals' cultural orientation, he feels that the will of the spirits will ultimately prevail even among higher-class groups. This is because he knows that the ancestors are a paramount force, and this is where my analysis differs, because I do not have the same deep-set knowledge. From my perspective and in my experience, class is the primary variable for understanding cultural tendencies as well as musical practices, taste, and goals for performance. Although Mhlanga is probably right that almost anyone could at some time "return to the spiritual side," black, middle- and upper-class Zimbabweans tend to do so much less frequently. To put it another way, people of higher class standing and people raised as orthodox Christians more often tend to operate from very different positions within which the spirits are not viewed as primary arbitrators of life.

Members of the African middle class often do not have the same level of knowledge of and cultural competence in indigenous lifeways and arts. During my year-long stay in Zimbabwe, my family and I lived in the modest, middle-class suburb of Mabelreign.[5] In the mornings I gave various neighbors rides into town and sometimes would play field recordings I had recently made of various indigenous styles. I found that my middle-aged neighbors could not identify many drumming genres, and did not recognize the sound of a *chipendani* (Shona musical bow). Some could not even recognize the mbira by sound, although it is, by now, one of the most famous indigenous instruments in the country. For the teenage and younger children in my neighborhood, indigenous Shona music was often more foreign than Congolese *soukous* or American rap.

*Bira* (ceremonies), commonplace in the lower- and working-class townships, were a rarity in my neighborhood and other, similar, black, middle-class neighborhoods according to musicians who played such events around town. This lack of familiarity and involvement with indigenous music and ceremony was common among the middle class during earlier decades as well (chapter 4). People raised in households and regions where such music and indigenous beliefs were not common have no reason to be familiar with them, or to consider them *their* culture, in spite of essentialist discourses to the contrary.

Class-based cultural distinctions are, of course, a relative matter. I have emphasized similar values and attitudes among myself and black, middle-class professionals that I knew—grounded in a common cosmopolitanism. The result was a basic familiarity and a fairly broad set of shared assumptions that belied radical cultural difference. Nonetheless, at times I would be surprised, for example, by a middle-class friend who feared returning to his rural home because of witchcraft as well as because of conflicting cultural expectations from his relatives. The concept of cosmopolitanism points to the common assumptions across geographical distance, but it also suggests that there will be differences in local branches of a given formation because of local conditions. People's dispositions are always complexly constituted and multiple—"cultural syncretism" is the rule, not the exception. Nonetheless, class-based tendencies can be identified and are the result of different types of life experiences.

### Syncretism as an Idea

The people from different class positions quoted above all agree that 'Zimbabwean culture' is 'in the middle'—is the result of some blending of indigenous and 'Western' or 'world' ideas, practices, and technologies. For Mr. Mhlanga and Mr. Chifunyise, however, it is not the same middle; or to put it more accurately, they approach 'the middle' from very different cultural positions which, in turn, give radically different spins to the nature of that middle ground and how it is constituted. The cultural syncretism that results from modernist reformism or economic concerns is of a very different order than that implied by the playing of mbira in a bar for money only if and when one's ancestors allow it. The point of distinction between class-based indigenous and cosmopolitan orientations is lodged in different notions of the prime forces shaping cultural realities.

Robert Kauffman made a similar point about musical syncretism not being a unitary phenomenon in Zimbabwe long ago (1970, 1975). He argued that the use of guitars according to indigenous Shona musical principles did not indicate westernization but simply the incorporation of a foreign object—what Appadurai (1996: 32) and many others refer to as *indigenization*. By the same logic, the incorporation of an mbira, an indigenous drum, or an mbira song into an electric band that operates largely according to cosmopolitan musical principles, practices, and goals does not in itself constitute heterogenization of the cosmopolitan sphere. Kauffman's point, and mine, is that the levels of meaning, value, and practice are more important than formal features for identifying different cultural formations.

## Indigenous Musical Aesthetics, Ethics, and Practice

As with the sense of family, home, and personal space, there are major distinctions between indigenous Shona and cosmopolitan musical sensibilities in Zimbabwe. To understand the impact of nationalism and cosmopolitanism, it is important to grasp the distinctive and valuable features of indigenous Shona music making at the levels of ethics, aesthetics, and practice. These distinctions can be framed in relation to what I think of as four very different modes of musical activity:

"participatory music," "presentational music," "high-fidelity music," and "studio music."

The most socially salient indigenous Shona music making, that which takes place in religious ceremonies and other communal contexts, is based fundamentally in participatory ethics. In his description of mbira performance at ceremonies, for example, Paul Berliner writes, "In its many aspects the *bira* is a communal affair; its music is the sum total of the contributions of all the members of the village who choose to participate" (1978: 190):

> Around the nucleus of mbira music and the basic supporting rhythm of the hosho, participants at the *bira* engage in three forms of musical expression: singing, handclapping, and dancing. In general, there is a great deal of freedom in the vocal parts (*huro, mahon'era,* and *kudeketera*) and participants join in the performance of singing at will. . . . The traditional vocal styles range from very simple to very complex patterns so that each individual in the village can perform at his or her own level of proficiency. . . .
>
> Active participation in the music is characteristic of the *bira*, and reflects the communal nature of the music, in which highly talented or professional musicians can express themselves without restraint within the same context as beginners. (1978: 191)

Berliner's comments about the ingrained communal-participatory ethos of indigenous Shona music making fit my experiences with musical occasions in rural Murehwa, Uzumba, and in the townships around Harare. His description also includes a variety of features, such as combining different levels of specialization, that are common to participatory traditions more widely.

### Participatory, Presentational, and Recorded Music

In "Musica Practica" (1977), Roland Barthes contrasts "music that is for playing" and "music that is for listening" as distinct types based on divergent qualities, aesthetics, and erotics of given composers and pieces. Inspired by this idea to think about musical fields as being defined by goals, role relations, ethics, and the processes of production, I have found four ideal types of music analytically useful: *participatory music, presentational music, high-fidelity music,* and *studio music.* These categories contrast musical arts along a series of continua involving distinct ideologies and goals of creation; a process-product continuum in relation to the conception of music; types of settings for

**Table 1.1** Ideal Types of Music Making

| Live Performance | | Recorded Music | |
|---|---|---|---|
| Participatory Music | Presentational Music | High-Fidelity Music | Studio Music |
| Goal: maximum sonic, kinesic participation of all present | Preparation of music for maximum interest for others | Recorded to index live performance | The Art Work without reference to live performance |
| Roles: little or no artist/audience distinctions; little or no mediation | Clear artist/ audience distinctions; people present mediated by stage, etc. | Artist/audience not in each other's presence; mediated by recording | Artists mediated by studio technology and spaces; artist/ audience mediated by recording |
| − Mediation | | + Mediation | |
| − Planning/control | | + Planning/control | |
| + Process-oriented | | + Process-oriented | |
| + Social interaction as central to the conception of music and "good" music | | + Sound component as central to the conception of music and "good music" | |

production and reception; different degrees of mediation; and the types of role interaction involved (see table 1.1). These, in turn, influence sound style in critical ways.

Musical participation may take many forms, for example, sitting in still, silent contemplation of a concert performance. Following Charles Keil (1987), Steven Feld (1988), and others, however, I use the term *participation* in the specific, more restricted sense of actively contributing to the sound and motion of a *group* performance event through dancing and gestures, singing and other types of vocalizing, clapping, or playing an instrument.[6] Participatory music is defined and shaped stylistically by the fundamental goal of inviting the fullest participation possible, and the success of an occasion is judged primarily by the amount of participation realized. In heightened participatory contexts, there is little or no distinction between performers and audience—there are only participants and potential participants. Nonetheless, participatory events may, and should, allow for different types of roles (e.g., instrumentalists, dancers) and levels of specialization. Participatory music tends to be process-oriented. Musical sound is shaped to fit participant needs, goals, and desires in the moment as well as to facilitate participation.

In presentational music, by contrast, artist/audience distinctions are emphasized in "live" settings by a number of means, including physical distance, stages, microphones, and agreed-upon conventions about who has the right to make music or dance. The primary goal of presentational music revolves around creating the best, most acceptable, most interesting (however these are defined) musical pieces specifically for a separate audience. Presentational music thus tends to be product-oriented: programs and pieces are often conceptualized as set, reproducible, items carefully organized and prepared in advance, although certain genres, such as jazz, differ in this regard. Sound is shaped to provide variety for maintaining audience interest; virtuosity is often emphasized to legitimate artist distinction as well as to create interest.

Recorded music partakes of some aspects of presentational music, such as product orientation and attention to intended, although further removed, audiences. Recorded music requires additional conceptualization. Based on the ideology and processes of production, two ideal types of recorded music might be identified: "high-fidelity music" and "studio audio art." High-fidelity recordings involve an ideology of previous or possible live performance; the recording is projected as being "faithful" to, or indexing, a live music experience, although the recording is understood to have been made in a studio. Atlantic soul recordings of the 1960s, sometimes even including "audience" sounds such as shouts and clapping, are an example of this category. In studio audio art there is no pretension to a prior or necessary live rendition; sounds are shaped and presented in ways that make studio technology and process explicit, and the resulting art object is the paramount concern. The Beatles's *Sergeant Pepper* album and some computer music are examples of this category.

I am aware that many musical occasions, styles, and products combine elements of the participatory, presentational, and the recorded modes—such as sing-alongs in concerts, karaoke, D. J. scratching, disco dance parties, or an individual presentational moment in a group participatory event. Karaoke is distinct from, say, Shona events in that it involves sequential as opposed to simultaneous participation, and it uses recordings. Live concert recordings bridge the high-fidelity and presentational types; field recordings might combine aspects of the participatory and high-fidelity modes when a participatory performance is recorded and issued.

Nonetheless, these ideal types do point to general distinctions in musical practice, style, and ethics, and sometimes pertain fairly specifically to actual situations. Music making among the Aymara in Southern

Peru and in indigenous Shona contexts in northeastern Zimbabwe both fit the participatory ideal type fairly closely, although sometimes in different ways (see Turino 1993 for the Peruvian case).

Like recordings, presentational music articulates with a modernist ethos and capitalism in that it emphasizes rationalist control of the performance, increased objectification of the art object, and the distinctions between artists and audience that make ticket and recording sales possible. Participatory music operates according to different ethics and results in different types of sounds. After the 1950s indigenous Shona music and dance increasingly became inserted into the presentational and recorded modes and, as we shall see, fairly predictable stylistic transformations resulted. A major thrust of this book is to document the processes by which participatory ethics, sounds, and movement become transformed into presentational and recorded forms in the context of modernist-capitalist cosmopolitanism. To this end, we must begin with a description of Shona participatory events, roles, ethics, and sounds.

## Indigenous Shona
## Participatory Events

Indigenous Shona music is sometimes performed solo for a person's own enjoyment and in a variety of informal settings. Here I want to concentrate on the music used in indigenous participatory group events such as religious ceremonies (bira, guva), weddings and funerals, and at more informal social occasions like beer parties and community (e.g., jit) dances.

Formal musical occasions are usually hosted by individual families, and they typically take place at the host family's home in the rural areas or townships (see Berliner 1978: 186–206 for a full description of bira). Ceremonies often begin around sunset and go into the next morning, or they may last for several days, especially if ancestors attending require it.

Going all night is important to the function of social bonding that often underlies participatory events. Staying up together, especially through the bleak hours from three to five A.M., can involve discomfort and sacrifice. In fact, some people do slip away to bed during these hours only to return around dawn, and special songs are sung during this time that recognize people by name who remain present and awake.[7] Because of fatigue, the music and dance may become more subdued during the wee hours. Various friends in Zimbabwe commented that the music and dance in ceremonies build in intensity and are best in the hour or so before dawn. This is also a time of special closeness among participants who supported each other through the long night. Participatory events that have evolved to create social unity often span long periods of time (more than a few hours) to extend contact and activities among participants, but also to require endurance, commitment, sacrifice, and to provide the pleasure of living up to one's responsibilities to others.

In ceremonies, the music and dance also build in intensity as they lead up to and reach the point at which a medium shows signs that her spirit is coming. This may happen at any time and depends on the will of the ancestor—some spirits come easily and quickly; others take a good deal of coaxing. When the medium shows signs, musicians will play harder and faster, the singing becomes louder and denser, and people may surround the medium, dancing with passion to help bring on possession. Thus, as in many participatory occasions, the dynamic ebb and flow of music-dance performance is molded to the needs of the participants and the goals of the event; it cannot be predicted or planned ahead of time.

For *bira,* the host family provides food and drink, often ritual 'seven-day beer,' as well as snuff for the ancestors. A typical event might have twenty or more participants. When possession is involved, people are packed into the relatively small space of a round house on the family compound or in the largest room of an urban home. Physical closeness aids in building participatory intensity; it is not a coincidence that possession activities typically take place 'inside the house.' Other events, like *guva* (grave ceremonies held a year after death), may include both inside activities involving possession and other dancing and festivities that take place outside. More casual events not involving possession often take place outside, and sometimes possession ceremonies in the townships are held on an outside patio if no room in the house is large enough to accommodate the guests.

## Musical Specialization
## and Professionalism

Relatives, neighbors, and friends are invited to formal family events, as are particular mediums and specialized performers if the presence of particular ancestors is hoped for. When a family has close ties to people who have the needed specialized musical skills, such as drummers or mbira players, the musicians may play in collaboration with the hosts or be given a gift. In other events, currently, dance-drumming groups or specialized musicians may be hired ahead of time to perform at family events beyond their immediate villages or neighborhoods. Paul Berliner

(1978) also reports part-time professional mbira players and spirit mediums for his period of research.

A key objective of this study is to trace the rise of musical professionalism in Zimbabwe. Throughout the book I use the term *professional* to refer strictly to income-generating activity, whether or not specialized skill is required, and *specialist* to refer to special skills and knowledge, whether or not money is involved. It is not known when the practice of performing ritual-possession music on contract for money first became widespread among indigenous musicians—as opposed to uncompensated collaboration, or being given gifts as a reciprocal gesture (Berliner 1998, p.c.). All three forms coexist currently. For music-dance genres not required to aid spirit possession, however, it is clear that professionalism began to emerge in the 1950s (chapter 2). Musical professionalism begins to be a widespread idea only in the 1960s (chapters 4, 7). By the 1990s, hiring performers of all types of indigenous music and dance had become commonplace, and a number of people had taken up these activities as full-time employment.

## Specialization and Participatory Ethics

The downplaying of performer/audience distinctions in participatory events does not imply that there are not different roles and degrees of specialization within the group. In fact, the most successful participatory traditions are precisely those that allow for different levels of specialization and that suit distinct interests (e.g., singing, instrumental performance, dancing). Traditions that only have simple roles, for example our campfire songs, offer few challenges and hence bore and perhaps ultimately exclude people who are particularly engaged with music and seek a challenge. Traditions that only include highly specialized roles exclude people who do not have the desire or time to master difficult parts. A good deal of indigenous Shona music, especially the type used in ceremonies, involves different levels of specialization so that everyone may participate at their particular level of interest and expertise. As Csikszentmihalyi (1988) has suggested, for deeply engaging, sometimes transcendental, "flow" activities, competence and challenge must be balanced to draw participants in fully and focus them without creating frustration. As in the Shona case, well-developed participatory traditions offer graded levels of specialization that can keep people engaged as they progressively develop more skills over time.

Mbira and other lamellophone performance requires a good deal of specialized knowledge, experience, and skill, as do various drumming styles. Advanced singing and dancing are also specialized roles. The playing of *hosho* (gourd or tin-can rattles), which accompany most indigenous Shona music occupies a middle-ground of specialization, as do average singing and dancing skills, the complex handclapping patterns so valued in Shona performance, and other instruments such as *ngororombe* panpipes. At the least specialized end, people may simply clap the basic pulse or do simple dance movements and vocal parts along with others.

It would be inaccurate to view this type of organization as consisting of "star" performers (drummers, mbira players) providing the "real" music with the contributions of others being more peripheral, as I initially did. Rather, several of my Shona music teachers explained that the situation was actually the other way around. The specialists have the *responsibility* of consistently providing well-played ground parts which are necessary to inspire fuller participation and simultaneous variations in the elaboration parts—it is difficult to dance, clap, or sing when a solid rhythmic and melodic-harmonic base are not in place.[8] Mr. Mhlanga once noted that if the best mbira players gave their most skilled performance at a ceremony but no one joined in, the performance would be deemed a failure. This is not to say that advanced mbira playing and drumming are not greatly appreciated; they are, but in ceremonies they are not ends in themselves. Rather they are the basis for inspiring participation among family, neighbors, and the ancestors. As Berliner commented, the music at ceremonies is the sum total of all participants' contributions.

The notion of *responsibility* for fulfilling a musical role in such a way that it allows and, ideally, inspires others to participate enables a clear understanding of aesthetics as part of a broader system of participatory ethics (Turino 1993; Sugarman 1997; cf. Peirce 1998: 200–203). Participation has to do with expressing a level of social commitment to the event and to the other participants through sonic and kinesic contributions. Greater responsibility accompanies specialized core roles. This is felt most acutely when there is difficulty in bringing a spirit into the ceremony, or when it is necessary to continue playing through the wee hours of the morning with fatigue and sore hands and throats, but it is also a responsibility for providing core parts in an accessible way throughout.

Ground parts played on drums, hosho, and lamellophones like the mbira, or choral parts that maintain the basic ostinato of a piece, must be firmly anchored as a foundation if other contributions are to be successful. Specialized ground-part musicians must curtail personal desires for more radical variations or elaborations that would confuse or exclude other participants (see Berliner 1978: 106–8). In Mr. Chigamba's case, he feels the need to curtail the performance of his own new compositions in ceremonies because "the ancestors won't know them"; if he played many of his original pieces, he would not be fulfilling his responsibility to the event.

Presentational performers also have a responsibility to their audiences, but it is of a different type. They must provide the whole of the music for others' enjoyment and edification, and this often leads to extensive elaboration of forms, stark contrasts, and virtuosic display to keep audiences interested. In capitalist-cosmopolitan contexts musicians also play by different rules. Modernist values emphasize new composition and originality as an acid-test for artistic standing (see chapters 7 and 8). Novelty itself is favored in modernist ethics, and new compositions also allow for the amassing of "intellectual property" and royalties for professionals within the capitalist sphere.[9] The responsibility of participatory specialists in Zimbabwe, by contrast, requires that they play familiar music and that they discipline their parts so as to allow even the most unskilled to join in, while inspiring more advanced people to do so. This leads to a type of *intensive* (within the form) variation and improvisation and has other major ramifications for participatory musical style.

### Shona Participatory Sound Style

Indigenous Shona music is based on cyclical forms with a constant rhythmic motion. Dramatic shifts in dynamics, melody, harmony, or tempo are avoided, although gradual accelerando is common. The rhythms themselves are often constructed through different parts pushing and pulling against each other to create tension and dynamism (Keil 1987); in two-handed hosho (shaker) parts, for example, the right hand often plays on the front side of the beat pushing the music forward, while the left hand lays back so that the music does not rush and a tension is created. A similar relationship is evident in the two drum parts of dandanda dance music: one drummer plays a repeated, driving triple pattern as the ground part, while the second drummer plays more laid-back elaboration patterns. This type of push-pull relationship is also often basic to the first (*kushaura*—to lead) and second (*kutsinhira*—to accompany) mbira parts.

*Interlocking* (placing the "notes" of your part into the spaces of other parts) is typical to the design of both ground and elaboration parts in much Shona music. Musical interlocking is a foregrounded, highly stylized version of other types of social interaction—like the temporal alternation and social give and take of a good conversation in daily life. Interlocking highlights individual contributions as well as social interconnectedness and sensitivity. Interlocking takes place from the microlevel of organizing women's single-handed hosho parts into a single gestalt, to the macro-level of the overall call-and-response form of the singing in dandanda music and other genres.

The texture of Shona music is typically dense, involving a good deal of overlapping of different parts. The overall semiotic effect is one of a sonic-social merging that resembles the physical merging of participants packed into the small space of a round house. More than this, dense overlapping of parts provides a kind of *masking function,* in which the individual contributions of neophytes will not stand out, making insecure entrances and contributions possible.

Adding to the density, intonational variation is relatively wide as compared to Euroamerican conservatory and popular music conventions. Like many features of participatory aesthetics, the preference for wide intonation may have developed through the dialectics of ethics and practice. Contemporary aesthetics are the result of past experience. We are socialized within particular soundscapes, and we want to hear, sing, and dance what we grew up hearing, singing, and dancing. In situations where everyone is encouraged to participate but not everyone is encouraged to specialize in music, relatively wide tuning variations are likely. When we grow up with this sound, it becomes the sound that is appreciated. Thus, although mbira makers could tune unison and octave keys on their instruments precisely, they typically tune such keys slightly wide to produce rich overtones and combination tones which resemble the dense quality of participatory singing. Incidently, this practice begins to change when makers build mbira for use in electric bands (see chapter 9).

In Shona participatory contexts, pieces do not have a predetermined form—a set middle and end, and planned dynamic shape. Gradual ebbs and flows of textural density and volume rely on the ad hoc contributions of participants and the requirements of the event at any given time. Short, repetitive, open-ended forms are often played for a long time—until people tire or the music doesn't appear to be working. Individual Shona songs and pieces have names and basic structures by which they are identified. Yet pieces are not conceived as set, predetermined "musical objects," for which all ensemble members' contributions are preplanned, rehearsed, and controlled. Rather the music is a flexible medium for a particular type of social interaction and *play.* This is one of the most basic conceptions that begins to change when indigenous music and musicians become involved in modernist-cosmopolitan settings and presentational performance.

Rather than leading to boredom, as it might for a quietly seated audience, the repetitive cyclical quality of indigenous music in Zimbabwe provides *security in constancy.* Cyclical forms and unvarying rhythmic and melodic-harmonic motion allow neophytes to join in without fear of the piece suddenly veering off in surprising directions, making their contributions awkward. The choice to play familiar pieces also helps inspire security, and in Shona ceremonies is crucial for bringing on possession because ancestors are more likely to come when the music they knew and enjoyed when they were alive is played—familiarity aids participation by both the living and the dead and concretely unites generations around the same music.

The constancy of a culturally appropriate, familiar rhythmic motion, and lengthy performance aids participants in reaching and sustaining a deep level of sonic-kinesic synchrony. Moving and sounding as one creates the potential for community members to actually experience unity, although not necessarily simultaneously. Stark contrasts are avoided so that once this state is reached it can be maintained. Since aesthetic-emotional pleasure is largely the result of locking in with one's neighbors through synchronized sound and motion, repetition and long performances actually lead to a heightened intensity of satisfaction rather than to boredom, as they might in a presentational event.

### The Semiotics of Identity
### in Participatory Performance

The special power of participatory music and dance to create group unity and identity is due to their nature as inclusive, collective activities that place the subtle signs of social interaction and relationships in the foreground. Following the semiotic theories of C. S. Peirce, it is through different types of *signs* (something that stands for something else to someone in some way) that people think, feel, act, and experience the world. Peirce elaborated a variety of sign types. Each potentially creates effects of differing quality, ranging from pure feeling or sensation to physical reactions to linguistic-based thought (see Turino 1999 for fuller discussion of Peircian semiotics and music).

Certain types of signs within the Peircian framework operate in particularly direct ways and are interpreted as being concretely and existentially part *of* or connected to what they signify. Other sign types, such as those largely comprising propositional language, are of a general, "low-context" nature (Hall 1977), and are often perceived to be more highly mediational, that is, *about* something else. Musical signs are usually of the more direct type.

Of particular significance for understanding participatory musical occasions are the signs Peirce calls indexical-dicents.[10] The indexical component of a sign functions through co-occurrence of the sign and what it signifies (its *object*)—for example, "Taps" and funerals. The dicent component indicates that a sign is interpreted as actually being *affected by* what it signifies. A weathervane is an indexical-dicent because its direction is really affected by the direction of the wind (*object*, what is signified) which touches (index) and moves it. We typically interpret facial expressions and other "body language" as signs that are the result of the inner state or feeling that they signify, and thus they are also indexical-dicents.

Because we experience indexical-dicents as being actually connected to and affected by what they signify, we usually interpret them as true and real—as fact—whether they are or not.[11] Our processing (interpreting) of indexical-dicents such as "body language" often takes place outside the realm of linguistic-based thought and focal awareness. We are directly affected by such "mood indicators" in others, although we often do not even explicitly notice we are being affected. Such signs produce effects at the levels of sensation and physical reaction that then may have further effects within a particular semiotic chain (see Turino 1999).

In participatory situations the myriad subtle signs of sonic and kinesic timing, attack, and mode of articulation are all influenced by, and produced in response to, these same types of signs from other participants. Like "body language," they are dicents because they are both the results of and the signifiers of the quality of social relations among and the shared cultural knowledge of the participants. They are thus felt as the reality of those relationships and shared knowledge, which are in turn the foundation of social identities.

During intense musical-dance moments in participatory occasions, indexical-dicents are at the center of activity and of a certain type of awareness; often in such events fewer signs of other types compete for attention. Especially in intense participatory moments these signs often generate a concrete, nonreflexive sense of perceptual reality, and are all the more powerful for this. Being out-of-sync is as distressing as being smoothly in sync is satisfying because we experience indexical-dicents in a direct sensory way as the actual state of social relations, which are so important to our senses of self, well-being, and belonging (Hall 1977).

When things are clicking in participatory occasions, direct kinesic and sonic response to others may well be felt as a deep type of communion and the reality *of* affective identity in contrast to the effects of more highly mediational signs *about* relationships and identity (e.g., propositional speech). In constructing the "imagined communities" of nation-states, it is precisely these direct signs of communal identity and experience that nationalists seek to harness to imbue that larger, more abstract identity with sentiment and reality (see chapter 5).

### Participatory Music
### and Cosmopolitanism

Many of the basic musical principles, practices, and style features of indigenous Shona music making are similar to those of other indigenous African groups and, in fact, share a number of important elements with participatory musical traditions elsewhere (e.g., see Keil 1987; Feld 1988; Turino 1993).[12] But participatory traditions represent minority and often marginalized cases in largely cosmopolitan countries like the United States and England, where presentational and recorded forms predominate—in terms of mainstream social value if not in terms of actual numbers of music makers (Finnegann 1989).

In indigenous Shona society, however, participatory occasions represent the center both in terms of social value and numbers. In such places music and dance are particularly valued as special media for sustaining deep relations among people and between the living and the dead, and are shaped accordingly. Participatory styles, practices, and values offer important alternative models for enriching life and community in places where presentational and recorded forms of music have become the predominant, or at least most highly valued, modes—as in the modernist-capitalist formation. The lesson is not that we should replace these other modes of music making with participatory performance, thereby reducing music's potentials, but that we should learn to recognize, reinvigorate, and more highly value a type of music making and dance that, in many places, has proven key to social health. Indigenous Shona musicians provide successful models for this alternative mode of music making.

Mhlanga's analysis that most Zimbabweans are culturally 'in the middle' suggests that there are still various distinctive cultural positions that serve as sources for tension and combination. In this chapter I have begun to sketch what these different positions might be and have suggested that there is not simply one middle ground. Indigenous participatory music making and spiritual practices remained vibrant in Zimbabwe during the 1990s, as did an array of other local musical traditions, lifeways, and ethical positions. The following chapters trace various lines of musical and cultural development, and the processes of their multiple intersections.

# Part Two

# Colonialism and the Rise
of Urban Popular Music

# Chapter Two

# Indigenous Music and Dance in Mbare Township, 1930–1960

Before the emergence of urban-popular styles in the Harare townships during the 1930s, Christian music and indigenous music and dances were the mainstay for African workers in town and on farm and mine compounds (Chinamhora 1987: 261). Throughout the twentieth century the Mbare market area has been the hub of a vibrant indigenous music and dance scene. In this locale, at least, indigenous performing arts did not suffer decline because of colonial oppression—in fact they were encouraged as safe recreational activities (see chapter 3). Formalized regional dance clubs and burial societies developed out of ad hoc social gatherings among Shona workers, and a number of traditions were commonly reported in the township from the 1930s on. The main indigenous Shona genres observed in Mbare were *jerusarema, shangara, muchongoyo, mbukumba, dhinhe,* and *dandanda,* as well as *njari, mbira,* and perhaps other lamellophones.

What is striking about this list is that, out of the many Shona musical genres that exist, the styles performed in Mbare are precisely the ones that have become canonized as the paramount national music-dance traditions of Zimbabwe. These dances were commonly featured in the nationalist rallies in the early 1960s and became the core of the repertoire of the National Dance Company after 1980. Through the agency of the National Dance Company and guitar bands, it is largely these genres that became most highly professionalized for club, tourist, and international performances after the mid-1980s. This is no accident.

63

The "rural" Shona instruments and dances in Mbare are by now the most famous in Zimbabwe because their prolonged presence in the city made them so. They were the styles most readily available for incorporation into colonial cultural projects during the Federation years and for diffusion by the mass media; likewise, they were most available to the urban-based nationalist leadership. In this chapter I describe the indigenous traditions performed in Mbare, and trace the development of one particular dance association—The Murehwa Jerusarema Club and Burial Society—as a detailed case study.[1]

## Regional Networks in the City

During the first half of the twentieth century, and even today, many urban workers regarded themselves as only temporary residents in the city and planned to return 'home' *(kumusha)* after earning enough money.[2] As is common among rural migrants in cities around the world, "homeboy networks" were established in Harare. That is, people often tended to socialize and form voluntary associations with others of their own regions. In the early decades of the century this was particularly true of migrants from Malawi and Mozambique. Being foreigners and further from home, these migrants formed the first formal dance associations and burial societies, a pattern that was later imitated by Zimbabweans.

Within regional networks people performed the music and dances from their homes. This served as an obvious link between people in Mbare and home. Music and dance activities also helped foster regionally based social relationships in the township. As with the Murehwa Jerusarema Club, dance associations often included the name of their home region in their titles (Murehwa is a rural district in northeastern Zimbabwe). Zimbabwean social identities were, and often still are, strongly based on region of origin; the concept of *musha* figures importantly here.

According to what older people told me, dancing appears initially to have been largely a normal continuation of social activities that they had done at home. People interviewed said that their regional dances were simply the ones that they knew and enjoyed doing, and it was 'natural' for them to continue performing them after they got to the city (e.g., Nyandoro, Zim92-32: 5). This manner of continuing village musical practices in Mbare contrasts, for example, with the situation among Aymara migrants in Lima, Peru, where I did research previously. Most of my Aymara friends in Lima had not performed the panpipe and flute music of their hometowns before migrating to the city. Rather, they became involved in a very self-conscious reappropriation of their hometown music in order to establish communities in Lima and to create regional identity for social and political purposes (Turino 1993).

Early on in Mbare, indigenous music and dance were among the few recreational activities available to African workers; people who had enjoyed dancing and playing at home simply continued to do so in town. As several people mentioned, however, dancing publicly in Mbare was also a way of making your mark as an individual and a group—it was a forum for "showing people what you could do." These comments point to the feelings of anonymity and strangeness that village people may have experienced in the populous and heterogeneous township. The regionally specific music and dance activities were a way to create a familiar space in town and to locate others from 'home.'

## Indigenous Dances in Mbare, 1930–1960

Kenneth Mattaka, a central figure in the Harare music scene since the 1940s, remembers that when he first started coming regularly to Mbare township back in 1937, he often saw a variety of groups doing indigenous music and dances in the open areas near the central market.

> When we came in those days, you see, there were traditional dancers. But these were not organized in the form of [formal] groups as such, you know, as we find today. They used to dance. Because we had people from Mozambique, they used to sing, you know, just to entertain themselves, not being organized officially. So we had people from Malawi, also they used to sing their rhythms, their songs and dances, and so on. And we used to have Shonas. Especially on Sunday afternoons, you'd find the whole of that area where the market is now, drum-beating was very common on Sundays. (Zim92-65: 6)

Confirming Mattaka's remembrance, a police document from 1938 indicated that "among the laboring masses in the urban areas and mining districts, tribal dancing was easily the popular leisure-time activity" (cited in West 1990: 224).

In the order he remembered them for the 1937–38 period, Mattaka specifically mentioned people from Tete, Mozambique, performing the *ngororombe* panpipe dance; people from Murehwa dancing jerusarema; the muchongoyo dance-drumming tradition from southeastern Zimbabwe; Malawians performing their (unspecified) songs and dances; and shangara, a Shona recreational foot-stomping dance which is practiced in central, southern, and eastern Mashonaland (Zim92-65: 6). In 1929, political activist Charles Mzingeli mentioned Malawian *nyau* dancers performing in the Salisbury township (cited in West 1990: 225–26).[3]

Describing the musical life in Mbare township during the 1940s
and 1950s, middle-class African journalist Lawrence Vambe wrote,

> The most obvious and outstanding gift of the people of [Mbare] was
> that of song and dance. Tribal dances were the pre-dominant form
> of entertainment and they displayed incredible variety: from the
> Shona, with their hectic *ngororombe* (reed), drum, and *mbira* instru-
> mental ensembles, to the Mazungendava of Nyasaland [Malawi],
> with their extraordinary pipe bands. These performances used to
> take place in the open-air at the Musika market on Sunday after-
> noons. (1976: 212)

Mr. Maluwa, a ngororombe musician from Tete, Mozambique,
who came to Harare in 1951, gives a similar description of musical
activities in Mbare. To the list of dances already mentioned, he adds
that mbukumba was performed during the 1950s (Zim93-76: 3). Like
Vambe, Maluwa also mentioned that mbira groups performed near the
Mbare market during the 1950s.

Patrick Nyandoro stated that his group from Murehwa used to perform dandanda and other dances as well as jerusarema during the
1950s and 1960s in Mbare; he indicated that people from Murehwa
had been performing these dances in the township in previous decades
(Zim92-32: 3). Nyandoro also noted that when he arrived in 1949 there
was a shangara group from Kwesha, a muchongoyo ensemble, ngororombe from Mozambique, and a Korekore group from northern Zimbabwe doing dhinhe. Also known as dandanda, dhinhe was originally
a ceremonial dance of the Korekore people (Zim92-32: 2). Nicholas
Kambiriri, a co-member with Nyandoro in the Murehwa Jerusarema
Club, said that he remembered mbukumba, shangara, and muchongoyo
being danced in Mbare from the early 1950s, in addition to his own
participation in jerusarema.

Working in Zimbabwe as a missionary and music specialist beginning in 1960, Robert Kauffman similarly reported an active indigenous
music and dance scene in Harare's township beerhalls. He did not
specify the specific dance traditions and locales in question, but he commented that before "1954, mbira players, and later guitar players,
would wander through the streets collecting people as they went. When
the crowds became large enough, they would gather in a home to continue playing while drinking beer" (1970: 201).

Most observers single out the Mbare market area as the site where
indigenous dance and music performances took place most frequently
in the city early on, although beerhalls were an alternative. The market
area was a logical place to hold such dances: it was centrally located

within the earliest, most active African location, and there were large public spaces near the market. It is also significant that Mbare was home and social center to the lower-class workers and the sector that was most transient between the city and rural areas. Upward class mobility and urban permanence—as indicated by a move from Mbare to Highfield in the late 1930s and 1940s, and to 'lower-density' townships with home-ownership schemes in the 1960s—seems to correlate with a decline of interest in indigenous arts and culture among the middle class before the nationalist period.

## A List of Mbare Dances

Taken together, the descriptions of indigenous music and dance in Mbare provide a fairly coherent list of traditions that were performed there between the 1930s and the 1960s. The styles mentioned, usually by at least two observers, were (1) Malawian dances, including nyau; (2) Mozambiquean ngororombe; (3) jerusarema; (4) shangara; (5) muchongoyo; (6) mbira; (7) mbukumba; and (8) dhinhe/dandanda. Shona ngororombe was only mentioned by Lawrence Vambe; there is no other corroboration for the performance of this style by Shona groups in Mbare. Not involved with music himself, he might have confused the Shona and Tete panpipe styles (see below). Only Nyandoro mentioned dhinhe and dandanda. Unlike Vambe, however, Nyandoro is well acquainted with specific dance styles and is probably a reliable source. In the case of dandanda, he was involved in the performance of this dance himself.

Of particular significance for this study, it was precisely the *Shona* instruments and dances performed in Mbare—jerusarema, shangara, muchongoyo, mbira, mbukumba, and dhinhe—that came to constitute the nationalist canon of indigenous Zimbabwean dances, and the genres most commonly incorporated by electric-guitar bands. Although equally at hand, the genres from Malawi and Mozambique were ignored by the nationalists. The absence of Ndebele traditions is also worth noting and may simply be the result of Ndebele urban migration being centered in Bulawayo earlier on.

Given the available information, it is difficult to know if the eight dances and ensemble types specifically mentioned were all performed throughout the 1930–60 period; mbukumba, for instance, seems to have come in later, during the 1950s. Ngororombe from Mozambique, jerusarema, muchongoyo, and shangara, the most commonly cited dances, were, however, mentioned from the 1930s.

It is also difficult to know, given my data, how many different groups were performing in Mbare during any given period, and if a number of different groups performed the same commonly cited dances during the same period. Radio (Rhodesian Broadcasting Corporation, RBC) recordings in the National Archives of Zimbabwe, for example, suggest that there were several jerusarema groups active in the city in the early 1960s.[4] By 1950 there were at least two ngororombe groups from Tete performing. The original Tete burial society had split into three groups by this time, with Tete No. 1 and Tete No. 3 performing the ngororombe panpipe dance, and Tete No. 2 specializing in *mafuwe* dance drumming (fieldnotes 6/16/91; 10/4/92; 10/11/92), a tradition not even mentioned in other accounts. As in the case of Tete ngororombe after 1950, and jerusarema in the early 1960s, several groups simultaneously may have been doing any number of the nine traditions commonly mentioned. Other dances, such as *mafuwe,* were probably danced but not mentioned in my sources.

## Description of the Performance Traditions

Indigenous Shona dances and instrumental traditions are still associated with specific rural regions and social groups. Parallel to the Nigerian Yoruba case described by Waterman (1990a), the use of 'Shona' as an all-encompassing ethnic category is a colonial innovation. Zimbabweans typically self-identify with more specific regional groups. The ethnolinguistic populations now grouped within the Shona category include the Korekore, populating a broad band across northern Zimbabwe; the Zezuru in the central region surrounding and south of Harare; the Karanga in the south central area; Manyika in the central-eastern part of the country around the city of Mutare; and the Ndau in southeastern Zimbabwe. The Kalanga, located southwest of Bulawayo, have been grouped within the Shona category, but this is sometimes disputed. The Ndebele are the main non-Shona group, and inhabit the southwest-central region surrounding Zimbabwe's other major city, Bulawayo (see Sayce 1987: 210). Bulawayo served as the urban center for the Ndebele, which may partially account for the apparent paucity of Ndebele performance activities in Harare during the colonial era, although this is no longer the case.

Historically each of these rural regions and groups had their own dances and instrumental traditions. Especially after 1960, the mass media and nationalist cultural programs helped to spread the knowledge and influence of certain instruments and dances to new regions. Before this, dances and instruments were more slowly diffused to new areas. In what follows I briefly discuss the major dances and music performed in

Mbare. The descriptions are based on my own observations in rural areas and the city between 1991 and 1996. I also used photo, film, and recorded data dating back to the late 1950s. The descriptions thus pertain to this time period and to both rural and urban performance; working-class dance associations in Mbare tend to be stylistically consistent with performers in their home areas.

## Ngororombe

One of the earliest organized dance groups in Mbare was a burial society from Tete, Mozambique, that performed ngororombe. Ngororombe refers to bamboo panpipes played in pairs (with two and three tubes) within a larger panpipe ensemble that performs in interlocking style. In the Tete tradition, men play the panpipes and provide the percussion with leg rattles. The interlocking technique is doubly conceived in that each member of a pair often alternates blown pitches on his panpipe with sung/yodeled pitches on vocables. These are juxtaposed with the sung and blown pitches of his partner in the following manner (b = blown pitches; s = sung pitches):

Partner 1: b s b b s b s –
Partner 2: s b s – b s b b

This part of the instrumental/vocal performance comprises a "chorus" section which is alternated with solo a cappella vocal sections sung by the group leader, which feature topical texts.

The term *ngororombe* also refers to the dance. The men comprise half a single-file circle rhythmically stamping their feet to sound the leg rattles. Women, playing hand rattles and singing vocables on the chorus section, compose the other portion of the dance circle. Whereas the men's movement is quite angular and features percussive footwork, the women's dance style is softer with more movement of the hips.

The ngororombe dance was learned by Shona musicians in the rural Murehwa, Uzumba, and M'toko districts of northeastern Zimbabwe from Mozambique.[5] The Shona manner of performance differs in that one or two tall drums *(ngoma)*,[6] played with the hands, are added to articulate the 12/8 rhythmic cycle. The Shona style is also different in that the panpipe and female vocal parts constitute a two-phrase ostinato that is continuous—there is no alternation of solo and chorus sections as in the Tete style (see Jones 1992: 53–59). Shona ngororombe performance is not typically associated with spirit possession, but rather is performed at weddings, parties, and *guvas*.[7]

Shona ngororombe performance was apparently not diffused to

Mbare, whereas the Tete style became known through its longstanding presence there. It is striking that in spite of the distinctiveness and beauty of the Shona ngororombe style it was not among the dances later canonized by the nationalists or taken up within the culture industry. I would guess that this was because Tete's prominence in Mbare led to foreign associations with the dance, making it less useful for nationalist purposes. Even more important, since Shona ngororombe ensembles were apparently not readily available in the city, this tradition—like so many other rural genres—was passed over in cultural programs organized by urban elites.

### Muchongoyo

Another dance commonly mentioned for Mbare during the 1930–60 period, muchongoyo, is associated with the Ndau people of southeastern Zimbabwe. Muchongoyo is a militaristic dance style modeled on certain Nguni dances of South Africa (Welsh-Asante 1993: 96). It can be performed with two different-sized drums, one of which is like a miniature tomtom, and the other like a small Western bass drum with two pitches. These are strapped to the bodies of the drummers accompanying the dance, and are played with sticks. The male dancers, partially bare above the waist, wear costumes usually made of furs, and they carry sticks or spears and shields.

In a hallmark part of the choreography, the men stand upright in a line with knees slightly bent and make a dramatically hard stamping motion (the leg raising up at the thigh, moving out to the side, with knee bent, calf perpendicular). Good performance requires total synchrony of movement among the dancers, whose feet powerfully hit the earth simultaneously. The executions of this motion are paced relatively slowly (legs alternated in different patterns) as cued by the drums. In her excellent description of the dance, Welsh-Asante describes this part of the choreography as "strong in terms of weight, vertical with regards to space, and heavy in relation to quality" (1993: 103). Other parts of the dance are more acrobatic in nature and are an overt exhibition of male virility. As performed in Mbare and currently in rural Zimbabwe, muchongoyo is largely thought of as a recreational dance.

### Shangara

Unlike muchongoyo, which because of its special drums and costumes requires group organization, shangara is a rather ad hoc social dance. The term *shangara* refers to fast rhythmic footwork often done by one or two people at a time within a circle or gathering of other participants and observers. Accompaniment can be anything from handclapping to

drumming or mbira with *hosho* (gourd shakers). The majority of Shona
music is based on a two-phrase ostinato with descending melodies and
fast triple-duple rhythmic combinations within a 12/8 metric framework. Any song of this type might be used for shangara. Since the dance
is rather loosely defined by the rhythmically intricate footwork, rather
than any musical or rhythmic characteristics per se, music in simple
duple meter was also sometimes used for shangara.[8] This genre is
frequently mentioned in early descriptions of indigenous dancing in
Mbare. Because of its loose, informal character, it was probably very
common in beer halls and impromptu get-togethers in the market area.
My guess is that the term was somewhat loosely applied to various types
of informal social dancing and singing much as the term *jit* or *jiti* is used
in villages today (see chapter 7).

## Mbukumba

Mbukumba resembles shangara in its emphasis on fast rhythmic footwork. The dance is strongly associated with the Karanga people in
south central Zimbabwe. It is accompanied by a single, seated musician
playing two short, pitched drums with his hands, and by songs in solo-
chorus call and response. The male and female dancers often dress with
"skirts" of furs hanging from the waist, and the men wear pointed fur
hats; all the dancers wear abundant leg rattles. The men and women
may enter the dance space alone, in pairs, or in small groups. Sometimes
all the participants dance in a single line (side to side), as well as in two
lines, with the men and women facing each other.

Regardless of the formation, the dance has two distinct parts: a
"rest" section in which the dancers minimize movement and subtly accent the triple division of the 12/8 meter with their feet; and an "active"
section in which the dancers forcefully stamp out various combinations
of duple- and especially triple-based rhythmic patterns in relative unison
with their feet and leg rattles. The drummer often simply accents the
triple division of the meter (single strokes on 1,4,7,10) in the "rest" section, and combines duple and triple patterns in the "active" section.
During active sections, dancers may also include leaps and forward and
backward steps. When the men and women are divided in two lines,
during the active section they pass through each other and then turn to
face one another once again during the rest section. Zimbabweans clas-
sify mbukumba as a recreational 'outside the house' dance.

## Dandanda and Dhinhe

According to Nyandoro, dandanda and dhinhe were occasionally performed during the 1930–60 period in Mbare, although they did not

have the prominence of the other styles discussed here. The probable reason is that both were originally 'inside the house' dances connected with spirit possession ceremonies, and thus did not lend themselves to outdoor recreational contexts. In rural Zimbabwe they are still 'inside the house' traditions; since 1980, however, dhinhe has been stylized for stage and tourist performances by the National Dance Company and its offshoots.

In Korekoreland, northern Zimbabwe, the terms *dhinhe* and *dandanda* are sometimes used as synonyms. People in the Murehwa district where I worked used the term *dandanda,* and this is the dance that I will describe as it is done in Mhembere village. Dandanda is performed on two short (about 2.5 feet), single-headed drums played with sticks by two musicians sitting on the floor or ground. One drummer plays a fast, repeated triple pattern, while the second drummer accents the compound duple feel of the 12/8 meter and plays variations, both leading and in response to the dancers. The women play single *hosho* (gourd rattles) each interlocking her part with that of her neighbor. Men and women form separate sections of the chorus. Their parts are responsorial, or alternated to form an overall two-phrase ostinato. Frequently the men's and women's parts overlap substantially, and include simultaneous variations on both parts. These elements and a slightly heterophonic approach to singing in general produce an extremely dense texture. Although a song may last more than thirty minutes for dancing in a ceremony, the texts may comprise only one line, repeated over and over, or only vocables.

In ceremonies, people dance in the center of a kitchen hut at will in no fixed order or number, although as a medium is moving toward possession, the singing and dancing often become more intense with more people entering in. The dance style is rather individual in terms of actual movements but includes relatively erect posture for both men and women (slightly forward from the waist), and the major emphasis is in the lower legs and rhythmic work of the feet. Some basic moves of this dance resemble the dancing done to mbira music in ceremonies, such as a short hop on one foot with the other foot moving back and up, pivoting from the knee. Sometimes graceful leaps and other acrobatic movements are performed. I never witnessed dandanda done in the townships, and only saw dhinhe done by professional "folkloric" troupes.

### Mbira Music
Two observers cited above, Vambe and Maluwa, mentioned mbira performance in Mbare by at least the 1950s, and Kauffman mentions

mbira music in township streets and houses in the 1950s. I use the term *mbira* to refer to a specific type of lamellophone associated with the Zezuru people of the central region surrounding and to the south of Harare. This instrument, known in the musicological literature as "mbira dzaVadzimu," is of particular significance to my larger topic because it was the repertory of this particular lamellophone that became closely associated with popular artists like Thomas Mapfumo. It was also this instrument that became almost synonymous with Zimbabwean music in the international imagination during the 1980s (Turino 1998). Beginning around 1960 the diffusion of the mbira expanded, and today it is the most popular lamellophone type in Zimbabwe.

The Zezuru mbira has between twenty-two and twenty-eight metal keys in three manuals, attached to a sound board and played inside a calabash gourd resonator. Unlike the majority of Shona songs comprising two-phrase ostinatos, the basic ostinato of classical mbira pieces is usually four twelve-beat phrases within 12/8 meter. A single player may produce three or more polyphonic lines on the bass, medium range, and high keys. The bass and medium range mbira parts often imply harmonic progressions, with one "chord" changing stepwise with each phrase, for example,

$$\|\colon G\ B\ D \mid G\ B\ E \mid G\ C\ E \mid A\ C\ E \colon\|$$

When mbira progressions are arranged by guitar bands, they specify major and minor chords:

$$\|\colon G\ Bm\ D \mid G\ Bm\ Em \mid G\ C\ Em \mid Am\ C\ Em \colon\|$$

Such harmonic progressions, explicitly realized on guitars and bass, and the 12/8 rhythmic movement of mbira music were incorporated by popular electric bands after the early 1970s, along with other features (see chapter 8). As with most indigenous genres, hosho typically supply the rhythmic ground for two or more mbira players who perform separate (*kushaura* "to lead" and *kutsinhira* "to accompany"), interlocking parts. In ceremonies and other occasions the mbira and hosho provide the basis for collective singing and dancing.

The mbira has strong associations with spirit possession and 'inside the house' ceremonial activities in certain regions. In an article written in 1932, Hugh Tracey notes that in addition to religious ceremonies mbira "are also used for secular amusement" (1969: 84). Mbira are currently played in a wide variety of contexts such as at rural beer parties, urban beerhalls, special family and community occasions (e.g., graduation parties), and more casual get-togethers among family and friends, as well as in religious ceremonies. As indicated by Vambe, Maluwa, and

Kauffman, secular mbira performances took place in the Mbare market area and township streets by at least the 1950s.

Variations in terminology, however, make it possible that earlier observations about mbira performance in Mbare were really references to Shona lamellophones other than the Zezuru variety. The mbira is distinguished from the other types—for example, *njari, karimba, matepe, hera*—by the number of keys and their arrangement, by performance techniques, and often by repertory (see H. Tracey 1969; A. Tracey 1970, 1972; Berliner 1978). They also differ in terms of their regional/social group and contextual associations.

Although most Zimbabwean musicians that I met simply referred to the different lamellophones by their basic names (mbira, njari, karimba, etc.), a practice I follow in this book, the term *mbira* is also used generically to refer to the different lamellophone types. Hugh Tracey (1969: 91) suggested that njari was sometimes "called by the general term 'Mbira,' the notes," referring to the fact that the word *mbira* also denotes one or more lamellophone keys. John Kaemmer (1975: 82) and Paul Berliner (1978: 9) also found that Shona people sometimes used the term *mbira* generically for lamellophones.

Hugh Tracey went on to make the case that mbira *should* be the generic label for African lamellophones generally because it was already used this way in an important lamellophone-playing region (1961: 20–21). His son Andrew, Berliner, Kauffman, and many other writers have followed his lead, and it has become common practice in ethnomusicological writing. The generic use of the term *mbira* requires qualifiers—for example, "mbira dzaVadzimu" and "matepe mbira" (A. Tracey 1970)—and these names have also become common in scholarly writing.[9] If Vambe and Maluwa were using the term *mbira* generically, as Kauffman surely did,[10] we cannot be certain of the particular instruments observed in Mbare in the 1940s and 1950s from their accounts.

Hugh Tracey commented that the njari was the most popular type of Shona lamellophone by the early 1930s (1969: 79). This may have been the instrument that was observed in Mbare. Harare is in the Zezuru area, however, and in 1932, H. Tracey commented that the only people he found making and playing mbira were the Zezuru of the Harare region (1969: 79). It is thus also likely that the mbira found its way into the capital's township. From oral reports I gathered, it is clear that the Zezuru mbira was played in the townships of Harare by the late 1950s and early 1960s. In an article published in 1963, Andrew Tracey commented that in Mbare Township (then called Harare) he knew "at least seven youngish men playing [mbira], whereas the njari appears to be played mainly by older men" (1963: 23). This comment suggests that the njari may have been played in the township in earlier decades; the implication was that the mbira was a newer arrival in the township.

### MBIRA AND THE DISCOURSE
### OF REVIVAL

Andrew Tracey goes on to say that the age of the musicians he knew in Mbare suggested a "revival of interest" in the mbira (1963: 23). Tracey's comment is significant because it is the first statement in the literature I know that points to an "mbira revival," an idea that becomes common in later literature and matches ideas about a general decline of indigenous arts during the colonial period and a nationalist revival (e.g., Berliner 1978: 240–41). My question is whether there was actually an mbira *revival*, or rather a new popularity and broader diffusion of this particular lamellophone which, before the 1960s, had simply been a small-scale tradition in regard to the number of players—similar to the status of other lamellophones today (Turino 1998).

The earliest hint of the problem again comes in the paper written in 1932 by Hugh Tracey, who suggested that at the time of his research the mbira was not a prominent musical tradition, as compared to the more popular njari. He writes, "The fact that the only people that I have so far found still making and playing the *Mbira* variety are the Zezuru of the Salisbury area, would indicate that they were possibly the originators of the instrument, though not necessarily in their present geographical position" (1969: 79). Here he is using the term *mbira* in the nongeneric sense. Elsewhere in the article he says that "the *Mbira dze Midzimu* are now [1932] so rare that it is impossible to determine with any accuracy their modes" (83), and later he says that the instrument "appears to be dying out" (95). Paul Berliner's description of the mbira tradition in the Zezuru region of Mondoro in the decades before the 1960s indicates that Tracey's depiction of the mbira as a small-scale, specialist tradition had remained stable; Berliner indicates that there were very few players, and they tended to be old men (1978: 240).

Hugh Tracey asserts that the Zezuru mbira is the oldest Shona lamellophone (1969: 78), and implies through language like "dying out" that it was formerly more prominent and widely diffused than during the time of his research, but it remains unclear why he thinks so. Andrew Tracey (1972: 94) suggests that the Karanga (directly to the south of the Zezuru region) formerly played "mbira dza vadzimu," and Berliner states more specifically that this was the case in the later part of the nineteenth century (1978: 30).

Be all this as it may, for the language of *revival* to be pertinent to
the Zezuru mbira, the instrument would have had to have been much
more commonly played previously, and then to have suffered decline.
No specific data that I know of indicates that this was the case. The
Zezuru type existed in earlier centuries (A. Tracey 1972) and may even
have been played in a different region, but this in no way indicates that
there were substantially more mbira players previously than Hugh Tracey found in the 1930s. Indeed, the fact that Hugh Tracey could find so
few instruments in the early 1930s suggests that it was a rather specialized, small-scale tradition, at least by the early twentieth century—just
after colonial domination began. It is also possible that the tradition
was never quite as restricted as has been reported.[11] The crux of the
matter is that we simply do not know what the status of the mbira was
formerly. *Why, then, assume prominence, decline, and revival?*

What does seem clear is that the popularity and diffusion of Zezuru
mbira music has continued to increase from the late 1950s through the
early 1990s in various waves that are discussed in turn in later chapters.
In this section I am concerned with the beginning of this process signaled by Andrew Tracey's comment above, and similar comments by
Berliner and Peter Fry (1976) about the increased popularity of mbira
in the 1960s. John Kaemmer also noted that the "Zezuru mbira" (his
term) had recently been introduced into the Madziwa Tribal Trust
Lands in north central Zimbabwe (Korekoreland) around the time of
his 1972–73 research, and that they "are played today by a large number of young men" (1975: 85). The hera had been the lamellophone
used for ritual occasions in the Korekore region previously, and is still
used there alongside mbira. The njari had also been played in Madziwa,
but by the early 1970s it was going out of style (1975: 86). In the
Murehwa region where I interviewed, the njari had been the most common lamellophone before mid-century but was later replaced by the
mbira.[12] People in Murehwa still identified the Zezuru region of Mondoro as its source, indicating that they did not think of it as local to
Murehwa. By the early 1990s, mbira had been adopted alongside the
hera in the Uzumba region. What appears to have happened around
1960 is a shift in fashion, or a new taste for mbira alongside other local
lamellophones, in regions where it had not been common previously.
This seems to resemble the earlier process of njari diffusion described by
Hugh Tracey (1969).

As discussed in the previous chapter, the rise in popularity ("revival") of the Zezuru mbira has usually been explained by black nationalism. In terms of time frame this fits; mass cultural nationalism was

initiated by Mugabe in 1960. Other factors, however, explain more clearly why *this specific lamellophone* came into fashion rather than other types (e.g., the hera or matepe, with their own documented longevity and ritual connections), and why the Zezuru type articulated with nationalism to the extent that it did. In a comment made during a talk at the College of Music in Harare in 1993, Andrew Tracey suggested that the increased popularity and diffusion of the mbira may have been due to the Zezuru people's proximity to Harare; this makes particular sense because the capital was the center of the mass media.

## MBIRA ON RADIO

By the end of the 1950s, African programmers and field staff of the Rhodesian Broadcasting Corporation (RBC) began recording a great deal of indigenous Shona music for airplay on African Service Radio (now Radio 2). Single-copy, 78-rpm discs were recorded by mobile units throughout the country as well as in the Mbare studios. My partial list of the RBC collection, recorded between 1957 and 1972 and housed in the National Archives, suggests that a good deal of lamellophone music was recorded during this period (135 sides), and mbira recordings were more common than other types.[13] Another large indigenous music category in my partial catalogue list was shangara with eighty-three sides. Other regional genres commonly performed in Mbare were recorded much less: jerusarema (circa 20 sides), mbukumba (circa 25 sides), muchongoyo (circa 20 sides). Since the RBC recordings of indigenous music were the main ones available for radio broadcast, the collection is a good indication of what was aired on African Service radio programs dedicated to indigenous music.

From the 1960s through the mid-1990s on the African Service (Radio 2), special weekly programs were dedicated to lamellophone music, while separate Shona and Ndebele programs played a variety of indigenous genres; in the Shona programs this also included lamellophones. Within the field of indigenous Shona music, then, lamellophone music was singled out for special attention by the radio staff. Variety programs also played local and international popular music on the African Service.

Mr. Mbofana, current director of Radio 2, was an announcer on African Service Radio in the mid-1960s. Although he worked under a white director, Mr. Bernard Gilbert, the musical content of his programs was basically up to him. He used to play a variety of music. As a member of the black middle class,[14] it was not unusual that he particularly liked "American music, like the Mills Brothers and that sort of thing." He went on to say, however, "But I used to like, um, you know, from our African point of view, I like mbira. Yeah, that's my favourite" (Zim92-19: 2).

TURINO:  I have noticed that in the Archive collection there are quite a few mbira recordings, Bandambira is there, do you remember him?

MBOFANA:  Yes I remember; he was an old man . . .

TURINO:  and then this man, Mr. Mude?

MBOFANA:  Oh yes! Hakurotwi. Yeah, we recorded him. Yeah, I was actually involved in producing him.

TURINO:  How did you find him? How did you find mbira players at that time?

MBOFANA:  You see, what we used to do is to put an announcement across the air, yeah, to say, any mbira players could come and see us here [in Mbare Studios]. Then we auditioned them in the studio. This is how we discovered most of the mbira players. And some used to come on their own, of course, because we were the only station.

TURINO:  And also the only place to record.

MBOFANA:  Exactly. I don't remember how Hakurotwi Mude came to us. But he was one of our best mbira players. He was fantastic! His music became very popular.

TURINO:  Did people write or call? How did you know?

MBOFANA:  Yes! I mean we have got like listeners' request programs and they used to request, for instance, for his songs. He was very popular at one time.

TURINO:  How much time during the week or even during the day would mbira music be played?

MBOFANA:  We used to play lots of mbiras. I can't give the details, the breakdown exactly, but there was lots of mbira music played. Even up to now, we've got special programs on mbira. (Zim92-19: 3–4)

In a later interview Mbofana directly stated that lamellophone music, and especially mbira, had received significantly more airplay relative to other indigenous styles since the 1960s (Zimb93-43: 1).

Mbofana's comments illuminate Andrew Tracey's suggestion that Zezuru proximity to the city was important to the increased popularity and diffusion of the Zezuru mbira. While different types of lamellophone music were recorded in the rural areas by the mobile unit during the late 1950s and early 1960s,[15] Mbofana stated that the majority of players came into the studio to audition and record, thus making Zezuru proximity to the city an important factor in terms of the number of mbira players recorded and aired over radio. The rise in prominence of the Zezuru lamellophone has a direct parallel in the realm of language; the Zezuru dialect of Shona "assumed the status of a prestige form because of its use in Harare and on the radio" (Sayce 1987: 212). It is also significant that shangara, a Zezuru tradition, was also recorded more often than other dance-drumming traditions.[16]

Although the rise of mass-cultural nationalism around the same time may be significant, the role of the colonial, state-controlled radio in diffusing mbira is certainly worthy of notice. The special attention to lamellophone music by the radio staff (special programs dedicated to this music alone), and their greater access to Zezuru mbira artists helped enhance the prestige, popularity, and diffusion of this particular instrument.[17] The widespread radio popularity of Zezuru artists like Hakurotwi Mude and Bandambira served as inspiration to others.

Both Chris Mhlanga and Tute Chigamba, who took up the mbira in the early 1960s, told me that they had been inspired by, and actually learned mbira music from, these radio broadcasts—especially the recordings of Bandambira. A number of later "mbira-guitar" players like Jonah Sithole also primarily learned mbira music from the radio (see chapter 8). The special Radio 2 programs dedicated to lamellophone music still serve as a primary source for diffusing the Zezuru mbira among young players in the rural areas and townships, and the popularity of the mbira, in particular, has been strengthened among young people by its incorporation into guitar bands (see chapter 9).

By the 1980s, the mbira was far and away the most famous and popular lamellophone in the country. As far as we know, this does not so much represent an mbira revival as much as a new flowering of this instrument. As with the other dances performed in Mbare, the Zezuru mbira's greater presence in the city seems to have been crucial to its rise in prominence over other lamellophone types. Radio and recordings—the mass media—have played a central role in making this formerly localized tradition translocal and ultimately transnational (see chapter 9).

### Jerusarema

The current fame of the jerusarema dance in Zimbabwe is also partially related to the mass media. Jerusarema music is heard constantly throughout the day to introduce the national news on radio and television. The rhythmic pattern played on the woodblocks within this genre resembles the old teletype sounds that used to index news broadcasts in many places—here a local form fits within a cosmopolitan practice in a particularly neat way. The dance has also become a favorite among professional "folkloric" troupes performing at tourist locations, festivals, and contests in the city. Jerusarema is typically performed in 'outside the house' contexts at *guva* ceremonies, at weddings, funerals, and at other family occasions in the rural areas. In Mbare it was performed early on for recreation in the open area around the market, where it is still done presently, along with beerhall performances and at other more formal events in the city such as dance festivals.

Jerusarema (*mbende* is another name for the dance) was introduced in Mbare by the 1930s.[18] It is closely associated with the Murehwa district in northeastern Zimbabwe. The dance is accompanied by two tall drums (ngoma) played with hands by a single musician; a pair of hosho (made from metal cans). In addition, the male dancers play woodblock clappers *(manja)* and sing two-phrase ostinato melodies in unison or heterophony on vocables. One or more men will also ornament the chorus singing with yodeling and melodic variations.

In the dance, men and women form two semicircles facing each other, with the drummer and hosho player standing behind the line of men. Like mbukumba, the dance consists of active and rest sections. Atypical of most Shona music, jerusarema has a simple duple feel (4/4) with the rest section beginning on the first beat of a two-bar period, and the active section beginning on a pick-up on the eighth beat leading into a series of drum patterns that last eight beats. The repetitive, interlocked manja parts and the drums start together on the anacrusis, and during the active section the drummer plays a series of formulaic or improvised drum patterns which are divided into two four-beat sections.

♫ | ♫♩♫♩♫♩♫♩ | ♫♩♫♩♫♩♩♪ ᴎ

Specific drum patterns are synchronized with the moves of particular dancers. In the rest section the drummer usually plays a soft holding pattern similar to the manja rhythm, and the woodblocks are silent; the singing continues through both sections.

The dancers move into the central performance space spontaneously in various ways: a single man or woman, two or three women, male and female partners, several sets of partners. Once people 'have gone in' they will dance for as long as they wish, usually between four and eight minutes. During the rest sections the dancers simply step or shuffle in place (partners facing each other); during the active sections a variety of choreographic moves are brought into play.

Jerusarema is playful in nature and may involve mime and brief mini-dramas to comment on the occasion at hand. For example, once when our group, the Murehwa Jerusarema Club, performed at a grave ceremony *(guva)*, one of the members rhythmically dug a hole with a shovel and another dancer laid in the hole and was buried as part of the dance. For the most part, dancers develop their own repertory of moves which have, over time, proven to be entertaining to the other participants. Men and women within a rural community or an urban dance association may form partnerships (i.e., they often 'go in' together) and develop their own routines. There are also certain stock moves that are commonly performed.

A standard movement for women involves a rapid hip motion, arms out to the side, and feet slightly apart and pigeon-toed as the dancer steps forward. In a classic male movement, the dancer goes down close to the earth squatting on both legs (on the pick-up before the active section). Then with the right leg bent, the left leg is thrust out behind him (at which point he looks like a runner at the starting line) repeatedly on the beat (1, 2, 3, 4, . . . ). Simultaneously the hands do a swimming, breast-stroke motion. The dancers in the Murehwa Club denied that this or other standard movements had any particular meaning. Most dance moves end in synchrony on beat eight of the active section, which is accented by the drummer. This beat often contains a kind of choreographic "punchline" for that active period. The quality of dancing is judged significantly by the imaginative and usually humorous ways that beat eight is punctuated with the body.

Various types of play between the genders is often included in the dance. Usually a couple's performance will end with the woman aggressively driving her partner back to the line of manja-playing men; she then struts back to her line with a smug look of victory. This part of the dance is interesting for the way it turns normal gender relations on their head.

In Zimbabwe generally, and certainly in indigenous Shona societies, women are extremely subservient to men. In domestic relations this is clearly portrayed in the custom, still practiced, of women going down on their knees and clapping hands when greeting or serving their husbands or fathers. In indigenous Shona practice, women were, and in some ways still are, legal minors. For example, when a husband dies, his wife, children, and property belong to the husband's family and usually one of the brothers takes the widow as an additional wife. Since the husband's family pays *labola* (bride price) for the woman, she and the offspring are regarded as being the responsibility of that family. Historically in rural villages, this practice was supposed to provide continued support and good treatment of the widow and her children; social pressures within a village probably helped ensure this "social security" function.

Presently in the city, at least, this custom sometimes has sinister results. In a case I was personally aware of in 1992–93, a widow and her children were threatened with being left without home, possessions, and care by a greedy brother-in-law who was attempting to take all the belongings but not the family. Another woman described in outrage how her brother-in-law began to speak of their future marriage while her husband was still in critical condition in the hospital; she did not want to marry him, and happily the husband recovered. Since 1980, national laws have been passed allowing widows to fight this custom in court, but many remain unaware of their legal rights. Given this background, the almost uniform portrayal of female dominance in jerusarema is curious.

When men and women dance together various other types of sexual play are sometimes involved. Older urban dancers and rural dancers will occasionally enact a subtle pelvic thrust toward each other, punctuating beat eight of the active section, as a joke. According to Murehwa Club members, this may be done in relatively private contexts—'late at night when people had had a bit to drink and no children were around'—but the members adamantly disapproved of performing this move 'in public.' Many Shona people are quite modest when it comes to sexual matters, and I was told repeatedly that it would not be proper to do this pelvic thrust movement in front of your in-laws (the ultimate acid test) and children. What is striking, then, is that a remarkably explicit pelvic thrust between partners became the very centerpiece of the jerusarema dance when it was later stylized for stage performance by the National Dance Company and its professional offshoots. This sexually explicit version of the dance remains a sore spot with conservative people from Murehwa. This controversy makes jerusarema a particularly good example for illustrating what happens to indigenous dances when they become canonized and standardized for stage performance (see chapter 9).

### Sunday in Mbare, June 1960

During the colonial period Africans had to have full-time jobs to stay in the townships, which meant that Sunday was the only day off for most. It was a day for shopping at the open-air market in Mbare, for drinking, music, sports, and other types of recreation. Many people talked about Sundays in Mbare during the 1950s and 1960s, and the following description is a composite drawn from their remembrances.

The curving roads that run through the township were filled with people on bikes, trucks, and cars, mainly people walking, women with children in tow. Domestic servants who lived in white suburbs and could get away, came streaming in. Men from the hostels stood about loitering or headed for the beerhall to meet friends. On the main road in from the city center there is a football stadium surrounded by rough fields of grass. In the fields and sand lots, boys and young men organized pick-up soccer. Others walked to the stadium to watch more formal games; a well-dressed group of men from Highfield walked from the bus stop to see the afternoon match. This same group planned to attend a formal concert at Stodart Hall that evening featuring De Black Evening Follies, a dignified event that even their wives could attend.

Broad lots of red sand and a few shade trees stood between the blocks of hostels, rows of houses, the market, and the central beerhall with its cement walls, floor, and tables. Sitting on the curb in front the beerhall a ragged man played musical bow with a can set in front of him for coins. Inside at one table a guitar player was surrounded by men who laughed at his jokes; at another, mbira and hosho players drew a crowd who move quietly to their music. At other tables acquaintances and friends passed large containers of African corn beer between them and ignored the music completely—the sound lost beneath the loud hum of voices.

The day was cool but the sun was hot. Under trees in grassy places around the edges of Mbare people congregated for church. Dressed neatly with white shirts, pressed trousers, and clean cotton dresses, one group sang, in neat homophonic style, songs that could be heard in a Methodist church in Des Moines. Under another tree people dressed in long white robes danced energetically in a circle and sang "Africanized" Christian songs loudly, call-and-response, to a pair of drums.

By the shade tree in a sand lot a few men from Murehwa showed up just before noon. They set two tall drums out in the sun to tighten the leather heads and set themselves under the tree's branches to smoke and wait. Others gradually appeared; the greetings were formal and in-clusive. The few women who came curtsied to the men with lowered eyes and then stood together, slightly apart. One man went to test the drums periodically, and others talked quietly about general events of the past week; although these people had known each other for years, little was said of a personal nature.

After an hour the drums were ready and were moved out to a clear space. Men carefully chose their wood blocks from a cotton bag. They lined up in front of the drums and began to sing; one man walking back and forth in front yodeled and encouraged the others. As the singing became louder, the yodeling man gave a sign and the drummer kicked in with well-known jerusarema patterns to the thunder of the manja; a man and woman moved out into the center space to dance. Suddenly a crowd of people appeared—loiterers, passers-by, children—and encircled the group as they danced. Under other trees, in other lots, mbukumba and shangara dancers gathered.

Sunday afternoon in Mbare.

## The Institutionalization of Indigenous Dance in the City

With a few exceptions, the early dancing in Mbare was done by ad hoc groups of people that simply came together informally for recreation; to quote Mattaka again, dances "were not organized in the form of groups and such, you know, as we find today." Rather, a few friends from Murehwa might go out into an open area near the market with a pair of tall drums and begin playing jerusarema, maybe around the same time each week. The drumming would attract a crowd, and others from Murehwa who knew and enjoyed the dance might join in. As time went on, a nucleus of people who danced together regularly solidified. The regional basis for such performance groups thus evolved around the particular genres as a matter of course.

### Burial Societies

In addition to these informal regional dance collectives, burial societies also performed indigenous dances in Mbare during the early decades of the century. The first burial societies in Harare appear to have been formed by migrants from Mozambique and Malawi. Members of Shona burial societies that I spoke with generally agreed that the model for such institutions came from preexisting societies from these countries. There is little dependable data on the proliferation of burial societies among Shona speakers in the Harare area, but by now they are quite common.[19]

Burial societies are a type of formal self-help organization and grass-roots insurance agency. Members pay monthly dues which are kept in a joint account to pay for returning the body home and funeral costs. Coverage varies depending on the charter of the specific society; funeral costs for the member, his or her spouse, and a specified number of the eldest children are often guaranteed.[20]

Burial societies are also a type of formal community network providing social and emotional support in times of illness, death, and economic problems.[21] In addition, the societies that I had experience with were social clubs, with members coming together to drink and socialize in a favorite beerhall on a weekly basis. A number of burial societies include music and dance groups. Whereas the membership of a burial society may range from twenty to over one hundred people, only a portion of the membership usually performs with the society's ensemble.[22] Along with being a recreational activity, the performances are an important mechanism for making the society known and attracting new, dues-paying members.

A number of dance and music groups that I encountered in Harare were affiliated with burial societies; others were just formalized dance or musical associations. The precise period when the ad hoc Shona dance groups of the 1930s began to evolve into formal dance associations or burial societies is not known, and probably varies according to the individual group. Clearly, however, formal dance and music associations existed at least by the early 1950s.

## Murehwa Jerusarema Club and Burial Society

The Murehwa Jerusarema Club that I joined is interesting in that it has gone through different phases of being an ad hoc group, a formalized dance association in 1952, and finally a burial society with an affiliated jerusarema ensemble in 1987. A closer look at the history and organization of this group will illustrate several issues and dynamics pertaining to indigenous dance ensembles in Harare. The group's history also illuminates a number of key issues—especially the rise of professionalism and involvement with nationalism—from a grassroots perspective.

When Patrick Nyandoro and Nicholas Kambiriri, the two oldest original members of the Murehwa Club, came to the city seeking work at the end of the 1940s, there was already a group of people from Murehwa performing jerusarema on an informal basis in Mbare. This ad hoc group of 'older people' had been dancing in the city for several decades. Moving into the Old Bricks Hostel in Mbare, both Nyandoro and Kambiriri joined in dancing soon after arrival, Nyandoro being related to one of the men who had been doing jerusarema there formerly. Nyandoro and Kambiriri had danced jerusarema at home before coming to Harare. I asked them why they continued dancing in the city and Nyandoro replied, "That was in, in a natural way, you see, because we were all born like that. That is why we didn't want to stop it, we continued doing it: playing, playing, playing until we formed the group" (Zim 92-32: 5).

In 1952, a formal jerusarema club was created with drummer Douglas Vambe as chairman and Patrick Nyandoro as secretary; other early members included Kambiriri and Richard Taruvinga. All the members were from the Murehwa-Uzumba area. Although in Murehwa villages the number of men and women who dance jerusarema together is relatively equal, there were fewer women in Mbare at the time, and through the early 1960s the club had only two female dancers (Zim 92-32: 7).

Nyandoro stated that they formalized the club because they wanted to become an identifiable ensemble with a stable group of performers who would become known in Mbare for dancing in a particular way (Zim92-32: 1). Apparently other groups had the same idea and began to formalize under specific names during the first half of the 1950s. According to Nyandoro, the Korekore dhinhe group was known as Pasipamambo, and the muchongoyo dancers became known as Mapongwana Muchongoyo. The Murehwa Club continued to perform outdoors in the Mbare market area regularly on Wednesday evenings.

The fact that they had become a stable, recognizable ensemble began to pay off years later. In 1958, during the Federation period, they were invited to perform before a white audience at the University of Zimbabwe along with the Mapongwana Muchongoyo group. In 1959, the Murehwa Jerusarema Club was invited to participate in a special training program. Nyandoro told me that an African-American woman was invited to Zimbabwe to train 'traditional' dancers to perform on stage. Over the course of several coaching sessions, the visiting artist introduced the idea of arranging the order of pairs entering the jerusarema circle, and made suggestions about choreography: "We were taught to dance in the theater" (Nyandoro Zim92-32: 4). As a part of this brief program, the Murehwa Club, the muchongoyo ensemble, and a shangara group performed a concert for a white audience at the Rainbow Cinema on Park Street in downtown Harare—indicating an interest in indigenous dance among whites during the Federation.[23]

Nyandoro and Kambiriri had nothing to say about the lasting effects of the training received from the American dancer, but according to Nyandoro, the exposure they received at the Rainbow Cinema led directly to another opportunity. In 1963, the Murehwa Club "was taken by the government to Domboshawa," a site outside of Harare, for a filming session. The Central African Federation Film Unit made two movie shorts, entitled *Ngoma No. 1*, and *Ngoma No. 2*, which featured the Murehwa Club.[24] Like the recordings of indigenous music made by the RBC, these films were part of a series sponsored by the colonial government documenting 'African' culture and arts.

The first ten-minute film featured the Murehwa Club doing their standard version of jerusarema twice (selections 1 and 3), with an altered, stylized version in between. Selections 1 and 3 were performed in normal fashion, including both the classic jerusarema moves and individuals' variations. In general these performances are remarkably similar to the way the group danced in 1992–93, indicating stylistic stability over this thirty-year period.

The middle piece on *Ngoma No. 1* was related to jerusarema by the "active-section" "rest-section" manja (woodblock) arrangement and by the manja patterns themselves. Atypically, the drummer played more continuously through both sections with patterns in a 6/8 or 12/8 feel (rather than in simple duple meter as is usual). The choreography included none of the standard jerusarema moves but rather leaps by the male dancers, resembling dandanda, and some graceful line choreography with synchronized swaying hip movements done by four men and the two women lined up front-to-back.

In the second movie short, the club leads off with a threshing song-dance, repetitively moving in a circle beating imaginary grain in the center with sticks. This is followed by a hunting song accompanied by the paired tall ngoma and manja; the drumming patterns resembled dandanda. The dance involved miming of hunting with spears and shooting guns. The third selection on *Ngoma No. 2* was basically free-style social dancing, although, oddly, some of the male dancers included classic jerusarema features such as the "breast-stroke" movement, something that is not usual in village jit or *jocho* social dancing.[25]

The two performances of jerusarema (selections 1 and 3 on *Ngoma No.1*) were energetic, imaginative, brilliant. The middle selection on *Ngoma No.1* was carefully choreographed and, from the coordination of this performance, appears to have been well-rehearsed. The American artist's coaching was probably involved here. By contrast, the selections on *Ngoma No. 2* appear haphazard and uninspired. Around this time the group primarily performed jerusarema in typical style and probably did so for hours on end without tiring of it, as is the case today. Their primary commitment to this dance is indicated by the name the club used by the early 1960s—Murehwa No. 1 Jerusarema Club.

Like most people in Murehwa, they also could perform social dances such as jit, and knew other types of music and dance from

Murehwa as well—threshing songs, hunting songs, and dandanda being common. My guess is that for the second film, the movie director
wanted different dances for variety, and on short notice the Club improvised the numbers on *Ngoma No. 2* during the session to oblige. According to Nyandoro and Kambiriri, the Club did not normally do these
dances, and judging from the performances on the second film, they had
not put much forethought into them and were rather awkward in their
execution. The effects of staging participatory music and dance, and the
pressure to supply variety that comes when indigenous ensembles perform on stage and screen is evident here. These films are an early example of this type of dynamic, which becomes more common in later
decades.

### The Rise of Professionalism
Making these movies was a particularly significant moment in the Murehwa Jerusarema Club's history because it was the first time that they
received payment for performing. As Nyandoro remembers, "We performed about three minutes, then we finished. This is the time we were
first given money; we were given sixty pounds. That was too good for
us!" (Zim92-32: 4).[26]

Before the 1960s the performance of indigenous dance was not associated in most people's minds with making money. For Nyandoro and
his group, this first experience of being paid planted the idea that it was
possible to earn income by dancing. In a number of conversations,
Nyandoro singled out this realization as seminal in his group's history,
and the emphasis he put on it suggests just how revolutionary an idea it
was at the time.

In other conversations Nyandoro indicated that the number of indigenous dance groups in the townships had substantially increased
during the 1960s. Rather than attributing this proliferation to African nationalism, as I initially had, however, he explained it in terms of
the new realization that money could be earned by dancing—an idea
passed by word of mouth within indigenous dance circles in Mbare.
Whether or not this is literally true for everyone involved, Nyandoro's
interpretation certainly provides new dimensions for thinking about the
"indigenous cultural renaissance" of the 1960s, and about professionalism as a new force within Zimbabwean musical life.

### Nationalist Activities
Throughout the 1960s and 1970s—indeed, to the present day—the
Murehwa Jerusarema Club continued to perform in the Mbare market
area and in beerhalls on a regular, often weekly, basis when they did not

have special invitations to perform elsewhere. Between 1960 and 1963, however, a new type of opportunity for performance emerged. The Murehwa Club along with the other indigenous dance groups from Mbare began to be called to perform at ZAPU's nationalist rallies and activities in the townships of Harare (usually Highfield) and other cities.

The older members of the Jerusarema Club expressed a variety of attitudes about their performance in the early 1960s nationalist rallies, and their responses mirrored those of other people I interviewed. Some people told me that they had supported the nationalists and so were glad to perform at the rallies. When asked if they *were* nationalists during the early 1960s people said things like, "Definitely. Because everybody could see the injustices that were done on the blacks." Other people, however, told me that they were not particularly involved with nationalism but were fearful that if they did not participate, repercussions (including violence, such as rocks through their windows) might follow. When asked if he had been a nationalist during the 1960s, one man replied:

> M:  Yes. You had to be. Because when you lived among people who were not housed in the houses of the whites [domestic servants], we were living with our people [in the townships]. So if meetings were organized, you had to attend.
>
> TURINO:  You had to attend?
>
> M:  Where else could you go? 'Cause, ah, they went house to house, asking for people to attend meetings, so one had to attend the meeting. You need to have a very strong reason not to attend.
>
> TURINO:  So the nationalists, were they forcing you to go?
>
> M:  Eh, I wouldn't say they were forcing people to go, but, ah, perhaps the force was inbuilt. You could, ah, tell on your own that, if I don't attend, perhaps something will happen to me. But it wasn't said to you.

Other musicians and dancers not personally involved with nationalism simply viewed political rallies as another invitation to perform and were not concerned with the nature of the occasion. When I asked Murehwa Club members why they thought the nationalists wanted them to perform at the rallies, the most typical reply was "to entertain the people"; Patrick Nyandoro simply replied, "I do not know what was in their minds."

This variety of attitudes about, and involvement with, the early nationalist movement is noteworthy. African nationalism in Zimbabwe has often been portrayed as a mass participatory movement or considered from the perspectives of the leadership alone without taking into account different grassroots motivations and positions (see Kriger 1992; Hobsbawm 1990).

In the years of state repression that followed 1963, holding large-scale nationalist rallies became impossible for banned revolutionary parties such as ZAPU and ZANU. The performance of indigenous music and dance in the city at events organized by these parties was not to be resumed until the first Independence Day Celebration on 18 April 1980. The Jerusarema Club and a variety of other indigenous dance groups performed at this and subsequent nationalist celebrations in the first half of the 1980s. Given the historically momentous nature of the first Independence Day Celebration, I was surprised by the casual way this performance was mentioned by Murehwa Club members, certainly relative to the way their first professional engagement was reported.

During the 1980s the Murehwa Club began to perform more frequently on a contractual basis for weddings, *guva* ceremonies, store openings, and a variety of other occasions both in the city and in rural areas. By this time performing for money had become commonplace, and they considered themselves a part-time professional ensemble. From the 1960s through the 1990s they have also continued to perform jerusarema purely for enjoyment most Sundays in the Vito Beerhall in Mbare when they did not have a contractual performance, which is to say, most of the time.

## The Split within the Murehwa Jerusarema Club

In 1987, a split occurred in the original Murehwa No. 1 Jerusarema Club, and an offshoot emerged—The Murehwa Jerusarema Club and Burial Society (MJCBS)—led by Patrick Nyandoro. Splits in burial societies and dance associations are quite common (Cormack 1983; Hall 1987). The reasons for such splits commonly include memberships that become too large to manage, disputes over leadership, and problems over finances.

In the case of the Murehwa Club several issues were involved. Nyandoro and some members wanted to become a burial society as well as a dance group, while others were reluctant to pay dues, and so the group split along these lines. Since then MJCBS has attracted new members who are only involved with the burial society. Other people, like Reason Muskwe (current chairman and main drummer) were already committed performers, and they joined the group both because they wanted the security of a burial society and because they wanted to 'dance.'

Conflict over the style of dancing was another cause of the Murehwa Club split, and it was the issue that MJCBS members most readily talked about. By 1987 the National Dance Company had begun to popularize the style of jerusarema with the pelvic thrust movement as a centerpiece of the dance. This move has become almost synonymous with jerusarema in the public imagination since the mid-1980s—it began to be what audiences expected, and some performers responded to those expectations. Members of Murehwa No. 1 Jerusarema Club began to include this movement prominently, indeed, the jerusarema instructor for the National Dance Company, Immanuel Maseko, had come out of Murehwa No. 1 Jerusarema Club.

Some of the more conservative members of the club, however, were upset by this style of dancing and wanted to discourage it. A dispute continues over the proper way to dance jerusarema between the members of Murehwa No. 1 and the newer MJCBS; the latter group still eschews overtly sexual movements. In one beerhall performance a member of Murehwa No. 1 Jerusarema Club "sat in" with MJCBS and began to execute the pelvic thrust movement. People became very angry and asked him to stop; the women he danced with, in particular, gave him a very cold reception.

When the splinter group became a burial society several things shifted. Nyandoro (secretary), Reason Muskwe (president), and others suggested that now an important reason for performing regularly in Mbare was to become better known and to attract more members. This is a common rationale for burial society performing ensembles. The strength, wealth, and security of a burial society depends on the number of dues-paying members, and continually enlarging the ranks becomes a priority. Like the Tete groups and other burial societies I encountered, region of origin is no longer a major criterion of membership for MJCBS; people from anywhere are welcomed and valued as long as they pay their dues regularly and fit socially with the warm, supportive, and respectful social style of the group.

Approximately a fourth of the thirty-six members of MJCBS are not from the Murehwa-Uzumba area,[27] and some of them have joined the eighteen or twenty members who dance regularly for the society. According to Nyandoro, who led and taught the dance in the early 1990s, the presence of performers who come from outside Murehwa has changed things. Since not everyone in the ensemble grew up with jerusarema, more guidance is needed, and there are larger differences in skill. Moreover, these members are not familiar with the other dances from Murehwa such as dandanda, which, according to Nyandoro, the group used to perform occasionally but no longer does.

Thus while regionalism no longer restricts membership, for financial reasons, belonging to a place and growing up with its traditions is still perceived as being a factor determining artistic competence. The tension here between the financial benefits of translocalism versus the artistic value of being rooted in a place and its lifeways provides a concrete microcosm of tensions defining Zimbabwean identities and music much more broadly.

Chapter Three

# The Settler-State and Indigenous Music During the Federation Years

Patrick Nyandoro and Nicholas Kambiriri remembered the Murehwa Jerusarema Club's performances for white audiences at the University and at the Rainbow Theater in the late 1950s with special clarity. When I asked them, independently, about high points in the club's history, both cited these performances and the films they made in 1963. Surprisingly, neither mentioned as high points their performances at the rallies for ZAPU in the early 1960s, the historic first Independence Celebration of Zimbabwe in 1980, nor the many other large-scale nationalist events they have participated in since. Perhaps those early performances stood out in their memories because they represented a radically new type of experience: on stage, for the mass media, for white audiences, and for pay.

These experiences and the increased number of indigenous dance clubs in Mbare during the 1960s were linked in their minds to the white Federation government rather than to black nationalism, as I had originally supposed from the literature. This led to some interesting interchanges like the following one with Murehwa Club members Patrick Nyandoro, Nicholas Kambiriri, and Reason Muskwe:

> TURINO: A little while ago, Patrick, you said that in the 1960s, and from then on, more and more dance groups came up in the city.
> NYANDORO: Yes, they came more, because, as we were always being picked up and called for dancing, we were just given a little

bit of money, and the people saw that: "Ah they are being
given money!" So they started creating their own . . .
MUSKWE: Clubs.
NYANDORO: Clubs, you see.
TURINO: But was it the nationalists that were giving you money?
NYANDORO: That was the nationalists.
TURINO: The nationalists.
NYANDORO: I mean, the government.
TURINO: The *white* government!?
NYANDORO: The white government, yes. In the 1960s they, Welensky
[Federation prime minister, 1956–1963], . . .
MUSKWE: Sir Roy Welensky, he was the prime minister of this coun-
try at that time.
KAMBIRIRI: The first one is Whitehead [prime minister of Southern
Rhodesia, 1958–62], Welensky was, eh, Federation.
TURINO: So the white government was giving you jobs?
NYANDORO: Oh, in their mind, I don't know what they were seeing.
MUSKWE: By that time, they were trying to please people.
NYANDORO: Yes, I think it, they saw something in front of them, you
see. We could not see anything, and they just called us.
(Zim93-78:9-10)

The Murehwa Jerusarema Club's invitations to perform at the University and the Rainbow Theater in the late 1950s and the Central African Film Unit's interest in 'tribal' dances were part of a larger conjuncture during the years of the Central African Federation of Southern
Rhodesia, Northern Rhodesia, and Nyasaland, 1953–63. Whereas formerly, in the context of harsh racist policy and attitudes, there would
have been relatively little interest in African arts and culture on the part
of the state and many white Rhodesians, during the Federation period a
discourse of 'racial partnership' emerged which opened a space for engagement with indigenous arts on the part of the state and white settlers,
and allowed for new attitudes on the part of the black middle class.

A consideration of Federation cultural programs and social alliances illustrates the working and spread of cosmopolitan ideas such as
musical professionalism, modernist reformism, and cultural preserva-
tionism. In this chapter we see how such ideas became more widely diffused in Zimbabwe. We also see how such ideas were reinforced because
of the nature of cosmopolitan networks and the social power and technologies of the individuals involved. A primary goal is to show how
various cultural attitudes and projects usually attributed to black nationalism got their start under the "liberal" colonial banner of 'racial
partnership.'

## The Federation

In Southern Rhodesia interest in amalgamating with Northern Rhodesia and Nyasaland was expressed by Prime Minister Huggins as early as 1935, because of the discovery of copper in Northern Rhodesia and for other economic reasons such as expanded "internal" markets and labor pools (Utete 1978: 52–53; Holderness 1985: 106). Economic advantages would clearly accrue to the more powerful Southern Rhodesians, whereas the small white minority in the north felt increasingly threatened and needed allies:

> Since the statement by the British Government that African interests in her colonies should be paramount, whites in Northern Rhodesia felt that they were expendable in the eyes of the British Government. In anger, they turned to Huggins for salvation, thus giving him support for his expansionist dreams. (Vambe 1976: 117)

Africans in the three territories opposed federation, sensing that it would strengthen Southern Rhodesian racist policies. Consequently, the Bledisloe Commission sent by the British Government concluded in 1939 that "amalgamation was premature. While conceding that the plan was beneficial in principle, [the commission] pointed out the differences in the native policies of the three territories," specifically mentioning Southern Rhodesia's discriminatory native policies, "especially in the field of labour" (Vambe 1976: 118).

In response, Huggins reversed his former stance on racial superiority and in a statement on native policy in 1941 urged white Rhodesians to aid the advancement of "their black fellow men, bringing them to their level of civilization" (Vambe 1976: 119). After World War II, efforts to create the Federation were renewed, and an official British report assessing the racial situation was issued in 1951. The report stated that

> the most striking conclusion which we draw . . . is the degree of similarity between the policies of the three Governments rather than the degree of difference. . . . Differences of policy still exist . . . but we believe that these differences, although important, relate largely to method and timing and that the ultimate objective of all three Governments is broadly the same, namely, the economic, social, and political advancement of the Africans *in partnership* with the Europeans. (quoted in Holderness 1985: 96; my emphasis)

And so the discourse of racial partnership came into common circulation, and the Federation was established in 1953 based on its promise.

While the more radical contingent of the African intelligentsia quickly rejected the sincerity of this gambit, and most Africans came around to their opinion before the end of the 1950s because no real political or economic change was forthcoming, in the beginning the idea of partnership did provide hope among black Zimbabweans. Speaking of 1953, subsequent nationalist leader Nathan Shamuyarira writes,

> It [was] a time of optimism in Southern Rhodesia. A week or so before, the British House of Commons had approved . . . setting up the Central African Federation. The chiefs from the northern territories might protest at being linked with our settler-dominated country, and the British Labour Party might express grave doubts. . . . But for most of the hitherto oppressed Southern Rhodesian Africans the prospect of federation with the British protectorates of Northern Rhodesia and Nyasaland seemed full of promise: *the new policy of partnership*, which was to be inscribed in the federal constitution, would bring to a speedy end the segregation, humiliation, and indignation which we had suffered for forty years, since Britain made the country a self-governing colony under settler rule. . . . Rhodesian whites would even of their own accord, inspired by partnership, pass laws which would let us share political power and economic privileges and enjoy social justice.
>
> This wasn't such a pipe-dream. The newspapers which catered to white readers were full of this spirit. (1965: 15–16; my emphasis)

The dream was not long-lived. Shamuyarira notes that a "major blow to African hopes of racial cooperation came in 1954 when the motion to outlaw discrimination in public places . . . was rejected in the Federal Parliament," and the "decisive blow" came in 1958 when the relatively progressive Garfield Todd was dismissed from the Southern Rhodesian premiership (1965: 22).

Many observers have commented that it was the crushed hopes over the failure of partnership, especially among the African middle class, that fueled the fires of nationalism and ultimately led the country to civil war. Yet during the Federation period, concrete social alliances were forged between members of the black middle class and white middle-class liberals in multiracial political and cultural organizations. In the political sphere, the idea of racial partnership was genuine among a small group of white liberals such as Hardwicke Holderness and Guy Clutton-Brock, who prophetically saw real racial cooperation as the only hope for a healthy future for Rhodesia (see Holderness 1985).

Although rhetoric about partnership was largely hollow and opportunistic for many politicians and business people, having become a necessary official position, it at least allowed a space for white liberals within colonial government and church programs. During the Federation various cultural projects were launched to 'preserve,' generate interest in, and 'develop' the 'disappearing' indigenous arts. These programs require a reconsideration of the orthodoxy about the colonial state's and missionaries' general oppression of African arts and cultural practices.

Upholding the standard view, Zimbabwean University Lecturer Fred Zindi quotes an interview with an African DJ of the 1950s who said, "Even if one wanted to play African music, there was very little of it around on record because the whites were unwilling to record." Zindi goes on to comment, "The European minority who ruled Rhodesia found itself permanently on the defensive. It was either their 'civilised' culture or the African's and each D.J. who wanted to keep his job was made to promote western music and culture" (Zindi 1985: 9).

While these statements may be emotionally satisfying because they fit the usual black and white "good guys versus bad guys" scenario that has often characterized the telling of Zimbabwean music history, they fly in the face of a good deal of evidence to the contrary. It is true that the white 'settlers' used the motif of 'western civilization opposing the uncivilized [Africans]' as part of their rationalization of domination (e.g., Godwin and Hancock 1993; Kinloch 1975: 108–9, 116). But it is not true that whites were unwilling to allow African music to be recorded and aired on the radio during the Federation years and afterwards, albeit for a range of political reasons.

### Indigenous Music on Radio and Recordings in the 1950s and 1960s

African Service radio broadcasting began in the region in Northern Rhodesia during World War II; African broadcasters were enlisted so that bulletins could be read to black soldiers stationed on the Angola border. In 1948, through an agreement among the three territories soon to be amalgamated, Lusaka became the focal point for broadcasting in African languages, while European broadcasting was centered in Harare (RBC n.d.: 3; Fraenkel 1959: 17). Under this arrangement the Federation Broadcasting Corporation (FBC) came into existence in 1958, replacing Central African Broadcasting Service (CABS), which had been programming African music and in African languages earlier. Kauffman states that Shona radio broadcasts began in 1954, a year after the founding of the Federation (1970: 201), with Lusaka as the main center. The FBC was replaced by the RBC in Zimbabwe after the breakup of the Federation in 1963, and African radio broadcasts (now on Radio 2) emanated from the Mbare studios.

The RBC was affiliated with the Rhodesian government specifically through the Department of Information within the Ministry of Information, Immigration, and Tourism (Gwata and Reader 1977: 13). While the broadcasting corporation was a parastatal organ, the Department of Information could control information flow and censor news and music programs when its officials felt program content was not in the interests of the state. With the exception of politically sensitive material, however, most of the decisions about programming and the collection of African music to broadcast were left up to the African Service staff, according to Mr. Mbofana.[1] Hence, the CABS, FBC, and RBC activities, described below, had implicit government acceptance.

### CABS and the FBC Period

In the early days of African broadcasting, CABS emphasized news and education; the use of radio was conceptualized as part of the 'civilizing' mission of colonialism. A pamphlet issued to justify the service in its early years stated,

> We believed that formal educational methods, taking perhaps two or three generations to produce a comparatively civilized African people capable of working reasonably well in the development of the territory, were too slow. . . . We believed that if broadcasting could reach the masses, it could play a great part in their *enlightenment*. (quoted in Fraenkel 1959: 17; my emphasis)

In addition to diffusing messages about enlightenment and modernity, African language and music programs were also intended to draw listeners to state-controlled forums so that 'natives' would not tune into subversive ideas from "as far afield as Moscow" (H. Franklin, CABS, 1949, quoted in Frederikse 1982: 96).

While African broadcasting supported a number of colonial agendas, under Michael Kittermaster, the Broadcasting Officer in the 1950s, the station also emphasized genuine respect for African music, stories, and drama. Individuals comprising "the state" do not necessarily think with one mind, and this was certainly true during the Federation period when there were competing orthodoxies about 'native affairs.'

The Lusaka station built up its own sound archives through weekly recording sessions with African artists both at the studio and with a mobile unit that traveled through the Federation territories (Fraenkel 1959: 56, 222). Many different types of music were recorded, including

village dance-drumming ensembles and karimba players, African guitarists, African 'jazz' bands, and village and church choirs (Fraenkel
1959).

Peter Fraenkel, who worked at the station during the 1950s, stated
that because of Kittermaster, "colour-discrimination was completely
unknown" among the black and white staff members at the station, and
Kittermaster defied the norms of segregation in his private social life as
well. For example, Fraenkel noted that Kittermaster

> entertained Africans at his house, and oblivious of the reactions of
> white passers-by and neighbors, showed them over his garden, and
> served them drinks on his open veranda. When my predecessor as
> 'programme assistant' proved unable to get on with Africans, Kitter-
> master curtly asked him to resign or he would be fired. (1959: 24)

Kittermaster also had a genuine interest in indigenous arts and cultures but had the good sense to let an expert African singer, guitarist,
and composer, Alick Nkhata, handle most of the musical auditions and
recordings (Fraenkel 1959: 56). Nkhata had formerly been employed as
a teacher, and later worked with Hugh Tracey; "Together they had studied and recorded traditional African music all over the continent. After
this training Alick had joined the CABS" (51). Nkhata's former role as
a teacher suggests middle-class status, and his training and traveling
with Tracey indicate a familiarity with cosmopolitan ideas about indigenous arts. Tracey was particularly dedicated to recording and 'preserving' African music (see Erlmann 1991: 1; Nketia 1998: 52).

### Class, Religion, and the Decline
### of Indigenous Music
Most of the music in the Lusaka archives came from the northern regions (Malawi and Zambia). In line with ideas about the tremendous
decline of indigenous music in Zimbabwe [Southern Rhodesia] resulting
from colonial oppression, Fraenkel writes,

> A thing that always worried Nkhata was the poverty of Southern
> Rhodesian music. Our liaison unit there used to send up two types
> only, religious ditties after the manner of Sankey and Moody, and
> imitation jive [South African 'jazz'] seldom of any merit. One day,
> when one of our Southern Rhodesian continuity-announcers was go-
> ing back South for leave, Nkhata suggested that he try and trace
> some traditional singers in his home district and persuade them to
> rehearse. We agreed to try and get a recording van to him when he
> had got a sufficient number of items practised. But from his home our
> announcer wrote us sad little notes: 'Nobody remembers the old

songs any more.' I could not believe him, and when he returned after
his leave, I questioned him:

"No beer-drinking songs?"

"People do not drink beer any more."

"Go on! Beer-drinking is the chief recreation all over Africa!"

"Not in our district any more. We are near a Seventh-Day Adventist Mission."

"So, don't they have any social life at all?"

"Oh yes. The mothers" union give a tea-party twice a week, and
they sing hymns." (1959: 57)

I assume that if there had been people who performed indigenous
Shona music in this (unspecified) region, they would have come forward
and identified themselves for the opportunity of performing for the radio—even if they were usually clandestine in relation to their Seventh-
Day Adventist neighbors. Thus, the view that there was major decline
of indigenous music and dance because of missionary activity seems to
pertain to this region and would ring true for the residents there.

The vibrancy or disruption of indigenous artistic practices must be
understood in relation to multiple histories, specific regions, and different subject positions. The class position and religious orientation of particular actors and observers are crucial variables for understanding this
multiplicity. Not being Zimbabwean himself, Nkhata's general impression of the "poverty of Southern Rhodesian [indigenous] music" most
likely resulted from the nature of the Southern Rhodesians working for
the radio who created this impression. Who were these people?

Following the passage quoted above, Fraenkel contrasts Northern
Rhodesian blacks with the Southern Rhodesians who worked with them
at the radio station in Lusaka. He describes the Southern Rhodesians
as more sophisticated in relation to European ways, as more money-
minded, and noted that "they sometimes looked down upon the North-
erners as 'uncivilized.'" He also says that "they seemed quite resigned
to their subservient role in society" (1959: 57). This characterization
suggests a partial internalization of settler attitudes and stereotypes of
blacks ('uncivilized') and a petite-bourgeois class position. It makes
sense that members of this mission-educated group would have been
hired by the broadcasting service in the first place—just as Nkhata's
credentials were partially due to his having worked with Hugh Tracey
and having been a teacher.

Since black, middle-class habitus was shaped significantly through
higher levels of mission and government school education and was characterized by the internalization of European social style, ethos, and aesthetics, the cosmopolitan members of this class were more likely to be

distanced from indigenous lifeways. The orthodoxy of colonial oppression and indigenous cultural decline may well have been *their* story; it was true to the degree that it had happened in their lives. In areas heavily involved with missions like the Seventh-Day Adventists, the decline of indigenous arts and practices apparently involved peasants as well. This is particularly important. Often coming from such regions, this paucity of indigenous arts would only fortify middle-class views about their *general* 'disappearance.'

The idea that 'traditional' arts were disappearing and needed preservation was also practically a truism and reason for being among many ethnomusicologists during that time. Thus this view had the weight of expert opinion behind it. Nkhata's close association with Hugh Tracey may have helped lay the foundation for his assumptions about the decline of indigenous Zimbabwean music. With phrases like "dying out," this style of discourse was already evident in Tracey's article written in 1932 (see chapter 2).

### "Culture Brokers," Cosmopolitanism, and the Making of History

The close association between Nkhata and Hugh Tracey and Nkhata's key role in shaping African music broadcasting provide an important glimpse of how early ethnomusicological ideas, such as the need for preserving 'the Traditional,' might have been popularly diffused and influential beyond scholarly circles. It also illustrates a basic point of this book: the people already involved with cosmopolitanism are usually the ones selected to speak for indigenous local groups by and to other cosmopolitans (see Brennan 1997).

In some cases, perhaps Nkhata's, such individuals may have a deep understanding of the different cultural and aesthetic positions involved, and thus can function well as "culture brokers" (Coplan 1982). As suggested in chapter 1, however, being 'African' or a black Zimbabwean does not guarantee knowledge of indigenous African arts. People raised in cosmopolitan middle-class households and neighborhoods or in regions near Seventh-Day Adventist missions may have little acquaintance with or interest in such arts. Being black is not a sufficient condition to make indigenous music *their* music; socialization and habitus are the operatives here. Thus the idea of "culture broker," or worse yet "native representative," should not be assumed based on essentialist ideas of race or regional heritage, although this happens too frequently in cosmopolitan circles.

The linkages between various types of cosmopolitan actors at CABS are particularly clear: Kittermaster, a white liberal working in a parastatal organization; Nkhata, a former middle-class African school teacher and musician turned paraethnomusicologist; Tracey, a white South African ethnomusicologist; and the young, missionized, middle-class Zimbabwean radio worker. The fact that these people found each other is no mere accident. Like the members of any sociocultural group, cosmopolitans are often more attracted to and more likely to *hire* other cosmopolitans because of shared assumptions and social style, as well as values about types of credentials and backgrounds. The similar ideologies and dispositions that bring them together are further fortified by their having been brought together. But because *authentic difference,* in this case racial and regional, is invoked, "outsiders" like Kittermaster can believe the poverty of Zimbabwean music because "insiders" like Nkhata and especially the young black Zimbabwean attest to it.

Members of the emerging black middle class usually had the greatest access to African mass media outlets—as workers at the radio and as writers for publications like the *Bantu Mirror* and *African Parade.* Within these contexts, they would logically diffuse the views of their own experiences, assuming them to be general. This is apparently what happened among the staff at CABS—from the Zimbabwe workers to Nkhata, from Nkhata to Kittermaster and other 'Europeans.' The radio, in turn, would help propagate views of the paucity of indigenous Zimbabwean music more broadly, either through comments made on the air, or simply by the music that was played. Technologies like the radio and written media have special potential to document, propagate, and 'naturalize' particular views—to make them history—and in southern Africa such technologies were typically guided by cosmopolitans.

Ideas about the poverty of indigenous Zimbabwean music were apparently true for the radio workers at CABS. In the Murehwa-Uzumba area, in M'toko District, and in the very heart of Mbare Township, however, there were various types of indigenous music and dance being performed vibrantly during the 1950s which were available for recording and for providing a different historical picture. These and many other Shona regional styles *were* recorded as soon as the African Radio Service moved to Mbare studios at the end of the Federation.

## RBC *Archival Holdings in Mbare*
Along with making the two film shorts for the Central African Film Unit in 1963, the Murehwa No. 1 Jerusarema Club recorded five 78-rpm

sides for the Rhodesia Broadcasting Corporation, one of which has long been used as the musical lead-in for the news throughout the country. These recordings are part of a collection of approximately 6,800 items (in 1993) formerly belonging to the RBC African Service but currently housed in the National Archives of Zimbabwe. Many of these items were 78-rpm sides recorded in the country between 1957 and 1972, both in the studio and by mobile units, as had been the practice in Lusaka formerly.[2] These 78s were not commercial issues; they were intended for radio play only.[3]

A wide range of styles was recorded. In what is only a partial printout of the collection catalogue I have 14 different Shona dance-drumming traditions (with multiple groups for each dance, 192 items); various types of agricultural songs; many mbira, karimba, njari, and other lamellophone selections (at least 135 items); ngororombe from Mozambique and northeast Zimbabwe (8 items); chipendani bow music (13 items); makwaya [syncretic choral singing] selections (52 items); church, school, and women's club choruses; acoustic guitarists-songsters (277 items); and many local urban-popular "concert" vocal groups and 'jazz' bands. The large number of groups recording indigenous styles between 1958 and 1964 indicates that the poverty of music suggested by Lusaka's Southern Rhodesian affiliates was not a general phenomenon at the end of the Federation period.

Rather than trying to squelch indigenous arts and culture, the white and black employees at RBC's Mbare studios had a prominent role in diffusing the sound of localized indigenous musics to a wider audience. In fact, the government-affiliated African Radio Service saw the preservation of indigenous arts as one of its missions. An RBC publication of the early 1970s stated,

> Indigenous cultures are in danger of being trampled underfoot in the march of progress. As an article of policy, the RBC nurtures African musicianship and a knowledge of folklore. The latest hits on the "pop" parade have their place in the schedules. So, too, does the tribal drummer, mbira, and marimba player. (RBC n.d.: 7)

Similar to the discourse of indigenous cultural decline and the need for preservation espoused by ethnomusicologists and black, middle-class nationalists in Zimbabwe, state cultural workers and educators as well as missionaries became involved in programs of musical 'Africanization' and preservation during and after the Federation years. These groups were similar in terms of class standing and attitudes, which prominently included cosmopolitan ideas (e.g., 'folklore'). They were also similarly affected by post–World War II liberalism and anticolonialism, of which the discourse of partnership was but one result.

## African Music in the Schools

The radio was not the only state-affiliated institution in Zimbabwe involved in promoting African music during the 1950s and 1960s. During the Federation period, a policy was initiated that explicitly encouraged the use of African music in the school curriculum for black students. While this idea was in keeping with the notion of 'partnership' specific to the Federation context, it was also gaining currency in other regions of Africa and must be understood in relation to shifts in the attitudes of liberal missionaries and government educators in different parts of the continent around the same time.[4] The use of African music was also a pragmatic answer to shortages of teachers qualified to teach European music in Rhodesian schools. As reported by James McHarg, who was in charge of the state's music curriculum at the time,

> Recently the Southern Rhodesia Native Education Department, faced with the need to make the best use of teachers of limited qualification, decided to issue for the five years of school work a syllabus containing daily subject matter. It was my task to prepare the syllabus in music, providing for two lessons each week. In the absence of any song book in the vernacular, yet surrounded by denominational hymn-books none of which could be prescribed and none of which was suitable for use, I decided to try to restore the emphasis in teaching to activities related to indigenous music. The music syllabus begins with movement to song, continues with mime, and attempts through the use of sol-fa syllables and the time names to impart skill in the use of staff notation. . . . While the subject of each lesson is suggested to him, the task of finding a suitable African song is his [the African teacher's] alone. . . . It is too early yet to say whether the scheme will succeed, but first reactions would indicate that the subject of music is now moving in the right direction, and indigenous music is being encouraged. (McHarg 1958: 48)

Throughout this article McHarg emphasizes the importance of local indigenous music as well as the teaching of staff notation so that local music might be better understood by outsiders and take its place in the international world of music.[5]

The implementation of this program, however, did not appear to have wide effects in many regions. One problem may have been that the program was based on the essentialist notion that blacks would naturally know indigenous music. Many school teachers, however, probably came from missionized areas like the home of the CABS employee discussed earlier. Such people were neither likely to be familiar with nor interested in indigenous music.

## Kwanongoma College of Music

In 1961, the Kwanongoma College of Music was founded as part of the Rhodesian Academy of Music in Bulawayo.[6] The college was initiated in part to respond to the needs of African education and shifts in the state's music education policies. Following McHarg's line of thinking, the goals of the new institution according to its director, Leslie Williamson, included

> training African musicians and, in particular, African music teachers. It is the first venture of its kind in Southern Rhodesia and, as will be seen from the Syllabus, the work done covers a wide field of studies in which indigenous music plays a large part.
> The use of specialist music teachers in African schools will enable the staff at present handling school music, to the best of their usually limited capacity, to be released for the work for which they have primarily been trained. . . . A contribution to the general teacher shortage will thus be made and, at the same time, Music, which means so much to the African people, will be handled by adequately qualified staff. (Williamson 1963: 48)

The syllabus was inherently cosmopolitan in orientation. For instance it included musical appreciation "of the great works of music of all countries" with a "special study of African music." It also included a study of European music theory and history as a universal base from which to understand all music.

The mainstay of the training was in performance: in voice, piano, guitar, African marimba, African drums, fife, and karimba. Emphasis in choral singing was on music "in the Vernacular and in English, progressing towards operatic and oratorio work and the development of the operatic medium within the African environment." The school also developed an African Drum and Marimba Orchestra in which "various combinations of instruments are integrated in the preservation, performance and development of African Music. Public performances are regularly given by choir and orchestra, giving valuable experience to the students" (Williamson 1963: 49).

While the marimba was not a common local instrument in Zimbabwe, the current diffusion of this instrument throughout the country in schools, restaurants, nightclubs, and tourist spots can be traced to Kwanongoma College. This was taking place as early as 1965:

There is no doubt that the social and artistic forces emanating from
Kwanongoma are beginning to make themselves felt. Four years ago,
only one performer on the Marimba (African Xylophone) could be
found in the Bulawayo African Townships, and he was an old man.
In August this year, no less than 70 young people at one of the Youth
Clubs gave performances on these instruments, under the guidance
of their teacher, a graduate from Kwanongoma. ("Notes and News"
1965: 80)

The Shona karimba was also taught at Kwanongoma, and its current
international popularity is also a product of the teaching that went on
there. Specifically through the work of Kwanongoma graduate Dumisani Maraire, the karimba has become widely diffused in the United
States; in the Pacific northwest, where Maraire resided for many years,
there is also a flourishing Zimbabwean marimba scene.

### Modernist Reformism

The goals and syllabus of Kwanongoma, like those of McHarg's music
curriculum, reflected a type of reformist approach to indigenous music
that was paralleled by African nationalists during the same period and
replicated by state cultural institutions and the Ethnomusicology Program at the College of Music in Harare after 1980. Through emphasis
on indigenous music taught within a European pedagogical framework—Western music theory, history, and aesthetics—and within a
modernist ideology of 'development,' the music was to be 'improved'
and made viable for cosmopolitan audiences.

Williamson's goals for Kwanongoma explicitly incorporated the
language of modernist-reformism. His program also reflected the spirit
of partnership which seemed to be moving towards a kind of multiracial
(multicultural) Rhodesian national sentiment among white liberals:

> The encouragement, too, of an informed study of the *worthwhile ele-
> ments* of indigenous idioms is a very vital necessity, if these are not to
> be brushed aside by a community subjected to the indifferent noises
> of modern mechanical reproduction imported from elsewhere.
>
> The discovery, by youth, of the *folk-music* to which it is heir,
> *together with a musical literacy* which will enable the art of various
> tribes and peoples to be understood, appreciated *and developed*, may
> play a large part not only *in creating a specifically Rhodesian art-
> form* but also in engendering a consciousness of true worth by con-
> tributing from African resources, some part of the make-up of the
> fully educated man. (Williamson 1963: 48; my emphasis)

In this passage the role of reformism for bringing distinctive (isolated)
indigenous forms into relation with national and cosmopolitan consciousness is particularly clear.

Ubiquitous within (but not limited to) nationalist movements, cultural reformism is based on the idea that a new culture or new cultural forms should be forged as a synthesis of the 'best' or 'most valuable' aspects of local indigenous lifeways and the 'most valuable' features of foreign or cosmopolitan culture. As in the case of Kwanongoma College, what typically happens in reformist projects is that distinctive features of local social and artistic practice are symbolically selected, objectified, and then 'developed' or 'reformed' in light of modernist ideas, aesthetics, practices, and contexts. The local elements selected tend to be surface features—an instrument, a costume, a song or dance form. But the distinctive local meanings, modes of practice, group organization, pedagogy, ethics, and aesthetics that underpin indigenous artistic practice are typically *not* considered among the features thought by reformists to be 'most valuable,' and thus are usually systematically ignored. This critique of modernist reformism in Zimbabwe could, I think, be applied equally to the recent trend of multiculturalism in schools in the United States.

While modernist reformism often has preservation of 'the traditional' as one of its rationalizations, it tends to preserve surface features only, while having a major transformational effect at the level of cultural practice and ethos. Because such reformers consciously engage with indigenous lifeways, and because they typically operate from a middle-class, modernist position themselves, their programs often have a more direct transformational effect than colonialist positions that disparage or simply ignore indigenous arts. Thus, beneath the guise of benevolent concern, reformism poses a direct challenge to indigenous lifeways and ethics. This is particularly true when such programs are backed by the economic resources of the state or other powerful institutions. Although not parastatal itself, Kwanongoma articulated with the state by training and supplying teachers.

As is typical of modernist reformism generally, at Kwanongoma special emphasis was placed on music literacy. Williamson stated that literacy "will enable the art of various tribes and peoples to be understood, appreciated, and developed"—as if people within the tribes and peoples did not already understand and appreciate the music they were developing. Who were the intended beneficiaries of this literacy program? The stressing of music literacy for village musicians who work within an aural framework is common among nationalist musical reformers in many parts of the world (e.g., Capwell 1991; Noll 1991; Chopyak 1987), as it was in Zimbabwe among the African middle class after the 1930s. This was part of a larger process of rationalizing (vis-à-vis European music theory) and objectifying formerly nonobjectified

practices. Granting prestige to concert performance was part of the
same process.

A basic goal for Williamson was "creating a specifically Rhodesian
art-form" through the blending of European technique, forms, and aesthetics with indigenous African forms—for example, "the development
of the operatic medium within the African environment." African cultural nationalists were advocating precisely the same type of thing, although using popular cultural forms (e.g., rock and the twist) instead of
opera as the cosmopolitan component in the reformist mix (see chapter 5). A kind of pan-'tribal' fusion was also suggested for the work at
Kwanongoma:

> Since several tribes are represented among the Kwanongoma stu-
> dents, an attempt is made to fuse the musical traditions of the
> represented groups. The most dramatic and influential part of the
> Kwanongoma training includes the playing on specially-constructed
> marimbas which are capable of playing Chopi, Lozi, or Venda music.
> The marimba is presently not a part of the Shona musical practice,
> but graduates of Kwanongoma have recently introduced the instru-
> ment into Shona communities with tremendous success. (Kauffman
> 1970: 198)

Such fusions are meant to militate against localism and 'tribalism,' and
these goals of the white-directed college were shared fully by their African nationalist counterparts from the late 1950s through the 1980s. The
nationalists had to link the various 'tribes' to the party and 'nation' if
they were to claim political legitimacy. In both cases, however, this
agenda was also simply the result of the translocal purview of a shared
cosmopolitanism (e.g., see the quotation from Chifunyise in chapter 1).

The college's emphasis on 'preserving' indigenous music and culture
was an important part of nationalist and African middle-class discourse
after the late 1950s (see chapters 4 and 5). This concern for protecting
'traditional' music from "the indifferent noises of *modern* mechanical
reproduction imported from elsewhere" was part of a broader modernist discourse among white ethnomusicologists, RBC directors, and some
missionaries for which the 'traditional/modern' dichotomy served as
fulcrum.

By 1964, Williamson felt that some of the college's goals were being
met by its graduates:

> Of the two who qualified for a diploma, one is now working in Youth
> Clubs in the Bulawayo Municipal Housing and Amenities Depart-
> ment and is developing an enthusiasm for indigenous music and its
> performance amongst the young people in one of the African town-

ships. The other remained at Kwanongoma for two more terms and has been busy working on transcriptions of indigenous songs and instrumental music. The need for material of this sort is very great indeed. . . .

News continues to come from Wankie about the valuable work being done by an ex-Kwanongoma student, Basil Chidyamatamba. His indigenous opera, first performed last year, received a repeat performance early in 1964. He is busy organizing the first Music festival to be held in the area, which will take place in August.

The students at the College have, in recent months, been called upon for a great deal of work outside their normal curriculum. As the only practising body of performers on a fairly wide variety of indigenous instruments, they have given public performances in various places, including an appearance on television. They have also provided the background music for two films and prepared a series of educational programmes for the African Broadcasting Service. (Williamson 1964: 117–18)

Indigenous dance groups in Zimbabwe, including organized urban dance clubs, tended to specialize in one or two dances from their home region; they typically performed these for hours without boredom. When the Murehwa Jerusarema Club was called to make the two films, they were required to introduce a number of different dances for variety, with uneven success. Williamson's suggestion that the Kwanongoma students were "the only practising body of performers on a fairly wide variety of indigenous instruments" is probably accurate for that time.

Community participatory occasions do not require the same variety of styles to maintain the interest of participants, since interest within the performance is in the doing. In cosmopolitan stage, film, and TV settings, however, variety is crucial to maintaining audience interest— both because of the lack of active audience participation, and because prolonged repetition (lack of contrasts) is not generally valued within modernist-cosmopolitan aesthetics. This is certainly true in European and American concert music with its constant variety of dynamic, tempo, key, and texture contrasts. While there are exceptions within this stylistic trajectory—for example, minimalism—its very character as a distinctive stylistic departure was based on the fact that it eschewed contrasts and favored prolonged repetition—in this case the exception proves the rule. So too, in popular theater and television, the alternation of different types of numbers is usually thought of as being crucial for entertainment. The cosmopolitan values of novelty and variety were taught at Kwanongoma and were basic to middle-class popular musical acts as well (see chapter 4).

Williamson is thus probably correct in suggesting that the Kwanon-goma students' successes in cosmopolitan contexts were due to their ability to reproduce a wide variety of styles. The state's National Dance Company took precisely the same approach after 1980, as have other professional dance groups who have followed their lead. The Kwanon-goma students were early forerunners of this trend, which has had major influence in the post-1980 period.

Because of Kwanongoma, a new type of delocalized, 'indigenous' music was being popularized among urban youth; it was being objectified and preserved in staff notation; new variety was being offered within single performances; indigenous operas were being composed; festivals were being organized; students were performing in concerts and on TV, films, and radio. Kwanongoma was succeeding as a conduit for this new brand of African music within the cosmopolitan world of which the college and the nationalists, who shared a number of the same goals, were a part.

## Municipal Social and
## Recreational Programs

Municipal organs, such as the Bulawayo Municipal Housing and Amenities Department, which employed Kwanongoma graduates, were another point of contact between whites, the black middle class, and indigenous arts. Large private industrial, mining, and agricultural concerns often sponsored company football leagues, 'tribal' dance groups, 'modern' dance bands, and dance occasions as a way of directing and controlling the leisure-time activities of their African workers (Mattaka, Zim93-96; fieldnotes, 4 August 1993).

Historian Michael West has suggested that to the extent that recreational activities for Africans were initially "organized from above, however, it was done by a private group, the African (initially Native) Welfare Society (AWS), not the state" (1990: 183). The African Welfare Society, founded in 1929 in Bulawayo, was a colony-wide organization constituted by white businessmen, missionaries, and government officials as well as members of the black middle class, and was specifically concerned with African recreational activities. A member of the Mashonaland AWS, located in Harare, commented, "an unoccupied native—like a European child or youth, is liable to get into mischief and be not only a nuisance, but a danger to himself and others" (1951 AWS document quoted in West 1990: 183); hence, in a distinctly paternalistic spirit, they organized sports and dancing contests as "an insurance against 'trouble'" (1935 AWS document quoted in West 1990: 183).

Mattaka stated that the African Welfare Society was "part of the [Salisbury] City Council. They were inviting all prominent people in the city, Africans and whites, so we had church representatives. All the religious ministers were members of that board. Plus all leading members in [Mbare] were on that committee" (Zim93-65: 8). The AWS was thus a site for interaction between whites and the emerging black elite, again with cosmopolitanism being the cultural foundation.

As time went on, the City Council took over a greater role in the area of African recreation, so that by the 1970s, as Gwata and Reader note, "The Salisbury City Council [was] by far the largest agency which provide[d] cultural and leisure facilities" for Africans in the townships (Gwata and Reader 1977: 10).

Beerhalls in the townships were the first venues for village music and dance performance constructed and run by the municipal governments; they have a long history (Kauffman 1970: 201). As they exist today, the beerhalls or beergardens are large, walled-in lots with cement tables and umbrellas, open spaces where performances can take place, and sometimes an indoor area with tables. Initially the municipal halls only sold the local millet beer. Before the Liquor Act was amended in 1957 (one of the few antidiscriminatory gestures to result from 'partnership')' Africans were prohibited from drinking European beer and liquor.

The money made at the beerhalls went to the City Councils, which theoretically used the profits to pay for improvements in the townships.[7] This was not the only positive attribute beerhalls had for the City Council. Gwata and Reader suggest a function of social control as well: "It is difficult to say what dissatisfactions would manifest in the male labour force if this tranquilizing outlet were not available" (Gwata and Reader 1977: 5). Lawrence Vambe, an astute, middle-class observer of Mbare life in the post–World War II period, wrote that the money spent at beerhalls took bread out of working-class children's mouths (1976: 193). In spite of the negative and usurious aspects of the beerhalls, they were, and remain, primary social centers for urban working-class men (Gwata and Reader 1977: 5).[8] They have been a major context for all sorts of itinerant musicians for many decades. By at least the 1950s, indigenous-dance clubs and burial societies began performing in township beerhalls (Kauffman 1970: 201) as well as out in the open in the Mbare market area, as they still do today.

Between 1950 and 1966, Kenneth Mattaka worked off and on for the Salisbury City Council organizing African musical performances and other entertainment activities in township recreation halls (Mattaka, fieldnotes, 4 August 1993). Other Africans involved in organizing social and cultural events in the townships were similarly associated with the municipal government. One such group, the Neshamwari (with friends), organized sporting activities, including weight lifting and body building, amateur boxing, hockey, and indoor games in conjunction with the municipality (Parade 1966b: 14; see also Gwata and Reader 1977: 10–12). Of particular significance for this study, they also originated the Neshamwari Traditional Song and Dance Festival, currently the most important festival for indigenous music and dance in Harare. In her study "Rhodesian African Cultural and Leisure Needs," Gwata draws attention to the Neshamwari Festival as the culmination of the year's Council-supported cultural activities.

### The Neshamwari Festival

The Neshamwari Festival was initiated in September 1966 by the Neshamwari group in conjunction with the Hostels Social Services Section of the Department of Community Services of the City of Salisbury (Parade 1966b: 14; Muskwe, p.c. February 1994). According to Reason Muskwe, who investigated the matter,[9] the original intent of the festival was to get "the single men in the hostels to take part in sporting and cultural activities through competition." Although originally it was to have been strictly a municipal event, the organizers decided to open that first festival to nationwide participation (Parade 1966b: 14), as is still the case today. Spanning a two- to three-week period, the Neshamwari festivals in the 1960s and 1970s included competitions for urban dance bands, choruses, and ballroom dancers, as well as rural and urban indigenous dance groups. The competitions were held in places like Harare [Mbare] Stadium, and Mai Muzodzi and Stodart Halls in Mbare (Parade 1966b: 14; Gwata and Reader 1977: 11). The festival doubled in size during its first three years, with 61 entries in 1966, 117 entries in 1967, and 124 in 1968, and participation increased in all the different categories (Parade 1969: 32). The Neshamwari Festivals, and the prizes promised, may have been one of the concrete reasons for the increase in urban indigenous dance associations reported by Nyandoro and others for the 1960s.[10]

The festival, perhaps the central official occasion in Harare to demonstrate an interest in indigenous performing arts, was held throughout the war years of the 1970s with financial support from the city government. In addition to trophies, the winners were also given cash awards by the Chibuku (African beer) Breweries (1973–present) and the City Marketing Department (1975–77; Muskwe p.c. February 1994). After

1976, the organization of the event shifted to the newly formed Salisbury (now Harare) African Traditional Association (HATA) with continued support from the city, the Chibuku Breweries, and after 1980 from the National Arts Council (Chifunyise 1987: 1).

As it evolved during the 1980s the festival came to its present form of being the largest competition in the Harare area strictly for 'traditional' musicians and dancers, and the most important context for performing such dances on a stage.[11] It is certainly the most important contemporary music-dance festival of the year for indigenous dance associations around Harare such as the Murehwa Jerusarema Club and Burial Society, who participate annually.

This important artistic showcase for staged indigenous music and dance was initiated and maintained in conjunction with the municipal government during the most oppressive years of white-settler rule. There is no contradiction. The colonial state supported such activities as a way to keep the 'natives' occupied. Nonetheless, this situation flies in the face of assertions that the colonial state sought to suppress the indigenous arts that only black nationalism could revive. On the contrary, indigenous artistic activities were fostered by the colonial state during and after the Federation years because, at worst, they were deemed harmless recreation, while among white liberals such as Kittermaster and Williamson they were regarded as positive elements for the region's multiracial cultural future.

## The Role of the Churches

Of all the arms of colonialism in Zimbabwe, missionaries have received a lion's share of blame for the direct oppression of indigenous Shona music and dance. There is good reason for this. Especially in the early period of missionary activity, indigenous music and dance seem to have been widely discouraged among people being missionized: (1) pragmatically, because certain forms were closely associated with the competing indigenous beliefs and rituals, and (2) more vaguely but no less powerfully as a part of the general ideology of European cultural superiority. The literature includes so many testimonies to this state of affairs that one hardly knows where to begin (e.g., Berliner 1978: chapter 9; Jones 1992: 29; Kaemmer 1989: 35; Kauffman 1970: 192; Maraire 1990).

Explaining early oppressive attitudes among missionaries, Axelsson writes that, after the reformation, Protestant denominations were particularly adamant about spreading their own particular style of worship so that there would be "a deeper sense of *universal* unity between [the young churches in Africa] and the old churches in Europe or America" (1973: 91). This universalist project would, of course, exclude African music from services. Ethnocentric views about the uncivilized nature of the "Dark Continent" also played a key part in the suppression of indigenous arts in the nineteenth and early twentieth centuries (Axelsson 1973: 91; McCall 1998). Against the backdrop of such generalizations, however, specific denominations articulated different attitudes toward African cultural practices (e.g., Jones 1992: 29; Kauffman 1970: 192; Ranger 1985: 256), as did individual missionaries, according to their personal dispositions, within a given denomination (e.g., Kauffman 1970: 192–93).

During the 1950s and 1960s there was also a more general reevaluation of the worth of African music for worship, and a shift toward the 'indigenization' of church music in Zimbabwe in several of the major denominations.[12] Significantly, this coincided with the state's discourse about partnership and with the rise of African mass nationalism. The liberalization of church policies represents a third, somewhat independent, stream which flowed very much in the same direction as the other two in relation to indigenous performing arts.

Axelsson's "Historical Notes on Neo-African Church Music" (1973; see also 1981) provides a good sense of the slow ideological transformation. He suggests that the first change—from total rejection to a paternalistic acceptance of African cultural practices—came through evolutionary thinking in anthropology. Axelsson quotes a 1914 article by a religious theorist, H. A. Junod, to make the point:

> Science has shown that primitive and semi-primitive peoples are passing through a phase of development through which our fathers also passed. . . .
> For the missionary himself, the study of the pagan system will be investigated with a wholly new interest. . . . He will no longer be the theorist teaching the ideas of a superior race, but the elder brother guiding his younger brethren towards the hill of holiness, where the Father bids all his children gather. (1973: 92)

Axelsson also suggests that the work of early ethnomusicologists, such as von Hornbostel's 1928 article, "African Negro Music," might have furthered a growing acceptance of African music on its own terms among missionaries interested in music (1973: 92).

Attempts to 'Africanize' church music were already in progress among Catholics and Anglicans in Central and West Africa as early as 1940 (Axelsson 1973: 93). In the Federation region, the real break with former attitudes of musical intolerance came after World War II; the missionary-ethnomusicology connections are particularly strong within this conjuncture.

Axelsson cites A. M. Jones, who worked in Northern Rhodesia, as one of the first missionaries in the area to express discontent over the demand for Western-styled singing in African churches (Jones 1948). In making his case, Jones reiterated earlier statements by von Hornbostel about problems of rhythm and speech tones in the use of European hymn tunes with vernacular texts. Jones went on to experiment with 'Africanized' church music and remained engaged with ethnomusicological research and writing.

By the late 1940s others began to follow Jones' lead in experimenting with African church music and publishing articles about approaches and problems. By the mid-1950s it had become a general focus of missionary concern and activity throughout the sub-Saharan region (e.g., Carroll 1954: 81; Louw 1956, 1958; Lury 1956; Parrinder 1956; Shaffer 1956).

The Roman Catholics were leaders in this activity. Axelsson quotes a 1939 statement by Pope Pius XII: "Respect for the particular genius of each race is the guiding star by which the missionaries should conduct themselves, and on which they should fix their attention constantly in their apostolic march" (1973: 94). These instructions were acted on in the following decades in different parts of the continent—Missa Katanga and Missa Luba being famous results. Similar sentiments were reiterated by Vatican II in the early 1960s, emphasizing that missionaries should respect and use local music in worship.

In early 1960, a Swiss Catholic missionary priest and musicologist, Joseph Lenherr, came to Rhodesia with the specific assignment of supporting the creation of music for worship based on local models by local composers—mainly drawn from the ranks of primary-school teachers and hence indicating a middle-class genesis. Dr. H. Weman came to Rhodesia from Sweden for the Evangelical Lutheran Church. He spearheaded a similar, earlier, program for this denomination on several trips after his initial visit in 1954. Axelsson goes on to note that "in 1960 a trained musician and musicologist, Robert Kauffman, was specially assigned by the American Methodist Board of Missions to Rhodesia for a period of five years in order to encourage the use of indigenous music in churches and schools" (1973: 99).

Kauffman ultimately suggested the use of adapted local secular songs and the creation of new songs based on local style for church music, and he generated workshops to realize this approach. Kauffman was followed in his work for the Methodists by John E. Kaemmer; both men subsequently became leading ethnomusicological authorities on Zimbabwean music, receiving their Ph.D. degrees in ethnomusicology in the United States in 1970 and 1975 respectively.

Axelsson and other commentators suggest that once the ball got rolling among white missionaries, it was the converted, 'educated' (i.e., middle-class) Africans who resisted the infusion of African elements into their church music: "Africans had been taught to despise their own musical heritage, and because of the long and deep infiltration of their culture by the mission societies, the young churches in Africa became proud of the 'Western guise' and cherished it" (Axelsson 1973: 93; see also Carrington 1954: 83). In a later article Axelsson emphasizes that some white missionaries became "puritanical" about 'Africanization' and wanted to reject any European elements in the music (1981: 2).

Ultimately, the activities undertaken by the different denominations resulted in a new type of "acculturated African art music." Axelsson characterizes the new style as including, from the African side: (1) responsorial singing; (2) descending melodies; (3) adherence to the tonal pattern of language; (4) the polyrhythmic structure based on equal and rapid time units grouped in cyclical patterns; (5) parallel harmonic motion using especially fourths, and fifths, but also commonly thirds; and (6) contrapuntal motion. Elements from the European side included adherence to Western tonality within the diatonic system, and extension of harmonic feeling in multipart music by the addition of thirds (Axelsson 1973: 101). Vocal timbre and techniques were probably also strongly influenced by European aesthetic values.

## Conclusions

All of the projects, organizations, and individuals discussed in this chapter had different agendas and varying positions in relation to racial partnership and African performing arts. While they were all tied institutionally to the colonial project, each must be considered separately.

Yet similarities in the goals and effects of the various programs, and especially their congruence in time, suggest a general ideological shift in the post–World War II era which dialectically affected each of the movements and brought them into concrete relations with each other. Kwanongoma graduates worked with municipal social programs and performed for the RBC, missionary musicians worked with or as music educators, and ethnomusicologists influenced the progression of events at various points—for example, Hugh Tracey's protegee at CABS, and A. M. Jones and Robert Kauffman in the missionary movement.

The central Rhodesian government's need to placate British fears about its racist policies led to the discourse of racial partnership. But whites in the central and municipal governments did not necessarily intend to celebrate indigenous African arts or racial partnership through their various programs. The central government wanted to control information access to Africans through CABS, the FBC, and the RBC. The shift in McHarg's music syllabus was, in part, to make up for the lack of expenditure on teachers adequately trained in European music. The municipal government of Salisbury (Harare) created the beerhalls and festivals to make money and to keep African workers safely occupied during leisure time. As a by-product of these specific agendas, the different reformist projects created a space that brought African performing arts within the state's purview and into translocal contexts more than ever before.

Unlike many state and municipal officials, some of the music educators, missionaries, and radio people were genuinely interested in indigenous performing arts and the well-being of Africans, even if paternalism sometimes lingered on. Some people were reacting to the contradictions of colonialism that had been underlined by the war against racist, imperialist Hitler, or by their own Christian faith, or by ideas of national sovereignty coming from the UN, India, Ghana, and a myriad of other sources. Although many whites in the Federation and Rhodesian governments demonstrated that they were not sincere about political, social, and economic partnership, people like Kittermaster and Holderness were attempting to use the spaces created by the state's own discourse of partnership to widen the cracks in its racist policies.

It would be a mistake to stereotype all white Rhodesians and to assume that they only had negative effects on local indigenous musics. Their role in the so-called African cultural renaissance of the 1960s has been largely ignored. In fact, the white-directed cultural programs worked in conjunction with black cultural nationalism because of a concrete class alliance between white liberals and members of the black middle class who led the nationalist movement. Deeper still, both groups operated from a similar class habitus and cosmopolitan cultural position that united them across racial difference and affected indigenous arts in similar ways. Regardless of differences among the people and programs, all were involved in creating some type of reformist artistic fusion or transformation that strengthened modernist cosmopolitanism. While some, like Kittermaster, questioned the racist basis of Rhodesian society, none questioned the *discourse of modernity* which set the intellectual parameters and the directions that the cultural programs were to take.

All of the relationships and programs discussed in this chapter were based in a common cosmopolitanism and suggest the ways that this particular cultural formation articulated people, regardless of race, to the 'civilizing,' mission of colonialism and later the homologous 'modernizing' mission of nationalism. As becomes clear in subsequent chapters, both these articulations contributed to the "passive" cultural revolution of capitalism.

Chapter Four

# The African Middle Class: Concerts, Cultural Discourse, and All That Jazz

Beginning in the 1930s, various types of urban-popular music modeled largely on North American and South African styles emerged in Zimbabwean cities. In this chapter I trace the rise of early African dance bands, "concert" performance ensembles, and other musical activities such as ballroom dancing. Although not exclusive to the African middle class in the townships, these styles were strongly associated with middle-class performers, audiences, and occasions.

Initially based on foreign musical sources, social conventions, and aesthetics, "concert," jazz, and ballroom were prime activities for the development of a distinctive local cosmopolitanism. This cultural position, defined as 'civilization' within colonial discourse, became the basis of corporate, middle-class identity before the rise of mass nationalism. Since many nationalist leaders and current government officials come from the ranks of the African middle-class, an understanding of this group's cultural practices and attitudes is key to comprehending musical nationalism before, and state cultural policies since, 1980, as well as popular music trends more generally.

## Race and Class in Zimbabwe

Among the black middle class, race and class identifications have been emphasized variably at different times. As demonstrated in this chapter, 'elite' Africans stressed their own *class* distinction from peasants and the black working class before mass nationalism, and played down the importance of color and geographical heritage ('race') for defining social categories. During the mass-nationalist phase of 1958–82, middle-class nationalist leaders minimalized African class distinctions and shifted to a 'national' identification based on color and African heritage—even while other members of the black middle class maintained the earlier position. After gaining majority rule in 1980, the African elite quickly reverted to *class*-based practices and identity. Alliances with the white economic elite were fostered throughout the 1980s, although racial distinctions continued to be invoked for specific purposes. During the mid-1990s, racial distinctions again seemed to be coming to the fore as the state and the African elite argued for the 'indigenization' (black leadership or takeover) of white-controlled local and transnational companies and land. Musical developments follow these shifts in emphasis between racial and class identifications in significant, and often predictable, ways.

### Race

The concept of race has no universally fixed objective parameters. At different times and places racial categories have been variably based on arbitrary physical characteristics, religion and other cultural practices, on geographical heritage, and on class standing; racisms and discourses about race can only be understood within specific historical circumstances (e.g., Gilroy 1987).[1] As a category, "race" is not a conceptual tool for social analysis; rather, it is the subject of such analysis. This distinction is crucial; to miss it is to take essentialist discourses of "race" at face value.

The social category "race" is nested within more general ideas about, and functions of, social difference, but the power of racial discourses that stress physical traits stems from the claim of naturalness and hence immutability. Emphasis on a "biological" definition masks the socially constructed, variable nature of race within relations of domination. The history of the black middle class in Zimbabwe illustrates a general phenomenon: struggles over the construction and redefinition of social categories involving "race" will emphasize or deemphasize criteria perceived as immutable, depending on the goals of particular groups within specific conjunctures.

Regardless of what else was said, *color* and *geographical heritage,* Europe versus Africa, were used by white Rhodesians to determine a racist hierarchical order affecting almost all realms of life. The white settlers also typically claimed cultural criteria as components of their construction of African/European difference. As is typically the case in colonial situations in Africa, the social hierarchy was legitimated by discourses about the superiority of the colonist culture; in Zimbabwe this was articulated in terms of degrees of 'civilization,' and the whites' civilizing mission—a component of social-evolutionary theory.

## Class

My conception of class involves structural positions in relation to control over processes and resources of economic production within market situations (class *in* itself). According to Bourdieu, class also involves the relative control over other types of capital: *cultural* (e.g., social style, aesthetic taste, 'manners'), *social* (connections), *educational* (degrees), and *political* resources that are valued within particular social fields and that may be "exchanged" or used to procure economic and other types of capital.[2] In combination with economic position, the social and cultural components of class may give rise to a corporate identity and shared aspirations (class *for* itself).

Colonial Zimbabwe (Rhodesia) was characterized by a multisphere class system. The white working, middle, and elite class system was legally elevated above and separated from the class system of people of color. In white Rhodesian constructions of blacks, *class* was a relatively minor issue; the general tendency was to lump all 'natives' into a single group. Colonial attitudes and policy varied at different times and among different individuals, however, regarding the desirability of creating an African middle class. Many settlers viewed 'natives' as only fit for labor. At other times, however, educational policies were created that fostered the creation of a black middle class that could serve as mediators between whites and the African masses (e.g., see Moyana 1989). Also the creation of different types of home-ownership schemes and townships around Harare, especially during the 1960s, signaled an official recognition of different black social classes.

Based on an early statement by Cecil Rhodes—"Equal rights for all civilized men"—a black class system emerged around levels of 'civilization' which were defined by degrees of European education and by the inculcation and display of European values, skills, and social-cultural style (West 1990: 391; Shamuyarira 1965: 51). Rhodes's statement was supported by the messages of mission educators who proselytized for modernity and progress as the keys to civilization. As we saw in chapter 3, African Service Radio was initiated by the colonial state with a similar mission in mind. As Africans became deeply socialized to European, American, and settler ways of thinking and acting—as these ways became their own ways—a new Zimbabwean cosmopolitan group emerged.

## The African Middle Class
## in Zimbabwe

Historian Michael West has written a detailed dissertation on the rise of
the African middle class in Zimbabwe (1990). Defining class in both
structural (in relation to the means of production) and cultural (the
emergence of a common *habitus*) terms, West strongly links the rise of
the middle class to mission school education and shows how it was primarily an urban-centered phenomenon (1990: 4–5). Covering the years
between 1890 and 1965, West persuasively shows that

> by the end of the period under review, there had emerged a self-
> conscious and corporate African middle class consisting of the more
> highly-qualified and better-paid teachers, preachers, clerks and, in
> the post-World War II era especially, businessmen, salesmen, social
> workers, journalists, nurses, doctors, lawyers and other profession-
> als. For the most part, the material basis of this class, especially in
> comparison to the white settlers . . . was not very considerable. Its
> members, however, were held together by a unity of purpose, that is,
> they had interests, aspirations and ideas that set them apart from the
> other major social strata in Southern Rhodesian society—namely,
> the dominant white settlers on the one hand and the African peas-
> ants and workers from among whom they emerged on the other.
> (1990: 2–3)

In light of the promise of "equal rights for all civilized men," the
emergent black middle class negated the importance of color and stressed
cultural attainment in their process of self-definition. Before the advent
of mass nationalism, the African elite had become a class *for* itself and
did not seem overly concerned with the position of the lower classes. As
the Reverend E. T. J. Nemapare put it in the *Bantu Mirror* in 1954, "The
trouble is that in Southern Rhodesia the social bar, *which I fully support,* is being taken for the colour bar, which no decent European or
African wants" (quoted in West 1990: 391; my emphasis). This comment suggests a desired class alliance across color lines and argues for
the validity of class stratification ("the social bar") within the African
population. Similarly, the protonationalist B. J. Mnyanda emphasizes
African class stratification based on cultural capital (levels of 'civilization'), and articulates corporate, middle-class aspirations: "Today,
the African people—particularly the educated and the civilised among
them . . . demand a place in the sun; and he who thwarts their legitimate
aspirations will do so at his own peril. By all means, let us have a 'culture bar' in place of the present colour bar" (1954; quoted in West

1990: 391). This comment suggests Mnyanda's own internalization of colonialist conceptions of civilization.

Although black Zimbabweans ultimately could not escape the way white projections of "race" structured African lives and livelihoods, as a class for itself the African elite attempted to contest and redefine racial discourse that lumped all 'natives' into one legal and social category. In regard to discriminatory liquor laws, for example,

> In the 1950s, as the black middle class became more clearly differentiated from other Africans, the call grew increasingly louder for legal access to "European" liquor and for the establishment of exclusive drinking facilities. Thus, in the 1950s, repeating grievances which were being voiced as far back as the 1920s, "Progressive Africans in Bulawayo . . . [became] indignant at the rough conditions and behavior of their fellow Africans at the Beer Hall," demanding "that better conditions be created by recognition of the City Council of the middle-class African." (quotations from the *Bantu Mirror* 2 June and 7 July 1956; quoted in West 1990: 190–91)

*Class* and *cultural criteria* were particularly important to Africans' attempt to refigure social categories precisely because these criteria allowed for the possibility of mobility, whereas *color* and *geographical heritage* apparently did not. Since the black middle class had only recently emerged from the lower strata, and since their own material distinction "was not very considerable," cultural markers of difference from other Africans—dress, language, artistic tastes, social style, access to European liquor—were all the more important to their corporate identity. Concerts, jazz, ballroom dancing, and European-style weddings were primary public arenas for articulating class distinctions until the early 1960s.

## The Emergence of Urban-Popular Vocal Music

In addition to the indigenous music and dances performed by members of the lower classes in Mbare during the 1930s, other urban-popular performance traditions were developing as a parallel sphere of activity among the middle class. As in many parts of colonial Africa, in Zimbabwe new urban-popular musical styles grew out of three types of colonial institutions: mission schools, churches, and military bands (Coplan 1978, 1985; Collins 1985; Waterman 1990; Erlmann 1991). From the 1930s through the early 1960s, Zimbabweans distinguished the new type of music by its basis in European, South African, American, and especially African-American models. Locally, the emergent styles were conceptualized as 'modern' and 'progressive' in contrast to the 'old,' 'traditional' indigenous traditions performed in villages and the Mbare market area.

### School Choirs

Many people who graduated from mission or government schools in the 1930s came to Salisbury to seek employment. Mbare was still the primary township at that time. Having been trained in choir singing in school, the graduates at first simply formed choirs in Mbare. As indicated by recordings in the National Archive and oral accounts, the choirs attached to schools were large groups which performed a variety of Protestant hymns, North American spirituals, choir music by middle-class South African composers, and secular songs from England and the United States (e.g., "Shortnin' Bread" and "I Ride an Old Paint"). The same sources suggest that the school choirs performed in a tightly arranged homophonic style with the voices in close synchrony in their articulation of distinct melodic phrases. Like the neatness of the musical execution, text diction was particularly clear, and the African-English accent resembled the speech style particular to the black middle-class.[3]

Since education was viewed as the avenue to class mobility and social progress, it is hardly surprising that school singing styles were thought to be progressive. David Coplan notes that for South Africa (1985), through this connection Euro-American and African-American religious and even urban-popular musical styles became associated with ideals of cultural development and progress within the ideology of modernity. A 1954 article in *African Parade,* the most widely read magazine among Africans in Zimbabwe (Stopforth 1972: 86),[4] states that

> since the early thirties Africans in Southern Rhodesia and in Salisbury in particular have made tremendous progress in all walks of life. Nowhere perhaps is that progress more manifest than in the field of entertainment. The existence of so many choirs modelled on the American Negro pattern in Harare [Mbare] is eloquent testimony to that progress. (*African Parade* 1954: 14)

European and American missionaries supplied the mainstay of African education. Perhaps on the basis of rather essentialist conceptions of race, it was often white educators who initially chose "the American Negro pattern" for black Zimbabweans. Whether or not a black diasporic or pan-African consciousness emerged later among the middle class, it was probably not the original impetus for the emphasis on what were regarded as relatively more sophisticated black styles from the United States and South Africa.[5]

## Makwaya

Mission and government school singing generated several offshoots, including adult choirs in the townships that maintained the school-singing style, the "concert" groups discussed in this chapter, and *makwaya*. Like the name itself, an Africanization of the English word *choir*, makwaya involved adaptation of performance practices learned in school (or from people who had been to school) according to indigenous aesthetic dispositions. In Zimbabwe, makwaya singing often combines triadic harmonies and some homophonic singing with indigenous practices such as responsorial organization, dense overlapping, and variations of individual parts. Any type of indigenous or foreign song might be labeled makwaya if sung in this distinctive syncretic manner.[6]

With the use of more relaxed vocal timbres, a more spontaneous approach to melodic variations, the inclusion of vocal exclamations and other sounds, and especially the denser overlapping textures, makwaya is clearly distinguished from school singing and the middle-class styles that emerged from it. On the other side, triadic harmonies, a somewhat more transparent texture, and relatively clearer phrasing distinguish makwaya from indigenous singing styles.

Makwaya thus represented a stylistic middle ground, but "the middle" was approached primarily from indigenous aesthetics and performance practices. Just as a little schooling did not qualify a person for middle-class standing if not accompanied by the prominent inculcation of modernist ethos and social style, makwaya lacked sufficient elements of control, organization, and "sophistication," and hence was contrasted with the musical styles like "concert" that became major indices of middle-class identity. "Syncretism" ('being in the middle part') is not a unitary phenomenon, and does not necessarily represent a prominent shift away from indigenous aesthetics and lifeways, as in the case of makwaya.

## The "Concert" Tradition, 1930s–1960s

By the mid-1930s an urban performance style which I will call "concert" grew directly out of the school choir tradition. Along with urban jazz and dance bands, "concert" remained the most popular musical style among middle-class Zimbabweans in Harare's townships until the early 1960s.

As "concert" emerged, an ensemble often involved fewer performers than the school choirs. While most "concert" groups eventually added instrumental accompaniment (e.g., some combination of piano, guitar, bass, traps, and winds), the focal point was usually a vocal quartet, quintet, or sextet. The style emphasized smooth, relatively transparent tonal harmonies learned at school and, like the school choirs, the repertories of "concert" groups included church hymns, African-American spirituals, and similarly styled choir music composed by South Africans. The "concert" repertory, however, quickly expanded to feature numbers styled after vaudeville and Tin Pan Alley, either directly from America or as filtered through South African performers; South Africans were important models for this Zimbabwean tradition.[7]

"Concert" performers began to incorporate dance and vaudeville-style skits in their shows and to define themselves as stage entertainers—a rather different conception than "choir member." As the tradition developed, "concert" artists emphasized variety in both the musical styles and formats that they performed, in line with the need for variation common to presentational traditions. Many of the major "concert" ensembles around Harare included people who originally had been trained in a group called the Bantu Actors, led by Kenneth Mattaka. An *African Parade* writer says that Mattaka's ensemble emerged as the leader in Mbare in 1937 and was

> one of the best entertainment groups Salisbury has ever had. The members came from the Glee Singers of Domboshawa [government school] led by C. S. Hlabangana. The group was first known as "Domboshawa Old Boys Choir," alias "Expensive Bantu." This went for three years. They won all the music competitions. (1954: 20)

Mattaka's ensembles remained a training ground for urban-popular musicians through the early 1960s. The young Thomas Mapfumo was one of the last prominent alumni. Mattaka was one of the first full-time professional popular musicians in Zimbabwe; otherwise his background and the attitudes he expressed were often typical of middle-class Africans of his generation.

### Kenneth Mattaka and the Bantu Actors

Mattaka was born circa 1916 in Malawi. His father and uncles received education and became relatively well-to-do farmers; they received titles to their lands by joining a newly established mission village in Malawi. Mattaka's father later migrated to various places seeking even better opportunities and finally landed a managerial position at a mine in Kadoma, Zimbabwe.

Kenneth began school at age ten in Malawi at a Church of Scotland Mission. It was there that he began his singing career:

> While I was at school, we used to have singing practices every now and then. Because our school used to open in December we used to sing Christmas carols and things like that. So we had a lady, Miss Fraser. She was our organist; she used to train us in singing. . . . This gave me a chance to learn reading music and all that. So each time I was on holiday, I would also go and team up with my friends. We would sing and repeat the songs we were singing at school. (Zim93-65: 2–3)

In 1932, Mattaka's father brought him and his brothers to Zimbabwe to study at Domboshawa, the country's first government school. At Domboshawa singing was taught in classes along with carpentry and farming techniques.[8] Several choirs were formed, and Mattaka was chosen for the lead choir because of his ability to read music. After moving to Mbare at the end of 1936, Mattaka and some of the men he had sung with at school were invited to perform at a Methodist Church fundraiser in the township. This led to other invitations to sing at concerts, and during 1937 they became so popular that "we found that a concert without our friends [his group] was a flop" (Mattaka Zim93-65: 4). Indicating the school affiliation, the group was first known as the Domboshawa Old Boys, but later they were called "Expensive Bantu"—*bantu* because, as Mattaka explained, they were not all Zimbabweans and *bantu* was a general term, and *expensive* indicated that they had class.

Mattaka soon took a leadership role, and in 1938 they "decided to draft a constitution which we handed over to the [City] Council. There was a body which was running all the African Affairs. We had to apply for an affiliation. So this was granted. Now we had a constituted body" (Zim93-65: 4). Exhibiting a different mindset from most of the more ad hoc village dancers performing in Mbare during the 1930s, this ensemble of school graduates felt the need to formalize the group and to become affiliated with the African Affairs branch of the municipal government. After drafting the constitution, they changed the name to Bantu Actors: "You see, we found we were not only going to be singers, but we were going to act as well. So we called ourselves Bantu Actors, as entertainers now" (Zim93-64: 4).

In the late 1930s and early 1940s the Bantu Actors performed South African and American songs, but Mattaka said that they did not sing many Shona songs.[9] They were careful to gauge the popularity of songs by audience reaction:

> MATTAKA: each time after a concert we would sit down and assess every-thing and see which number, you know, did not appeal to the audience.
> TURINO: Were the American songs and the English songs popular?
> MATTAKA: They were. And people liked that, because in those days, you know, when they are from school, people used to feel very proud of you. You see? So when you sing and it shows some-thing advanced and so on, well, people would really want to hear your voice again or hear the song again. (Zim93-65: 5)

Mattaka's statement suggests a new type of shared aesthetic among Africans who had been to school—an appreciation of advanced music as an articulation of the group's position and aspirations. Mattaka repeat-edly contrasted the advanced music of his ensemble with indigenous Shona music and the syncretic makwaya style:

> MATTAKA: Now makwaya is what we found before I started, I brought in this change I'm talking about with the Bantu Actors. We found the makwaya type of singing. Yeah, where one person leads and the others keep repeating.
> TURINO: Answering? Call and response?
> MATTAKA: That's it. And they'll clap hands and, you know.
> TURINO: So that was more traditional in a way?
> MATTAKA: Eh, not quite, because it started from schools out in the rural areas. Teachers used to teach singing, and that, so it became common. So you'd find also grown-ups you know, organized themselves in this, in the same form. So they used to call that makwaya. . . . But then we brought in now better singing, where we could read notes, we could read staff notation. You see, then that became the difference (Zim93-65: 7). . . . In those days, people used to appreciate if you sing good songs. You know, musical, and all the parts in, and all the harmony. Educated people used to appreciate that. The makwaya was just a sort of shouting sort of singing. Different, not well com-posed. (Zim93-65: 17)

As a product of a certain type of education, musical literacy was deemed important by Mattaka and other members of the middle class. Having "all the parts in, and all the harmony" likewise indexed a stan-dardization and sophistication that were important marks of distinc-tion. Yet the role of these features for defining class position goes be-yond the conscious display of prestige practices; they were part of the cultural position that constituted being middle class.

Peircian semiotics help clarify the distinction I am trying to make. In the construction of a new identity unit—ranging from youth subcultures to nations—leaders of the movement can design new emblems and practices to define the group, and participants can consciously take on these emblems in the act of joining up. As in Zimbabwe, such is often the case with incipient nationalist movements. In such instances the signs involved are iconic-rhemes, signs interpreted as representing social possibilities (Turino 1999). The operation of constructing identity is still fresh enough to be perceived by participants, and the practices are not yet a "natural" or authentic part of the habitus, although the goal is to make them so.

When practices that indicate social identities emerge organically out of the habitus of participants, a different perceptual process involving indexical-dicent signs is operating. An indexical-dicent is a sign for which the *object* (entity signified) is implicitly understood as actually affecting the sign (wind and weathervane), and hence is interpreted as the reality or true nature of the object. With indexical-dicents the interpretive process takes place in a particularly direct, unreflexive way outside the realm of language-based thought—as with the effects of body language. For Mattaka and his educated audiences, musical literacy and well-crafted harmony appear to have been indexical-dicent signs. Here musical literacy and carefully orchestrated harmonies were the products of the same cosmopolitan habitus which they signified, making them particularly direct, authentic, reality-laden signs for middle-class identity.

An emphasis on music notation has often accompanied peoples' internalization of a modernist position in many parts of the world—regardless of whether this technique was necessary for learning and transmitting music or not (e.g., Capwell 1991; Buchanan 1995; Noll 1991; Chopyak 1987). Music notation was the first technology through which musical sounds and practices could be (partially) objectified and sold (Ellingson 1992). The importance of music notation derives from the modernist-capitalist tendency to base the legitimacy and, indeed, the reality of a practice on its transformation into an objectified form.[10] In the musical realm, recordings represent a more advanced stage, and videos more advanced still, of the same objectifying function formerly fulfilled by scores: transforming ephemeral human-sound-motion-relationships-thought (*music*) into a reproducible product.

As with the white music educators during the Federation period, Mattaka's emphasis on notation fits with the related modernist tendencies of standardization, 'rationalism,' objectification, and 'universalism' (see especially Buchanan 1995 for parallels). Rather than interpreting Mattaka's emphasis on staff notation, standardized harmony, and tight vocal arrangements merely as external prestige markers—cultural capital dependent on display and admiration—my claim is that their importance derives from their deeper significances and correspondences to his and his audiences' commonsense ways of understanding the world. Mattaka's and other middle-class peoples' remarks about these practices lead me to believe that they were indexical-dicent signs, that is, signs of the authenticity of the group to the group itself—the very mortar of identity.

### De Black Evening Follies

Mattaka's Bantu Actors was the training ground for some of the most important "concert" acts of the 1940s and 1950s. Mattaka recounted how he was continually "compelled to bring in some new blood" (Zim93-65: 4, 7) because his performers would drop out due to time conflicts, loss of interest, or because they split off to form their own groups. He reformulated the Bantu Actors for the first time in 1939, approaching four people who were in school at Waddilove Mission Station. These performers included Moses Mpahlo, Samuel Gotora, Elisha Kassim, and a fourth, a young woman, whose name Mattaka could not remember. Instead of searching out replacements for his group among the multitude of singers around him in Mbare, he approached a group of young people who had been trained in singing at a mission school.

Mpahlo, Gotora, and Kassim stayed with the Bantu Actors until 1943, when they joined with Renny Nyamundanda and others to form perhaps the most famous of all the "concert" ensembles: De Black Evening Follies (Mattaka Zim93-65: 8). Performing between 1943 and the 1960s, De Black Evening Follies had a number of personnel additions and changes. At various times they worked with female singers such as Joyce Ndoro and Christine Dube. The most famous addition was the great singer, dancer, and comedian Sonny Sondo (also from Waddilove mission school), who became the lead singer in Mpahlo's group between 1946 and 1953.

In an interview with Joyce Makwenda, Moses Mpahlo, the leader of the Follies, recounted, "We did not have guitars to start with. We used to stamp our feet to produce the rhythm." According to Makwenda, most of their early songs were jazz 'copyrights' (pieces composed and previously recorded by someone else) and the songs of the Mills Brothers (1992b).[11] Mpahlo stated, "I wouldn't say we used to write music as such. What we used to do is . . . take two, say, tunes, and we combined them together. We then composed our song from those two tunes" (quoted in Makwenda 1992a). According to both Mattaka and Mpahlo, original composition was not particularly valued within the "concert" tradition during the 1940s and 1950s. Sonny Sondo, however, did compose both music and lyrics, and the Follies added completely original songs to their copyright material after his arrival (Guvi 1964: 28; Makwenda 1992c).

Over the course of their career, De Black Evening Follies performed a wide variety of genres and styles based in the cosmopolitan popular music of the day. In the 1940s they began in a style based on the Mills Brothers and the Ink Spots, and these models remained an important component of their style into the 1960s. The Mills Brothers influence is heard in the prominent use of a swing rhythm produced by a vamping guitar, by the tight, smooth vocal harmonies, and the creative use of precisely enunciated vocables, often sung by backup singers to accompany the lead. American 'Negro' groups like the Mills Brothers and the Ink Spots were a logical choice for mission-trained Zimbabwean "concert" musicians. The sweet, highly controlled sound of these American ensembles certainly projected an image of refinement that was emulated by Zimbabweans in stage manner, dress, and sound, just as the jazz rhythm was considered progressive, and the prominence of vocables familiar.

Throughout the 1950s South African jive was also a major influence in "concert" groups' style, as were South African vocal groups such as the Manhattan Brothers. *Parade* music writer Biz Kameat states that most of the "concert" groups in Zimbabwe were modeled on the Manhattan Brothers (1966a: 11).[12] The South African connection is complex, however, because groups like the Manhattan Brothers were also modeled on the Mills Brothers and other North American groups (see Coplan 1985: 135). Ultimately, Zimbabwean ensembles sounded more like their South African counterparts than they did the original North American models although the original Mills Brothers influence is readily apparent. The texture of a Mills Brother's performance tends to be more transparent, and the rhythm crisper than the slightly denser, more relaxed sound of the Follies or the Manhattan Brothers. The Africans' use of a somewhat looser vocal timbre and technique seems key to the difference, as is the influence of distinctive rhythms in southern Africa.

By the end of the 1950s the Follies were doing chacha and 'rumba' numbers, apparently influenced by the international "dance-craze" diffusion of Cuban music, which also influenced African ballroom dancing.

While Congolese guitar-band rumba became very influential in Zimbabwe around this time, I consider the Follies' use of Latin American dance music to be part of a broader trajectory: their stage show was more in the style of a Carmen Miranda or Desi Arnaz presentation. For example, a 1961 film clip of De Black Evening Follies features Joyce Ndoro in a grass skirt singing "Gori Gori," a dance-band rumba, with three clownish, male backup singers in "Latin American" vests. Ndoro's vocal style and body movement and the antics of the backup vocalists seem to have been influenced by Miranda for this presentation (film housed in National Archives of Zimbabwe; hear also "Sono Sami" Gallo G.B.1658A).[13]

Simangliso Tutani, Jacob Mhungu, and other veteran Zimbabwean musicians have commented that American films were as influential as 78-rpm recordings for learning foreign styles. Tutani said, "We used to see a few American groups on films that were played on Saturdays. We'd see pictures of groups like the Mills Brothers, the Negro Brothers, who'd do dance routines, so that even our music changed later on" (quoted in Makwenda 1992a). Miranda (and Arnaz) films were a likely source for De Black Evening Follies' Latin style of presentation.

As rock and roll became popular in Zimbabwe at the end of the 1950s, the Follies incorporated it. In 1960 they recorded a wonderful version of "Long Tally [sic] Sally" which, although distinctly southern African, certainly maintains much of the original energy of Little Richard's recording in contrast to, say, Pat Boone's cover version. The Follies apparently learned the song from the Little Richard recording and, while their enunciation of song texts was usually very precise, in this recording the lead singer slurs over words he apparently did not understand (National Archives of Zimbabwe, ZBC 78 collection #311b). In a 1961 Central African Film Unit clip in which the Follies performed this song, the lead singer did a good imitation of Elvis's choreography—up on his toes, wobbling in at the knees.

Mpahlo described a typical Follies performance as a "variety program" in which they juxtaposed many different kinds of music and arrangements. A quartet number might be followed by a full sextet vocal performance or a vocal solo backed by three or four vocalists doing do-wop or crooning accompaniment. The primary musical attention was on singing with smooth timbres and carefully arranged triadic harmonies. By the late 1940s, instrumental accompaniment (like the vocal style) would vary according to the nature of a given song. The core of the instrumental accompaniment was solo guitar or guitar with traps and stand-up bass; a saxophone might be added for a rock and roll number; sax, clarinet, and other winds for a 'jazz' or jive piece; and Latin American percussion instruments would be brought in for 'rumbas.' The rhythm section was very competent and would swing softly behind the singers. When winds were added, they would mainly join the chorus or riff between vocal lines; extended guitar or wind solos, as in North American jazz, were not a prominent part of the style.

Following the tradition of the Bantu Actors, the Follies also did comic skits, what Mpahlo called "sketches," between musical numbers. For example, Mpahlo described one of their skits as follows: "We did a serial called Chabata. It was about a person who had his *zango* [talisman or good luck charm], called Chabata. At the end Chabata died, and we went to the extent of bringing the coffin onto the stage" (quoted in Makwenda 1992b). The sketches sometimes involved comic dialogue between two or more performers who often dressed clownishly in hobolike garb.[14] There is a strong parallel here between the way middle-class Zimbabweans represented lower-class Africans and the way nineteenth-century minstrels depicted blacks, or the way hillbilly performers sometimes depicted rural whites during the 1920s and 1930s in the United States—as cultural others available for parody.[15]

By the late 1950s the "variety show" sometimes also included Shona village dances. In a Central African Film Unit short from 1960, the Follies performed three pieces. A slow Mills Brothers–influenced vocal number was performed in tuxedos, followed by the rumba "Gori Gori" discussed above. The final number was a performance of jerusarema. A member of the ensemble announced, "We hope you have enjoyed our *modern* music, and now we are going to show you some of our *traditional* dance"; the "traditional/modern" dichotomy was clearly part of their thinking. Five male performers, dressed in the typical skirts made of skins, danced with Joyce Ndoro while a sixth man played the tall *ngoma* (drums). Their singing of jerusarema, including the yodeling technique, was quite good, sounding as it might in any village performance. They did not appear comfortable or familiar with other aspects of the tradition, however. They clapped their hands instead of using woodblocks. The clapped patterns, drumming, and the dancing bore little resemblance to jerusarema as it is normally performed, suggesting that they were more adept at learning foreign vocal genres than unfamiliar instrumental and dance styles. The addition of indigenous dances to their shows must have become standard by the late 1950s; in 1959, *African Parade* music writer "Mr. Music" describes De Black Evening Follies as "experts in typical tribal dances, rumba, and rock 'n' roll" (*African Parade* 1959a: 14).

As stage entertainers, De Black Evening Follies stressed variety. Costumes, ranging from tuxedos to skins, as well as instrumental accompaniment and vocal style would be changed in keeping with the given genre performed. Whereas Mattaka had stressed "progressive" (i.e., European, American, and South African) music, as did the Follies, by the end of the 1950s, local genres were also being incorporated into their show to provide a contrast to their mainstay of 'modern' music.

The Follies appear to have been unusual among the "concert" groups in actually staging indigenous dances in their shows. The use of local Shona music as an additional style to draw from among a wide range of international genres, however, was not uncommon among Zimbabwean urban dance bands by the late 1950s. Mass nationalism was barely getting started in 1959, and it seems an unlikely inspiration for the Follies' incorporation of indigenous dances. The white-led musical reformist movements of the Federation period were a more likely impetus, as is demonstrated at the end of this chapter.

### Other "Concert" Artists

In 1953, Sonny Sondo left De Black Evening Follies to form the City Quads with Sam Matambo, Titus Mukotsanjera, and Steve Mtunyane (Chinamhora 1987; Guvi 1964). According to an *African Parade* music writer, the City Quads was, along with the Follies, the most popular "concert" group in Salisbury in the late 1950s (1959a: 14). Their recordings from the 1950s on Polydor/Gallotone suggest that they continued in the light, jazzy, Mills Brothers style, accompanied by guitar, traps, and bass (e.g., Gallo GB. 3172). One of their pieces, released around 1960 and based on an African-American spiritual, was perceived as being a political song—"When Will the Day of Freedom Come?"[16] Other prominent "concert" artists included the Epworth Theatrical Strutters,[17] Bulawayo-based groups such as the Golden Rhythm Crooners and the Cool Four, and Dorothy Masuka.

Dorothy Masuka was Zimbabwe's first international singing artist. She got her start performing in South Africa in a style resembling that of Miriam Makeba, and she actually worked with Makeba, Hugh Masekela, and the Manhattan Brothers there. She returned to Zimbabwe during the late 1950s and early 1960s to perform and record, backed by the Golden Rhythm Crooners (Chinamhora 1987: 240, 263). She also recorded several sides for RBC African Service Radio backed by the Harare Hot Shots, a local African dance band. These recordings included a jive piece sung in Xhosa and a sentimental song, "A Boy on a Dolphin." She cites Ella Fitzgerald as an influence, and she sang this

English song in the silky smooth style of an American torch singer with practically no "foreign" musical or verbal accent. She later moved to England and toured in Africa, Europe, North America, and Asia (Chinamhora 1987: 240). Because of her international reputation, Masuka is often considered the first lady of Zimbabwean music, but her presence in the country during her peak years was actually rather brief; she lived outside Zimbabwe from the mid-1960s until 1980.[18]

Finally, it is worth mentioning that Harare had its own minstrel, or 'coons,' troupe called The Capital City Dixies. A South African coons group, Coons Carnival, successfully performed in Mbare at Stodart Hall in 1958 (*African Parade* 1958: 12). In 1959, a recent European immigrant, Eric Williamson, was inspired by the South Africans to seek out talent in Mbare and start a troupe there. Complete with blackface, top hats, and tails, the Capital City Dixies performed popular music in the Tin Pan Alley style, rumba, rock and roll (including a cover of "Kansas City" renamed "Capital City," ZBC #2164B), and "variety skits" (Rusike 1960: 38–39). While the Dixies' costuming and use of blackface was unique, the group fit squarely within the "concert" tradition; ensembles like De Black Evening Follies had also borrowed from minstrelsy, especially for their skits.

## "Concert" and Cosmopolitanism

The repertory and stage act of De Black Evening Follies and other "concert" groups may be thought of as cosmopolitan at various levels. Most obviously they drew on and juxtaposed styles and pieces from a variety of Zimbabwean and international sources. The foreign styles they chose were often cosmopolitan in their own right. For example, while 'the American Negro pattern' was emphasized early on, the African-American models selected—spirituals, the Mills Brothers—were precisely those that were heavily based on cosmopolitan aesthetics and were already incorporated into cosmopolitan markets and cultural loops. Moreover, the African-American styles were often diffused to Zimbabwe after having been shaped by South African groups like the Manhattan Brothers.

A parallel case can be made for the diffusion of Latin American styles incorporated into "concert." Rather than picking distinctive local Latin American genres and pieces, they chose models that had already been aesthetically shaped and commercially mainstreamed in the United States, Europe, and Asia.[19] Congolese adoption of Cuban music may have also been an influence. The point is that "concert" groups did not draw on idiosyncratic foreign local styles—delta blues from the United

States or Cuban *son* as played in Cuba. Being tied into cosmopolitan loops by their own dispositions, they selected styles already available within cosmopolitanism. Even indigenous Zimbabwean genres like jerusarema were already being tied into cosmopolitan spheres through the cultural discourse and projects of the Federation era such as Kwanongoma, radio and film broadcasts, and "folkloric" performances at the Rainbow Cinema and the University. As middle-class "concert" performers combined these sources and put their own linguistic (many songs were translated into Shona) and musical slants on 'copyrights,' the style became locally generated and distinctive—that is, cosmopolitan in the sense I am developing.

### Cosmopolitan Concert
### Conventions

The ethics and aesthetics of "concert" performance and reception were also grounded in cosmopolitan conventions for concert-hall presentations. As entertainers, the Bantu Actors, De Black Evening Follies, and other "concert" ensembles performed almost exclusively on stages for well-dressed, sit-down audiences in municipal recreation halls on weekends, rather than in churches or beerhalls. Audiences paid between a shilling and two shillings and sixpence to enter.[20] Mattaka singles out educated Africans as being particularly appreciative of the style, and specifically identified the audience as middle-class Africans (Zim93-65: 7).[21]

In describing concerts in the 1940s and 1950s, William Saidi of the Milton Brothers, another "concert" ensemble, stressed the importance of the stage, of dressing well, and the respectable atmosphere at concerts:

> I don't go out to these musical shows [nowadays] too much, they are different from what we had. . . . There was the stage, and, you, the singers, the entertainers, were on stage. The audience they sat *quietly*. They came dressed up in their *best*. People brought their wives! their mothers-in-law!! to a concert which went on from eight o'clock to half past eleven. And it was an evening that had a lot of class. (quoted in Makwenda 1992a)

Mattaka also commented with real appreciation on the polite, refined atmosphere at these events. During concerts, the hall would be silent— "You could hear a pin drop"—suggesting the adoption of European concert conventions. Jeremiah Kainga, a guitar player and dancer who joined the Bantu Actors in 1947, noted that "we were called Actors because our concert shows were full of variety. We did not have amplifiers, but our voices were heard by people even at the back of the hall. The audiences were so quiet that if you dropped a coin, everyone in the hall would look at you" (quoted in Makwenda 1992d).

Mattaka was accurate when he contrasted his and other "concert" groups' performances with indigenous music making. A more radically different modus operandi from typical indigenous Shona occasions couldn't be imagined with their ethos of group participation and aesthetic preferences for densely overlapping, interlocking parts, buzzy timbres, spontaneous vocal interjections, and dancing. Formal differences between indigenous music making and "concert" correlate with the distinct goals of presentational performance which, in turn, are grounded in basic ethical and aesthetic differences between African middle-class concert-goers and Zimbabweans strongly grounded in indigenous lifeways.

Indigenous Shona music is cyclical and open-ended, and pieces are played as long as the situation requires or the participants desire. In "concert," relatively short pieces in prearranged closed form (i.e., having a set beginning, middle, and ending) were presented. Open-ended forms emphasize music as a process of interaction tailored to the needs of specific people and moments, whereas the emphasis on closed, prearranged forms points to a conception of music as a set art object.

At an indigenous ceremony, one or two genres and rhythmic grooves are typically performed all night. The long, repetitious performances help participants get into rhythmic synchrony with each other and maintain an experience of actual physical unity through dancing, clapping, and singing. *Variety* of musical style and format of presentation (e.g., comic skits alternated with serious musical numbers) was a major value and point of pride in the "concert" tradition. This correlates with presentational stage music generally as a mechanism for maintaining interest for a seated audience not actively involved with the music making or dancing.

The dense overlapping textures and feathered approach to phrasing, the practice of interlocking parts, the buzzy timbres (bottle caps on mbira, the ever-present hosho), and the wide intonational fields of indigenous Shona performance are similar to participatory traditions in many places, but contrast fundamentally with the modernist-cosmopolitan aesthetics upon which the "concert" tradition is based. In indigenous performance as the spirit moves people, feathered entrances, melodic variations, shouts, whistles, ululations, clapping patterns, are added and are considered a necessary part of successful music. It was precisely this spontaneous rather free-wheeling style of indigenous music making that Mattaka explicitly criticized as "a shouting sort of singing, different, not well composed" (Zim93-65: 17). Such styles are actually an affront to people who are attached to order and control.

Within middle-class ethics, the lack of control, organization, pre-planning, variety, and lack of *distinction*—between sounds as well as between artists and audiences—make indigenous participatory style objectionable. Given the testimonies of "concert" performers and audience members, I believe that they were not merely imitating the colonizers' concert conventions and aesthetic preferences as a conscious ploy to be recognized as 'civilized.' This was not merely a matter of display. Rather, people involved with "concert" were shaping their behavior ("You could hear a pin drop"), performance style, and expectations based in an emerging class habitus among 'people who had been to school.' They created, performed, and enjoyed "concert" because of how they had been socialized and *who they were*. At this point the use of the Mills Brothers' style and repertory, the matching tuxedos, and silent audiences are not an imitation of foreign practices, but are a locally generated form of cosmopolitanism. The ethical elements of sharp role distinctions, planning and control, and the conception of pieces as set, reproducible objects point to an articulation specifically with modernist-capitalist cosmopolitanism.

### End of an Era

By the mid-1960s the "concert" tradition was all but dead. Some "concert" artists have suggested that the shows died away because of the volatile political climate surrounding the government crackdown on African nationalism after 1963, especially following Ian Smith's Unilateral Declaration of Independence (UDI) from Britain in 1965 (e.g., see Makwenda 1992a). The suggestion that government repression dampened the scheduling of concerts, however, does not fit with the fact that recreational events such as the Neshamwari Festival and other performance occasions continued to be supported by the municipal government after 1966, and throughout the war years of the 1970s.

Other observers suggest that African nationalism caused the decline of the "concert" tradition without specifying how. For example the *African Parade* writer Tinos Guvi explained Sonny Sondo's move to Zambia (circa 1960) by saying that "with the advent of African nationalism, patrons to concert shows decreased to an untold low" (1964: 28). It is clear, however, that the nationalist leadership was in no way hostile to "concert" ensembles; such groups were actually invited to perform at nationalist rallies and festivals during the early 1960s (see chapter 5).

Rather than being direct causes for the decline of "concert," African nationalism and government oppression can only be understood as part of a broader, more ambiguous shift in middle-class, black Zimbabweans' "structures of feeling." When the discourse of 'partnership' was seen for the sham it was, and with UDI and the coming of war, the time for the polite, sophisticated, 'civilized' ethos celebrated and embodied by "concert" was weakened. The taste for 'sophisticated' cosmopolitan music and dance activities did not disappear completely among the African middle class, however, as indicated by the continued popularity of ballroom dancing through the 1970s.

Perhaps the best explanation for the decline of "concert" is simply that cosmopolitan styles had changed and that after twenty years, the school-choir-cum-Mills-Brothers-cum-vaudeville model was no longer in vogue and could no longer capture the imagination. *Parade* music writer Biz Kameat asks, "What killed [the concert groups]?"

> Above all, the failure of Rhodesian bands to compose their own music, which had become a duplicate of the music from the South [Africa], taken, in most cases, from the Manhattan Brothers and other troupes which toured the country so many years ago.
>
> And because of this, the fans began to be bored, and restless, the halls began to empty, . . . and that was the end of showbiz.
>
> Since then, and thanks to the rock 'n roll, . . . the young of the country have taken to the guitar, and a drum. (1966a: 11)

The Follies adoption of rock and roll around 1959 may be seen as an attempt to stay current, as was their staging of jerusarema; both were forecasts of major popular musical trends to come. Just as Perry Como was gradually swept away by Elvis and Chuck Berry in the United States, guitar bands grounded in rock and roll—but incorporating elements of indigenous music—replaced the "concert" ensembles by the late 1960s in Harare (see chapter 7). Also by the mid-1960s the cosmopolitan value of artistic originality became increasingly important and was to have a major impact on the creation of unique Zimbabwean genres by the Mapfumo generation in the following decade.

## Urban Dance Bands and Instrumental African Jazz

Although "concert" groups, and certainly their instrumental accompanists, were tied into jazz, urban dance bands playing instrumental African 'jazz' and cosmopolitan popular music are part of a different trajectory.[22] In British colonies the training of Africans in military bands spawned local dance bands and sometimes, as with Highlife in West Africa, emergent styles (e.g., see Coplan 1978: 98; Waterman 1990:

42–43). The origin of many instrumental dance bands in Zimbabwe can be traced directly to the British South African Police Band and, later, to the Prison Band—both native to Zimbabwe. Often the dance band musicians of the 1940s and 1950s were actually moonlighting Police Band members who, because of their state-supported musical day jobs, were the first significant group of full-time professional musicians in the country.

When the British South African Police Band was formed in Zimbabwe in 1939, the idea of using only African musicians was met with skepticism and controversy. The ensemble soon proved its worth, however, and by the mid-1950s, it was reported that "no important occasion is complete without this band of over twenty men in gorgeous uniform. They play at most civic and private functions, including dances for Europeans. When the [British] Royal Family went in 1947, they provided music" (*African Parade* 1955b: 7).

At the time the Police Band was formed, it provided one of the main institutional contexts in which Africans in Zimbabwe could learn European wind instruments and obtain instruments.[23] The band played genres ranging from military marches and British patriotic music for parades and state occasions to cosmopolitan ballroom dance music and jazz. The Police Band, still active today, was the training ground for some of Zimbabwe's leading 'jazz' musicians of the 1940s and 1950s, such as Benedict Mazura, August Musarurwa, the Harare Hot Shots, and the City Slickers. Lawrence Vambe notes that the instrumentalists who accompanied De Black Evening Follies (and presumably other "concert" groups in Harare), such as trumpeter Jona Mbirimi, were also trained in the Police Band (1976: 213).

### August Musarurwa and Tsaba-Tsaba

A particularly prominent alumnus of the Police Band, August Musarurwa is one of Zimbabwe's most revered 'jazz' saxophone players and composers.[24] After graduating from high school and working as a clerk, he got a job as a police interpreter. For an African to complete high school was quite an accomplishment for that time, enabling Musarurwa to move into relatively good jobs such as clerking and interpreting, all of this suggesting middle-class standing.

From his position as interpreter with the Police, August Musarurwa applied and was accepted in the Police Band in 1942, where he received training on saxophone and gained musical literacy. After leaving the band in 1947 for health reasons, he moved to Bulawayo, where he started the Cold Storage Band, later renamed the Bulawayo Sweet Rhythms Band, comprising two banjos, two saxophones, trumpet, traps, and bass (*African Parade* 1955b: 7).[25] It was with the Bulawayo Sweet Rhythms Band that he recorded his famous piece "Skokiaan" for Gallo Records (GB11 52.T; Coplan 1985: 154). "Skokiaan"—the word for strong, illicit alcohol sold in informal drinking places in African townships—became an international hit in the mid-1950s; it was re-corded by Louis Armstrong under the title "Happy Africa," by South African groups under the original title, and as far away as the Domini-can Republic, for example, the merenge version by Antonio Morel y su Orquesta (Austerlitz 1997: 59). A 45-rpm recording of "Skokiaan" by the Bulawayo Sweet Rhythms Band was even released in the United States by London Records (n.d., 45-1491).[26]

"Skokiaan" thus exemplifies the emergent, synthetic nature of cos-mopolitanism, and jazz as a cosmopolitan genre, in a particularly clear way. Although still associated with its African-American or American origins, by the post–World War II era jazz had been diffused to many places in the world, had taken root, and had given rise to myriad local variants. Musicians like Musarurwa who became involved with jazz and contributed to local creation were already tied into cosmopolitan loops, in his case through colonial schooling and the Police Band. Mov-ing beyond mere imitation of foreign models, Musarurwa and other southern African musicians created their own brand of "jazz" or "jive" and pieces that could then feed back through cosmopolitan loops (re-cordings, tours) to "The Source" (Armstrong) as well as to multiple other sites with their own local variants (the merenge version in the Do-minican Republic). Musarurwa's contribution was attractive to and *constructive of* cosmopolitan jazz both for the "local" southern African difference that it provided and for its base in and similarity to the larger tradition that allowed for its recognition and inclusion.

In South Africa "Skokiaan" was recorded by Nico Carstens en Sy Orkes (Columbia B.E. 294), and by Johnny Johnston and the Johnston Brothers (Decca F. 10369). A sheet music version with words by Tom Glazer was published by Gallo in 1952, and was identified as a South Af-rican, rather than Zimbabwean, song. On the sheet music, "Skokiaan" is translated as "happy happy." Armstrong's title may have come from the opening of the song text backed by this erroneous translation. Glazer's words fit the romantic, exotic imagery found in many popular songs drawn "from the margins" into cosmopolitan circles—for example, Tin Pan Alley treatments of Hawaiian, Latin American, and Asian im-agery and sources during the first half of the twentieth century:

Ho Ho, Far away in Africa, happy, happy Africa, They sing a-bing, a-bang, a-bing, Oh They have a ball and really go. SKOKIAAN, Ho Ho. Take a trip to Africa, Any ship to Africa. Come on along and learn the lingo, Beside a jungle bungalow. The hot drums are drummin', The hot strings are strummin', And warm lips are blissful. They're kissfull of SKOKIAAN, Ho Ho. If you go to Africa, Happy, Happy Africa, You'll linger longer like a king—Oh Right in the jungle-ungleo. (Gallo #10925, 1952)

Given that savannas, forests, high plateaus, mountains, and deserts characterize southern African topography, the romantic, "jungle-ungleo" imagery is particularly striking. Similar to the way 1980s "worldbeat" is unified as a phenomenon by constructing everything outside of cosmopolitanism as a single unified otherness, in the 1940s and 1950s one tropical paradise was designed to fit all.

Musarurwa performed a type of African jazz that, although identified as "jive" on Gallo record labels, was known popularly as *tsaba-tsaba* (or *tsava-tsava*).[27] Tsaba-tsaba was a style associated with the urban working class in southern Africa. In Zimbabwe it was associated with "tea parties"—a euphemism for weekend dance parties where skokiaan alcohol was sold—that took place in the townships, mining compounds, and large farms. Tsaba-tsaba was performed by solo acoustic guitarists or small guitar bands with hosho and other indigenous percussion instruments (see chapter 7), as well as by larger groups including guitars, saxophones, bass, and traps (Vambe 1976: 188). Lawrence Vambe also associates more organized jazz bands like Musarurwa's with middle-class African ballroom dancing (213).

According to most Zimbabweans I spoke with, tsaba-tsaba originated in South Africa and was imported into Zimbabwe on records and by returning migrants. Describing tsaba-tsaba in South Africa, David Coplan writes,

> By the 1940s, the latest popular, working-class dance music combined African melody and rhythm with the rhythms of American swing, jitterbug, and even Latin American rumba and conga. Developed by black South African bandsmen, the new style was called tsaba-tsaba. It is played in duple time, and its rhythm has several distinctive African/Afro-American features, including rushed second and fourth beats, the freedom to accent any of the four beats, and a poly-rhythmic sense of two beats against three. (1985: 152)

Coplan cites Musarurwa's "Skokiaan" as a "classic *tsaba* dance tune" (1985: 154).

"Skokiaan" has a four-bar I–IV–I–V progression in 4/4 meter, with the banjos strumming a ♪♪♩♪♪♩ figure throughout. The main melodic strain (A) begins with a long held trill (anywhere from one to three bars) played by the sax on the dominant pitch; extended trills later became a trademark of Musarurwa's style. The trill is followed by an undulating, descending melody. The A strain is contrasted with sections of riffing that follow the harmonic progression fairly closely (often based on simple arpeggiation) before the main melody returns. Toward the end of Musarurwa's recording there is a short trumpet solo which is overlapped by Musarurwa's sax toward the end; otherwise the melody is carried by the sax.

Musarurwa's later "jive" or "tsaba-tsaba" pieces[28] were similar to Skokiaan in harmony and form. Consistent with South African jive, they were grounded on a simpler swinging guitar vamp: consistent eighth notes with the accents on two and four, although beats two and four are sometimes slightly anticipated, as Coplan observed. In Musarurwa's music there are frequent phrasing shifts between melodic placement and the guitar vamp accents within the same performance, a primary source of interest. In Chapter 7 we will return to tsaba-tsaba in the context of acoustic guitar music and the history of the jit genre.

### Dance Bands

During the 1950s two of the best-known instrumental dance bands in the Harare area were the Harare Hot Shots and the City Slickers.[29] Both groups comprised moonlighting musicians who worked full-time for the Police Band and, perhaps due to this training, were very similar in instrumentation and approach. The Hot Shots, recording as early as 1954 (Trek D.C. Records, *African Parade* 1954: 9), performed with two saxophones, trumpet, trombone, guitar, bass, and traps; solos were usually taken by the trumpet, guitar, and sax. The City Slickers differed in that they had three saxophone players, and the main soloing was done by these musicians. Both groups performed the popular dance music of the day, including rumba, foxtrots, quicksteps, waltzes, and rock and roll.

Depending on the piece, their styles could be quite varied. The Hot Shots in particular did many South African jive pieces. Both groups sometimes used New Orleans–style texture and effects (collective improvisation and heterophony, comical trombone slides) as well as big-band-style soloing against a horn chorus and a smooth swing feel (e.g., Hot Shots' "Rockin' Thru the Rye" RBC #1357A). If vocals were involved, the piece might have a Tin Pan Alley sound of the 1940s, much like some "concert" groups (e.g., the Slickers' "My Dream Boat" RBC #1232A). Sometimes pieces combined these different elements in rather interesting ways. For example, "City Slickers' Rock" (RBC #2059B) sounds like a less-than-sober tourist Dixieland Band in the French Quarter having fun with a stereotypic 1950s rock and roll song.

In addition to their international fare, both the Hot Shots and the City Slickers sometimes arranged indigenous Shona songs. For instance, in 1961, the City Slickers recorded a version of the extremely popular Shona song, "Chemutengure" for African Service Radio (RBC #1245B). I have heard this song performed in Zimbabwe in many ways, including on mbira, karimba,[30] chipendani, guitar, accordion, and vocally (makwaya). As typically performed, this song is classically Shona in its features: an ostinato composed of two moderate-to-quick 12/8 phrases, descending melody, and call-and-response text form. The Slickers, however, performed the piece instrumentally as a ballroom-style waltz in which the traditional melody is rendered so slowly that it is hard to recognize.

Chartwell Dutiro, mbira and saxophone player for Thomas Mapfumo from the mid-1980s through the early 1990s, told me that his uncle Davis Musango played trumpet and did arranging and composing for the Hot Shots. In the late 1950s and early 1960s Musango would occasionally base 'jazz band' pieces on local Shona songs. Like the Slicker's version of "Chemutengure," however, Dutiro noted that when the Hot Shots got done with the arrangement, the piece was pretty far from the original (Fieldbook II: 38c). Dance-band renditions of indigenous songs paralleled De Black Evening Follies staging of indigenous dances at the end of the 1950s. Given the predominantly black, middle-class audiences for "concert" groups and dance bands like the Hot Shots and the City Slickers, 'traditional' additions to their repertories suggest the beginning of new interests within middle-class audiences around that time.

### The Beginnings of Professionalism in "Concert" and "Jazz"

Even the biggest "concert" stars from the 1940s through the 1960s were not professional musicians in the sense of earning a living from performance.[31] Sonny Sondo, one of the most successful, required a day job in Harare to sustain himself. Echoing many others in the "concert" tradition, Sam Matambo of the City Quads stated that they performed for the love of it and that the group actually earned very little from performances (in Makwenda 1992a). The money they did make usually paid expenses or went to charities (an idea supported in various *Parade* articles). Mattaka stated that the Bantu Actors kept the money earned from concert ticket sales but that it basically went to cover expenses; this use of their income was actually monitored by the African Welfare Society with whom they were registered (Zim93-65: 8).

When Sondo moved to Zambia (around 1960) and worked for a mining company as beer hall supervisor by day and led a mining-company-sponsored singing group by night, we could say he became a full-time professional in the entertainment business. Kenneth Mattaka had a similar position earlier in Mbare. Africans had to have proof of employment to live in Mbare township since the city was legally a white area. When Mattaka stopped working as a dispatch clerk at the *Herald* because of ill health in 1948, he "had to report to the government." In 1949 he petitioned the City Council for a permit to stay in the township with the work status of professional entertainer, and it was granted (his former involvement with the AWS was probably helpful in this regard). Mattaka stated that there were no other full-time professional musicians or entertainers in Mbare at that time (Zim93-65: 10–11; field-notes 4 August 1993). In 1955 he began performing magic along with music and dance and thus became a kind of "one-man variety show."

Beside performing with the Bantu Actors and a second group, The Mattaka Family, in Mbare, he also organized African recreational activities for the City Council. Throughout the 1950s Mattaka was hired by mining companies and farmers to entertain their workers in rural areas. In 1952, Lever Brothers hired him as an entertainer to tour the country and promote their products. Between 1966 and 1973 Mattaka worked full-time for the Bata Shoes Company, performing throughout the country and, as part of his program, providing "lectures" on the health benefits of wearing shoes (fieldnotes 4 August 1993). In this way Mattaka earned a living as a performer, and his style of urban entertainment was brought to the rural areas. He was not alone. By the 1960s a few other bands and entertainers got involved with similar promotional activities and traveled throughout the country.

Mattaka's claim of being the only full-time professional African musician/entertainer in the Harare area during the 1950s is perhaps not literally true. The members of the Police Band and its splinter groups also worked as full-time musicians, and there may have been other isolated cases I am unaware of. The general point stands, however, that urban-popular music and dance performance was primarily a nonprofessional or part-time professional activity well into the 1960s. Many "concert" performers did not even seem to have professional aspirations. Rather most described their activities as a beloved avocation— art for art's sake.

The changing of the Liquor Act and the gradual expansion of bars and nightclubs for Africans after 1957 is an important part of the explanation for the rise of black professional musicians. Because of extreme racial segregation for most of Rhodesia's history, white venues were largely closed to black performers, and whites, who had more money to spend, rarely attended black shows or events. There was simply less money in "the system" for African music performance. As Lawrence Vambe observes about "concert" performers,

> Unfortunately, there were then [in the 1940s and 1950s] only two public halls, and because they were not allowed to perform in the European places of entertainment, these groups found themselves severely limited as to the space and the number of times they could give performances. (1976: 214)

Given this situation, professionalism probably didn't seem like an option, and in any case, it does not even seem to have been desirable given some "concert" performer's middle-class attitudes about respectable employment—as an avocation, performance was respectable; as a profession, it was not.[32]

In the indigenous sphere of music making, specialist lamellophone players and drummers were sometimes paid for performing at ceremonies, although we don't know when this practice began or how common it was in the decades of the 1940s and 1950s. With the exception of a handful of musicians attached to the establishments of full-time ritual healers, however, few would have considered indigenous music and dance a full-time or even a consistent part-time professional activity. Until the second half of the 1960s, then, it was not a commonsense idea that music/dance performance could or even should be a profession among the African middle class, any more than it was in indigenous society.

### Ballroom Dancing

The Police Band and its offshoot ensembles like the City Slickers and the Hot Shots played for white dances. These groups, and others like them, also played for African ballroom dancing. In describing the music scene in Salisbury Townships since the 1930s, Lawrence Vambe wrote, "For those who aspired to keep up with the times there was no doubt that the most popular form of music was the European ballroom dance variety. Both the players and the public took to it with all the passion and energy they had" (1976: 212–13). In this same passage, Vambe also linked August Musarurwa's ensemble with ballroom dancing. Vambe associates the taste for ballroom dancing with the ideology of modernity, and

Kenneth Mattaka specifically identified it as a middle-class African activity. What was surprising to me was that Mattaka considered domestics and hotel workers to be of the middle class, thus suggesting that cultural and social style rather than occupation and economic standing were his primary criteria for class identification (Zim93-65: 10). Mattaka related how the first Africans to become interested in ballroom were domestic and hotel workers who used to watch white people dance, and

> then, when they went home on weekends [to Mbare], they would have dancing competitions. Yeah, so eventually they had dancing clubs in Harare [Mbare]. . . . We used to invite white judges to come and judge their competition and all that. But you find most of those [dancers] were waiters and cooks. (Zim93-65: 7)

In his study of the rise of the African middle class in Zimbabwe, Michael West writes,

> For elite Africans, . . . ballroom dancing was the preferred dance form. Ballroom dancing was encouraged by the AWS [African Welfare Society] which, in the 1940s, established a national dancing cup that was keenly contested by dancers from the major urban centers. The annual competition for the dancing cup was more than just a big party, however; it was also a major social event, an opportunity for aspiring middle-class Africans to put themselves on display. (1990: 222)

The African Welfare Society (AWS), considered ballroom dancing, like sports, a healthy recreational pastime for Africans. For many African participants, it was a prestige activity of "a better class of people." Such attitudes changed slowly among the black middle class, and the story of Mr. H is telling in this regard.[33]

Mr. H became a Ministry of Education and Culture official involved with organizing indigenous dance activities after independence. As a youth, he had been peripherally involved with *chinyambera* (an indigenous social dance) in his village, but he began his real career in the arts as a ballroom dancer in Harare before independence. Speaking of the situation as late as the early 1970s, Mr. H recalled that

> after school and coming to the city, before independence, I started learning some classical dances such as, you know, ballroom dancing, here in town. Ballroom dancing and Latin American dances and such—chachacha, the rumba, the samba, the jive, the pasodoble— all those I learned when I came to town. It interested me before independence. I learned this from some schools here in town. You know, mainly white schools who were teaching these dances. So

before independence the, of course, colonial mentality that we all
had, if you were a ballroom dancer, you were a special person.

And so, at that time I intended to put my chinyambera knowledge, which I got from my village, under the table, for a reason. Because during the colonial days, you had to be accepted in society.
*Even in our own African society you had to, you know, to portray
some kind of Western culture.* So people who were doing ballroom
dancing, like myself and others, were great people, you know, in
society. . . . Ah, so, we had, I had no option but to, you know, that
was the order of the day, that was the cultural setup of the day, influenced by, ah, colonial mentality. (Zim92-29: 1–2, my emphasis)

Ballroom dancing was done in African nightclubs when they
opened after the liquor laws were changed in 1957, but the real centers
of activity were contests held at various times of the year from the 1940s
through the 1970s. Organizations like the Salisbury African Ballroom
Dancing Association took over from the AWS in sponsoring the major
contests. Men dressed in suits or tuxedos and women in formal gowns
competed at different levels—novice to professional—in the "four major dances": waltz, quick step, tango, and foxtrot. There were also contests to determine the best dressed. From the 1940s through the 1970s
such contests were typically held in the municipal recreation halls in
Mbare, Highfield, and other townships and were judged by white Rhodesians (Mattaka Zim93-65: 7; *Parade* 1977a: 8). The presence of white
judges is a significant indicator of the aesthetic standards. These events
attracted large crowds of black spectators as well as contestants through
the 1970s, as is evident from photos in *African Parade*.

The size of ballroom events, and Mr. H's description of himself and
other ballroom dancers during the 1970s suggests that the 'colonial mentality' remained strong among some members of the middle class even at
the height of the nationalist war. Since the nationalist leadership also
hailed from the middle class, there was clearly a divergence of positions.
Nationalism and the radical politics required to wage war created splits
in corporate, middle-class identity—fissures which can be seen emerging
in the early 1960s. Yet these are surface differences relative to the ideology
of modernity, which remained a common basis for black, middle-class
worldview among political conservatives and radicals alike.

## Modernity, Tradition, and
## Middle-Class Cultural Discourse
## in *African Parade*

While African radio was directed at all class-strata, publications like
*African Parade (Parade)* and the *Bantu Mirror* were largely of and for
the black middle class and are thus interesting windows to the cultural

positions of this group. Several trends emerged from my comprehensive survey of articles about music, dance, art, and cultural identity, as well as letters to the editor in *African Parade* monthly from 1954 through the 1970s.

As might be expected, the main music and dance topics covered by the magazine in the pre-1965 period were local "concert" and jazz ensembles, dance bands, ballroom dancing, and foreign artists—the music of interest to the middle class. What is interesting, however, was the way indigenous music and dance were discussed when they were included. In the late 1950s and early 1960s, the black middle-class writers of *Parade* exhibited a lack of familiarity with indigenous arts, treating them as strange exotica. I am convinced that this was the result of a real cultural distance from indigenous lifeways. The articles in *Parade* provide additional evidence that by the 1950s some members of the African middle class were culturally more unified with modernist cosmopolitanism than with indigenous Africans. The discourse of modernity with its concomitant traditional/modern dichotomy were important fulcrums of middle-class thinking, as a review of *Parade* articles will illustrate.

The first article about indigenous music and dance that I encountered in *Parade* was published in February 1959—"City Tribal Dancing Display," by M. E. Kumalo—about an event in Bulawayo. Kumalo writes,

> The MacDonald Hall Club room was packed to capacity with people of all races, and they were held spell-bound by the art of the performers, which at times seemed to have something *weird* about it. These *antics of ancient days* came timely to close a most eventful year in the music and entertainment sphere. There was no jazz, no rock 'n roll of the *modern world*. Many spectators left with the firm conviction that these tribal dances are a form of entertainment which should be encouraged to keep in existence because they have their own special appeal and charm in the entertainment sphere. Add to them a touch of *modern stage craft*, they will please any audience. (15; my emphasis)

The reformist desire for 'modern' stagecraft and preservation are particularly striking in this passage. These ideas fit precisely with white liberal cultural programs of the Federation period; the multiracial composition of the audience is significant in this regard. The traditional/modern dichotomy was central to Kumalo's thinking. He distanced himself from 'traditional' arts, calling them weird antics and relegating them to the past. Yet Kumalo felt that indigenous dances should be kept in existence for their charm, if and when reformed for the entertainment sphere, that is, for cosmopolitan consumption.

Although indigenous music and dance had not been mentioned in any of the previous issues of *Parade,* in the same February issue there was a report by "Mr. Music" about The All-African Music Festival of 1958, organized by the Cultural Syndicate at Stodart Hall in Mbare. Mr. Music writes,

> To many a curious ordinary music fan, the Syndicate was organizing the greatest variety concert ever held in Central Africa, and they were probably quite right in their expectations. But by the *more sophisticated man and woman, particularly the Europeans,* it was expected that the All-African Music Festival would consist mostly of *traditional African music* as portraited [sic] by the anthropologist and others who bemoan the passing of the African as he appeared *in the days of yore.* It was expected that such African traditional music instruments as the mbira, . . . the drum as it beat *in the jungle,* and many others would be seen heard and enjoyed. . . . The stage of the Stodart Hall was garlanded with very little that suggested it was the *jungles of dear old Africa* come to *modern Salisbury.* It was mostly a grouping of several modern jazz singing troupes and individual artists and a collection of *modern* jazz music instruments of the Western World. (1959b: 22; my emphasis)

Mr. Music mentions that there was only one indigenous dance included in the festival, muchongoyo, and that the curtain raiser, "the Call of the Jungle," was organized by singer Dorothy Masuka in order "to lend an African jungle setting to the festival."

The festival turned out to be "the usual mimicking of European *modern* music—the Elvis Presleys, the Bing Crosbys and the rest of them."[34] Mr. Music was disappointed, as he assumed sophisticated people, especially Europeans and anthropologists, would be. He implied that such people "expected something original—real traditional African music, which is said to be wonderful by most of those who know it." At the end of the article, the Cultural Syndicate secretary Herbert Munangatire, is quoted as saying that at next year's festival (1959) "there will definitely be more African traditional music and dancing" (*African Parade* 1959b: 22).

Like Kumalo, Mr. Music indicated a new interest in indigenous music and dance among the African middle class, although the festival organizers had not been prepared for it. This trend has already been suggested by De Black Evening Follies performance of jerusarema, and jazz bands' arrangements of indigenous songs around exactly the same time.

In a dramatic reversal from former middle-class attitudes that ignored or disparaged indigenous arts as a "shouting sort of singing," Mr. Music suggested that the ability to appreciate indigeneous performance was actually a mark of *sophistication*! He directly links this attitude to Europeans and anthropologists, rather than to the nationalists or some other source. This new appreciation was grounded in Federation-state and missionary cultural programs, as well as in the opinions of white liberals who attended indigenous performances such as those at the University, or the Rainbow Theater (see chapter 2), or the event at the MacDonald Hall Club reported by Kumalo.

During the Federation years, some white liberals had a sincere interest in making 'racial partnership' work. White liberals were directly associated with members of the black middle class in various multiracial organizations, and these two groups would have attended staged performances of indigenous dance together at theaters and the University. It is not hard to imagine that in their desire to be known as liberal, white 'multiracialists' might have emphasized their appreciation of 'authentic' indigenous music over urban-popular styles. This was certainly evidenced in Kwanongoma director Williamson's statements. Likewise, Axelsson noted that some of the missionaries who were involved with the 'Africanization' of church music became "puritanical" in their insistence on authenticity and purity (1981: 2). White liberals' enthusiasm for indigenous arts would have been influential among black cosmopolitans during the late 1950s.

At the same time, Mr. Music distanced himself from indigenous African lifeways. He writes that indigenous music "is said to be wonderful by most of those who know it"—as if he and his middle-class readership did not. He did not approach indigenous arts as his own traditions rediscovered. Rather his interest in them was like that of other cosmopolitans—anthropologists, connoisseurs of primitive art—who were sophisticated enough to value "original," "authentic" expressions of a disappearing primitive Other. Like Kumalo, Mr. Music relegated indigenous music and dance to precivilized time and place: the jungle in the "days of yore" in contrast to 'modern' forms and artists. The passing of the indigenous was lamented but also assumed—in spite of the vibrant dance scene in nearby Mbare and elsewhere. For the rest of 1959, Mr. Music and the other *African Parade* music writers returned to discussing ballroom dance contests and concert artists like Dorothy Masuka and the Hilltones. The Syndicate's festival was not held again in the following years.

In the January 1960 issue of *African Parade* a new music column, "This Music Business—from Charlie," began with a defense of indigenous music, indicating its growing acceptance among the black middle class:

Each time somebody talks to me about African traditional music, I get the sickening feeling . . . that some of our musicians have got really screwed-up ideas. . . . "That traditional music!" one of my quaint acquaintances told me the other day. "It's just beastly. Why, I wouldn't like to be seen or heard singing that music which sounds like a buffalo-stampede. Man, we've got to move with the times. We've got to have modern music for modern times."

The music of my grandpa is something I am very proud of. In fact, whether they bring the can-can dance, cha-cha-cha or just old-fashioned rock 'n roll, there's nothing to beat my old grandpa's music. (27)

Charlie went on to note that Harry Belafonte "brought the [United] States to a standstill" by singing calypso tunes, "the music of his ancestors; the music of the early ages." Charlie also reported that the "concert" group the Golden City Dixies did not get a good reception during their tour of the United Kingdom because they concentrated on songs "that Bing Crosby has long forgotten he ever sung. . . . But," he argued, "if it had been a group of traditional dancers, let's say nearer home, the Shangani [muchongoyo] dancers, you would have found Fleet Street working overtime just to keep up with the excitement" (*African Parade* 1960). So here again, the argument for valuing indigenous arts is based on the perception that sophisticated Europeans appreciated them.

Charlie concluded on a preservationist note: "I wonder what the troupes think about preserving African traditional music. Trouble is everyone is getting so urbanised that some of them have forgotten what exactly a plough looks like" (*African Parade* 1960: 27). The "everyone" here was the writer's own social group, and more specifically his urbane readership, rather than the peasant majority who were certainly still well acquainted with ploughs. This style of writing is but one example of how cosmopolitans' control of mass media helps construct their particular experience as general history.

In February of 1960 the article "Preserve and Improve on Our African Tribal Music" was published. In this essay, Mr. Wilson Shamuyarira, a middle-class teacher and choir master, set out to teach the black Zimbabwean readership of *African Parade* about indigenous Zimbabwean music in very basic terms. He began by explaining that African music was *functional,* for hunting, grinding, herding, and so on, much as Alan Merriam had in an article about African music the year before. I am not suggesting any direct influence between Merriam (1959) and Shamuyarira, but would point out that the Zimbabwean teacher seemed familiar with the standard ethnomusicological treatment of

African music at that time. The author went on to define such exotic
Zimbabwean instruments as the drum, the mbira (defined as a harp),
and the musical bow (defined as "a single-string piano"). The rest of the
article makes the case that young Zimbabweans should preserve and
improve village instruments and traditions:

> A man who despises his own tribal culture is not fit to live on this
> earth. There is a lot that can be done to bring the tribal music in line
> *with other nations' advanced type*. All the musical instruments could
> be renoverted [*sic*] and improved. At concert meetings a number of
> 'zvipendani' [musical bows] all of varying lengths could be organized
> and render a harmonious melody. (1960: 78; my emphasis)

The striking thing from my vantage point is that this middle-class
teacher felt the need to explain what a drum or mbira was to the *Parade*
readership who, at the very least, could have encountered these instruments in the Mbare market area on a weekly basis. His manner of explanation was also suggestive. The mbira was described as a harp and
the chipendani (musical bow) "a one-string piano," suggesting this
writer's perception that his readers would be more familiar with European instruments than with local ones. In this article, the goal of modernist reform is particularly clear—the desire to "bring the tribal music
in line with other nations' advanced type."

The rest of the *African Parade* issues of 1960 through May of 1962
either reported on "concert" and "coons," or did not discuss music at
all. After May 1962 the magazine begins to cover nationalist rallies and
musical events (discussed in the next chapter), and for several years village music traditions come up for discussion more frequently, although
they never receive the same amount of attention as urban-popular
bands.

It is significant, however, that beginning around 1962, indigenous
arts begin to be discussed in *Parade* in a new way. They are often still
presented as exotic, "of the past," and in need of preservation. But other
middle-class writers begin to discuss indigenous music as a normal,
commonly practiced *contemporary* part of Zimbabwean social life (e.g.,
the article about njari player Simon Mashoko, *Parade* 1965: 17). In a
pivotal 1962 article, "African Traditional Music Is a Reflection of African Personality," the author, M. Mushwe, is caught between the old
modernist view that indigenous music "is disappearing" and a new
recognition that indigenous culture "is strong still." His ambiguity on
the matter is directly reflected in the writing as he constantly shifts between past and present tense when discussing contemporary indigenous

traditions. Yet a new recognition among the middle class that indigenous performing arts are a normal rather than exotic aspect of social life seems indicated.

Rather than being the result of any fundamental change in the levels of indigenous performance activity between 1958 and 1962, what appears to have happened is that white liberalism and black cultural nationalism simply opened certain people's eyes and ears to what had been going on around them all along. In my view this awakening among certain members of the black middle class is the primary basis of the much celebrated nationalist cultural renaissance. The renaissance was thus partially true, but it later became generalized by the discourse of nationalism. The decline of indigenous culture was also partially true; that is, it was true in certain regions and among certain groups. It was generalized, however, by the very logic of modernity.

### The Modern/Traditional Dichotomy

As Foucault has shown, the power of discourse is that it sets the parameters and premises of what *can* be thought and articulated. Throughout these *Parade* articles, 'old Africa,' 'antics of ancient days,' and 'the jungle' are contrasted with 'modern' arts (rock and jazz) and places (Salisbury, London). Within the discourse of modernity, 'the Traditional' must be perceived as old and primitive because it is constructed as the binary opposite of 'the Modern,' everything that is current and forward-looking. The discourse of modernity functions to construct particular cultural formations (modernist-capitalism, modernist-socialism) as potential universals because they define and are defined by the totality of contemporary time.

As I suggested in my introduction, the traditional/modern dichotomy is a product of the social-evolutionist root of the discourse of modernity itself. When thoroughly ingrained, as with these middle-class *Parade* writers, this manner of thinking defines indigenous arts as obsolete. This construction of reality itself creates the need for preservation—regardless of the fact that indigenous arts were still commonly being practiced among other contemporaneous groups as close by as Mbare. In such situations, the apparently benevolent cry for preservation is part of the same message that portrays indigenous lifeways as disappearing, and indigenous social groups and occasions as invisible or irrelevant.

In Zimbabwe, cosmopolitans who held modernist views included middle-class African journalists, teachers, and performers like Mattaka, as well as white missionaries, liberals, and government officials. These people were aware of the expert opinion of anthropologists and ethnomusicologists who bemoaned the passing of 'the Traditional,' and they all helped reinforce this truth for each other. Since they also controlled the institutions and media for the mass diffusion of knowledge, their perspective gained greater official momentum and historical weight with repetition and with time. The modernist assumption that indigenous culture is passé becomes a self-realizing idea when repeatedly taught to, say, indigenous young people—what teenager wants to be passé? The rise of black cultural nationalism, still grounded in modernist perspectives, added other dimensions to this dynamic with its new goals for cultural reform.

## Modernist Cosmopolitanism and the Middle Class

Before the 1960s, elite Africans exhibited a distance from indigenous arts. They either felt that they had 'progressed' beyond them, as expressed by Mattaka and other "concert" performers, or they simply expressed a lack of interest in or knowledge of them, as illustrated in *African Parade*. In some cases this distance was part of a conscious strategy of mobility; in others, however, the lack of familiarity with indigenous arts was the result of a particular type of socialization.

Mr. H's personal story gives some indication of how strategic distance may simply have been a matter of individual choice. He consciously moved away from the indigenous practices of his village because of his desire to be accepted within middle-class African society after moving to Highfield. Mr. H's apparent consciousness of strategic choice, described from the hindsight of the independence period, parallels the stories of many people across class lines.

The Zimbabwean CABS employee discussed in chapter 3 represents another type of case. When asked by his supervisors to record indigenous Shona music for the radio on a sojourn to his rural home by a Seventh-Day Adventist mission, he found no indigenous music to record there. The CABS worker may not have been 'putting indigenous lifeways under the table'; apparently they were not practiced in his region and thus were simply not a part of his experience. When he returned to the Lusaka station empty-handed with reports of the disappearance of 'traditional' Shona music, he was just stating the facts as he knew them.

Since middle-class standing is typically tied to greater degrees of education, usually mission education, proportionately greater numbers of the African elite may similarly have come from areas where indigenous arts were not commonly practiced. Different denominations and individual missionaries showed varying degrees of tolerance for indigenous cultural practices (see Ranger 1984, 1985), but even liberal missions propagated modernist ethos and practices instead of indigenous lifeways as a matter of common sense.

Socialized in such areas, the CABS employee, *Parade* writers, and others like them came to be a separate cultural group within the black population. The main point is that they were not simply imitating European cultural ways, nor feigning ignorance of indigenous practices— that is, trying to be something they were not. Rather, they *were* the local black Zimbabwean branch of modernist cosmopolitanism because of their socialization. This distinction is an important one.

In discussing the movement to 'Africanize' church music, Axelsson echoes other observers of the 1950s and 1960s when he notes,

> When finally African music started to be introduced into the Christian worship, however, a most *astonishing* problem arose. Many African Christians did not seem to wish to have *their own music* in the church. The reason for such opposition can be understood only by appreciating the [negative] impact of the initial mission approach. (1973: 93; my emphasis)

Black Christians may have rejected indigenous music in church for a variety of reasons. For some, regardless of class position and aspirations, music associated with indigenous religion may have conflicted with deeply held Christian beliefs, as is still the case today. For others, like Mr. H, who grew up in an indigenous area, there may have been a conscious or semiconscious move to separate oneself from indigenous lifeways and to take on a "Western guise" as a display for prestige.

Yet for others, like the CABS employee and the *Parade* writers, the rejection may also have involved the fact that they did not regard indigenous styles as "their music." There is no reason why they should if they grew up in areas where it was not commonly performed. In spite of Axelsson's well-meant astonishment, identity, cultural practice, and aesthetic taste are not essentially tied to color, but to life experience. For cosmopolitan Zimbabweans, indigenous music was not a major part of that experience; it was simply not "their music."

Nonetheless as cultural outsiders, cosmopolitan Africans did begin to gain some appreciation for indigenous arts by the end of the 1950s— lessons initially learned from 'sophisticated' Europeans, anthropologists, and Federation cultural programs. With the emergence of mass cultural nationalism after 1960, the revaluing of indigenous arts among the middle class began to be generated from this cosmopolitan-based political movement as well. In both cases indigenous arts were approached through modernist reform. On this and other points, white-liberal and black-nationalist programs converged around 1960 to influence cultural attitudes among the black middle class and ultimately the Zimbabwean population more broadly.

Dandanda dancers, Mhembere Village, Murehwa, 1993
(All photos are by Thomas Turino)

Vito Beerhall, Sunday morning, 1993

Murehwa Jerusarema Club and Burial Society performing jerusarema
in Vito Beerhall, Mbare Township, 1996

Murehwa Jerusarema Club and Burial Society, performing jerusarema
in Vito Beerhall, Mbare Township, 1996

Mbira players in Vito Beerhall, Mbare Township, 1996

Street musician
playing musical
bow outside of
Vito Beerhall,
Mbare Township,
1993

Chris Mhlanga, Highfield, 1992

Homemade guitars,
Uzumba District, 1993

Casper Muskwe with
homemade guitar,
Uzumba District,
1993

Joshua Dube Hlomayi and Sinyoro Jackson Chinembere, Harare, 1993

Thomas Mapfumo, Joshua Dube Hlomayi, guitar, Harare nightclub, 1996

Thomas Mapfumo,
Harare nightclub, 1996

Thomas Mapfumo and
band members at the mall
in downtown Harare

# Part Three

# Musical Nationalism

# Chapter Five

# Music, Emotion, and Cultural Nationalism, 1958–1963

It is not uncommon that times of social and political upheaval follow "liberal" periods when people's expectations for advancement are raised and then dashed. The Federation promise of partnership, coming as it did with the waves of African nationalism across the continent and the formation of multiracial political organizations at home, initially raised middle-class hopes for social change. Hopes were quickly dimmed. White liberals in multiracial organizations did not have the power to effect major legislative transformation. As Bhebe notes, a few concessions were made, such as the change in the liquor laws, modification of the Land Apportionment Act, which resulted in some additional acres of African land, as well as "virtual abandonment of the Land Husbandry Act, modification of the powers of the hated Native Affairs Department, and the restoration of some of the Chiefs' powers." He also suggests, however, that early nationalists rejected these concessions, "calling them inadequate crumbs falling from the rich man's table" (1989: 50–51). The 1961 constitution entrenched settler privilege.

As the ultimate blow, the rightist Rhodesian Front Party came to power and proclaimed the Unilateral Declaration of Independence from Britain in 1965. Many black Zimbabweans saw Britain as the avenue for future majority rule. Indeed Britain was putting some pressure on white Rhodesia to clean up its racist policies and was negotiating African franchise as a condition for granting independence. After failed negotiations with Britain over this and other matters, the Rhodesian Front Party, led by Ian Smith, proclaimed "Unilateral Independence" from

Britain in order to stem outside interference in Rhodesian affairs, especially on racial matters. These events along with stepped-up political oppression after 1963 made it clear to increasing numbers of black Zimbabweans that the whites would not share power and privilege without a fight.

The response was nationalism in a rather orthodox form. The first stage is what Partha Chatterjee (1986) has called nationalism's "moment of departure," when the nationalist leadership emerges, goals of the movement are established, and the effort to define the "nation" is initiated. This last objective integrally involves *cultural nationalism*—the fashioning of a national 'culture' and images of the nation. In Zimbabwe this phase lasted from approximately 1955 to 1965. The second phase is the "moment of manuever," involving the nationalists' military or political efforts to take control of the state (1966–80). The third phase, "the moment of arrival," is initiated upon the successful takeover of the state, and involves continued cultural, economic, and political efforts to link the general population to the ruling nationalist party and the state (after 1980 in Zimbabwe).

Many studies outline the political history of African nationalism in Zimbabwe, of the political parties involved, and of the war (e.g., Banana 1989; Frederikse 1982; Kriger 1991, 1992; Lan 1985; Martin and Johnson 1981; Ranger 1985; Shamuyarira 1965; Utete 1978; Vambe 1976). In this chapter I am specifically interested in the cultural and ideological positions of the nationalist leadership and in the ways cultural and musical nationalism were developed and used to further the goals of the political movement during the moment of departure. I am also interested in the ways cultural nationalism interfaced with trends that were already in motion (e.g., cultural reformism of the Federation period) and the manner in which cultural nationalism of the early 1960s set the stage for things to come.

## Nationalism as an Idea

The contemporary idea of *nationalism*—a political ideology and movement to make "nation" congruent with state—is relatively recent, only emerging at the end of the eighteenth century in Europe and the Americas, and diffused worldwide on the back of European colonialism in the nineteenth and twentieth centuries.

In the abstract, after gaining the upper hand militarily, black Zimbabweans could have decided to return to precolonial, smaller-scale forms of social organization (as some Zimbabweans would have actually preferred), or they could have innovated a federation of localist groups or some other political alternative to the nation-state. Given that by the 1950s nationalism was deeply accepted as an ideology of political legitimacy within cosmopolitan thinking, however, the option of forming an alternative social formation did not really come up for serious discussion among Zimbabwean nationalists. For example, in the 1960s the Zimbabwean nationalist leader Ndabaningi Sithole noted that "some political architects have suggested that the old traditional system is perhaps the best for Africa" (1968: 173), but he rapidly dismissed this idea based on the ideology of political legitimacy involving national sovereignty. He also noted,

> Practically all the present African political leaders came to power, not under the *traditional* system, but under the *modern* political system. African leaders cannot discard the present political system without discarding themselves. In any case, what is this African traditional system? In my view the traditional system merely represents a *lower level of political evolution.* (1968: 173; my emphasis)

Presenting an insider's perspective from the nationalist camp, Sithole's comments underline a basic point of this book. The nationalist leadership was not simply imitating a foreign political model; they were acting from the basis of their own cultural position, which included ideas about the genuine legitimacy of national sovereignty and their place in the 'modern' world. They could not discard nationalist ideas (the 'modern,' 'present' system) without discarding themselves. Sithole's statement also exhibits the social-evolutionist ideas that underpin the ideology of modernity itself. As a key symbol in this ideology, the term *modern* is used unreflexively to assert an all-pervasive 'present,' whereas the 'traditional' is relegated to an inferior historical past.

In truth, to be a player in the contemporary world scene nation-state status is practically requisite for recognition: 'legitimate' political units join the United *Nations,* not "United Tribes," "United Bands," "United Neighborhoods," or "United Villages." Inter*national* relations, trade agreements, loans, and artistic exchanges take place, by definition, among nations. Hence, in terms of both internalized cosmopolitan ideas and objective conditions, the drive toward nation-state status was the logical path for the middle-class African leadership in Zimbabwe.

## *Nationalism and Modernity*

Scholars studying nationalism from as widely divergent perspectives as those of Anthony Smith and Partha Chatterjee generally trace its rise in the colonial world to a local "middle group" (a local elite between the

colonialists and the masses) who have inculcated the cosmopolitan discourse of modernity. Typically this takes place through standardized
languages, education, and mass media. Summarizing the "modernization" theories of nationalism, Smith writes,

> Nationalism is the product of a new type of education, which first
> affects a small disaffected minority within the traditional society, the
> "intelligentsia," and then spreads to other groups, using the mass
> media and literacy to reach the masses. This novel type of education
> is radically opposed to the traditional elite or folk varieties. It stresses
> secular, utilitarian values, [and] is linguistic in form. . . . It opens up
> undreamt of vistas, [and] subjects all ideas to the tests of reason
> and observation. . . . It replaces precedent and myth and custom
> by the habit of critical inquiry, technical efficiency and professional
> expertise. . . .
>     The vanguard of "modernisation" is the intelligentsia, and the
> modernising intellectual of the Western Enlightenment is the proto-
> type. (1971: 87–88)

Here Smith offers a good description of key components of modernity
which underpin the emergence of nationalism. Gellner also ties nationalism to modernity and the need for a flexible work force in industrial
societies, which is supplied through standardized education (1983). For
Benedict Anderson, the "imagined community" of the nation-state is
also realized through standardized language, "print capitalism," and
educational pilgrimages (1991).

More critical in stance, Partha Chatterjee does not want to see nationalism in India and other parts of the colonial world as a mere modular imitation of a European phenomenon. Yet Chatterjee recognizes that
nationalism *"produced a discourse in which, even as it challenged the
colonial claim to political domination, it also accepted the very intellectual premises of 'modernity' on which colonial domination was based"*
(1986: 30). This statement is central to my understanding of the Zimbabwean nationalist leadership. As indicated by Sithole's comment
above, a modernist-cosmopolitan position was prerequisite for the
adoption of nationalism as an idea. Like Chatterjee, I also suggest that,
by the 1950s in Zimbabwe, nationalism was not simply a product of
imitating European Enlightenment models. By this time, the ideas of
nationalism were deeply ingrained and internally generated by the black
cosmopolitan leadership.

Moreover, nationalism had been diffused among and continually
shaped by local groups worldwide so that this doctrine had become
truly cosmopolitan. Thus, Robert Mugabe learned key nationalist ideas

and strategies from Ghana and China, as well as through his own colonial-mission education, and postsecondary education.

Like most students of nationalism (e.g., Hobsbawm 1990: 10; Seton-Watson 1977: 439; Gellner 1983; Smith 1971), Chatterjee links nationalist leaderships in colonial situations to local cosmopolitan elites. A survey of the biographies of the African nationalist leadership in Zimbabwe confirms that they fit the description of a cosmopolitan "middle group" (between the colonial rulers and the masses). The great majority of the leadership had at least received mission education. A good number studied at institutions of higher education in South Africa, Great Britain, and the United States, including Canaan Banana (U.S.), Gordon Chavunduka (U.S.), James Chikerema (S.A.), Josiah Chinamano (S.A.), Herbert Chitepo (S.A., U.K.), Elliot Gabellah (U.S.), Morton Malianga (S.A.), Robert Mugabe (S.A.), Abel Muzorewa (U.S.), Joshua Nkomo (S.A.), George Silunkika (S.A.), Ndabaningi Sithole (U.S.), Leopold Takawira (S.A.), and Edson Zvobgo (S.A., U.S.). Other leaders had received less formal education but became "self-made men" through private study or enterprise. George Nyandoro, a founding member of the City Youth League in 1955 and secretary general of ZAPU, 1963–70, received only seven years of formal education at St. Mary's Mission in Salisbury but qualified as an accountant privately (see Nyangoni and Nyandoro 1979: 444–47). Although receiving little formal education, Maurice Nyagumbo became a successful small businessman (Nyagumbo 1980).

## Colonial Education: Learning
## the Doctrines of Nationalism

Many nationalist leaders have been quite explicit about how they learned the doctrines of nationalism as the preferred solution to colonial oppression. They point, first and foremost, to mission education, and their descriptions firmly support the theoretical generalizations advanced by Gellner, Smith, Anderson, and others about the formation of nationalist ideology.

In 1968, Ndabaningi Sithole, the first president of ZANU, wrote that most subjects taught in mission schools emphasized the value of 'modern' European civilization. In the area of history, however, this backfired if it was meant to support colonial domination:

> The study in African schools of European, English, and American as well as African history, has had a profound influence upon African people. The European struggle for liberty, for religious toleration,

for freedom of thought and expression, and European resistance
against tyranny thrilled the African students. . . . 'Please tell us about
Mr. Government-of-the-people-by-the-people-for-the-people'(Abraham Lincoln). European, American, and Indian heroism thrilled African students. They admired the firm stand against tyranny. But
sooner or later the African admirer sought to overthrow the tyranny
of his European hero. (Sithole 1968: 90)

Nathan Shamuyarira, a key nationalist figure, echoes this position exactly. He states that while some nationalists viewed the missionaries as
part of the imperialist structure of domination, "All of this is ironic,
since it was the provision of education by the missionaries which directly caused the growth of African nationalism. The Church's teachings
of equal human dignity before God provoked African desires for self-
determination" (1965: 143).

Attending the mission schools had other effects. As African teachers became politicized, schools became diffusion points of nationalist
doctrines and ideas (e.g. Smith and Simpson 1981: 19–20). Supporting Benedict Anderson's idea about schools being part of the political
pilgrimages that helped define pan-regional "imagined communities,"
Zimbabwean observers note that schools were places where students
from all over the country met to share ideas and began to construct a
common "national" identity. The teaching of the colonial language, it
was argued, rather than being antinationalist, was crucial to nationalism, since it broke down 'tribal' and regional barriers that stood in the
way of constructing "the nation" (e.g., see Sithole 1968: 92–94).

Sithole goes on to suggest that colonialism itself had a crucial positive role in generating the nationalist movement. Nationalism depends
on the inculcation of the cosmopolitan worldview which was diffused
by colonialism. Sithole's comments closely resemble Benedict Anderson's general observations about the birth of nation-states as imagined
communities:

It is seen, then, that colonialism has created a radio-audience and a
television-audience. It has created a reading public. It has created a
press-writing and reading public. It has created a travelling-public by
land, sea, and air. All these four kinds of African public are still growing every year. The tendency has been the creation of a comparatively
well-informed and enlightened African public, and a focusing of the
world's problems on the public consciousness of the African people.
The African public that existed before the introduction of the radio,
the press, the train, and the motor-car was highly localized. Particu-
larism is now in many places giving way to *universalism.* Colonialism

gave birth to a new brand of African, a non-tribal African: in short, a national African. (1968: 99; my emphasis)

Underlining a basic theme of this book, Sithole suggests fundamental causal links between colonialism, cosmopolitanism, and nationalism.

On the basis of a comparative historical analysis, Hugh Seton-Watson has argued that "Almost all struggles for national independence have been inextricably connected with class struggles" (1977: 439). In Zimbabwe the African middle class had the sharpest sense of what was at stake in the struggle for majority rule. As the group that would take over from the white settlers on behalf of the general population, they also had the most to gain. I do not believe, however, that the fever of African nationalism in the 1960s and 1970s was simply the result of cynical class-based opportunism (e.g., see Astrow 1983); rather, it came out of a historically specific combination of middle-class cosmopolitan worldview, a logical response to oppression, and political idealism. Yet the nationalist response, with its necessary populist component, certainly contrasts with earlier elitist attitudes among the African middle class, and with the multiracial elite class alliances forged after 1980.

## African Political Organizations and the Middle Class

Before World War II, African political organizations such as the Rhodesian Bantu Voters' Association fought for legistative changes that would specifically benefit the middle class, including an African franchise based on sufficient levels of education. West concludes that the middle-class leadership did not represent "popular concerns" (1990: 320; see also Shamuyarira 1965: 30–31). During the Federation years, the middle-class leadership became involved with interracial organizations, the main political institutions that were trying to effect change at that time. Many black leaders never intended 'partnership' to be generalized; the African participants were to be only those who had achieved sufficient levels of 'civilization.' Black union leaders, too, were of the middle class, and the rank-and-file generally considered them too conciliatory to be effective (Astrow 1983: 21–30; Brand 1976: 61–62).

When middle-class leaders finally came to grips with the fact that neither their attainment of 'civilization' nor their conciliatory political activities would lead to advancement, they turned to a nationalist strategy (Shamuyarira 1965: 21). As a result of both the ideology of nationalism, which requires a nation as the basis of political legitimacy, and the fact that the middle-class was not large or strong enough in itself to make political gains, an alliance with the general black population came to be seen as necessary. Doing a complete about-face from former elitist positions, in the early 1960s middle-class nationalists began publicly to play down African class differences and play up racial unity as the prime strategy for political and economic advancement. Nonetheless, in spite of this facet of nationalist discourse, class remained a fundamental defining feature of the movement.

## Class and the African Nationalist Leadership, after 1955

The Salisbury City Youth League (formed 1955) is often considered the key forerunner to Zimbabwean mass-nationalist parties. Zimbabwean nationalist Nathan Shamuyarira emphasizes that "perhaps most importantly, the City Youth League grew as a common-man movement; it rose from the people rather than starting with the recognized leaders of former times" (1965: 40). He refers here to the fact that the organization was led by George Nyandoro and other individuals not considered to be of the middle class, such as James Chikerema[1] and Paul Mushonga. In the opening meeting of the City Youth League in Mbare, Chikerema attacked African middle-class moderates, telling the approximately five hundred people in attendance to "forget the tea-drinking multi-racialists" (Shamuyarira 1965: 28).

This populist position alienated established political and union leaders and proved to be an obstacle to the League's efforts to form a national organization. Maurice Nyagumbo notes that

> the indifferent attitude of nationalists in other cities frustrated the efforts of the League leaders during the rest of 1956. . . . The three leaders had come to sincerely believe that if an *African graduate* were to lead an African political party, all the African intellectuals would join and there would be no criticism from them. These three people [Nyandoro, Chikerema, and Mushonga], . . . believed that they did not have sufficient education to lead the people. (1980: 106; my emphasis)

When a meeting was finally arranged in Salisbury to form a national party in 1957, it almost fell apart because the three League leaders wanted an African graduate to lead, and no one readily acceptable was on hand. They even asked the white liberal and prominent multiracialist Guy Clutton-Brock to lead the meeting. The Youth League leaders' insistence on an African graduate, and failing that, a white liberal, suggests the depth of the class-based prestige system instilled by colonialism, even among people well on their way to rejecting colonialism. Guy Clutton-Brock intelligently refused to lead the meeting, and

> asked why Chikerema could not chair the meeting. He did not see the need for a change in the leadership; he believed that the Youth League leadership was the right one and should be preserved. After Chikerema had explained the need for an African graduate to lead the new party, Mr. Clutton-Brock . . . said that the Africans of this country should guard against opportunists, those who were self-centered and had no love for their country.
>
> Despite these warnings from Mr. Clutton-Brock, . . . the three leaders made up their minds that the new party had to be led by an African graduate. (Nyagumbo 1980: 107)

Mr. Joshua Nkomo, who was on hand, was chosen for the task and was elected president of the new Southern Rhodesia African National Congress (1957, banned 1959). Nationalist leadership positions remained in middle-class hands thereafter. Nkomo went on to lead the subsequent countrywide nationalist parties: the National Democratic Party (NDP, formed 1 January 1960, banned 9 December 1961); and the Zimbabwe African People's Union (ZAPU, formed 16 December 1961, banned 20 September 1962, but continued underground and as the Peoples' Caretaker Council). Nkomo remained the leader of the main nationalist party until the Zimbabwe African National Union (ZANU) split off in August 1963 under the leadership of 'African graduates' Ndabaningi Sithole as president, Leopold Takawira as vice president, and Robert Mugabe as secretary-general. Mugabe, of course, was later to emerge as the leader of ZANU-PF and ultimately of the new nation-state after 1980.

## Middle-Class Leadership
## and the Masses

The middle-class leadership knew that they were not necessarily in touch with the opinions of the masses, and Shamuyarira states that the crucial problem in the early 1960s was finding a way to bring 'the people' into the discussions shaping the nationalist movement (1965: 192). Shamuyarira provides a telling anecdote about the paternalistic gap between the middle-class leadership and the masses:

> Effective discussion [between leaders and masses] is difficult to organize, but it is better for all in the long run to go through those difficulties, than to feed the masses on slogans. A fiery young nationalist once remarked in a joke that the masses were incapable of liberating

themselves. But he nodded in agreement when his colleague retorted: "At least they know who can liberate them." (1965: 193)

There is much debate about the degree to which the masses were really integrated into the nationalist movement during its height in the 1970s (e.g., Ranger 1985; Lan 1985; Kriger 1991; Manungo 1991); I cannot take up this problem here. It may be worth noting, however, that in a survey of eighty-seven people living in Highfield township conducted at the close of the 1960s, Stopforth found a rather low level of connection with the nationalist leadership. In response to the question, "Who represents African political opinion?" only 4.6 percent responded African Nationalists; 5.7 percent responded Institutional African; 3.4 percent responded Chiefs; 1.1. percent answered Moderate Multi-racial; 1.1. percent answered European Conservative, and a rousing 55.2 percent answered "nobody" (1972: 93). Highfield was famous as a center for African nationalism during the 1960s.

## Cultural Nationalism, Emotion, and Music: The Making of a Nation

The early protonationalist and nationalist organizations of the 1950s, the City Youth League (1955–57) and the African National Congress (ANC, 1957–59), won popular support by direct confrontations with the hated District Commissioners in the rural areas, by mass political actions like the famous bus boycott of 1956, and by criticizing the Land Apportionment Act, animal destocking, and unequal educational opportunities (e.g., Bhebe 1989: 64). At the time of its founding, however, ANC president Joshua Nkomo was still talking in terms of "true partnership, regardless of race, colour or creed" (cited in Shamuyarira 1965: 46). Thus, these organizations had not yet fully settled on the need to create a new, unique, separatist nation, and had not yet begun to mobilize cultural nationalism.

The real shift from the discourse of partnership to the idea that Africans should rule themselves came with the National Democratic Party (NDP, January 1960–December 1961). It is significant, then, that the NDP also initiated cultural nationalism.

### Robert Mugabe, the NDP, and the Rise of Cultural Nationalism

The accounts of Nathan Shamuyarira, Sithole, and other Zimbabwean nationalists of the time suggest that it was not until Robert Mugabe returned to Zimbabwe in 1960 and took the post of "publicity secretary" of the NDP that the party began to emphasize mass cultural nationalism. Mugabe had lived and worked as a school teacher in Ghana between 1958 and 1960. Kwame Nkrumah had invited literate Africans from other countries to teach, work, and learn about their recently successful nationalist movement, so as to inspire similar political movements in the visitors' home countries.

It was in Ghana that Mugabe began to understand colonialism in Marxist, class-based terms, and where he began to understand that nationalist movements needed widespread popular support to succeed. Speaking at his first mass protest rally (in response to NDP leaders being arrested) in Mbare after returning from Ghana in 1960, Mugabe is quoted as saying, "The nationalist movement will only succeed if it is based on a blending of all classes of men. It will be necessary for graduates, lawyers, doctors and others to accept the chosen leadership even if they are not university men" (Smith and Simpson 1981: 27). Although the middle-class basis of the leadership did not change, this rejection of class privilege received a rousing response from the audience (ibid).

Even before living in Ghana, Mugabe came to realize the importance of *emotion* as a key element in nationalist movements, but this idea was confirmed by his Ghana experience. His biographers Smith and Simpson write that from the "relatively humble position" of NDP publicity secretary,

> Mugabe proceeded to carry out a major cornerstone of policy which was to be of lasting importance to the nationalist movement in the years ahead. . . .
> His aim was to consciously inject emotionalism into the thinking of the nationalists. From his experience in Ghana he recognized that support for the movement would have to rest on something more than just intellectual attraction for men like himself. To win broad-based support among all Africans in Rhodesia, the struggle had to be made part of the people's daily life. The barrier between political activity and all others had to be broken down. The people must be made to recognise politics without the taboo of thinking that it wasn't their domain.
> He appealed to their emotions and to their spiritual and cultural values. He encouraged them, through party publicity, to value their heritage (Smith and Simpson 1981: 37)

Nathan Shamuyarira also links Mugabe's role in the NDP with cultural nationalism, music, and emotion. As a firsthand observer and prominent nationalist leader, he is worth quoting at length:

The NDP added one important factor that had been singularly miss-
ing in Rhodesian nationalism: *emotion.* Nationalism is basically
emotional, and has to be to succeed. At times—particularly in early
years—it should be blind and blinkered if it is to establish its
principles. . . .
    The work of building an emotional appeal was left to the NDP
particularly one of its able new officers, Robert G. Mugabe. . . .
    From the position of publicity secretary, Mugabe proceeded to
organize a semi-militant youth wing. . . . [The] Youth [Wing] started
influencing and controlling some party activities. Thudding drums,
ululation by women dressed in national costumes, and ancestral
prayers began to [be] feature[d] at meetings more prominently than
before. A public meeting became a massive rally of residents of a
given township. The Youth Wing, with a small executive taking
charge of units of fifty houses in each township, knocked at every
door on Saturday evening to remind residents about meetings. Next
Sunday morning, thudding drums, and singing groups again reminded the residents, until the meeting started. . . . At the hall, Youth
Leaguers ordered attendants to remove their shoes, ties and jackets,
as one of the first signs in rejection of European civilization. Water
served in traditional water-pots replaced Coca-Cola kiosks. By the
time the first speaker, a European in bare feet, took the platform, the
whole square was a sea of some 15,000 to 20,000 cheering and
cheerful black faces. The emotional impact of such gatherings went
far beyond claiming to rule the country—it was an ordinary man's
participation in creating something new, a new nation. (Shamuyarira
1965: 67–68)

Shamuyarira's firsthand description suggests how music, clothing,
prayers, and other cultural gestures were used to generate attendance at
the early rallies, to infuse them with meaning, and to create enthusiasm
for the cause. This enthusiasm was not necessarily uniform, and the
house-to-house visits by the Youth Wing members were perceived as
intimidation by some township dwellers (see chapter 2). Nonetheless his
description certainly captures the energy and excitement that many
must have felt in the moment at these rallies.
    Mugabe's idea of establishing a youth wing was directly based on
Nkrumah's Youth League. The new emphasis on cultural drama as a
way of linking the masses to the middle-class leadership was also most
likely inspired by his Ghana experience (Smith and Simpson 1981: 27,
37). This strategy was a novelty in Zimbabwe in 1960, and Shamuyarira's comment that the emotional appeal of nationalism at first "should
be blind and blinkered" at least contains hints that a conscious manipulation of the masses was involved.

The historian Ngwabi Bhebe also describes Mugabe's central role in initiating cultural nationalism. As already suggested by Shamuyarira's description, Bhebe notes that Mugabe emphasized sacrifice and the rejection of dependence on European cultural goods:

> On a cultural level the [NDP] party, on Robert Mugabe's initiative, tried to inspire the spirit of "self-sacrifice," which was marked by a rejection of European luxuries and habits and by emphasis of African culture in attire, music, diet, drinks, and religion. This was supposed to inspire pride in African culture and was calculated to cultivate a spirit of self-discipline and to reduce unnecessary dependence on the whiteman....
>
> In that context the NDP can be credited with having started to build a liberation culture and language, which was to culminate in the famous songs of liberation. (1989: 101)

Mugabe and the NDP were responsible for initiating the construction of a separatist "nation." Here, nation-building is a consciously designed process of getting people to invest themselves in a new identity called "nation" which in turn derives its basis from a relationship to the nationalist party and to the idea of nationalism itself. Since "nation" is a rather abstract idea, it also has to be grounded on concrete emblems and practices that come to be defined as "national culture."

### Language, Music, and Cultural Nationalism

In reading Benedict Anderson's celebrated analysis of nationalism, *Imagined Communities,* I was struck by the fact that he focuses on the role of language to the almost complete exclusion of other semiotic domains and practices until his chapter on patriotism (national sentiment). There he returns to a key question posed in the introduction about why people might be willing to die for an imagined community, and in his discussion of patriotism, the emotional underpinning of nationalism, he begins to discuss music, song, and poetry.

This association is not coincidental, nor is it unique to Anderson. When discussing music, he points to the "experience of simultaneity" in unison singing, just as I have suggested the importance of music and dance as media for communal synchrony (see chapter 1; Turino 1999). Although he begins a tentative approach to issues of the arts in relation to emotion in nationalist movements, Anderson quickly retreats to the power of language. He argues that the apparent "primordialness of languages" helps people imagine the nation as primordial. He writes,

"Nothing connects us affectively to the dead more than language" (1991: 145).

In Zimbabwe, however, it is music as much as language that serves as a link with the dead. Drumming, mbira, or hera music call the ancestors into ceremonies so that verbal conversations can take place. Music and dance create the emotional charge that helps possession to take place and, during nationalist rallies, allow people to begin not only to *imagine* the nation, but to have the experience of being part of it.

Like Anderson, most writers on nationalism pay primary attention to the creation of a common language as the basis of nation-building. The roles of music, dance, dress, and visual arts have received much less detailed attention in general studies of nationalism. Scholars tend to ignore something that nationalist leaders seem to grasp intuitively: that the emotional force of nationalist movements is generated through the use of nonpropositional semiotic domains.

In fact, in early Zimbabwean efforts to create a nation, clothing, food, music, dance, as well as *performative* (indexical) speech such as political slogans and 'ancestral prayers' were more central than the use of propositional speech or any emphasis on a unified language.[2] Following Mugabe's lead, the Zimbabwean nationalist leadership seemed keenly aware that these other realms of social and artistic practice held the key to generating the emotion that nationalism required. It is worth pausing to consider why this might be so.

### Emotion and Meaning in Musical Indices

Propositional speech—and political speeches offering detailed information and propositions—are likely to inspire a certain type of mental process involving language-based reflection that does not tend to generate "blind and blinkered" emotion. Music, dance, clothing, food, and performative speech, in contrast, typically function semiotically as icons and indices, and the indexical nature of these media especially augments their emotional potential.

In Peircian terminology, an *index* is a sign that is related to its *object* (what it signifies) because of co-occurrence between the sign and object in the actual experience of a perceiver. Among sports fans, the national anthem might be an index for baseball games because the anthem is always played at the start of games. Through other actual experiential associations (e.g., with Fourth of July parades), however, the anthem can also simultaneously become an index for nationalist celebrations and ultimately, through the use of language in such contexts, for "nation."

Indexical signs, then, are associational and particularly context-dependent; they lack the generality of linguistic signs (there are no dictionaries for indexical signs). Indices are dependent on personal as well as shared experiential associations over time, and these facets give them a more affective, personal, or group-specific, quality ("our song"), as well as variable semantic character, because people's experiences and associations differ. The affective potential of a given index obviously depends on the emotional salience of the entity signified in a person's life. Kitchen smells that call forth childhood, a musical index of "home" when one is far away, or a song that calls up the memory of a deep romantic attachment may be more potent than music associated with elevators.

In addition, indices may signify multiple things simultaneously: the collection of varied associations over time creates a "semantic snowballing effect" (Turino 1999). This facet also adds to semantic ambiguity as well as affective potential, since signs calling forth densely layered meanings often initially create complex effects which we experience as feeling. The multiple semantic references of such signs can potentially produce semiotic effects (*interpretants*) in the perceiver which are too complex to be initially processed through linear, linguistic-based thought—the type of process often inspired by propositional speech and glossed as "rational." Rather, the effect of signs with multiple simultaneous objects is often a jumble of various nonrationalized sensations, *experienced* as feelings, although certain objects of the sign may be foregrounded in focal awareness more than others, depending on the context. If a given index calls forth a thick complex of vague sensations behind more foregrounded associations, the sign will tend to have greater emotional salience.

Particularly important, while the words in propositional speech are signs *about* something else, and we often recognize them as mediational signs (we don't mistake the word *tree* for an actual tree), indices are often experienced as signs *of* the experience or entity stood for. They are experienced as part of the reality that they signify. Hence, the nationalist use of indigenous Shona drums as indices of the village, or of indigenous Shona life, appear as direct facets *of* that life, not propositional statements about it, which would usually create a different type of response. It is this "reality potential" of indexical signs,[3] their intimate, personal quality resulting from dependence on individual and shared-group experience, and the "semantic snowballing effect" that begin to account for the power of indices to create emotion in political movements.

The semantic snowballing effect has particular utility within political movements. Through repeated use of a preexisting index in a new context, a sign may take on additional layers of meaning. Thus, for example, the jerusarema dance has long served as a potent index of "Murehwa" and of "home" *(musha)* for many Murehwa migrants in Harare, and for "Murehwa" among Zimbabweans generally. If jerusarema is performed repeatedly at nationalist rallies accompanied by verbal messages about "nation," "party," and other nationalist imagery, the dance can also become an index for the rallies, the party, and later, through these associations, for the linguistic concept "nation."

Thus, the dance potentially can come to simultaneously signify "Murehwa," *musha,* "political activity," and "nation"—fusing these things within a condensed sign vehicle. If such images (*objects* of the sign) become standardly fused within, or gathered around, a particular index—as through repeated performance of jerusarema at nationalist rallies—the multiple objects of the sign potentially become indexically related to each other in the minds of perceivers through the sign.

It is important to reiterate that the effects of layered indices are experienced as direct and as real, rather than as more obviously mediational signs. The linguistic proposition, "People from Murehwa are part of the nation," may call up an assessment in verbal-based thought: "yes," "no," or "not me." Because condensed indices emerge organically from an individual's actual layered experience over time, however, the connections between the multiple objects of an index such as jerusarema— "Murehwa"/"rallies"/"nationalists"/"nation"—are typically not perceived as propositions about a relationship, but may be felt within memory as the existential fact *of* the relationship.

The entity signified by the word *nation* is particularly general and abstract. We cannot point to (index) or create an iconic sign that resembles the object of "nation." We cannot gather up all the people in one place that compose the "nation," and even if we could, that would not exhaust what is encompassed by the symbol. Precisely for this reason, concrete indexical emblems must become associated with the word and idea "nation" to bring it to emotional life and into reality—"I pledge allegiance to the *flag,*" first and foremost, and only then "to the republic for which it stands."

In this discussion I have been concentrating on the semiotic *potentials* and *tendencies* of indexical signs. I must also emphasize that because indices are extremely context-dependent and highly personal, the effects they create in a perceiver are difficult to control, resulting in heightened polysemy. Arguments over the orthodox semantic range of most words can be settled by referring to a dictionary. There are no such authoritative meanings for indices. The successful manipulation of indexical signs for political purposes can have powerful results, as Shamuyarira has already suggested, but there can be no guarantees about those results. An analysis of some specific nationalist events will deepen our consideration of the connections between musical signs, emotion, and the political goals of the ZAPU nationalist party.

## ZAPU, Cultural Nationalism, and Mass Rallies, 1962–1963

By the time the NDP was banned for fomenting outbreaks of violence, civil disobedience, and strikes (Bhebe 1989: 102–3), cultural nationalism had become a stable component of the political movement.[4] ZAPU (formed December 1961) took up where the NDP had left off, and its president, Joshua Nkomo, adopted the cultural strategy Mugabe had set in motion with the NDP; Mugabe stayed on as National Publicity Secretary for Information in ZAPU. During 1962 and 1963, mass rallies became primary contexts where images of the nation were established. Indigenous cultural emblems and themes were used in combination with indices of modernity in ZAPU's outreach to the general population. Music and dance were particularly central to these events.

### Celebration of the Founding of ZAPU, 1962

A celebration for the founding of ZAPU was held on 4 March 1962 at Gwanzura Stadium in Highfield. The *Parade* headline for the article describing the celebration read, "ZAPU Endeavours to Blend the Old and the New" (Supiya 1962: 8, 53, 58). Although this was a rally launching a new nationalist party, the *Parade* reporter, Stephen Supiya, stressed music and dance activities above all others. He begins his article as follows:

> The most significant part of the whole celebration was the introduction of African tribal dances, such as Mbira (Shona), Kotsore (Manyika), Mbukumba (Budya), Muchongoyo (Shangan), Shangara (Zezuru), and Gure (Makorekore), and many other bits and pieces which added variety to the occasion.
>
> Another significant aspect was the opening of the Celebrations by Ex-Chief Munhuwapayi Mangwende of Mangwende Reserve, near Salisbury, who is well known as a staunch supporter of African Nationalism. (53)

The sky was clear and the sun shone brightly on the day of the rally. The fifteen thousand people in Gwanzura Stadium cheered continually through the opening speech by Magwende who likened ZAPU to a new-born baby son: "May God and all our ancestral spirits bless this great son of Zimbabwe who has come to life" (*African Parade* 1962: 53). The Mbukumba Dancers then immediately took the stage dressed in their 'tribal' skins and bird feathers, their dance accompanied by drums. "In this feature many were taken back to *old Africa,* and this will remain in the hearts of those present for quite some time" (53). Bare to the waist, muchongoyo dancers came next, doing their acrobatic, virile dance; and "In another hair raising feature, they jumped up and down and moved on their stomachs like lizards."

Muchongoyo was followed by De Black Evening Follies, who performed a rock and roll song, a 'tribal dance' with Joyce Ndoro on the microphone, and finally a rumba. Next up were the Shangara Dancers, who sang and danced "in a most tribal way." The ZAPU officials, dressed in suits and ties, were then quickly introduced, followed by a short speech by Dr. S. T. Parirenyatwa (deputy president of ZAPU). Immediately afterwards the Kotsore Dancers "invaded the platform," followed by an mbira group performing "Nhemamusasa." The Cool Four, a Bulawayo-based concert group, concluded the stage program with a rock and roll piece. The celebration ended with the entire crowd singing "God Bless Africa" together, a short prayer, and then before dispersing peacefully, they chanted "ZAPU! ZAPU! Freedom!" long and loud from every corner of the stadium.

Although this event was to celebrate the founding of a new nationalist party, the main activities revolved around music, dance, performative speech by the ex-chief, and only brief introductions and words about the party by the deputy president. Judging from Supiya's impression of the event, ZAPU's rally was carefully orchestrated to attract people to the party and to create emotion. For this reason, music and dance, rather than propositional political speeches, were the main activities programmed.

The event was also designed to create an inclusive image of the nation-to-be. Dances associated with different indigenous groups were juxtaposed, as were "concert" ensembles performing 'modern' rock and roll and rumba—styles associated with modernity and the middle class. It is significant that Supiya emphasized the specific 'tribal' associations of each indigenous dance and music genre performed. In this event, as in other nationalist rallies, indices of various social groups were combined to create a unified image of the nation: taken as a whole, the

ZAPU rally was constructed to represent iconically what that imagined entity might look, sound, and feel like. Visual art, literature, and, in this case, music-dance performance often function as iconic-rhemes, signs interpreted as representing possible objects (Turino 1999). This type of sign can help bring the imagined into being by presenting the possibility (of the object = nation) in a concrete, perceptible form. This is all the more powerful when affective indices of peoples' actual homes and allegiances are used to construct the broader iconic sign.

The rally was orchestrated so that it moved from presentational performances, speeches, and introductions on a stage to a participatory finale in which everyone could sing the national anthem and chant party slogans together. The presentational portion provided a series of images and verbal messages about ZAPU and the nation; the various juxtapositions within the larger context would tend to inform the meanings attached to specific musical indices.

Supiya suggested that the musical performances on stage captivated the audience and left them "stunned," but it was the collective singing and chanting at the end that probably provided the emotional, feel-good climax of the event. At this participatory moment, those present had an opportunity to release the excitement built up throughout the program. The social synchrony created through mass singing and chanting would help concretize, through actual participatory experience, the very images of inclusion and unity fashioned within the presentational portion of the program.

It is not hard to imagine that many participants may have been deeply moved by singing "God Bless Africa" and chanting "ZAPU ZAPU Freedom!" together with thousands of others. The memory of particularly strong emotional moments—a memory in and of sensations—itself becomes indexically linked to the larger context of which the moments were part. If, later, such sensations become indices for the programmed nationalist images and messages, participants might come to *feel* a powerful investment in the party and nation; this was the explicit intent of the leadership. Similarly orchestrated events between 1960 and 1963 were meant to help fortify such associations between affective experience, party, and nation.

## Of Modernity and Tradition
Supiya's reporting of the dances at the ZAPU celebration resembles the same middle-class distance from indigenous arts exhibited by other *Parade* writers at the time. His comment that the Mbukumba Dancers took many people "back to Old Africa" invokes the temporally based

traditional/modern dichotomy that seems to have influenced the design of the event as a whole. His headline, "ZAPU Endeavours to Blend the Old and the New," captures the party's agenda of cultural reformism— combining the 'best' of 'old,' indigenous culture with 'modern' cosmo- politan culture—evident in the musical programming of indigenous dancers and "concert" artists.

Supiya's comment about "Old Africa" also suggests that, beyond indexing particular regional groups, Mbukumba and the other indige- nous dances also served simultaneously as more general indices for an earlier, precolonial Africa, at least among middle-class observers such as himself. New national cultures are often depicted as ancient primor- dial components of the land, as Anderson, Gellner, Smith, Herzfeld, and other students of nationalism have remarked. Building time depth into the image of new nations strengthens the legitimacy of claims about sovereignty.

Time depth is commonly provided by linking earlier local civiliza- tions and their "high cultural" remains to the new national culture. In Zimbabwe, the art and architecture recovered archaeologically at the Great Zimbabwe ruins served this purpose in nationalist discourse. Equally important, contemporary cultural and artistic practices branded as 'traditional' become indices of a primordial past because of the dis- course of modernity itself. Typically in Zimbabwe, 'the traditional' had been depicted as being of a primitive, inferior past—recall Sithole's comments about 'traditional' political systems quoted earlier. In specific nationalist contexts, however, the significance of the traditional/mod- ern dichotomy was inverted to serve a different function: the ancient temporal associations of 'the traditional' remained but were given a new positive value in relation to claims of legitimate ownership of the territory.

### Zimbabwe Festival
### of African Culture

By May of 1963, the idea of cultural nationalism in an unabashedly reformist mode had become more widely diffused in Harare. In that month the Zimbabwe Festival of African Culture was held. The event was explicitly designed to identify and define, as much as celebrate, a uniquely Zimbabwean national culture. Held at Gwanzura Stadium in Highfield, the festival was organized by the Zimbabwe Traditional and Cultural Club, the cultural arm of the nationalist party. An article in the liberal South African journal *Drum* (1992: 173) describes the

Zimbabwe Traditional and Cultural Club as "a movement that arose from the ashes of the burnt-out nationalist bandwagon of 1962." One of the club's organizers, Davies Mugabe, is quoted as saying, "Our aim is simple but terribly urgent. *We are a people who need a unity and an identity.* We need to assert the dignity in ourselves and our past and not turn to a secondhand shoddy copy of other people's cultures" (173; my emphasis).

The festival organized by the club was "a show of the culture, the art, the craftsmanship, the food, the music and dance, and the dress of the people of Zimbabwe" (*African Parade* 1963b: 8). As background to their goals for the festival, the chairman of the Cultural Club stated that

> the year 1963 was a year of the *renaissance* of Zimbabwe. We sin-cerely believe that our land *was* one of the greatest centres of culture, and that culture lies within the mud huts of our villages and in the national archives of this land.
>
> We are descended from the great civilization of the Manomo-tapa Empire which even today enriches the archives of this land and literature of the Portuguese and Arab peoples. Let that be known by those who wish us ill or well. Let those who pour scorn and derision on this our modest beginning, know that we shall work untiringly to make Zimbabwe the heart of African culture. (8; my emphasis)

This passage is significant as a very early articulation of the idea of a nationalist-inspired cultural renaissance, a motif that would later be-come common in both nationalist and ethnomusicological thinking.[5] It also exhibits common features of nationalist discourse in establishing time depth for "the nation" through the reference to an ancient parent civilization and the social-evolutionist notion that this civilization con-tinues in the mud huts of contemporary peasants. At the same time, the statement establishes the new Zimbabwean nation within an inter-national perspective, as in the reference to the Portuguese and Arab peoples.

The Zimbabwe Festival of African Culture included a clothing show, and the *Parade* reporter commented that "the main aim of the show was *to find* a new dress that could be called the 'Dress of Zim-babwe,' in the same way the fur hat has now become the hat of Zim-babwe" (1963b: 8; my emphasis). Although the nationalist leadership almost always dressed in suits and ties for public occasions, during the previous few years they had begun to wear roughly fashioned fur hats resembling those used by certain indigenous dance groups (e.g., Mbukumba dancers). These hats became a widely recognized index of nationalist activism, a trend that expanded beyond the core leadership.[6]

In response to cultural nationalism, a discussion had emerged in the black press about creating a national costume that would be distinct from the western clothes most people wore. The festival's clothing show was designed to settle this problem, although national dress was to remain almost strictly a women's issue. The clothing show was divided into two contests,

> one showing the multifarious national costumes that are today put on by African women in the name of 'national dress' and another showing what the women of Zimbabwe really put on a hundred years and more ago. From this array it was hoped that designers would create a dress that is inspired from ancient Zimbabwe and yet of modern Zimbabwe. (*Parade* 1963b: 8)

The reformist idea of creating a new national culture by combining the ancient and the modern is readily apparent here. The contests, however, did not succeed in settling the matter of a national costume; in fact, newspaper articles and letters to the editor were still being written debating this subject during my stay in 1992–93.

Along with the clothing show, there was an African cooking contest which included "real African beer," the type brewed by families for ceremonies. There was no attempt to modernize village dishes, but the quality of indigenous food was legitimated by modern experts: "Two doctors of great repute went through the food stuffs. All they could say was: 'We don't know why the Africans have abandoned this wonderful food for buns and bread. There is a lot more food value in these'" (*Parade* 1963b: 9).

The festival included a show of "both modern paintings and traditional arts [carved stools, axes, walking sticks]." But the *Parade* reporter emphasized that "Dances of the Zimbabwe of old and of today were the highlights of the day" (*Parade* 1963b: 9). The music-dance performances included muchongoyo, mbukumba, shangara, and jerusarema ensembles; the first two were rural groups, the latter two were urban-based ensembles; jerusarema was danced by the Murehwa Jerusarema Club.

In addition, the Zimbabwe Traditional and Cultural Club's own affiliate ensemble, the Hurricanes, performed. Although the Club was formed to champion 'traditional' culture, their own affiliate band consisted of two electric guitars, bass guitar, traps, and significantly, "tribal drums" (*Drum* 1992: 173). The *Parade* reporter described the

Hurricanes' music in the following terms: "Theirs is a combination of modern jazz, the twist, the maddison, rock 'n' roll together with the music of the years of yore which in the end come to one: The Gallop, the dance of Zimbabwe" (1963b: 9).

### The Gallop
The reformist approach to music and dance exhibited at ZAPU's 1962 founding ceremony involved the juxtaposition of "the old and the new" through an alternation of indigenous dance ensembles and established "concert" groups. Only a year later, the *gallop* emerged as an attempt to create a unified genre that fused local indigenous elements with 'modern' cosmopolitan styles and instrumentation. Whereas urban dance bands such as the City Slickers had already been doing this to some degree, the gallop represents the first conscious attempt to create a new reformist national genre in which "the old and the new" were integrated as a hallmark of the style. The Hurricanes also foreshadowed important popular music trends to come in their integration of indigenous instruments ('tribal drums') within a rock band context.

The gallop was a flash in the pan. No one questioned during my 1992–93 fieldwork remembered the term or the style. The first reference in print to the gallop that I could find was in the May 1963 *African Parade,* an article entitled, "The New Dance of Zimbabwe: The Gallop." The article describes the genre in the following terms: "It is something unique and yet not new. It is the chachacha, the twist, and the rhumba put together. In the old days it used to be called 'chinungu' or 'chikende.' But today they call it the gallop" (84). *Chinungu* was a local village term used to refer to the musical genre that would later become known as jit (see chapter 7). This reference suggests a stylistic connection between the gallop and jit (a fast 12/8 dance music), but I have little else to go on. The only other journal references that I was able to find were a description of the Hurricanes, published in *Parade* two months later, but with no musical detail added, and a description in *Drum* (1992 [July 1963]: 173): "A great range of creations was paraded as the [Traditional and Cultural] club's own band, the Zimbabwe Hurricanes thumped out a throbbing, shuffling rhythm."

In the entire RBC collection of 78-rpm records in the National Archives, I found only one piece designated as "Instrumental Gallop." It was a piece by the Harare Mambos guitar band, "Mambo Goes South" recorded at Mbare studios in 1966. It sounds like a combination of South African mbaqanga—heavy bass, a I (4 beats), IV (4 beats), V (8 beats) progression in moderate tempo—with chacha rhythmic flavor, and 1960s rock guitar style. Beyond a possible rhythmic connection to jit, and the presence of indigenous drums, I have no way of knowing what the indigenous Zimbabwean elements were supposed to be in the Hurricanes' rendition of the gallop; none were apparent in the 1966 gallop recording by the Harare Mambos.

Like the nationalists' failed project to create a national costume in 1963, the gallop didn't take. But it is important in that it marks the beginning of an explicit attempt to use the fusion of indigenous and cosmopolitan elements as the defining feature of a new musical style, a trend among electric-guitar bands that was to culminate in the work of artists like Jackson Phiri, Thomas Mapfumo, and Oliver M'tukudzi a decade later.

## 'Culture' for the Masses, 'Politics' for the Elite

A front-page article in the African *Daily News* (30 July 1962) reports on Nkomo's return from a trip abroad. It begins,

> Mr. Joshua Nkomo knelt in front of Salisbury Airport terminal building today to receive a war-axe, sword, and knobkerry from 90-year-old Mr. Nyamasoka Chinamhora, uncle of Chief Chinamhora. With the presents went this charge: "Take this sword and these other weapons of war, and with them fight the enemy to the bitter end. Let the time be the same as those days when we used to keep as many cattle as we wanted. Also let it be that we shall plough wherever we like and as we like."

A second article in the same paper outlined Nkomo's political statements made at a separate press conference at the airport upon his return. Four main points were made:

> [1] That those who do not support the United Nations resolution "initiated by ZAPU's three million supporters" must leave the country; [2] That there will be no elections in Southern Rhodesia under the new Constitution "while we live"; [3] That there will be a Congress of his Party within 60 days; and [4] That he would "quit the present form and nature of politics" in the country if self-government and independence on the basis of universal suffrage was not attained within a time to be given at the Congress.

After the press conference, Nkomo led a procession of his followers through Mbare to Gwanzura Stadium in Highfield, where a mass rally was held. A third front-page article described the rally; in its entirety it read:

> Mr. Joshua Nkomo, the ZAPU leader, urged more than 50,000 of his followers who attended a reception held in his honour in the Gwan-

zura stadium this afternoon to maintain their traditional dances and music.

The ZAPU leader, who received presents ranging from a spear to two cockerels, was entertained to different types of African traditional music.

The *Daily News* coverage of Nkomo's arrival, his press conference, and the rally makes it appear as if ZAPU's president had two very different styles of message and presentation, depending on the intended audience. When the event was for the masses, pat statements about land, cattle, traditional music, and dance were at the center. When it was for the press—that is, for a middle-class African, a white, and even an international audience—he spoke of the UN, the constitution, internal ZAPU issues, and made an only slightly veiled threat of revolution. Events for the "masses" were largely orchestrated in emotional-traditionalist terms—fur hats, walking sticks, music, and dance, the ninety-year-old chief's uncle. The political issues presented at such events were reduced to basics, as if it were assumed that people would not understand or be interested in the complex issues of nationalist politics.

The preceding description of the mass celebration for the founding of ZAPU and data about other mass rallies point to the same interpretation, as does Shamuyarira's comment that "nationalism is basically emotional, and has to be to succeed. At times—particularly in early years—it should be blind and blinkered" (1965: 67). It is true that the nationalist parties had to capture the general population's imagination if the movement was to go forward, yet the same type of class-based paternalism that had long characterized African political and labor leadership seems evident in the two faces of ZAPU.

On 8 January 1963, six nationalist leaders who had been restricted to a remote rural area for four years returned to Harare. The City Youth League leaders, George Nyandoro and James Chikerema, were among them. Huge crowds greeted them at the train station with songs, drumming, and dancing. Later in the day the restrictees were treated to a celebration in Highfield, where they were entertained by the Murehwa Jerusarema Club and Muchongoyo Dancers among other urban-based, indigenous dance ensembles. The celebration was organized by the ZAPU-affiliated Traditional and Cultural Club, and music and dance were the main activities of the day (*African Parade* 1963c: 11–14).

This manner of reception seems to have come as a bit of a surprise to Nyandoro and Chikerema, who had been out of the center of action for four years. Chikerema, considered one of the truly populist and relatively radical early nationalists, addressed the audience at the Highfield celebration in the following terms:

> The receptions we have been accorded since our arrival here have been formidable and remarkable. The people's love of our traditional culture is encouraging. But it must be made absolutely clear that this is not all there is to it. We must have absolute unity and loyalty to our leaders and must learn to be disciplined, and only then can we be proud of ourselves and can achieve our goal quicker and easier. (*African Parade* 1963c: 14)

Chikerema had gone into detention in 1959 before Mugabe had initiated cultural nationalism. When he returned he was startled by the festival-like atmosphere created by ZAPU's style of outreach to the general population. From the sternness of this statement, it appears that Chikerema was not totally pleased with the way things had gone. Chikerema considered himself outside the educated African elite. From this position, he may have had greater faith in the general population's capacity to face the complexities and hard realities that liberation would require.

Like Chikerema, Mugabe, too, had stressed discipline and self-sacrifice within cultural nationalism, but in ZAPU's efforts to mobilize support, energize it with emotion, and forge a separate national identity, they had not tempered the emblematic and celebratory use of local music and dance, fur hats, and seven-day beer with the sterner political realities of nationalist struggle. In the end, Nkomo's manner of relating to "the people" bore the marks of paternalistic simplification which, in the second half of the 1960s, limited people's understanding of, and commitment to, the movement.

Indeed the very musicians and dancers who participated in the rallies were not always clear about why they had been invited to perform, beyond the fact that they were there "to entertain the people between speakers." Some performers did not consider themselves nationalists, but even those who did lacked a detailed understanding of what the party was doing (see chapter 2). Once again, this points to a gap between the elite leadership and the general population: 'culture' and emotionalism for the masses, politics and propositional speech for the elite.

## The Decline of Overt Cultural Nationalism

The 1960–63 years represent the most intense and overt period of cultural nationalism within the country before independence; the May 1963 Zimbabwe Festival of African Culture was perhaps the most public and explicit apex of this moment. Shortly after this, overt cultural nationalism faded as an issue of importance as the leadership was faced with graver problems. In August 1963 the nationalist movement was thrown into turmoil as ZANU (Zimbabwe African National Union) split with ZAPU (PCC) over questions of tactics and leadership (during this period, ZAPU was temporarily renamed People's Caretaker Council, PCC, after ZAPU was banned in 1962). Violence erupted between the followers of the two parties, and the white state capitalized on this situation. In 1964 there was a government clampdown on both ZANU and PCC (ZAPU); both parties were banned and many of the leaders were arrested and detained. The government declared a state of emergency. The hope of an overt mass nationalist movement led by the revolutionary parties was temporarily weakened.

Government oppression was continually stepped up in the following years, and ZAPU and ZANU continued underground and began to prepare for war. A battle between ZANU guerrillas and government forces in April 1966 at Sinoia (Chinoyi) marked the beginning of the armed struggle. The period of public celebratory mass rallies directed by the leading revolutionary parties was over.

Although short-lived, the 1960–63 period of intense, public cultural nationalism directed by the NDP and ZAPU made its mark in subtle yet lasting ways. A new reformist vision of what it meant to be a 'modern' yet distinctive Zimbabwean was initiated and demonstrated *by* Africans *for* huge numbers of urban Africans. This was done through speeches, the print media, and performance, as when Nkomo accepted an indigenous-style axe after descending from an international flight at the airport. By all accounts, however, music and dance were at the center of cultural nationalist activities.

Images of an inclusive black nation were created through music-dance performance in the mass rallies. Preexisting indices of specific local groups, of different classes, and of 'the traditional' and 'the modern' were indexically linked with each other, with the party, and with the idea of nation. In the rallies, participatory singing and chanting were also used to actualize experiences of unity and emotion; the social unity and semiotic fusions realized through the rallies could be experienced as iconic for the nation itself. In this way music and dance served as a medium for both creating the "nation" and for charging this identity with emotion. I have offered evidence that this was the conscious objective of the nationalist leaders.

The fact that nationalist rallies and events largely took place in Highfield and other urban townships suggests that the creation of national sentiment was probably strongest in these areas. A major question remains about how deeply nationalist discourse and *national* sentiment had penetrated the rural areas by the 1970s. Stopforth's survey of Highfield residents at the end of the 1960s suggested that even there—a major location for the rallies—few people openly identified the nationalist leadership as representing their political interests. In my interviews with people who performed at or attended the rallies, about half said they identified with the nationalists at the time. Fear might be taken into account when interpreting Stopforth's findings; hindsight and romanticism might be taken into account when interpreting mine.

If there was disillusionment with the nationalist movement during the second half of the 1960s, it might partially be due to the very hopes raised by the captivating rhetoric, emotion, and the optimistic images of "people power" created in the rallies. As Chikerema warned about the festival-like atmosphere of nationalism during the early 1960s, "This [was] not all there [was] to it." While creating an emotional investment in images of "the nation" is certainly important to nationalist movements, combining this strategy with hard-core political education would have probably helped build a more sustainable movement. The ZANU-PF leadership came to develop this combination successfully in the 1970s, thus partially moving away from the paternalistic attitudes that had characterized the African political and labor leadership for many years.

## 'Cultural Renaissance' and National Sentiment

Although the early nationalist rallies did not uniformly succeed in linking the general population to the party leadership (to nationalism and nation) in a lasting way, they did further the process of fortifying pride and interest in indigenous arts and culture among the portion of the population that had not been socialized in indigenous lifeways. The 'cultural renaissance' touted by the nationalists in 1963 was primarily relevant only to such people since the bulk of nonmissionized peasants and workers (e.g., the members of urban indigenous dance groups) had largely remained involved with indigenous arts and lifeways as a matter of course. The revaluing of indigenous arts among cosmopolitan Africans had already been initiated by the liberals and missionaries during the Federation period. It was given a new, more powerful, impetus under the banner of nationalism because within this movement other aspects of black self-interest were also involved.

After the 1964 clampdown, the renewed pride in "Africanness" produced by the white-Federation/black-nationalist conjuncture continued to filter through and become established among the urban population. Insofar as such feelings were *national* sentiment (rather than *lo-*

*calist, 'tribal,'* or even vaguer *African* sentiment), it was the NDP-ZAPU movement that initially provided the "national" framework.

Regardless of the specific type of sentiment involved, what is significant for later developments in Zimbabwean urban popular music is that early cultural nationalism, in conjunction with Federation cultural programs, helped foster and diffuse a new aesthetic preference for *syncretic* artistic and cultural styles. Whereas foreign and indigenous arts were once perceived as contrasting aesthetic spheres, after 1960 reformist-driven syncretism increasingly begins to be conceived as a legitimate basis for artistic and cultural practice in its own right.

This conjuncture set the stage for new tastes in music among urban audiences, which in turn inspired the creation of indigenous-based guitar-band styles like those performed by Jackson Phiri, Thomas Mapfumo, Oliver M'tukudzi, and the Green Arrows in the 1970s. It laid the groundwork for the current acceptance of syncretic cultural identities as the norm, and for state-generated cultural reformism after 1980.

# Chapter Six

# Musical Nationalism and
# Chimurenga Songs of the 1970s

Nationalist movements have affected musical developments throughout the postcolonial world in powerful ways, yet the processes of musical nationalism have received very little direct theoretical attention. In historical musicology the concept of *musical nationalism* typically involves the use of local "vernacular" or "folk" elements and themes within cosmopolitan styles, especially the classical music traditions of Europe, North America, and Latin America. This usage designates a style category rather than specific types of musical-political processes. Frequently, ethnomusicologists have used the term to refer to phenomena that are somehow bound up with national sentiment, but without consistently distinguishing between nationalism and national sentiment or specifically analyzing the functional relationships between the two (e.g., Manuel 1987, 1994; Díaz 1996; Austerlitz 1997; Bohlman 1988). A number of ethnomusicologists, however, have focused on musical nationalism in relation to political nationalist movements and state nationalist projects (e.g., Capwell 1976, 1991; Buchanan 1995; Noll 1991; Wong 1984); my use of the concept is part of this line of development.

I define *musical nationalism* narrowly as the conscious use of any preexisting or newly created music in the service of a political nationalist movement, be it in the initial nation-building stage, during the militant moment of maneuver, or during and after the moment of arrival to build and buttress the relationship between the general population and the state. This purely functional-processual definition precludes the possibility of deducing instances of musical nationalism from style alone.

The consciousness of a nationalist function applies to the user, not necessarily to the artists or originators of a piece or style. Thus, by this definition, musical nationalism is extremely context-specific; including a performance by De Black Evening Follies or the Murehwa Jerusarema Club in a nationalist rally in the early 1960s was a case of musical nationalism; contemporaneous "concert" or beerhall performances by the same groups were not.

This definition is useful because it focuses attention on the nexus between music making and the actual type of political movement denoted by the term. This conception helps the analyst concentrate on what is at stake in the use of music within such movements, as well as on the dialectical political and musical effects. It draws attention to the common motivations and processes that shape musical styles and occasions among different instances of nationalism (e.g., the need to link diverse groups to the nation; reformism). This conception also helps to distinguish the relationships between different types of motivations, musical processes, and contexts that result in styles often misrepresented as nationalist.

In the preceding chapter I analyzed various roles of musical nationalism within processes of nation-building during the moment of departure. In this chapter I focus on a most explicit form of musical nationalism, ZANU's *chimurenga* songs, 'songs of the struggle,' during the moment of maneuver—the war years of the 1970s. I am interested in the types of cultural, political, and military work these songs accomplished during the height of the Liberation War, and the ways the song texts paralleled official party discourse and agendas. ZANU receives the lion's share of attention since that party was most highly engaged with cultural nationalism during the 1970s and gained control of the state after 1980—a development we follow in relation to cultural nationalism in later chapters.

## The Military and Political Fronts of the War

The Battle of Sinoia, on 28 April 1966, is often used to mark the beginning of the guerrilla war for majority rule. Seven ZANLA (ZANU's Zimbabwe African National Liberation Army) soldiers died in direct confrontation with Rhodesian forces. In 1967 a joint ZAPU-South African ANC force lost heavily to the vastly superior Rhodesian Army in conventional warfare, making it painfully apparent that different tactics would have to be used (Martin and Johnson 1981: 9–11).

Whereas ZAPU's major alliance was with the Soviets, ZANU turned to China for training and support; their first group of five soldiers went to China for training in 1963, and this was to continue throughout the 1960s. ZANLA became committed to Maoist principles for fighting the war, and the central principle was that victory would only be obtained by a thorough politicization and mobilization of the masses, especially the peasantry. The military leader Josiah Tongogara received training in mass mobilization and guerrilla strategy and tactics in Bejing in 1966, and he trained the early cadres working in the northeast (ZANLA's first main operational zone) to be political commissars as much as fighters (Martin and Johnson 1981: 11, 81).

Since ZANLA depended on the peasantry for food, shelter, young people *(mujibas)* to supply information and aid, as well as new cadres, they concentrated major attention on the ideological, cultural, front.[1] So did the Smith regime, which conducted a major information campaign about the evils of the "terrorists" *(magandanga:* "murderers, people who kill for no reason") and communists.[2] The guerrillas were trained to win the peasantry over through Maoist principles of correct conduct for soldiers, a concern with local grievances, and by educating people about the causes and need for the war against colonialism.

Certain individuals in ZANU's army received special training to become 'political instructors.' Their responsibility was to teach other cadres how to teach and relate to the masses, and to convey messages from the leadership in Mozambique to the people and guerrillas inside Zimbabwe. They also had to know what was going on at the front and to diffuse this information. Comrade Chinx became a 'political instructor' who specialized in using songs to carry out these functions and to boost morale among the troops and villagers in Zimbabwe.[3] A popular guitar-band leader after 1980, Chinx first became well known to Zimbabweans as a major chimurenga song composer and chorus leader over ZANU's Voice of Zimbabwe radio during the second half of the 1970s.

### Recruitment
By December 1972, ZANLA had made enough progress in gaining popular support to initiate a new, more decisive phase of the war with their attack on Altena Farm some fifteen kilometers from Chiweshe Tribal Trust Lands in the northeast. The movement had come a long way from the early days of the 1960s when ZANU and ZAPU had to resort to press-ganging Zimbabwean residents in Zambia to fill their ranks (Martin and Johnson 1981: 23). By 1978 the number of recruits

for the Patriotic Front armies had begun to swell; ZANU and ZAPU had joined forces in the Patriotic Front in 1976.

In the rural areas enlistment was accelerated by the increased penetration and presence of the guerrillas. Recruiters also worked to enlist urban workers and students. Young people's specific reasons for joining up were probably as numerous as the recruits themselves, but the growing strength of the guerrillas and the oppressive atmosphere created by Smith's government made enlistment an increasingly viable response to long-standing frustrations. Comrade Chinx's story about why he joined ZANLA is probably not atypical.

As a secondary student in Bulawayo in 1972, Chinx won a scholarship competition to go to England to study. He wanted to become a medical doctor. "But the visas, all those, you know, bureaucracies from the regime, you know, retarded the whole process, and I couldn't go." Feeling trapped and frustrated, the nationalist cry, "Smith, give us our country," now resonated in a new way (Zim96-4: 1). After leaving school Chinx went to Harare and got a job with an engineering firm. He became involved with the union to improve working conditions and pay. Chinx came to feel that the middle-class union leadership was in collusion with management, and that no progress would be made. Again he felt deeply frustrated (Zim96-4: 3). During this time he and some fellow workers were approached by recruiters for the ZANU guerrillas. He went home to Rusape, in eastern Zimbabwe, to tell his parents that he had decided to join the comrades. They begged him not to; a younger brother had recently left to join ZANLA and they felt that this was enough sacrifice for one family. During this period in Rusape, Chinx met with the guerrillas and, after a grilling to test his commitment, was accepted. Later his own parents' homestead was burned by Rhodesian forces, some youngsters were killed, and his parents came to support his decision to fight. Chinx went for training at a camp in Mozambique and in 1976, through a special course with eight other men, was made a political instructor.

## The African National Council and the Patriotic Front

From the period of 1971 to 1979, ZANU and ZAPU were not the only African political and military organizations operating. A number of attempts at negotiating a political settlement with the Smith regime were undertaken by various groups during this period in parallel with the military efforts of ZANU and ZAPU.[4]

The African National Council (ANC) was an important organization formed in 1971 to unite the various nationalist forces under the leadership of Bishop Abel Muzorewa. At first with the support of other nationalist groups, and acting on behalf of the detained nationalist leaders, Muzorewa attempted to negotiate settlements with the Smith government for majority rule (Chambati 1989: 149). In 1974, Muzorewa signed an agreement with Smith without consulting the ANC Central Committee, at which point ZANU and other nationalist leaders rejected the agreement and severed ties with the ANC (153–54).

Further reunifications, instigated by surrounding Frontline States, and political splits within the ANC were to follow. Joshua Nkomo led a faction of one such split, ANC (ZAPU), and in 1975 this group too attempted negotiations with Smith. Chambati remarks, "The idea of negotiating with Ian Smith was repugnant to the ZANU leadership; hence it sowed seeds of distrust which was to characterise relations between ZANU and ZAPU for a long time, and particularly between Robert Mugabe and Joshua Nkomo" (1989: 157).

In spite of this distrust, the Frontline State leaders finally succeeded in unifying the two revolutionary organizations of the nationalist movement, ZANU and ZAPU, within the Patriotic Front in 1976 as these groups stepped up the war effort. Within the country, Muzorewa continued to work with Smith and signed another agreement with him in 1978. In a last-ditch attempt to maintain white dominance and head off externally administered negotiations with the Patriotic Front, Smith made Muzorewa titular prime minister of Zimbabwe-Rhodesia in 1979. During this period of "internal settlement" and joint Smith/Muzorewa leadership, bombings of the guerrilla camps in Zambia and Mozambique were intensified, dooming the political future of Muzorewa and the ANC once majority rule was achieved (Chambati 1986).

While Muzorewa does not fare well in contemporary accounts of Zimbabwean revolutionary history, it should be noted that even toward the end of the 1970s he had support among African conservatives in Zimbabwe. Within the country, censored press coverage—both white and black—downplayed the increasing power of the Patriotic Front armies and the state's growing fatigue with the war. Some Africans within Zimbabwe remained convinced that Muzorewa's "partnership" strategy was the path most likely to succeed. Even on the eve of the elections in which Mugabe was elected, *Parade* pushed Muzorewa as a front runner and depicted Mugabe as an untrustworthy radical who was not a serious contender.[5]

During a 1993 interview with a black, middle-class friend in the music business, I asked about a particular artist whose reputation had been hurt because of associations with Muzorewa during the late 1970s. When I asked if the musician had really supported Muzorewa, to my surprise my friend replied: "Tom, back then we were *all* for Muzorewa!" The people included in the "we" remained unclear, and while this is probably an overstatement, it alerted me to the fact that current histories minimizing Muzorewa's popularity during the late 1970s might also be overstatements (e.g., see Chambati 1989: 154).[6] The point to remember as we turn our attention to the militant nationalists is that there were multiple political orientations in the 1970s, just as there were ballroom dancers, apolitical rock bands, and revolutionary chimurenga choirs, each representing different cultural and political orientations.

### Party Discourse and Cultural Nationalism in the 1970s

During the period of severe state repression and censorship, 1964–79, statements and articles explicitly about or expressing African cultural nationalism largely disappear from the black popular press and media (see Frederikse 1982: 24–31). The two leading nationalist parties, ZANU and ZAPU, occasionally released written policy statements on the issue of constructing a new national culture, but even in their documents and media presentations this topic received little attention relative to political and economic issues and war news as the struggle progressed (see Nyangoni and Nyandoro 1979).[7]

In the few official statements that were issued, a reformist approach to constructing a new national culture was still being articulated, thereby representing a major point of continuity with the discourse of cultural nationalism of the early 1960s. As we saw in the previous chapter, during the early 1960s some nationalist leaders actually gave credit to missionaries and European-style education for inspiring nationalism and models for future national development. By 1963, other black Zimbabweans were beginning to criticize the churches as institutions of cultural domination (Fry 1976: 111), foreshadowing the predominant nationalist discourse of the 1970s.

During the 1970s, missionaries, European education, and everything else associated with colonialism were officially recast, in black-and-white terms, as part of the processes of domination by a wartime enemy. For example, writing in 1969 and published in ZANU's official *Zimbabwe News,* Lazarus Mpofu states, "Christianity has been used as the subtle instrument to destroy Zimbabwe culture. By one stroke every form of African culture has been called heathen and therefore full of evil which bars an individual from entering heaven after death. This form of blackmail has now been seen through" (Mpofu 1978: 14). While this antimissionary attitude is understandable in the context of the violent struggle for majority rule, it becomes problematic in relation to the positive roles some missionaries played during the war. It is also problematic in relation to the missionary-educational backgrounds and cosmopolitan dispositions of the nationalist leaders themselves. This attitude is also striking in relation to the fact that a great many of ZANU's and ZAPU's chimurenga songs were based on Christian hymns.

A ZANU document, "MWENJE No. 2. ZANU's Political Programme," issued from Lusaka on 1 August 1972, contains one of the party's few clear official statements on cultural nationalism. The fact that this document continued to be quoted in relation to ZANU's cultural position through the end of the 1970s suggests that it was a major policy statement. It also suggests that ZANU cultural policy did not evolve very much, at least in official discourse, during the 1970s. The eighth article, "The New Zimbabwe Culture" states that

> eighty years of colonization have warped the minds of our people and shaken their confidence in themselves by a process of cultural alienation. The settler stage, screen, mass media, literature, school and church, have combined to create a false impression that a foreign culture was good and our own was bad. Consequently, *our rich cultural heritage has been lost* and at times despised by the young generation which has been indoctrinated and intoxicated with western cultural values. (Nyangoni and Nyandoro 1979: 261)

Here, as elsewhere, ZANU spokesmen assert a major loss of indigenous culture, paralleling similar views expressed earlier by ethnomusicologists such as Hugh Tracey (1969), by the middle-class writers of *Parade,* by the African Service radio staff in Lusaka, and by Williamson at Kwanongoma College. The nationalist leadership came out of the educational background that they depict as evil and which, in earlier accounts, was actually credited with giving rise to nationalism. In ZANU's statement, by rhetorical turn, it is "the young generation which has been indoctrinated and intoxicated with western cultural values"; this generation certainly included the leaders themselves.

In earlier chapters I have suggested that there was not a major decline of indigenous ethos and artistic practice in some rural areas, and among certain portions of the urban population (see Kaemmer 1998: 755). In the ZANU document, the suggestion of categorical loss served to dramatize the evil of the enemy, but it does not stand up well to historical evidence for all regions and population groups. Modernist ideas about cultural loss were still perpetuated by the ZANU state, although for slightly different reasons, throughout the 1980s, and they are still repeated in recent accounts of Zimbabwean music (e.g., see Bender 1991; Zindi 1993). What I am suggesting here is that nationalist discourse, as a part of the larger cosmopolitan discourse of modernity, has helped maintain and diffuse the orthodoxy about indigenous cultural decline.

The ZANU policy statement continues,

> In a free, democratic, independent and socialist Zimbabwe the people will be encouraged and assisted in building a new Zimbabwe culture, *derived from the best in what our heritage and history has given, and developed to meet the needs of the new socialist society of the twentieth century.* We are prepared to learn from the accumulated experience and refinement of mind, morals and tastes *from other peoples and cultures in the world,* especially those from other parts of Africa and use such knowledge to improve and enrich our own. But our culture must stem from our own creativeness and so remain African and indigenous. (Nyangoni and Nyandoro 1979: 261)

This statement is orthodox reformism at its core. It recommends the fashioning of a "new" culture by "modernizing" "the best" aspects of the indigenous heritage and by fusing them with elements "from other peoples and cultures in the world." The universalist, cosmopolitan perspective that serves as a basis for reformism is noteworthy here. In keeping with militant African nationalism, borrowing from the colonizer's culture is played down, and borrowing from other African models is favored. The value of cosmopolitan contexts for cultural practice, learning, and diffusion such as the screen, the stage, mass media, literature, and schools is not questioned. Rather, they are portrayed as neutral channels—when used by colonial rulers they were bad; used by the nationalists they will be positive tools.

The promised turn to socialism as the basis for social-political organization itself confirms the importance of European-initiated cosmopolitan models. In Zimbabwe, socialism represented a clear oppositional stance vis-à-vis capitalist colonialism. It fit with the populist necessity of the nationalist movement. Moreover, China was an important ally of ZANU, and the Soviets supported ZAPU. Echoing other nationalist leaders, Ndabaningi Sithole rejected indigenous political models as "merely represent[ing] a lower level of political evolution" (1968:

173; see chapter 5). Political choice seems to have been circumscribed by available modernist-cosmopolitan models because of the cultural dispositions of the leadership; among these, socialism was the only logical modern alternative to capitalism. This conjuncture illustrates the analytical importance of conceptualizing distinct, coexisting cosmopolitan formations.

### Mass Media,
### Communities, and Nations
The ZANU document continues as follows: "The emphasis of Zimbabwe's new culture will be on the community. The new screen, stage, mass media, literature and schools will project the richness of our community life and the role of the individual in it" (Nyangoni and Nyandoro 1979: 261).

Students of nationalism such as Anderson, Smith, and Gellner have suggested that state educational systems and the mass media are the primary mechanisms for producing the translocal cultural homogeneity necessary for the very existence of nations. Typically these institutions are understood to erode local distinctiveness and community. This paragraph of the 1972 ZANU document, however, states that mass educational institutions and media will be used specifically to support community life. What emerges here is one of the central paradoxes of nationalism: the need to celebrate local communities while simultaneously undermining their localness in order to produce relatively homogenous citizens who will give primary alliance to the nation-state.

Benedict Anderson's celebrated phrase "imagined communities" is useful because it draws attention to the abstract, rather fragile, character of national sentiment. Identities and personal allegiances are more firmly grounded in local relationships—face-to-face or potentially face-to-face relations—such as the family, neighborhoods, and other local groups that maintain their own distinctive lifeways. The foundation and affective force of these relationships are based on shared experiences and concrete interactions—and are realized most powerfully through indices and dicent signs—which are more difficult to produce at the level of nation-states. As Zimbabwean cultural nationalism illustrates, nationalist movements use indices and symbols of concrete social groups such as the family and local communities to imbue the concept of nation with sentiment and, indeed, reality. Nationalists also typically need distinctive features of local communities to distinguish their nation-state from others within the "global family of nations."

Nationalism thus depends on concrete local communities, but it is also threatened by them. If people give their primary allegiance to local groups, the existence of the nation as an identity and political unit is weakened. Moreover, local groups can claim "national" standing and seek independence by the very logic of nationalism itself—the axiom that each distinctive cultural unit ("nation") should have its own state.

Mass media and educational institutions are critical for establishing shared knowledge and experiences—once the province of local groups—on a mass scale. Mass communication competes with distinctive local identities by creating the indexical signs of concrete relations and knowledge at the level of the translocal nation. ZANU's allusions to community in the paragraph cited are precisely of this created, "imagined," translocal type. Yet in other activities, such as the use of indigenous dances in rallies to index specific groups, Zimbabwean nationalists also have had to engage with actual local communities.

## Cultural Nationalism and Shona
## Religion During the War

During the war, one of the focal points of cultural nationalism involved the local religion and spirit mediums (Fry 1976; Lan 1985; Martin and Johnson 1981: 74–75; Ranger 1982, 1984, 1985: 199–213). While Ranger makes it clear that some spirit mediums chose to buttress their own political power by aligning themselves with the Smith regime, others viewed the guerrillas as potential allies (1982; see also Lan 1985).[8] The mediums were (are) considered the rightful 'owners of the land,' had an investment in indigenous ways of life, and, acting for/as the ancestors, were responsible for the well-being of local people. The ZANU cadres asserted that they shared these same concerns. The settler government had made it a policy to co-opt chiefs and headmen for indirect rule. Consequently, many had lost legitimacy in the eyes of local populations who were in conflict with the government primarily over access to land, state-enforced agricultural methods, and restrictions on cattle. Spirit mediums of Shona religion, which had remained strongest in subsistence-peasant, and liberal-mission areas (Ranger 1982), however, maintained a special legitimacy as local leaders.

Mediums who aligned themselves with the nationalist movement became focal points for ZANU guerrillas within the Maoist program of infiltrating and mobilizing the peasantry. Martin and Johnson observe that "Urimbo, ZANLA's first provincial commander, and Chimurenga, the operational commander of ZANLA forces . . . swiftly recognized the importance of the spirit mediums in the north-east" (1981: 75), especially for recruitment. As Ranger explains, the mediums played a twin role of helping the guerrillas gain the trust of local populations while simultaneously putting checks on guerilla behavior so as to protect local people (Ranger 1982: 367).

## Mbuya Nehanda

The ZANLA guerrillas usually became involved with mediums of spirits of headmen and chiefs who were the 'owners' of particular areas of land (Ranger 1982: 366). ZANLA leaders, however, also appealed to the spirit of Mbuya Nehanda, who had much more widespread signifi-cance.[9] Nehanda's medium, a woman named Charwe, along with the medium of the spirit Kagubi played major coordinating-leadership roles in the African uprisings of 1896—'the First Chimurenga.' Nehanda's medium was allegedly one of the last rebel leaders to be captured; she and the Kagubi medium were tried and executed in March 1898 after the rebellion had failed.

Over time, Kagubi, and Nehanda in particular, came to be pan-regional symbols of resistance and martyrdom in both oral tradition and in nationalist literature and discourse of the 1950s and 1960s. Tra-dition has it that on the scaffold, Nehanda predicted the second war of liberation with the statement that "my bones will rise" to fight and take back the land from the Europeans (Lan 1985: 6–7).[10] In this way she became a link between the 1896 uprising and the war of the 1970s—'The Second Chimurenga.' The use of the word *chimurenga* to denote the second war stems from the 1896 uprisings. According to Peter Fry (1976: 49), the medium of "Kagubi began to be known as *Murenga* which became almost synonymous with the rebellion itself."[11] The use of the term *chimurenga* for the war of the 1960s and 1970s is based in this usage and semiotically linked the two uprisings.

In 1972, ZANLA guerrillas met with the old woman who was then the medium of Nehanda. Realizing her symbolic and spiritual impor-tance, they convinced her to help them wage the war and then carried her back to the Chifombo guerilla camp in Mozambique, where she blessed and guided the soldiers. Josiah Tungamirai, Chief Political Commissar of ZANLA, stated that

> Mbuya Nehanda was ZANLA's most important and influential re-cruit in those early days. 'Once the children, the boys and girls in that area, knew that NeHanda had joined the war, they came in large numbers.' NeHanda, in Tungamirai's view, was then the most pow-erful medium in Zimbabwe and other mediums followed her in join-ing the guerrillas, recruiting for ZANLA, and pointing out 'sell outs' in the villages. (Martin and Johnson 1981: 78)

Martin and Johnson describe how Tungamirai, raised as a Christian, did not at first believe in the powers of Nehanda and other mediums, but through interaction with them became converted (1981: 76 – 77). Lan notes that "many [guerrillas] who started the war as skeptics [because of their Christian education and backgrounds] were believers before the end. Some, though they did not believe, saw the success of the strategy [of forming alliances with mediums] and did not interfere" (1985: 147).

### Chaminuka

Another focal culture hero of the nationalist movement was the spirit Chaminuka. Pasipamire, the medium of this Shona spirit, was a very powerful figure in the 1870s. He died at the hands of King Lobengula's Ndebele soldiers in 1883, and apparently no medium of Chaminuka was active in the 1896 uprisings (Ranger 1982: 349, 351).

Ranger weaves a very complex and intriguing tale about how the figure of Chaminuka was projected by both white and black nationalist writers as a Shona culture hero, beginning with Arthur Shearly Cripps 1926 book, *Chaminuka: The Man Whom God Taught*. According to Ranger, various white scholars—including Michael Gelfand, writing about Shona religion, Donald Abraham, a scholar of Shona political history, and Paul Berliner, writing about mbira music—helped cement the centrality of Chaminuka in Shona cultural history. It is especially significant that these scholars worked with Muchatera Mujuru, who claimed after 1934 to be the medium of Chaminuka.

In Ranger's account, Muchatera Mujuru attempted to enhance his own power by placing Chaminuka at the center of Shona religious, political, and cultural history, and by gaining the endorsement of the white intellectual establishment. The publications of Gelfand and Abraham helped to cement Chaminuka's central importance. For example, Gelfand largely reported Mujuru's own vision of Shona religion in *Shona Ritual with Special Reference to the Chaminuka Cult* (1959):

> At the head of the tribal spirits is Chaminuka and under him are a variable yet large number of tribal spirits . . . who care for large regions or provinces. . . . The lesser mhondoro are intended merely to carry messages or news of events to the greater ones, who in their turn report to Chaminuka. . . . It is believed that all the spirits receive instructions from Chaminuka. (quoted in Ranger 1982: 352)

In this account, Chaminuka, like Nehanda, had a transregional significance, and when the nationalists were looking for broad, unifying emblems for the nation and for the glories of the indigenous past, Chaminuka was enlisted as a culture hero. The central role of Chaminuka in Shona history was also projected in the writings of nationalists such as Nathan Shamuyarira, Herbert Chitepo, and Lawrence Vambe from the late 1950s through the 1970s.

It seems odd, then, that ZANLA guerrillas, who typically allied themselves with powerful spirit mediums, openly confessed to killing Muchatera Mujuru in January 1977. They did so because Mujuru had sided against the nationalists, and because his mediumship was contested on various fronts (Ranger 1982). The ZANLA soldiers dispensed with a man they claimed was a false medium, and who, through his association with the powerful image of Chaminuka, posed a major threat. They did not dispense with the image of Chaminuka, however. ZANLA guerrillas named a war zone after him as well as after Nehanda, and used his name as a rallying cry throughout the struggle.

The strong identification of Chaminuka with Shona ethnicity might also have influenced ZANU's selection of him as a culture hero. In spite of the distinctly antitribalist nature of nationalist discourse, the two main protagonists for political power in Zimbabwe were strongly divided along 'tribal' lines: ZAPU came to be associated with an Ndebele following, and ZANU with the Shona. The centerpiece of the early Chaminuka story was how he predicted the coming of Ndebele raiders into the Shona area in the pre-Colonial period, and how he was killed by them. Nathan Shamuyarira's account of the Chaminuka story clearly suggests Shona identification, and so is worth quoting at some length.

> Mashona reaction [to the defeat in 1896] also looked to the past for comfort, and took as *tribal* hero the tall, bearded prophet Chaminuka who had lived at Chitungwiza. . . . Many legends are told of how, in the 1880s, Chaminuka warned his people of the approach of Matebele raiders, as well as excelling all as a rainmaker. . . . The Mashona have always honoured him as a great prophet and symbol of their tribe's resistance. The legends took on extra significance, though, after the formation of the City Youth League, when George Nyandoro particularly dwelt upon his memory in speeches as a binding factor in resisting the settlers. (1965: 28–29)

## Christian Elements

The images of local ancestral spirits, of Nehanda and Chaminuka, and of a distinct Shona identity, come up in ZANU's chimurenga songs as major themes. Christian imagery rarely came into the texts directly, as one might expect within the cultural nationalist movement. Of the musical resources used for ZANU's and ZAPU's chimurenga songs, however, approximately 50 percent of my sample are Christian hymns.

ZANU's official position attacked the churches as arms of colonial domination, but in fact "it would not be possible to say that nationalism as a whole was anti-Christian" (Ranger 1985: 328). Just as individual mediums took different sides during the war, some missionaries supported the guerrillas and played important roles in resistance to the state, as different missionary groups had throughout the colonial period (Ranger 1985). Comrade Chinx explained that the oppressive role of missionaries was really in preaching meekness and forgiveness so that people would not stand up to the racist injustices of colonialism. He went on to say, "We had missionaries who helped us [ZANU] a lot, whom we couldn't say were enemies. Of course, enemies could be my brother, you know! As well as a missionary, but friends could be another missionary as well as a brother, you see" (Zim96-4: 11). ZANU in particular was interested in forming links with all the people, some of whom were Christians. Many of the guerrillas, and certainly the military and cultural-nationalist leaders, often had mission school backgrounds. Hence, they were not averse to using cultural elements from Christianity that would help them solidify relations with Christians and that were part of their own background; the use of hymns as the basis of chimurenga songs is one of the most striking examples of this.

## Music and the Politicization of the Masses

Two venues were central to ZANU's efforts to educate, mobilize, and recruit the masses: the radio and all-night *pungwes* (clandestine political gatherings); in both contexts chimurenga songs had a prominent role (Lane 1993). Already by 1970, ZANU and ZAPU had pro-party radio programs broadcast into the country which were allegedly effective in inspiring recruitment (Martin and Johnson 1981: 77). ZAPU's "Zimbabwe People's Voice" was broadcast from Lusaka, Dar es Salaam, Cairo, and on Radio Moscow. The most important ZANU programs were known collectively as "The Voice of Zimbabwe" broadcast out of Radio Mozambique in Maputo. Much of the programming involved war news, political speeches, and education. Several programs on "The Voice of Zimbabwe," however, included chimurenga music. The "Chimurenga Requests Programme" (Saturday 8:15–8:30 P.M.) was so popular that in 1979 another fifteen-minute music program was added (8:15–

8:30 on Tuesdays)—Nziyo Dzechimurenga Ingoma Zempi Yenkulu-
leko (Revolutionary Songs)—which was "a selection of songs depicting
the stages and development of Chimurenga" (see Frederikse 1982: 104).
In an interview with Julie Frederikse, a Rhodesian Special Air Service-
man described the Chimurenga Requests program as follows:

> Sure, I heard that radio broadcast from Maputo. A lot of it was silly,
> broadcasts of victories that you couldn't believe. But that "*Chimu-
> renga* Requests" programme! It was very effective propaganda, be-
> cause of the songs and the emotion put into it. . . . It was totally
> different to our "Forces Requests" programme. That was just mo-
> rale-boosting, whereas "*Chimurenga* Requests" gave a really rous-
> ing, spiritual feeling. It had everyone singing. I've come across Afri-
> cans in the bush, sitting around the radio, singing. (1982: 105)

### Pungwes

One of the most important means for politicizing the masses and gaining peasant support were the *pungwes* (all-night gatherings). After a
group of guerrillas had established themselves in a given area, they
would require all the local people, with the exception of the sick and
disabled, to attend these clandestine gatherings out in the bush. People
who did not want to attend would be forced to do so both for the sake
of full local participation and fear that they might inform on the gathering. Political speeches and lectures were delivered, and pungwes were
occasions for discussions about local problems and grievances. Comrade Zeppelin, ZANLA political commissar, stated that talking to the
people about getting land back was their "major political weapon,"
and ZIPRA (ZAPU's army) political commissar Colin Matutu noted
that at pungwes they focused on local issues and grievances and how to
solve them:

> You don't talk about the capitalist state or the socialist state to them
> [local people]. What mattered to them was how to do away with their
> grievances at the present time. . . . That political jargon is left to docu-
> ments and other things. When you are dealing with the masses you
> have to talk about relevant issues on the ground. (quoted in Freder-
> ikse 1982: 61)

In this description of political education at pungwes one gets the
sense of small-scale, subsistence peasants still largely operating in relation to localist identities and concerns rather than with a national identity. The goal of ZANLA and ZIPRA political education was to con-
vince the peasantry that local concerns could best be addressed through

the nationalist struggle. I agree with K. D. Manungo, who writes that "each of the classes within the peasantry had its own form of grievances against the settler system, and they therefore saw the guerrillas as representing a new hope of changing the system" (1991: 120). This does not necessarily mean, however, that people with local purviews began to think in national terms because alliances were formed with the party. Indeed, my own interviews with people in Murehwa-Uzumba, as well as published sources (e.g., Ranger 1985; Kriger 1992) indicate that localism often remained strong among some rural people into the 1970s and beyond. The formation of local alliances with the nationalists—the formation of a hegemonic bloc with the nationalists in the leadership role—rather than a general, unified national consciousness is probably a better description of what occurred among many peasants. This distinction is crucial for cultural analysis.

In addition to political speeches and education, the pungwes also centrally involved music and dance. Although some people interviewed by Frederikse in 1980 indicated that they were not always happy about being required to attend these all-night sessions, many mentioned that they enjoyed the music and dancing once there (1982: 60–62). The ZANLA political commissar, Zeppelin, commented that "we used to sing songs at *pungwes* because it helped to boost morale. Traditionally our people always liked singing, but this singing had some political content to it. Often people would get more from this singing than they did from all the talking. We called them '*Chimurenga* songs'" (Frederikse 1982: 61).

## Chimurenga Songs

The chimurenga songs associated with ZANU radio broadcasts and the pungwes grew up with the war in the late 1960s and during the 1970s. Composers, who were themselves party political instructors, set new, explicitly political texts to a variety of preexisting musical styles and melodies for educational and informational purposes.

I do not know specifically when the term *chimurenga* first came to be used to designate a musical genre, but it originally referred to ZANU's and ZAPU's politicization songs during the early to mid-1970s. By the early 1980s, the category *chimurenga music* was extended to the political songs of electric guitar bands performing inside Zimbabwe (e.g., see Pongweni 1982). The first evidence I have for Thomas Mapfumo's use of the term to identify his electric guitar-band style comes in a 1980 interview with Julie Frederikse (Zimbabwe National

Archives tape #ATC 0078; Frederikse 1982: 106). For obvious reasons this term would not have been used openly by bands within the country during the war years.

After the mid-1980s, the term *chimurenga music* became a commercial genre designation for indigenous-based electric music with or without political lyrics, a usage largely coined and diffused by Thomas Mapfumo and others who followed his lead. Because of Mapfumo's prominence, this usage was supported by the Zimbabwean and international media, and the term became most strongly associated with his music. In this chapter, however, I am only concerned with chimurenga music in its original sense: the songs created and used by ZANU and ZAPU, during the war years.

My description of 1970s chimurenga songs is based on the few recordings of "The Voice of Zimbabwe" programs I was able to hear in the National Archives; eighteen selections on the LP recording of the ZANU (ZANLA) Choir produced outside the country in the 1970s, *Pamberi ne Chimurenga;*[12] and four recordings by Dorothy Masuka and the (ZAPU) Zimbabwe National Choir (LSM Records, R-1). My musical sample from the 1970s (twenty-four pieces) is thus limited, but the ZANU recording was produced by the party's department of Publicity and Information and was presented as representative of their repertory. Comrade Chinx, a major ZANU chimurenga song leader and composer, confirmed that the selection on ZANU's LP was representative of their chimurenga songs of the 1970s (p.c. July 1996).

The four ZAPU Choir recordings from the 1970s that I have are all in a homophonic, hymn-based, style with triadic harmony, clear, smooth vocal timbre, and exact syllabic enunciation of the text. These performances are very professional, with precise coordination between the members of the choir, and they are studio recordings. The presence of Zimbabwe singing star Dorothy Masuka as lead vocalist represents a continuity with ZAPU's use of "concert" artists in the early 1960s; these selections did not include indices of indigenous music.

The selections on the ZANU recording have a very different quality. Judging from the wind noise audible on a few of the recordings, at least some of them were made outside, probably in the guerrilla camps in Mozambique. The performances here are less rehearsed and more relaxed; they sound like people just getting together to sing informally rather than a tightly rehearsed choir. The recordings reminded me of nights singing informally around a fire at ceremonies with the Murehwa Jerusarema Club; much the same quality and range of repertory were present. This interpretation was confirmed by Chinx, who described the singing he led—in the camps, in pungwes, and on the radio—as involving informal ad hoc groups. He told me that after he composed a song that was to be aired on the radio, he might teach it to twenty comrades for the broadcast, "But in the bases, or in the front, it could be a section of seven, a section of fifteen, ah, a plateau of over thirty. All right, you could sing together, anyone who will be there [and] knows which song to sing" (Zim96-4: 7). This description suggests a participatory ethos as the basic modus operandi for ZANU's chimurenga songs.

## Composition and Style

Eight of the twenty ZANU Choir recordings from the 1970s in my possession are hymn-based; seven are makwaya in call-and-response format with primarily unison singing by the chorus (with occasional fifths).[13] In addition, however, a school song, a jitlike social dance-drumming song, a story song, a *majukwa* spiritual dance-drumming song,[14] and "Taireva," an mbira piece, were also included on the ZANU recording. This breakdown matches Chinx's general description of the musical repertory and the way preexisting tunes and styles were chosen to set new texts.

Chinx told me that he and other chimurenga song composers would use any preexisting tune that fit the text they wanted to compose:

> TURINO: So it didn't matter what melody you used?
> CHINX: No. As long as you saw it fit. We had our songs here at home before the liberation struggle. And when we were there [at home before the war], we would come and say [sings] "Wai, moze, moze," meaning "We are greeting you, we are greeting you, we have come, your children." But here [during the war], we weren't singing like that, like it was just folk song, you see. Everyone sang jit songs. You could even use all what we had. . . . But all we did was to know a song, then take off those words which didn't mean what we were doing [during the war], and put in the meaningful ones! So that's how I even came to be a nice composer. (Zim96-4: 9)

Well-known tunes were used to facilitate learning, but Chinx indicated that he wasn't particularly conscious of this at the time. Rather, he assumed that the songs that were well known to him would be well known to everyone. As a boy he had been involved in church music as well as jit and other recreational dance-drumming traditions; these genres provided the mainstay of his melodies (Zim96-4: 11–12).

TURINO: When you picked melodies yourself, as a composer, did you ever think, "I want to choose a melody that everybody knows?" Did that matter to you?

CHINX: Yeah, it mattered. So that you could teach them faster.

TURINO: So did you think of that yourself?

CHINX: No, I didn't. We just heard, you know, because we were church-goers. Everyone, nearly everyone had to go to church, everyone.

TURINO: In Rusape [his home]?

CHINX: Mostly, even here in Harare, even everywhere. . . . And you would know, if I sing this, one is hooked by the church, but what is sung there is today's happening [war news]. So straight away you have beaten two birds with one stone, because he, she, will just go along with the theme or the melody, yes. (Zim96-4: 10)

In this statement we get a sense of the instrumentality of familiar music as vehicle for imparting new information and ideas. The hymns facilitated this process for people already "hooked by the church."

TURINO: What you're saying is, that there was no contradiction between being a nationalist and using church songs, it was okay?

CHINX: There wasn't any contradiction because what I was saying was "Ndinoda hondo" [I want war] instead of "Ndinoda Jesus" [I love Jesus]. . . . We would just take that ready song, ready melody, and put those words along. We didn't like any war, but it had come and we can't do anything unless we have to go against this war. So we have to fight the war, instead of "I love Jesus," though I love Jesus. So Jesus is just a brother whom we just put aside and said, "Please forgive us for this time, let us finish with this." (Zim96-4: 11)

Sometimes the form of the original text would be maintained with words substituted. Chinx also commented,

The kind of melodies, now, are from the Nhemamusasas, these mbira music you have. The jerusaremas, the shangaras—everything! That's where every melody, you know. We could take off [he sings] "ngororombe, ngororombe," or "nhemamusasa, nhemamusasa" and put in "chimurenga, chimurenga" instead, you see? And put "sabiehdu, sabiehdu," meaning submachine gun. (Zim96-4: 8)

While several of the pieces on the ZANU recording used drum and hosho, and one used mbira accompaniment, the main emphasis was on vocal performance. Chinx indicated that the use of instruments was even rarer in the pungwes than it was in the camps.

TURINO: In the pungwes did you use instruments too?

CHINX: No, not even a single instrument.

TURINO: Never?

CHINX: Never, ever. Unless otherwise, the conga. Yeah, the drum. We could even say, "No, we [are] liberated, we have the conga!" But the conga could also, you know, say to the enemy, we're here, so [put us] in danger, of course. But there were zones now which were liberated in such a way that we could even show that we are hitting them [the drums], and you can come, and we can still fight you back.

TURINO: On that early record there was one piece with mbira.

CHINX: Okay.

TURINO: So in the pungwes you didn't use mbira?

CHINX: No, we couldn't. (Zim96-4: 8)

He went on to say that occasionally someone might be present who would have an mbira, "Some of our, you know, ancestral representatives [mediums]. We could have those ones and we could play a nice piece" (ibid). At such times they might learn new melodies which they could use later for chimurenga songs.

The genres that provided the predominant basis for ZANU's chimurenga songs (hymns, makwaya, story songs, school songs, jit) were most often those that had longer, elaborated texts and featured a more syllabic approach in group text delivery. These characteristics contrast with indigenous genres where vocable singing predominates and with traditions where heightened overlapping of different vocal and instrumental parts is the rule (e.g., ceremonial mbira performance, jerusarema, dandanda, ngororombe). The clarity of text delivery and the elaboration of political themes was paramount to the function of chimurenga songs. For this reason, composers may have been predisposed to genres associated with longer texts and syllabic singing. Chinx did not mention this criterion, although it might be implied by his comment that any melody would do "as long as you saw it fit."

Especially in pungwes, the songs and dances were used to inspire group participation. Listening to the ZANU Choir LP of chimurenga songs, I was struck by the fact that the quality of the singing and drumming as well as the indigenous genres performed were those that would be typically heard in a wide range of 'outside the house' (more recreational) village social occasions, including singing around the fire during a *guva* (grave) ceremony, at beer drinks, weddings, and funerals. That pungwes often went all night provided an additional point of resemblance to the customary way of performing indigenous ceremonies and parties. Church songs were also linked to common group-participatory occasions. The music and dance may have helped people to link the pungwes to these other, more normal, social events.

Through the use of familiar melodies and familiar settings for performance, the ZANLA cadres could put new political ideas in old comfortable vehicles. The testimonies I have already cited make it apparent that singing was many people's favorite part of the pungwes; thus, they were effective tools for involving people in these events.

## Chimurenga Song Texts

While the very act of engaging people in song at pungwes was of political importance within ZANU's Maoist strategy, it was the song texts that allowed the party to diffuse its official goals, attitudes, positions, and needs. The songs were, above and beyond everything else, an educational tool.

Comrade Chinx noted that the content of his song texts derived from several sources. He would compose songs based on speeches by the ZANU leadership and on things learned in political training. In addition, however, he traveled back and forth from the camps in Mozambique to the front. Some of his texts contained current events in one place, broadcast over radio to the other. For example, through his travels he might learn of enemy tactics in one area, such as the poisoning of wells, and then write a song warning the people in other areas to guard their wells. He also saw boosting morale at the front, in the villages, and in the camps as one of his major roles.

### SONGS FOR TEACHING MILITARY
### AND POLITICAL DOCTRINE

One of the most commonly heard ZANU chimurenga songs was "Nzira Dzemasoja Dzekuzvibata Nadzo" ("The Principles of a People's Soldier"). According to Eddison Zvobgo, deputy secretary of ZANU Publicity and Information Department, this song was played every night on "The Voice of Zimbabwe" before the news (Frederikse 1982: 212). The music is in the style of a hymn sung in homophonic texture with triadic harmony. A leader lines out the text, which teaches Maoist principles for the right conduct of a soldier:

> Soldiers have a code of conduct by which they live;
> Listen properly to all these rules.
> We must not exploit or rob the masses
> Let us return to them the property taken from the enemy.
> Educate the masses in a clear way
> And they will understand the policies of the party.
> Pay fair prices for everything that you buy
> Return anything that you have confiscated for military reasons....
> We must not engage in promiscuity while waging a
>     revolutionary war.

We must not harass prisoners of war. . . .
These are the words of wisdom handed down to us by
   Mao Tse Tung, the Revolutionary sage.
            (trans. Pongweni 1982: 9–10; Frederikse 1982: 212)

Another hymn-based ZANU song, "Zvinozibwa NeZanu" briefly
tells the history of ZANU: of how "The sons and daughters of Zimbabwe came together to form a Party," and how they "chose Mugabe
to lead the people." It told how "after our leaders left the country, we
followed them, one by one in small groups until there were many of us."
The song tells of how nationalist leaders were jailed and murdered, and
concludes, "Now we are armed to the teeth, Our soldiers are spoiling
for a fight" (trans. Pongweni 1982: 20).

Other songs, like the makwaya-based piece "Tora Gidi Uzvitonge,"
were intended to inspire recruitment. In this song, the important martyr
from the First Chimurenga, Mbuya Nehanda, tells the people to take
up arms and liberate themselves, and Herbert Chitepo, a martyr from
the Second Chimurenga is linked to her by being placed in the same
paradigmatic slot in the text:

Solo:  NeHanda died with these words on her lips,

Chorus:  "I am dying for our country."
         She left us one word of advice,
         "Take up arms and liberate yourselves."

Solo:  Chitepo died with these words on his lips,

Chorus:  "I am dying for our country."
         His word of advice was, "Take up arms and
         liberate yourselves."
            (Trans. Pongweni 1982: 27)

## HISTORY, KINSHIP, AND NATION

Connecting the First and Second Chimurenga—as in "Tora Gidi Uzvitonge" through the substitution of Chitepo for Nehanda—was a centerpiece of ZANU's cultural nationalism during the 1970s. The same
poetic strategy was used in "Titatireyi"—an indigenous Shona melody
sung in makwaya style. In this text, ZANU's singers appeal to the ancestral spirits to protect the guerrillas. The use of an indigenous-style
melody for this appeal to the ancestral spirits may be significant—ancestors respond to the music that they knew when alive. Yet Nehanda is
appealed to in hymn-based songs as well, so the correlation between
ancestor imagery and indigenous tunes is not consistent; Chinx implied that this type of text-tune correlation was not explicitly followed.
In "Titatireyi," Takawira and Mugabe are replaced by Nehanda and
Chaminuka:

Nhandi vaTakawira mudzimu wedu baba . . .
Nhandi vaNeHanda mudzimu wedu baba . . .
Nhandi vaMugabe mutungamiri wedu . . .
Nhandi vaChaminuka mudzimu wedu baba . . .
                      (Pongweni 1982: 51–52)

This linking of the First and Second Chimurenga gave the nationalist movement and the "nation" itself the mantle of historical depth. Constructing the image of the primordial nation—"we" were here before and will be here after—was common to Zimbabwean cultural nationalism from the start. As suggested earlier, Nehanda and Chaminuka were significant as nationalist emblems because of their pan-regional character.

The device of paradigmatic substitution that links these different historical figures was also used to construct the image of the nation. A section of the ZANU song "Chimoto" (Flame), for example, repeats two lines six times: "Nyika yemadzibaba / Nyika yeZimbabwe." The first line may be translated literally as "Land of our collective fathers" (or "Land of all our fathers in general"); the second line means "Land of Zimbabwe." Pongweni translates "Nyika yemadzibaba" as "Our Fatherland," which may well have been the meaning that was intended (1982: 42–43). Benedict Anderson, among others, has drawn attention to the common use of the image of "fatherland" or "motherland" for imagining the nation and for expressing patriotism:

> Something of the nature of this political love can be deciphered from the ways in which languages describe its object: either in the vocabulary of kinship (motherland, Vaterland, patria) or that of home. . . . Both idioms denote something to which one is naturally tied. As we have seen earlier, in everything 'natural' there is always something unchosen. In this way, nation-ness is assimilated to skin-colour, gender, parentage and birth-era—all those things one cannot help. (1991: 143)

Anderson's comment parallels my observations about the way nationalists attempt to index the emotional bonds of face-to-face groups (families, neighborhoods, villages) in the construction of the nation.

Zimbabwean peasants were and are spiritually tied to the land of their ancestors, as the concept of *musha* indicates. People with an indigenous mind-set are also tied to specific family ancestors and regional or lineage spirits. Like the pan-regional character of Chaminuka and Nehanda, the use of the more general phrase "our collective fathers" ("our fathers in general") extends the notion from a local to a national plane. The concept of "fatherland" is drawn from a pool of images within cosmopolitan nationalist discourse. In another ZANU chimu-renga song, "Hapana Chavo," Pongweni translates the phrase "Nem-huri yeZimbabwe" as "Zimbabwe nation" (1982: 11–15). This phrase, which literally means 'family of Zimbabwe' (*mhuri* = family), again suggests the imagery of kinship that Anderson alludes to, and it also suggests the lack of a suitable Shona word and concept to denote "nation."

SHONA IDENTITY,

PARTY, AND NATION

In "Hapana Chavo," another interesting paradigmatic substitution is made early on in which the notion of "nation" becomes replaceable by the party ZANU-PF:

| | |
|---|---|
| Chimurenga chakarwiwa | The Liberation War was fought |
| Chakarwiwa neZANU PF. | ZANU PF fought the war. |
| Chakarwiwa naniko? | Who fought? |
| Nemhuri yeZimbabwe | The family [nation] of Zimbabwe |
| Chimurenga chakarwiwa | The Liberation War was fought |
| Chakarwiwa neZANU PF | ZANU PF fought the war. |

Here and in other ZANU songs, this party is singled out as the main political and military protagonist in Zimbabwe's present and future; the other main participant in the Patriotic Front, ZAPU, goes largely un-mentioned, as if groundwork was already being laid for the elections that were ahead. This is particularly clear in a ZANU song featured on their LP, "Ndiro Gidi" (It's the gun): "We sing the praises of ZANU / The party which will rule Zimbabwe / It shall come to power in Zim-babwe" (trans. Pongweni 1982: 66).

While ZAPU songs and Ndebele pieces were sometimes aired on the "Voice of Zimbabwe," an Ndebele presence was not well incorporated into ZANU's vision of the nation, as expressed in chimurenga songs and within ZANU cultural nationalism in general. The emphasis on Chaminuka is particularly significant in this regard. In spite of most na-tionalists' official antitribalism, ZAPU was associated with the Ndebele people just as ZANU was most closely identified with the Shona. Hence, this difference led to an inherent party rivalry that began in 1963 and was exacerbated in the 1970s. In the chimurenga song texts, it is clear that ZANU constructed itself as the future of the nation, and the na-tion was often presented as the Shona majority. It was the courting of this majority that brought ZANU to power in the 1980 elections; ZAPU only carried the Ndebele areas. This split also led to violence

between the ZANU State and Ndebele dissidents between the early
1980s and 1987.

## IMAGES OF MODERNITY

While some of the images in chimurenga songs evoke the past and the
"natural" foundations of the nation (ancestors, family, land), others
speak of cosmopolitan technology, of new fertilizers produced in Zimbabwe, of the electricity that comes from the Kariba Dam, and of the
imperialist appropriation of Zimbabwe's resources (e.g., in "Hapana
Chavo," Pongweni 1982: 11–15). In the song "Mukoma Takanyi,"
traveling by bus and airplane is equated with basic human rights (Pongweni 1982: 45).

In "Tora Gidi Uzvitonge," as in other songs, the lyrics emphasize
the guerrillas' prowess with technologically sophisticated weapons like
"anti-airs" and submachine guns. The text of the hymn-like makwaya
song "Zvikomborero" (Blessings), for example, says, "The subma-
chine-gun is my weapon I can use it so well, it's like my toy," and "I can
even dig up a mortar bomb, Yes, that too. / These blessings are now
mine I count them, father" (Pongweni 1982: 30). In this case it is not
hard to imagine the type of word substitutions described by Chinx for
transforming a Christian piece into a chimurenga song.

In these songs, ZANU discourse combines a plea to the ancestral
spirits for help and power while realistically recognizing the importance
of cosmopolitan technology as a source of power: "We are singing
about the gun / It shall rule Zimbabwe" (in "Ndiro Gidi," Pongweni
1982: 66); "We know this from reading Mao's works / Who states in no
uncertain terms 'Political power comes from the barrel of a gun'" (in
"Mukoma Takanyi," Pongweni 1982: 46).

## The Local, the National, and the Cosmopolitan

The images combined in ZANU's chimurenga song texts are extremely
consistent with the party's stated program of cultural nationalism,
which involved the reformist fusion of indigenous and cosmopolitan
elements. In the chimurenga songs, images of the vadzimu (ancestral
spirits) are closely linked to specific locality, while Chaminuka and Nehanda project ideas of a translocal Shona society—the national. Collectively, the ancestral spirits were intended to communicate the ideas of
historical depth and, particularly powerful among peasants, inalienable
ties to the land. Like the living mediums who aided the guerrillas, the
ancestors were real focal points for rallying local collective sympathies.

ZANU also necessarily framed the new nation within a 'modern' cosmopolitan context and was prepared to learn from other societies. In song, Mao Tse Tung is termed "The Revolutionary Sage," and Nyerere of Tanzania and Samora Michel of Mozambique are beloved allies as well as role models. The cosmopolitan model of socialism is rhetorically projected as the future of choice in contrast to settler capitalism, European and American imperialism, or some other indigenous solution that might have been invented.[15] Thus, the economic, political, and technological fields were defined as the "most valuable" cosmopolitan features within the reformist mix.

In the songs, the struggle itself was positioned in a pan-African and a broader global context. In "Vanhu Vose VemuAfrica" the ZANU Choir sings,

> Masses of Africa please listen . . .
> Let us assert the supremacy of the masses
> Both of this country and Asia, Latin America, and of Africa
>     generally.
> In our struggle with the enemy
> Our guardian spirits [midzimu] please bless us.
>                               (trans. Pongweni 1982: 62)

Again, this text is basically a restatement, in poetic form, of ZANU's official policy; indeed as Chinx noted, ideas for his song texts sometimes came from his leaders' speeches and from political training. "Vanhu Vose VemuAfrica" sounds very much like a passage from ZANU's policy document "MWENJE No. 2" (1972):

> ZANU's foreign policy is determined by two cardinal principles: to fight against imperialism and to unite with all other progressive forces in the world. The enemies we fight against are both local and international. There would be no logic in fighting imperialist tentacles in Southern Africa, then supporting or condoning them in the Middle East, South-East Africa or Latin America. Progressive forces are engaged in a titanic global conflict with imperialism and capitalism. ZANU has thrown its weight on the side of progressive forces. (Nyangoni and Nyandoro 1979: 263)

By their very nature, nations and nationalisms must be understood in an international context, just as they must also engage with the local.

### The Twin Paradoxes of Nationalism

Earlier in this chapter I suggested that the very existence of the nation-state is both dependent on and threatened by actual local communities. Distinctive local groups are necessary because they provide the emblems that distinguish the nation from other nations. They provide the affective bases of identity and belonging which nationalists then attempt to harness to the idea of nation through the transformation of localist indices. Neighborhoods and villages also provide tax-paying citizens and potential army recruits.

But because nations are abstract and because they require primary allegiance from a major number of citizens to function, their existence is simultaneously threatened by more concrete local groups. Nationalist discourse holds that distinctive cultural lifeways are the basis of nationhood, and this idea potentially places distinctive local groups on par with the nation-state itself. As Herzfeld (1997) has suggested, nationalism potentially creates its own separatist rivals.

The other major paradox is that nation-states are also simultaneously dependent on and threatened by cosmopolitanism. As we saw in chapter 5, the very idea of nationalism, and its more concrete programs and mechanisms, are learned from and based on cosmopolitan models. Nationalism *is* a cosmopolitan idea and program. But there is more to it than this. Social identities exist through similarities and oppositional contrasts. We articulate (foreground) a given part of our social identity in relation to who and what we are *not* within a basic context of similarity. Thus, when meeting a person of the same local group (Zezuru) and general region, we might distinguish ourselves in terms of village or family. When meeting an Ndebele person from Bulawayo, we might identify ourselves as being Shona speakers from Murehwa. When meeting a North American in London, we might identify ourselves as Zimbabwean. The existence of a given national identity depends on the existence of other nations and national identities—other social units of the same categorical type.

The nationalist push to create a nation-state is also based on the desire to join the global "family of nations." To be recognized as a nation, nationalists must construct their new social entity to be recognizably like other nations—with national languages, anthems, flags, sports teams, dance companies, and similar state apparatuses, as well as *international* airports and memberships in *international* organizations like the United Nations.[16] Homologous state apparatuses are necessary if my president is going to be able to talk to your president, my minister of finance to yours, my diplomat to yours.

At the same time, for identity to operate at this level, each nation must distinguish itself, or it will cease to exist in relation to other nations. It is here where local, indigenous (noncosmopolitan) emblems must be brought into play. Nationalism involves the fashioning of a *somewhat* distinctive cultural unit within an overall framework of similarity. Modernist-cosmopolitanism gave rise to nationalism in the first place and provides the basic underlying structures of similarity. Local-indigenous groups supply distinctiveness, sentiment, and in places like Zimbabwe, the majority of potential citizens.

The nation-state cannot exist without both the local and cosmopolitan poles of social conceptualization, just as nation-states are also threatened by localism and cosmopolitanism. Cultural nationalism balances one pole against the other, and new nations in the colonial world are typically fashioned through the combination of local and cosmopolitan elements within the process of modernist reform. We have already had abundant Zimbabwean examples of this dynamic in the preceding chapter; it is central to the combination of styles and images in chimurenga songs as well.

## The Role of Musical Nationalism

The chimurenga song texts were, along with political speeches and discussions, a way to teach people about ZANU's official positions. The songs were a particularly powerful medium for doing so. Because singing and dancing are a primary form of recreation and religious celebration in rural villages, these media were attractive and encouraged popular participation. As indices of typical occasions, singing and dancing helped integrate the new pungwe contexts within rural social life. Because the songs were repeated often (e.g., "Nzira Dzemasoja Dzekuzvibata Nadzo" was broadcast every night) and the texts involved a great deal of internal repetition, they were a good means of cementing ideas in people's minds.

Repetition, poetic devices such as parallelism and paradigmatic substitution, and the use of familiar tunes make song texts easier to remember than speeches. Through both iconic and indexical semiotic processes, paradigmatic substitutions in the texts help create new bundles of association and meaning. The First Chimurenga is linked to the Second, giving the nation time depth; the nation is concretely linked to family, and ZANU is portrayed as synonymous with nation; contemporary leaders are made iconically equivalent to ancestral spirits and culture heroes through paradigmatic substitution.[17]

Perhaps most important, because the songs involved group unison or homophonic singing, as well as some interlocking and overlapping techniques, they created the direct, concrete sense of social synchrony—of singing together and being together. This direct sense experience is fundamental to creating a visceral, emotional, aesthetic power that comes to be associated with the meanings communicated through the texts and ZANU-framed events. The songs seem to have resonated with people in Zimbabwe. Descriptions of the effects of the chimurenga songs provided earlier—in pungwes, singing around the radio in the bush—support this interpretation of their affective power.

Like the musical nationalism of the early 1960s, the chimurenga song tradition combined indigenous and cosmopolitan elements and images, but by the mid-1970s they were often integrated into the same pieces: references to machine guns and ancestors set to a church hymn. The same forces that generate syncretism were also operating here. As in the early rallies, for the music to pragmatically represent, attract, and involve a broad range of Zimbabweans, a corresponding range of well-known styles and pieces was needed.

Chinx's description of the composition process suggests that there was not a great deal of conscious manipulation of musical materials for emblematic purposes. That is, he did not self-consciously link certain types of texts and tunes—mbira music to sing about ancestors, and hymns for references to modernity. Analysis of my sample bears this out. The emphasis was on choosing tunes and styles that he knew well and that metrically fit the text he wanted to compose. The syncretic chimurenga style was largely the product of who the composers were, in conjunction with the pragmatic needs of the party during the moment of maneuver.

Chinx noted that occasionally they would meet an mbira player in the field and learn a song, but this was not a genre he was very familiar with or that ZANU composers often used. Contrary to a common perception outside Zimbabwe, mbira music was *not* a prominent aspect of party chimurenga songs during the 1970s, just as it had not been particularly prominent in the rallies of the early 1960s. Reflecting general contemporary perceptions, Kaemmer writes that "near the end of the colonial period, indigenous music, particularly that of the mbira, became an important symbol of Shona identity. The mbira and related ancestral-spirit rites helped politicize rural people" (1998: 756).

Spirit mediums and indigenous religion were important components of ZANU's cultural nationalism and military tactics. In light of the actual nature of ZAPU's and ZANU's musical nationalism, however, it seems that the emblematic importance of the mbira has been overstated. Indeed Kaemmer goes on to accurately describe the musically eclectic nature of party chimurenga songs (1998: 757). As I will explain in chapter 9, overemphasizing the nationalist role of the mbira may be the result of cosmopolitan interest in this particular instrument in hindsight accounts produced during the 1980s and 1990s.

## Reformism and
## Participatory Ethics

The reformism underpinning ZANU's cultural nationalism of the 1970s differs in one critical way from all the other examples of modernist reformism that I discuss in this book. All the reformist cases blend indigenous and cosmopolitan cultural forms and themes; in the other instances, however, indigenous forms and practices are largely extracted out of communal-participatory contexts, segmented from participatory ethics and aesthetics, and then recontextualized within cosmopolitan presentational and objectified formats (mass media, stage arrangements, scores, recordings, schools, song books).

In contrast, because their function was to inspire people to become involved and participate, ZANU's chimurenga songs were, above all else, designed to maintain the ethics and sound qualities of participatory art so central to indigenous Zimbabwean music making. Even in their most objectified form, the ZANLA Choir recording, ZANU's chimurenga song performances maintained a relatively open, relaxed feel, as if someone had simply turned on a tape recorder in a pungwe or a guerrilla camp.[18]

Hence in this case of reformism, a kind of inversion took place whereby cosmopolitan ideas and forms (e.g., hymn melodies, triadic harmonies, the ideas of machine guns and nation) were incorporated within an alternative participatory aesthetic and mode of practice without subverting the most fundamental bases of their alternity. This case, then, exemplifies Shamuyarira's statement that Zimbabwean cultural nationalism should borrow "valuable foreign elements" but make them truly community-strengthening and participatory. Only in such instances can we speak about the local heterogenization of cosmopolitan culture at anything but the superficial level of forms.

# Part Four

# Guitar Bands and Cosmopolitan Youth Culture

Chapter Seven

## On the Margins of Nationalism: Acoustic
## Guitarists and Guitar Bands of the 1960s

If you mentioned chimurenga music to worldbeat fans in Tokyo, Sidney, Berlin, London, New York, or Champaign-Urbana in the 1990s, the songs of Comrade Chinx and his ZANU chorus would probably not spring to mind. Rather they would most likely visualize the crouching, dreadlocked figure of Thomas Mapfumo clutching the microphone in front of his band, the Blacks Unlimited. They might hear in their minds' ear the brilliantly polished, transparent arrangements of classical mbira pieces such as "Dande" performed with electrified mbira, hosho, electric guitars, keyboards, traps, and bass, or a jit song with horn riffs punctuating Mapfumo's vocal lines. Along with the Bhundu Boys and Stella Chiweshe, Mapfumo is the leading international exponent of the most unique urban-popular music genres to come out of Zimbabwe. As a result of the worldbeat marketing of Mapfumo, and aspects of his own history, this style has come to define musical nationalism and the national music of Zimbabwe in the cosmopolitan imagination.

The nationalist association is partially based on the fact that a number of guitar bands, Mapfumo's among them, began performing political songs about the guerrilla war after 1974. Mapfumo and others continued to emphasize the war and the politics of liberation as themes in their self-presentation to national and especially international audiences through the 1990s. For example, the name Bhundu refers to the bush and is a reference to the guerilla fighters. Mapfumo coined the term *chimurenga* as a commercial genre designation (e.g., for his record label) in the mid-1980s. The term has, by now, become synonymous with guitar-band music based on indigenous Shona genres, although some Zimbabweans, especially ex-combatants, contest this usage. In 1988, Stella Chiweshe recorded songs called "Chimurenga" and "NeHondo" (war) on an international release (*Upenyu Ambuya*, Upenyu Productions SHL 1003), thus adding the motif of black liberation to her more prominent identification with spirituality—both are canonic features of worldbeat imagery.

For those who simply think of *musical nationalism* as the incorporation of vernacular elements within cosmopolitan genres, the music of Mapfumo, Chiweshe, and the Bhundu Boys could easily be conceptualized as such based on style alone. Indeed, their music seems identical to the usual products of modernist reformism, the process which typically underpins cultural nationalism. As we saw for the Federation period, however, there may be other motivations for reformist-driven syncretism which may or may not articulate with nationalism. The development of indigenous-based guitar-band music was, in fact, shaped by the intersection of several factors: 1960s cosmopolitan youth culture and the emergence of professional aspirations among musicians; nationalism in the 1970s and 1980s; and the desires of worldbeat fans in the 1980s and 1990s.

This chapter provides a history of early, indigenous-based Zimbabwean guitar music and guitar bands. I begin with a general introduction to the two genres—mbira-based pieces and jit—which stand out as the most famous and most common, respectively, within indigenous-based guitar music. We then turn to a consideration of acoustic guitarists in the pre-nationalist period. Paralleling "concert" and jazz ensembles in time, these lower-class itinerant guitarists were, like their middle-class counterparts, fundamental forerunners to the later electric bands. The chapter concludes with a discussion of the rise of teenage guitar bands and the emergence of their professional aspirations in the context of 1960s cosmopolitan youth culture.

The extensive career of Thomas Mapfumo is, in various ways, paradigmatic for the history of Zimbabwean guitar bands. His early work is discussed at the end of this chapter, and his career during the war years of the 1970s is considered in chapter 8. Chapter 9 discusses his work in the context of worldbeat during the post-1980 period. In each of these phases, Mapfumo is discussed in relation to a number of other artists who were working simultaneously in similar ways. Mapfumo made music history, but not from conditions of his own making; especially in the early phases, he was only one of various innovators.

## "Mbira-Guitar" Music

Beginning around 1974, guitar-band renditions of mbira music and jit became relatively solidified stylistically. Since one purpose of the next two chapters is to trace the somewhat independent emergence of the different musical features of these genres, we begin with a general description of them so that important stylistic innovations may be recognized as we progress through their histories.

Throughout the 1970s, the instrumentation in bands that played the "mbira-guitar" style comprised guitars, bass, traps, and occasionally horns, electric organ, and additional percussion.[1] In the early to mid-1980s electric keyboards became common. After 1986 guitar bands began to incorporate actual indigenous instruments, especially the twenty-two-key Zezuru mbira, ngoma (tall single-headed drums), and hosho (shakers). Although there were a few forerunners, such as the Harare Mambos (1983?), and acoustic guitarist Pamidze Benhura (1980), Mapfumo popularized the mixing of mbira with guitars in a band context. He told me that he first used an mbira in his band in 1984 on "Chemera Chaunoda" on the *Mabasa* LP (Zim92-23: 4–5); the inclusion of one to three mbira became permanent in Mapfumo's Blacks Unlimited in 1986. By the early 1990s many bands playing Shona music commonly included mbira, ngoma, and hosho with traps and electric instruments—pointing to the gradual, yet continuous, process of "indigenization" which has characterized this guitar-band trajectory from the beginning.

Guitar-band mbira music is based on the 12/8 metric-rhythmic structures of mbira pieces, with the drummer strongly accenting beats 1, 4, 7, and 10 on the kickdrum and playing hosho-like triple patterns on the highhat. Guitar-band renditions range from moderate to quick tempos (e.g., ♪ = 120 to 150). The genre is also defined by four-phrase harmonic-melodic ostinatos, either of an actual mbira piece or in close imitation of mbira-style progressions. This basic structure is rendered by the bass and guitars, and later also by keyboards and electric mbira.

Mbira-based chord progressions are at once unusual *and* familiar within cosmopolitan popular music and are one of the distinguishing as well as attractive features of the style. Although only implied by the mbira parts, when translated to the guitar the resulting progressions typically shift between major and minor chords and create a harmonically unstable feeling which moves the basic ostinato forward relentlessly. Three chords are typically played in each 12/8 phrase, with one chord changing stepwise each phrase. The first chord is usually held for half the bar, and the other two chords are held for three eighth notes each.[2] Progressions from mbira classics like "Karigamombe" or "Nyamaropa" are frequently used (the keys chosen here are arbitrary): G Bm D | G Bm Em | G C Em | Am C Em. This progression is used for both mbira pieces mentioned and for various others. The starting point of this and other mbira-based progressions is rather flexible and may be used and perceived in a variety of ways. For example, a song might start on what I have here as the second, third, or fourth phrases. The pattern of substituting one chord stepwise per phrase is common in mbira-based chord progressions generally.

Within the conventions of contemporary cosmopolitan popular music, such juxtapositions of the major and minor are commonly employed to create feelings of bittersweet ambiguity, mysteriousness, and restlessness, but also feelings of strength (e.g., "Every Breath You Take" by the Police). It is easy to understand why such progressions—distinctive and yet familiar—would have proven attractive to worldbeat audiences, and why these harmonies would have fit with and supported the imagery surrounding artists like Mapfumo and Stella Chiweshe (see chapter 9).

In this genre the lead guitar repeats high descending lines like those played on the high keys of the mbira, or it may play other types of lines (e.g., rock-style). Bass parts are often modeled on those of the bass keys of the mbira. The keyboards are typically used to play the accompanying kutsinhira mbira part, which follows one beat behind or interlocks in other ways with the first (kushaura) part played by the bass and guitars. This style also frequently incorporates the "damped guitar" technique in which the palm of the right hand partially mutes the plucked strings, creating an mbiralike guitar timbre. The use of Shona vocal techniques such as *huro* (high yodeling) and *mahon'era* (low, soft, vocable singing) is another feature of mature guitar-band mbira music (see Berliner 1978 for a detailed description of mbira music and vocal styles).

Guitar-band artists continually compose new songs over this rather standardized musical base, just as North Americans have created an infinite number of songs over several standard blues progressions. The songs include indigenous-style texts, of a mosaic[3] or narrative character, and they tend to be highly repetitive. Songs may have a loose verse-refrain structure (i.e., the refrain coming at irregular intervals) or simple-strophic form (no refrain), but because the music is ostinato-based, the approach to melody and setting lyrics can be irregular and rather free, much like indigenous mbira music. Texts by artists like

Mapfumo may be substantially new or may primarily be composed of preexisting lines, but are typically some combination.

While classical mbira pieces became one model for guitar-band compositions after the mid-1970s, the label "mbira-guitar music" is a bit of a misnomer when applied to the entire repertory of a guitar band. Bands typically performed a wide variety of indigenous Shona songs and genres, including jit, agricultural, war, dance-drumming, beer-drinking, and topical songs.[4] For example, songs associated with jerusarema dancing were performed by electric bands in the late 1960s and by Mapfumo in the late 1980s and 1990s. We should remember, then, that mbira-based pieces and jit are simply two specific types within the broader category of "indigenous-based guitar-band music."

## Guitar-Band Jit

Along with indigenous-based pieces and original compositions that do not fit neatly into any genre category, popular artists like the Green Arrows, Oliver M'tukudzi, and Thomas Mapfumo perform music that would be widely identified in Zimbabwe as *jit* or *jiti*.[5] Other artists such as Paul Mpofu and the Bhundu Boys have come to be identified primarily with the jit genre, although they too do a variety of genres and styles.

Hallmark characteristics of mature guitar-band jit are found in its temporal structure. Guitar-band jit is in 12/8 meter with the drummer strongly accenting the first of every three eighth-note groupings on the kick drum, and playing consistent triplet patterns on the highhat in rapid tempo (a range of $\flat$. = 158 to 184 is common). The songs are most typically based on a I–IV–I–V harmonic ostinato with each chord held for one 12/8 bar and a pronounced bass line accenting beats 1 and 7. If one focuses on the bass, it is possible to hear the entire rhythmic-metric structure in 4/4 with the bass playing half notes on 1 and 3, the kick drum hitting quarter notes (e. g., $\flat$ = 184), and the chords still changing every bar. These two ways of hearing the rhythmic structure are displayed by contemporary dancers, although the 12/8 framework appears to be felt as primary; each rhythmic "feel" is also significant in terms of oral data about the emergence of jit.

As I will explain, jit was originally derived from South African urban styles such as *marabi, tsaba-tsaba,* and *jive,* terms that Zimbabweans almost treated as synonyms for South African urban music of the 1940s and 1950s (see chapter 4). In South Africa this music was characterized by a 4/4 metric framework, a swing feel, and tempos ranging from $\flat$ = 126 to 176, the upper range of which was comparable to jit. South African urban-popular music from Mbube of the 1930s to the jive of Spokes Mashiyane of the 1950s commonly utilized a I–IV–I–V progression with chords changing every bar (or half bar depending on how you feel the basic pulse).[6]

Guitar-band jit is defined by the combination of the typical Zimbabwean two-phrase 12/8 structure with a South African chord progression and simple duple framework. When listening to guitar-band jit, if one orients the overall rhythmic-metric feel to the bass part (rather than the 12/8 structure emphasized by the kickdrum and highhat), one can hear the South African influence clearly.

The other prominent instrumental feature in contemporary guitar-band jit is a single-line, lead guitar ostinato accompanied by a less pronounced second guitar ostinato, or arpeggiated chords to accompany vocal parts. This approach to guitar playing was most likely derived from Congolese-rumba guitar styles. The overall range of the guitar parts tends to be in the middle and higher registers. Extensive instrumental sections (usually variations on the basic lead ostinato) are interspersed with the vocal sections. The instrumentation for jit music is heavily guitar-oriented, although bands that have horns and keyboards, and that later incorporated village instruments, may use them on jit songs as well. The vocals are in a rather sweet, smooth, high singing style without much or any use of indigenous vocal techniques (perhaps another Congolese influence). The texts are strophic and cover a wide range of topics from current events and moral teachings to songs about romantic love.

### The History of Jit:
### Urban Associations

By the 1980s jit had become associated in young Zimbabweans' minds with village recreational dance-drumming as the original source for the electric band style. The development of guitar-band jit was thus understood as identical to the process of incorporating mbira and other indigenous genres into electric band repertories. Actually, the history of the term *jit*, and of the style itself, is more complex. The development of jit—involving South African harmony and rhythms, rural Shona rhythms and texts, and influences from Congolese rumba—illustrates how international and rural-urban interchanges can influence the emergence of a new local genre. The history of jit also illustrates the nature of generational memory and the way musical meanings shift over time. Since the history of jit is largely unknown in Zimbabwe, and the sources for the term and style are contested, it is worth going into the background of the genre in some detail.

From what I can gather from interview and recorded sources,[7] *jit* was a term originally associated with urban South African genres, such as marabi, tsaba-tsaba, and jive (or South African 'jazz'). These styles were diffused to Zimbabwe by the powerful South African recording industry, by touring South African artists, and by returning Zimbabwean migrant workers (Mattaka, p.c. 4 August 1993). The term *jit-jive*, still occasionally heard, indicates this connection.[8] Mr. Mbofana, current head of Radio 2, who has had a long career in African radio programming in Harare, offered the following opinion: "I think jit is a development from jive. . . . I remember one song which used to say, 'We will sing jiti and jive.' Ah, you know, so they combined jit and jive. See what I'm getting at? So jit, I think, was part of jive. Just a word that was coined . . . so it was jit and jive" (Zim 93-43: 14). Mr. Mbofana said that this took place sometime around the middle 1960s. Veteran "concert" performer Kenneth Mattaka, however, dated the term *jit* to the early 1950s. While he said he couldn't be sure, he thought the style might have come from South Africa: "I think it came together with jive and jazz and all that." He describes jit as being played on acoustic guitars during that period (Zim93-65: 1). Other long-time musicians in Harare, such as Jackson Phiri, also linked jit to South African jive and jazz and placed its emergence at the beginning of the 1950s (Zim93-44: 5; Zim93-40: 24). Thomas Mapfumo adds that *jiti* "is not a Zimbabwean word as such. There's no such word as *jiti*. This is South African" (Zim93-46: 3).

Acoustic guitar players performing during the 1950s and 1960s provide further clues to the links between Zimbabwean jit and South African styles and terms such as *jive, marabi,* and *tsaba-tsaba.* In describing his own music during the 1950s, Jacob Mhungu said, "Well, we were playing tsaba-tsaba, which is now called jit" (Zim93-87: 1). The acoustic guitarist Sinyoro Jackson Chinemberi linked tsaba-tsaba, jive, and jit stylistically, saying that "tsaba-tsaba beat is part of jit. Tsaba-tsaba's like jit, and jit is like jive, but jive is slower" (Zim93-72: 19). Faster South African jive was comparable to jit. By saying that tsaba-tsaba was part of jit, and jit was like jive, however, he seems to be pointing to the way the 12/8 structure became superimposed on the South African 4/4 meter.[9] The latter is less dense rhythmically, and hence might be perceived as "slower." Mr. Chinemberi told me that when he began playing guitar in 1954 the term and faster style of "jit was there already" and that people were already requesting jit: "They just were into jit, no they say, Ah jive is not all right, we need jit!" (Zimb93-72: 6). This comment makes sense if, by this time, the 12/8 rhythm was already incorporated, thereby making the music familiar and attractive to the Zimbabwean peasants and workers who comprised the audiences for acoustic guitarists.

RBC recordings of Shona acoustic guitarists, such as Nguaru Mapundu, Pamidze Benhura, Marko Takaingofa, and many others during the late 1950s and the 1960s give the terms *tsaba, marabi, jive,* and *topical songs* interchangeably on the labels for pieces that, in tempo and rhythmic style, are identical to contemporary rural and electric-band jit. I played these acoustic guitar recordings for a variety of contemporary musicians who identified them rapidly and unproblematically as jit. One South African feature that remains a part of contemporary guitar-band jit—the I–IV–I–V harmonic ostinato—was featured in the acoustic guitarists' music. Yet the 12/8 rhythmic structure came to dominate in Zimbabwean guitarists' versions of the South African genres. The right thumb powerfully accented the triple division on bass notes, fulfilling the same function as the kickdrum in guitar bands.

Jit may have grown out of or been inspired by urban South African forms, but by the 1950s Zimbabwean acoustic guitarists had already transformed the temporal structure to conform to indigenous Shona musical preferences for compound-duple rhythms. It was this transformation, in combination with the South African harmonic progression, that signaled the birth of contemporary jit as a unique genre. As described later in this chapter, these itinerant acoustic guitarists typically came out of rural villages and traveled constantly between the rural areas, provincial towns, and cities, playing for tips. Unlike middle-class "concert" and jazz performers, these acoustic guitarists (and their lower-class patrons) were grounded in indigenous Shona aesthetics and yet were acutely aware of urban styles. They were thus the group most likely to have created jit, and they were also a likely source for diffusing urban musical ideas, and terms like *jit,* to the rural areas.

Around the time that the term *jit* was becoming current as slang in Harare (1950s), it was also being taken up in the villages of Mashonaland East and Central. For a number of villages that I have information about, it appears that the term was superimposed on preexisting recreational dance traditions that originally had different names. In Nyamutubu, Murehwa, for example, people told me that what is now called *jiti* was formerly known as *serenda.* In Reason Muskwe's area of Uzumba, they called young people's informal dance parties *choir,* and he said that the songs, drumming, and dance done at such occasions are what people now call jit (Zim93-73: 1). Patrick Nyandoro, who grew up in a village near the town of Murehwa, said that in his area what is now known as jit was previously called "concert." According to Nyandoro, the music was purely vocal with hand clapping at first, but people began playing drums during these informal occasions during the 1940s. The late mbira player and singer, Mondrek Muchena, told me that in his home region what became known as jit was previously called *chinungu,* although he thought that the term *jit* was already in use by the 1950s. Similar cases were reported for other villages.

From these accounts, it appears that it was the term rather than a specific musical or dance style, per se, that was adopted from the urban sphere in rural villages. A few rural people in Murehwa told me that jit dance and music came to the villages from the city: many rural people did not have guitars, so they simply played jit on drums and hosho. Since the acoustic guitarists' versions of urban South African jive, marabi, and tsaba had already been influenced by rural Shona rhythms, however, the direction of influences must, at the very least, be seen as circular.

It may be significant that in both Muskwe's and Nyandoro's villages, the name *jit* replaced what were already foreign terms to refer to recreational music, dance, and occasions. That is, the term *jit* seems to have been superimposed on what were already perceived as syncretic styles. John Kaemmer (1975: 106–7) describes jit in the rural northeastern area of Madziwa as a young people's recreational dance-drumming tradition incorporating I–IV–V harmonies; he categorizes it, along with makwaya, as 'modern' *(chimanjemanje)* music. Hence, while in some places the term *jit* was simply superimposed on preexisting indigenous musical and dance styles and occasions, elsewhere it replaced terms that already had 'modern' or urban associations.

Strikingly, the term *jit* or *jiti* was never used as a genre designation by the RBC staff for labeling the "jit-like" marabi, jive, and tsaba recordings of Zimbabwean acoustic guitarists during the 1960s. This suggests that either the term had not yet come into official or music-industry parlance, or that the guitarists were not defining their music as *jit,* a slang word at the time, for the RBC recording sessions. In fact, out of 6,833 78-rpm sides recorded by the RBC African Service Radio between the late 1950s and the early 1970s, the term *jiti* comes up only for two sides by the same rural dance-drumming group, a 1972 recording (#10534 A+B). This, and other indications discussed below, suggest that by 1972 the term *jit* had already taken on largely rural associations among urban dwellers.

*Generational Memory
and Rural Associations*

Unlike the older urban musicians interviewed in 1992–93, younger people in Harare commonly associated jit with the dancing and drumming that they had experienced in villages as children; they considered jit 'traditional' music, and typically didn't mention any South African or urban connections. For example, Bothwell Nyamhondera, musician, engineer and producer at Gramma Records in Harare, told me that "there's different forms of traditionalism. Mbukumba [dance] is the one based around the Mashingo province, and then there's the jiti. Yeah, around Murehwa . . . all traditional" (Zim93-50: 1). The young RTP (Record and Tape Production) marketing executive George Natonga said,

> Jit, to me, is music that was played by children or kids. Out there in rural areas. At night when the moon is bright, shining and you go out and sing some songs, and clap your hands and dance. That's what used to be called jit. "I'm going for jit." That means, that's where you're going to, that kind of dance. (Zim93-49: 17)

In 1968, the electric-guitar band M. D. Rhythm Success released a single, "Sevenza Nhamo Ichanya" (Gallo GB 3739), in jit style. This record featured an indigenous ngoma (tall single-headed drum) and village drumming style prominently in the mix and in a percussion solo, indicating the association of rural drumming with jit among these urban dance-band musicians by that time.

Apparently the term *jit* was not used in the music industry in Harare during the 1970s to refer to urban musical styles. For example, Steve Roskilly, a recording engineer and producer at Shed Studios in Harare, said that from the time he came on the scene in 1975 until the Bhundu Boys began to use the term *jit* for their music in the mid-1980s, "it was never bandied around within the record industry" (Zim92-20: 6). The word *jit* was maintained in the rural areas, however, explaining the rural 'traditional' associations among younger Zimbabweans. In the mid-1980s, the Bhundu Boys wanted to find a label for the music they were doing and chose jit—which by that time had its rural 'traditional' connotations. After that point it became a genre category for marketing a certain style of music played by electric-guitar bands, as well as a grassroots term in the rural areas.

Given that young urban musicians cite a rural source for electric-band jit, and given the close tempo and rhythmic resemblances between contemporary village jit and that played by the guitar bands, it seems probable that the latest wave of urban jit is indeed partially rooted in village musical style. As noted, this was already true for the acoustic guitarists of the 1950s and 1960s.

Regardless of the original South African associations with the term and the different rural, urban, and international sources for the musical style, guitar-band jit developed as a uniquely Zimbabwean genre. Jit also remains a common and vital social activity in the villages in Mashonaland East and Central. In this context it is a rather free-form social dance played in fast 12/8 meter with drums, hosho, and group singing in informal settings. The term *jit* referred as much to the type of occasion as to any set musical style.

Jit was the type of informal recreational music and event, both in rural areas and in urban beer halls, that provided a point of entry and a space for the itinerant acoustic guitarists of the 1940s, 1950s, and 1960s. It was the acoustic guitarists from Mashonaland that probably first created jit and that first adapted classical mbira pieces and other indigenous genres to this instrument. These 'box guitarists' or 'one-man bands' were thus key to the development of Zimbabwe's most unique and popular guitar-band genres.

## Early Acoustic Guitarists

Brian Chinamhora traces the emergence of Zimbabwean urban-popular music to Zimbabweans' adoption of several European instruments, including the zither, the banjo, the harmonica, and the accordion in the 1930s (1987: 261).[10] As part of this same development, the acoustic guitar became a major instrument for Zimbabwean musicians by the mid-1940s. Kenneth Mattaka suggested that these instruments were first brought to Zimbabwe by returning migrant workers from South Africa, and he corroborates Chinamhora's account that guitars became common in Zimbabwe somewhat later than the other instruments mentioned (Zim93-96: 1–2).

### The Itinerant Guitarists

While guitars were used in middle-class "concert" and African jazz groups, in this chapter we are concerned with the distinct realm of itinerant acoustic guitarists who moved between rural areas and cities playing for tips at beer halls or for hire for farm owners and mining company bosses. Many worked as laborers on the farms or mines and would entertain the other workers at night. Sinyoro Jackson Chinemberi, for example, told me how in the mid-1950s his farmer-employers would pay him three dollars to play guitar, accompanied by hosho, at all-night

dances for the other workers (Zim93-72: 2). Like many acoustic guitarists, Chinemberi also worked his own subsistence plot in the Tribal
Trust Lands but would travel at off-times to earn cash playing guitar at
"tea-parties" (gatherings where liquor was sold), in beer halls, on trains,
and on the street in towns. In rural areas such as Murehwa, the guitarists also played in ad hoc 'nightclubs'; temporary walls were erected in
an open area, and an entrance-fee was charged to drink and listen to the
guitarist inside.

These acoustic guitarists were thus mobile peasants and members
of the agrarian and industrial work force; the audiences for this music
were from the same classes. Along with Police Band musicians, these
itinerant guitarists comprised one of the first sizable groups of Zimbabwean musicians to seriously consider music as a cash-generating activity. Among conservative indigenous villagers, Christians, and members of the African middle-class, these itinerant guitarists often suffered
from being stereotyped as drunkards, woman chasers, and marginal
characters, a status they still have today.[11]

Gallo Records sent up mobile recording units from South Africa to
record Zimbabwean guitarists, especially musicians based in Bulawayo
like George Sibanda (Mhungu Zim93-87: 6). During the 1950s and
1960s the African Radio Service in Zambia and Zimbabwe recorded a
large number of acoustic guitarists, indicating that this music was both
widespread and popular. From the recordings still available, it appears
that by the late-1950s the acoustic guitar, usually a Gallotone model
from South Africa, had all but replaced zithers, manufactured banjos,[12]
and harmonicas as the instrument of choice for itinerant musicians. A
handful of accordionists (both piano and button varieties) were still
performing during the 1960s and still perform today, but in the heyday
of the 'box guitarists,' from the late 1940s to the mid-1970s, there must
have been a great number of players in Zimbabwe. I know of seventy-
five Shona and Ndebele acoustic guitarists whose recordings, made
between 1958 and 1972, are housed in the National Archives of Zimbabwe. I assume that there were many more guitarists who did not
record for the RBC African Service Radio or for Gallo S.A. during this
period.[13]

### Style and Repertory

My interview data supports Chinamhora's suggestion that the early
guitarists began by playing the local village music that they had grown
up with. In the course of their careers some would expand their repertories to include various international styles (1987: 261–62). Country

music from the United States was the foreign style that was most influential early on. Chinemberi, Mattaka, guitarist Jacob Mhungu, and others told me that the early guitar players were influenced specifically by Jimmie Rodger's records, originally diffused from South Africa. "The people who used to play guitars were adopting the Jimmie Rodgers style. Yodeling, and all that, that was also common" (Mattaka, Zim93-96: 1). South African urban styles (jive, tsaba, marabi) were also adapted by the guitarists. By the late 1950s, as Cuban-influenced Congolese rumba and chacha became popular in central Africa, these genres too were performed by Zimbabwean acoustic guitarists.

Since the guitarists often played for tips or were paid a few coins to play a requested song, some became outstanding, versatile entertainers with large repertories and varied performance gimmicks at their command. Some, like Mhungu, updated their style and repertories as fashions (and requests) changed. Others, like Chinemberi, specialized in a single guitar technique and style, and maintained it over many years. Many of the acoustic guitarists composed their own songs using formulaic melodies, and lyrics that combined original lines or strophes with a common stock of lines based on widely known Shona proverbs, images, and themes. There never was a single, unified, Zimbabwean acoustic guitar style or repertory, but rather a plethora of approaches. In what follows I discuss some of the major performers, stylistic trends, and guitar techniques with the understanding that individual players might cross stylistic lines and genre boundaries.

## Guitar Styles Derived
### from the Americas

Jeremiah Kainga was among the first generation of Zimbabwean acoustic guitarists recording between the late 1940s and the early 1960s. Kainga recorded two styles primarily: country guitar, based on Jimmie Rodgers, and blues. Although a few Zimbabwean acoustic guitarists played with a plectrum, Kainga, like the vast majority, played with a two-finger right-hand technique—thumb (T) and first finger (1st). On the songs based on U.S. country music, he performed a simple bass(T)-strum(1st), alternate bass-strum pattern, sometimes inserting the trademark Jimmie Rodgers strumming pattern at cadences. Kainga mainly borrowed the country guitar style while maintaining his own rich, smooth, baritone vocal style with only a trace of "country" twang and no Rodgers yodeling. His melodies and chord progressions were somewhat erratic and original, as compared both to American country music and other Zimbabwean guitarists.[14]

A number of Zimbabwean acoustic guitarists followed the American model more closely. For example, "Ndakamirira Nguva," by Clement Jumira and Amon Pikaita, is a North American country-style tune and includes an exact imitation of Rodgers's strumming style and yodeling;[15] Phinias Tshawe's "Whisper Your Mother's Name" is an even closer imitation of Rodger's guitar, melodic, and vocal style, including yodeling.[16]

Although Jordan Chataika started his career later (1960s–70s), he was one of the most important Zimbabwean guitarists; he first played acoustic and later electric guitar. Chataika primarily performed country music and country gospel. The hymn roots of American country music made it both familiar to Zimbabweans and attractive to Christians like Chataika; he had many predecessors and contemporaries in the country and gospel lines, including Israel Tendayi, John White, Elias Timba, Peter Lewanika, Lovemore Dambaza, Baboth Bomba, and John Zimonte.

Blues was also sometimes played by Zimbabwean solo acoustic guitarists. Along with his country tunes, this was Jeremiah Kainga's other major recorded genre. Rather than using standard eight-, twelve-, or sixteen-bar blues progressions, however, Kainga's blues pieces consisted of standard boogie bass riffs played over the tonic chord for vocal sections, with other chords occasionally being introduced during instrumental interludes.[17] While other Zimbabwean acoustic guitarists played some blues-based pieces, this was a minority style as compared to country and gospel. By the end of the 1950s, a number of guitarists also recorded rumbas, complete with someone tapping the Cuban *son* clave part on a bottle and the performance of a 3 + 3 + 2 bass line on the guitar. This, too, remained a minority style among acoustic guitarists, although it was simultaneously all the rage among urban dance bands and "concert" ensembles.

### The "Common Practice"
### Acoustic Guitar Style

Some of Kainga's more famous contemporaries of the 1940s and 1950s, including Josaya Hadebe and George Sibanda, developed styles that were much less idiosyncratic and less directly imitative of American and other foreign models. Hadebe and Sibanda represent a distinctive yet widely diffused African approach to acoustic guitar resembling West African palmwine, East African guitar playing, and Congolese acoustic guitar styles.[18] In fact, Hadebe's playing is very similar to one of the best-known Congolese acoustic guitarists—Jean Bosco Mwenda, who was recorded by Hugh Tracey in 1949. There appears to be a direct link: Bosco Mwenda has cited the early Zimbabwean guitarists among his first influences (Wald 1992: 11).[19] Hadebe and Sibanda, Gallo recording artists, may well have been among these influences.

Like Jean Bosco Mwenda, Hadebe and Sibanda played with the two-finger right-hand technique. The thumb played a strong, driving (downbeat) bass part—either playing the roots of chords, or at times playing more independent bass lines. The first finger was sometimes used for picking clear, chord-based melodic and harmonic parts in the high strings, and was sometimes used for strumming the higher strings. In this guitar style, a repetitive chord progression (e.g., I–IV–I–V; I–IV–I–IV; I–V) functioned as an ostinato for the vocal melody, and the pieces are often in simple duple meter. These musicians tend to play in the keys of C and G in first position, allowing for extra melodic activity on the first two strings with the first and fourth fingers of the left hand. Unlike Sibanda, with his smooth, controlled vocal style, Hadebe sang with a louder, somewhat harsher voice, and, in the tradition of itinerant musicians, would sometimes include comic falsetto effects, laughter, and speaking parts over the guitar ostinato.

Later performers in this "common practice" style from the 1960s, such as Fidelis Magomere and Soche Dube, commonly emphasize plucking rather than strumming. Whereas Sibanda and Hadebe often plucked only ornamental figures in the high strings, Magomere, Dube, and others typically pluck the entire sung melody on the high strings of the guitar in unison with the voice and against the independent bass part. For these performers, then, the use of the guitar becomes more melodic and polyphonic in conception.

Listening to recordings of this guitar style with experienced Zimbabwean musicians such as mbira players Chris Mhlanga and Tute Chigamba, it became clear that while it was not associated in their minds with indigenous Zimbabwean genres, they considered the style uniquely Zimbabwean. Mr. Mhlanga, for example, told me that Sibanda's style was 'traditional' in the sense that it was absolutely typical of rural acoustic guitarists in Zimbabwe. He said, "It is not a style that is played elsewhere, and it was not used in the cities, it was not a part of the urban jive" (p.c. 5 March 1993, fieldbook III: 49). While to my ear the Sibanda-Hadebe line resembles more widely diffused African acoustic guitar music like West African palmwine and Congolese styles, Mhlanga's comments suggest that Zimbabweans consider it an emergent, syncretic style original to their country.

## Indigenous-Based Guitar Music

The most important forerunners to the indigenous-based guitar bands of the 1970s and 1980s were a group of acoustic guitarists who specialized in performing local Shona music. This was the group that transformed South African jive and tsaba into jit. Judging from available recordings, this group of guitarists was numerically the largest as compared to those in the Sibanda-Hadebe line and those who imitated American styles.

The great majority of acoustic guitarists grew up in the rural areas, and even guitarists who later turned to other styles frequently began by performing their local village music. The well-known guitarist from Masvingo Province, Jacob Mhungu, for example, told me that he had been a *chipendani* (bow) and lamellophone (probably *njari*) player in his rural home, but in 1949 was inspired to take up the guitar after he had seen movies with country and western performer Tex Ritter at a mission school. He taught himself to play guitar, first on a homemade instrument with a tin-can sound box, and later on his uncle's Gallotone guitar. Unlike many Zimbabwean guitarists, he developed a three-finger right-hand technique, and invented his own tunings. He soon turned to country music, and later to African jazz, but he also remembers doing a lamellophone piece and other local-village songs on acoustic guitar during 1950 and 1951.

During the 1950s and 1960s, Zimbabwean acoustic guitarists performed the whole gamut of indigenous genres, including drum, mbira, and matepe songs used in ceremonies for the spirits; weddings songs; beer songs; war songs; threshing songs; story songs; and game songs, among others. They would arrange the guitar accompaniment to the original or slightly modified melodies and texts. Like guitarists in the other styles, they would typically play with two fingers in the right hand, either strumming chords or plucking melodies, or both, with the first finger against a driving bass part (usually the roots of chords on main beats, e.g., the dotted quarter in 12/8) played with the thumb. Many of the great performers in this style, including Marko Takaingofa, Ngwaru Mapundu, Pamidze Benhura, and John Nkomo sometimes fingered the chords with the left hand, but frequently they played with a slide, or bottleneck—a piece of metal or glass used to slide over and stop the strings. When playing bottleneck, they typically tuned their guitars to open G (D, G, D, G, b, d) allowing them to pluck parallel fifths, fourths, and octaves in keeping with typical indigenous Shona harmonies. Also well matched to indigenous aesthetics, the bottleneck technique produces a buzzy timbre (the strings vibrate under, and sound against, the slide).[20] Zimbabweans produced a sound with the slide more akin to rougher delta-blues players in the United States in contrast to the smoother style of country or Hawaiian slide guitar. Nonetheless, the few Zimbabwean musicians who had an opinion on the matter stated that the technique had been learned by listening to American country music and to Hawaiian music (e.g., Mhungu Zim93-87: 7), and that these influences had come up through South Africa, which was the diffusion point for foreign recordings.

Although some of the indigenous genres required the guitarists to play in simple duple or triple meter, the majority of indigenous-styled pieces were performed in 12/8 with a feel that would presently be identified as jit. As I explained earlier, while many of the guitarists of the 1950s and 1960s referred to this music using South African terms like tsaba-tsaba, jive, and marabi interchangeably, musicians hearing the RBC recordings in 1992–93 immediately identified the music as jit. Pre-existing indigenous songs of many types were fit to the jit rhythm and to cyclical chord progressions (e.g., I–IV–I–V, I–V, I–IV–I–I). Dance-drumming songs performed 'outside the house' at *guva* ceremonies, weddings, and other social occasions were a type commonly fit to jit-style accompaniment—thus linking this guitar style, and jit itself, to village social dancing.

Music usually played on the Zezuru mbira was also adapted to the acoustic guitar, usually using slide technique. Plucking parallel fourths and fifths, standard mbira harmonic progressions in four 12/8 phrases (e.g., G, B, D / G, B, E / G, C, E / A, C, E) were performed *without* the major and minor thirds that would be added by later electric-guitar band musicians. This type of guitar arrangement was used to accompany ceremonial songs such as "Karigamombe" and "Baya wa Baya" (e.g., John Nkomo's "Haruna" RBC #9544A). Other ceremonial music was adapted to the guitar as well. For example, in 1967 Ngwaru Mapundu recorded "Uya Uone Zvinoita Mhondoro" (full text: "Come and see what the 'Lion-Spirit' is doing") for the RBC (#9909A). According to Chris Mhlanga, this was originally a ritual song from western Mashonaland accompanied by drums. There were also relatively rare experiments of adapting other instrumental styles to the guitar. James Cubai, from southern Zimbabwe, for example, imitated a musical bow for his "Shangaan Guitar and Vocal" piece "Deva" (Columbia YE6011).[21]

## Acoustic Guitar Music, Nationalism, and Modernity

As the practice of performing indigenous Shona music on acoustic guitar emerged, it had nothing to do with national sentiment or a conscious program of cultural reformism. Guitarists simply, and quite un-self-consciously, adapted the music that they and their audiences knew and liked to a new instrument. This point is worth underlining. These acoustic guitarists were doing basically the same things that would later be consciously connected to reformism, national sentiment, nationalism, and professional career goals. That is, they were combining indigenous Shona and cosmopolitan musical elements in guitar performance: this was the basis of the gallop in 1963, and of Mapfumo's music after 1974. Yet the acoustic guitarists' performance of indigenous music preceded mass-cultural nationalism and apparently did not involve such meanings and motivations.

What is less clear is how colonial ideologies of modernity influenced early acoustic guitar players. Generally, it has been assumed that Zimbabweans were drawn to guitar because of the prestige of western culture (e.g., Kaemmer 1989; Brown 1994; Zindi 1985), and in some cases this may be true. Yet for rural guitarists, I am not convinced that the inculcation of modernist values can be simply assumed, even when a Tex Ritter movie was the original inspiration for learning the guitar. There are other reasons why a rural lamellophone or bow player like Mhungu might be attracted to the guitar beyond the lure of modernity. For example, it is louder than the bow, it is more versatile than the bow, and in some ways even than the mbira or njari. For providing simple accompaniment, the guitar is certainly easier to learn and play than mbira or njari. Mhungu indicated that he was attracted to the guitar because everyone was playing 'mbira' (lamellophones), and he wanted to be different. S. J. Chinemberi and several others interviewed said that they took up the guitar simply because they liked it. Such explanations do not take us very far.

While my sources provided a good general picture of the early itinerant guitarists,[22] they cannot address the subtle questions of why individuals might have been attracted to the guitar in the first place. My impression is that previous scholars do not have any more data than I do pertaining to this issue; thus blanket associations of the guitar with modernity should at least be questioned, as Kaufmann (1970, 1975) has already suggested.

I do know that when interviewing "concert" performers and ballroom dancers, ideas about modernity, the prestige of European culture, and images of sophistication and refinement were very consciously and openly attached to these middle-class traditions (see chapter 4). This was not true for the relatively few older acoustic guitarists that I spoke with about their choice of instrument—no one voiced such connections. Moreover, in the hands of itinerant 'one-man bands' the acoustic guitar had negative associations among the African middle class. These issues at least raise questions about any unitary modernist meaning or prestige attached to this instrument.[23]

### Song Texts

Performers like Takaingofa, Mapundu, Nkomo, and Benhura, who specialized in jit-based pieces and other local Shona genres, sang in typical village style using the *huro* (high yodeling), low *mahon'era,* and speech-like *kudeketara* techniques (see Berliner 1978: 115). Their song texts, which were a combination of standard formulaic lines and original lyrics, covered a wide range of topics, and served a number of functions for the performer as well as audience. Marko Takaingofa's piece "HwaHwa Hwemuno" (RBC #804B, 1960), is a jit piece played without slide. Some of the translation of this mosaic-styled text follows:

> There is plenty of beer here
> It is just not being given out
> Like it's coming from far away. (×2)
>
> Husband you astound me
> Husband you are mischievous
> You left the child in the fields
> Uprooting trees.
>
> Husband you astound me
> You are grossly irresponsible
> You left the child working the fields
> Uprooting trees.
>
> It is a song sung by the elderly
> When they are drunk and staggering
> When they enjoy singing
> They will be __?__ .
>
> I liked the song very much
> If you play it to the elderly
> Even a hidden pot of beer
> Will be taken out and offered
> To the people to drink.
>
> It [beer] is plentiful here.
> It is as if it is in a very deep hole
> Which is out of reach.

Variants of these same verses follow. In this beer song Takaingofa offers criticism of the hosts' lack of generosity as well as a moralist commentary on lazy husbands who leave their children unattended while drinking. As a musician who played for tips and drinks, the last two verses may be a hint to patrons to be generous with him.

In a narrative song Takaingofa discusses difficulties young people have getting married in traditional Shona society:

> Tell me tell me
> There is nothing (×4)
> Tell me tell me
> Why you rejected me
> There's nothing
> Tell me tell me
> There is nothing (×6)
> There was a certain boy
> Who was in love with a girl
> He loved the girl so much
> And the girl so much loved him
> They loved each other
>
> Now the boy got into a serious problem
> When he decided to marry
> The girl sincerely loved him
> He realized that he was in difficulties
> He said "What shall I do with her?"
> The parents will not accept marriage
> Without me paying the bridewealth
> Now the boy was clever
> He said "I will not tell the girl
> That I no longer love her"
> I'll tell her some other reasons
> Of course that was not good
> Now the boy did well
> He realized that if he took too long
> Deceiving this poor girl
> Well knowing that he couldn't afford
> The bride-wealth
> It could cause a crisis later on.
> Tell me the reason
> There's nothing (×18).

Guitar players applied this type of moralizing message to various sorts of problems. The great guitarist Ngwaru Mapundu sings, "I can't be proposed to by a loafer / With boots sewn with wire / I can't be proposed to by a drunkard / With pockets full of beer / Wire wire wire wire wire wire / He is full of wire (×2) / He has come he has come / Ngwaru Ngwaru has come" ("Rona" RBC # 10522B, 1971). Another standard feature of these texts is the high degree of repetition of a given line or set of lines. Indeed, the text of Ali Vintiware's song "Nyoka Mumba" simply consists of the repetition of a single couplet, "If you see a snake in the house / There are some rats" and variations of this line (RBC #1082A, 1960).

Another of Takaingofa's songs in jit style, "Chaminingwa" (RBC #1841, 1961), repeats the common theme of losing one's parents or being alone in the world: "All my kinsmen died, [vocables] / Who will I dance with / [vocables] . . . / Who will I share my troubles with?" This theme, incidently, was used by Thomas Mapfumo, reinterpreted as a political song in the late 1970s, although here it did not have political connotations.[24]

Mosaic-formulaic texts are common in village singing and among the guitar players who specialized in indigenous music. John Nkomo's "Haruna," a slide-guitar version of an mbira piece similar to "Karigamombe," has the following mosaic-style text:

He has no mother, [vocables] (×3).
Swearing by my mother.
Dance.
He has no mother, [vocables].
You Rahwadigwa, don't dance haphazardly,
Dance properly,
We are doing this for our deceased friend.
Oh my kin, I'm performing a dance that attracts my future wife.
He has no mother, [vocables]
. . . . . . . . . . . . . . . . . . . . . . . . .
This is dire poverty, [vocables].
. . . . . . . . . . . . . . . . . . . . . . . . .
This is the Shangara dance of our fathers
    which was commonly done at home during beer parties where beer
    was sold.

The same kinds of text themes and forms were common within the other acoustic guitar styles as well. In fact, it is not possible to strictly correlate specific types of texts or topics with a given guitar style. For example, in 1966, Jordan Chataika used an American, country-based tune and guitar style to accompany a plea to an ancestral spirit: "Great ancestor don't be vindictive / Don't kill your children / Others are happy / Great ancestor don't be vengeful." In the style of indigenous Shona performance, the entire text is a repetition of this stanza, with variants. Conversely, lyrics about 'modern' topics such as motor cars or trips to Johannesburg might be set to an indigenous tune.

In general, Shona acoustic guitarists drew on the same common stock of text lines, themes, and forms as other indigenous performers and as later guitar-band composers would. The acoustic guitarists' lyrics often touched on hardships and poverty, and even occasionally commented on race relations. These songs, however, offered no political solutions. One thing that does change with the guitar bands of the 1970s is the common insertion of political commentary into popular songs.

A few of the 'box guitarists' went on to become popular band musicians and to produce political as well as other types of songs in the 1970s. For example, in 1978 Jordan Chataika recorded "Tirwireiwo Mwari" with his electric band, the Highway Stars. In this song he asks Mwari [the Creator] to "Fight for us, for we might perish," and says, "What you did in Maputo [referring to Mozambique's independence] / Come and do likewise here in Zimbabwe." Chataika also continued to record popular gospel and country songs with his band during the 1970s. Most of the acoustic guitarists, however, did not adapt to the times and simply slipped into obscurity as electric-guitar bands rose in popularity in the late 1960s.[25]

After the 1970s, boys in the townships and rural areas may still have begun their careers with homemade guitars or manufactured acoustic instruments, but they have tended to see this mainly as a stepping stone to the real thing—an electric guitar to be played in a band so that they can make records and travel to England, Japan, and the United States, like Thomas Mapfumo.

### Early Electric Guitar Bands and Cosmopolitan Youth Culture

By the second half of the 1960s electric-guitar bands had replaced the "concert" ensembles in popularity, and the acoustic guitarists were on their way out. Rock and roll and Congolese rumba—two foreign musical styles which featured electric guitars, bass, and drum kit—were becoming extremely popular in Harare by the early 1960s, and were important inspirations for the shift. In the late 1960s a third influence on Zimbabwean guitar bands, *mbaqanga* from South Africa, took the country by storm.

### *Mbaqanga and Congolese Rumba*

Mbaqanga is a South African style accompanied by electric guitars, bass, traps, and often saxophones. The music is typically in simple duple meter, in moderate tempo, and based on repeated harmonic progressions using the tonic, subdominant, and dominant chords, or bow-inspired pieces involving the alternation of chords a step apart. Mbaqanga music is marked by an extremely prominent bass line, and it was this feature that most influenced Zimbabwean band music. This instrumental style was typically used to back vocal-dance groups like the Mahotella Queens, with two or more female singer-dancers and a male "growler." [26] Ensembles of this type toured Zimbabwe in the mid- to late-1960s. While the female singer-dancers generated the most excitement and popularity for mbaqanga groups, approaches to bass playing had the more lasting influence on Zimbabwean guitar bands.

Congolese guitar music—*kwasa kwasa,* or simply 'rumba,' as it is often called—has been a prominent music tradition in Zimbabwe since the late 1950s. The style emerged from the Democratic Republic of the Congo (formerly Zaire) and is now known internationally as *soukous,* although this term is not commonly used in Zimbabwe. During my visits to Zimbabwe in the 1990s, Congolese guitar music resonated throughout the townships and black middle-class neighborhoods constantly and was one of the most popular styles in the country. Internationally acclaimed artists like Kanda Bongo Man as well as lesser-known groups performed regularly in Harare, and a weekly television program was dedicated to this music.

Congolese guitar bands began coming to Harare in the late 1950s because of better economic conditions there. Their effect on the local music scene was so pronounced that Brian Chinamhora has claimed that the Congolese guitar bands' "highly successful performances heralded the decline of Zimbabwe's popular music for the following 15 years." He goes on to suggest that "to survive, Zimbabwean artists had no option but to abandon their own music and switch to playing rumba" (1987: 263). These are overstatements, because most bands, even those from the Democratic Republic of the Congo, played a variety of music, including rumba, chachacha, the twist, rock and roll, soul, and local Zimbabwean genres by the second half of the 1960s. Chinamhora's statements, however, do underline the important and lasting influence of Congolese 'rumba' in Zimbabwe. According to Jackson Phiri, a member of an early rumba group in Harare, the Congolese musicians were initially influential in Zimbabwe because they arrived with a highly developed approach to electric guitar performance as compared to the youthful local electric guitarists of the mid-1960s (Zim93-40: 7).

One early Congolese ensemble that settled in Harare in the 1960s was the Lipopo Jazz Band. Coming from Leopoldville (Kinshasha), Lipopo sought their fortune in Zambia's Copperbelt and in Lusaka before settling in Harare in 1964 (*Parade* 1964: 55). They were originally an

eight-piece, guitar-based band led by Joseph Mudendi that, at first, sang
in Lingala and played rumba in the Congolese style of the late 1950s
and early 1960s. At that time many of the features of the Cuban *son* (the
basis of Congolese rumba) were still explicitly stated, such as the classic
son clave pattern, the 3 + 3 + 2 bass line, and a two-part form with a
verse-chorus section followed by a responsorial *montuno* section. These
features were combined with long, sweet, lyrical guitar lines played over
accompanying guitar ostinatos.[27]

Once they decided to settle in Harare, Lipopo recruited local singers
such as Jackson Phiri (a lifelong Malawian resident in Harare) to sing
in various languages, including English, Shona, and Chewa. Phiri was
also experienced in composing and singing rock and roll, soul, South
African kwela, and local genres from Zimbabwe and Malawi. Lipopo's
repertory was thus expanded to appeal to a wide range of tastes in their
long stint at the Federal Hotel in Harare. When the Congolese members
of Lipopo were deported in 1969, Phiri took over direction of the ensemble. It later was one of the first groups to play classical mbira music
in an electric-guitar-band format, and under Phiri's direction Lipopo
became the training ground for several prominent Zimbabwean guitarists (see chapter 8).

### Rock and Roll and the Rise
### of "Youth Culture"

"Concert" groups wishing to remain current, like De Black Evening Follies, were already incorporating rock and roll into their acts with good
imitations of Elvis and Jerry Lee Lewis by 1959. For "concert" and African jazz ensembles, performing rock and roll was simply a continuation of their general practice of imitating North American–based and
cosmopolitan music trends—something they had always done.

The rise of Zimbabwean rock and roll bands as distinctive entities,
however, was linked to the spread of 1960s cosmopolitan youth culture
and the broader post-World War II phenomenon of conceptualizing
youth as a separate cultural category. Although initiated in places like
the United States, Britain, and Europe, these trends fit my conception of
cosmopolitanism precisely in that they were diffused among and had
similar effects in local sites of production throughout Latin America,
Africa, Japan, and many other places.

Because of strict age hierarchies in indigenous Shona societies, there
was (and often still is) a general feeling that young people should be seen
and not heard. While there might always have been some grumbling

about the shortcomings of young people among the elders (a universal phenomenon?), in Shona societies "youth" had not been conceptualized as a distinctive cultural category with separate mores, tastes, and styles before the 1960s. Early in the decade, however, a new social definition of urban "youth" or "teen" culture emerged in Zimbabwe as something apart; the Zimbabwean version fit cosmopolitan models in the use of rock and roll music and dance as focal points of distinction and identity.

During the 1950s, urban-popular musical styles like jazz and "concert" did not mark generation-gap distinctions. In 1959, for example, an *African Parade* music writer noted that "jazz seems to have come to stay, and it has made its powerful appeal to the old as well as to the young" (1959a: 14). Likewise, in 1964, a *Parade* music writer commented that "teens and oldsters alike" shared an interest in jazz. But this writer went on to say that when the Lipopo Jazz Band performed rock and roll, they were specifically "trying to give youth some sense of belonging to a musical group which helps youth to escape from the domination of adults." Echoing the generation-gap discourse of the North American and British press, he noted that "there has been talk that rock and roll annoys most parents in the suburbs" (*Parade* 1964: 56).

Another *Parade* reporter hinted at the emergence of a separate teen identity in the black townships. Describing the "teen-time" dances organized in Mbare, Highfield, and other township recreation halls every weekend during the early months of 1963, he says, "I am sure you all remember the first time that teen-time, the whites' side of it, appeared on television. . . . But six months after that somebody thought that it would be grand if someone provided the African teens with their own teen-time, although it would never get on to television (*Parade* 1963a: 15). He went on to describe the rock and roll, twist, and chachacha at "teen-time" dances in the townships, and the sloppy dress of the teens. Similar to press coverage of teen activities elsewhere, the *Parade* writer commented on how drinking and sexual activity were becoming a problem at these events, which, he felt, needed *much* more supervision.

In the course of the 1960s, early rock and roll, the twist, and R&B artists like Ray Charles gave way to the Beatles and North American rock and soul artists of the late 1960s and 1970s as primary influences. This shift was accompanied by the new imagery and discourses of hippie and African-American countercultures. In Zimbabwe, hippie and "Afro" clothing and hair styles were adopted by urban Zimbabwean youth, along with a new interest in smoking locally grown *dagga* (marijuana) and institutions such as rock festivals. The bands that played the festivals took names that were inspired by cosmopolitan youth culture and that emphasized the generation gap, freedom, and love—the "Odd Generation," "The Gipsy Band," "Love Generation." The Zimbabwean festivals were directly compared with their famous forerunners at Woodstock and the Isle of Wight in the local press (e.g., *Parade* 1971b: 34).

Around 1970, in keeping with liberal hippiedom, rock festivals in Zimbabwe became large-scale, multiracial affairs attended by "Africans, Europeans, Asians, and Coloureds." [28] Whether because of their multiracial character, or worries about pot smoking and rebellious behavior, the festivals drew major criticism in the white press and from rightist Rhodesian Front MPs (see *Parade* 1971b: 34).

During and soon after this period when the Love Generation was getting it together at multiracial rock festivals, white and black youth began to be recruited and trained to kill one another in ever greater numbers as the Liberation War intensified. Perhaps partially inspired by hippie ethics, there was resistance to the Rhodesian war effort among some white youth. I found a few rather quirky 1970s antiwar songs performed by white bands in the National Archives, and heard stories about white resistance to joining the army, although I do not have any accurate sources for assessing the size of this phenomenon.

Multiracial events and bands decreased in visibility after the early 1970s, but they did not disappear entirely. Even during 1976, approaching the hottest period of the war, there were a few multiracial bands like Soul & Blues Union, a Harare-based ensemble that performed soul and motown, South African mbaqanga, and Jamaican reggae. The band incorporated aspects of North American youth culture as well as black power discourses, and the leader of the group, Boykie, was quoted in 1976 as saying, "We are primarily a soul group. Soul music is Black music, and Black music is beautiful." The band wanted to convey the message that "music has no colour bar" (*Prize* 1976: 6). By identifying with blacks, the two white members of Soul & Blues Union may have represented a minority among Rhodesian youth, but we are reminded again of the heterogeneity of white racial attitudes.

### Youth Culture and
### Musical Professionalism

Images from cosmopolitan "youth culture"—the Beatles, North American rock stars of the late 1960s—were instrumental in fostering dreams of professional music careers and of wealth and international stardom among young Zimbabweans. Previously the idea of a full-time professional career in music was simply not part of most people's common-sense view of what was possible or even desirable. As more and more musicians in Britain and the United States assumed the status of culture heroes and became famous for the wealth they earned through music (the Beatles were particularly important in this regard), ideologies of what it meant to be a musician shifted throughout cosmopolitan popular music circles, including the urban youth of Zimbabwe. This new association of musical performance with wealth had significant consequences because it was accompanied by an expansion of the local record industry in Zimbabwe.

Whereas the cream of the "concert" and 'jazz' bands had made some commercial recordings with South African firms, primarily Gallo, as well as with the noncommercial RBC, the first Zimbabwean record company did not emerge until 1959. In that year, Teal Record Company (Central Africa), Ltd. was incorporated in Bulawayo on 23 September, in association with Lonrho (Teal later becomes Gramma Records). Gallo Records (SA) opened Musical Distributors (Private), Ltd. in Bulawayo on 5 December 1962, which became Gallo (Rhodesia) (Private) Ltd. on 1 July 1972 (the name was changed to Zimbabwe Music Corporation [ZMC], Ltd. in June 1985).[29] During the 1970s, local record production and promotion, especially of 45s, was greatly expanded by these companies in Zimbabwe. The companies were searching for new local African talent and markets; this helped create the sense that there was a future in the music business, especially among younger musicians.

Popular music researcher Joyce Makwenda has stated that professionalism in Zimbabwean popular music really begins with the "Mapfumo-M'tukudzi generation."[30] It was precisely this generation that was so strongly influenced by the cosmopolitan youth culture phenomenon of the 1960s. The large and rather unrealistic number of people presently trying to work as full-time musicians and dancers in Harare is the result.[31] Thus, it was not just cosmopolitan musical styles that were influential in Zimbabwe; rather, it was the whole image complex linking music with money and status that, perhaps just as profoundly, altered musical values and practices among young people around Harare. Along with the earlier change in the liquor laws, the opening of new African nightclubs, and the emergence of the local recording industry, it was this ideological shift that helped spur the boom of music professionalism and, ultimately, the desire to enter the transnational music market.

## Electric Bands
## and the Adaptation of
## Indigenous Music, 1966–1970

By the mid-1960s, making a living with music had entered the realm of the possible and the desirable. Cosmopolitan youth culture also inspired a new demand for Zimbabwean musicians to develop original styles and material. This shift, in conjunction with music professionalism, influenced the course of popular musical developments in important ways.

Within the "concert" and jazz traditions, Zimbabwean popular musicians had largely imitated foreign styles; moreover faithful reproduction, not originality, had been valued as a result of cultural competence ('civilization'). The "concert" performers I spoke with, even those who did compose, did not place much emphasis on composition. The valuing of reproduction rather than originality was more common in indigenous Shona societies as well, although for different reasons. In indigenous ceremonial contexts, for example, it was (and is) important to play older music faithfully in ways familiar to the ancestors, rather than new compositions and styles, in order to bring spirits into a ceremony (T. Chigamba, p.c., March 1993).[32]

In 1960s cosmopolitan youth culture, however, a unique style and original compositions became necessary for artistic standing. While this trend began in the rock world with people like Buddy Holly and Chuck Berry, Bob Dylan and the Beatles served as more famous models for the host of emergent singer-songwriters and rock composer-musicians. Following suit, after the mid-1960s, Zimbabwean music critics, musicians, and fans increasingly demanded originality from local artists as a prerequisite for artistic standing.

This emphasis on originality inspired some young Zimbabweans to turn to local indigenous sources. In 1966 nineteen year-old Rocky Costain Jabvurayi of Highfield was bent on a professional career as a guitarist singer-songwriter. As reported by *Parade* music writer Biz Kameat, Rocky was

> filling the vacuum in music which local artists have failed to fill because their music has not been theirs. They relied on popular hit parade songs [covering foreign music], rather than creating something they can claim [to] be their own.
>
> For, at 19, Rocky is setting a pattern whereby he hopes one day to be a boss on his own. *Selling his music at prices which can enable him to make a living of his own.* . . . He says, "I want to be the first African composer in Rhodesia who makes good."

The two brothers [Rocky plays guitar and sings with his brother Freddie] hope *to make it in the big time* soon, and Rocky's main ambition, is to *compose African traditional music* so that it too can last more generations to come. (Kameat 1966b: 40; my emphasis)

Apparently Rocky's career never took off, and he slipped into obscurity.[33] I wonder how many other young people of that time, who did not happen to get picked up by the media, shared Rocky's ambitions. Rocky's goal, however, illustrates that the idea of "making it big" in a music career was becoming more common by the mid-1960s. Indeed, most of the young guitar-band musicians discussed below for the 1966–70 period shared similar aspirations in contrast to the previous generation of "concert" performers. Rocky's comments also suggest that musicians were beginning to turn to indigenous music as a viable source for original material and style, and that he thought 'traditional' style would give his compositions longevity. The *Parade* article also makes it clear that Rocky's motivations for turning to indigenous musical sources were largely professional and artistic. Thomas Mapfumo and other big stars of the 1970s developed this same logic and course of action about a decade later (see chapter 8), but even in 1966, Rocky was not alone in hitting on this strategy for achieving professional success. Between 1966 and 1970 a number of electric-guitar bands recorded indigenous Shona songs along with rock, rumba, and South African genres.

The programs of music reformism during the Federation period set the stage for "concert" groups and jazz bands to incorporate indigenous pieces into their repertories by the end of the 1950s. From the 1950s on, indigenous music played on acoustic guitars could be heard frequently in beer halls and on African Service Radio. There had been the mass celebrations of cultural nationalism between 1960 and 1963 and the flash-in-the-pan gallop in 1963. By the mid-1960s, the general effects of Federation reformism and cultural nationalism came together with young musicians' professional aspirations and search for originality to support the inclusion of indigenous music within the guitar-band format. The idea of doing guitar-band renditions of indigenous songs simply seemed to be in the air.

By 1966, the black Zimbabweans responsible for labeling the 78s at RBC studios in Mbare had already come up with the genre category 'traditional adaptation' to refer to village songs being arranged and played with 'modern' instruments—electric guitars, bass, and traps.[34] Groups that recorded 'traditional adaptations' with the RBC between 1966 and 1970 included the Harare Mambos with Green Jangano, the

Springfields with Thomas Mapfumo, St. Paul's Band, All Saints Band, the Beatsters, the Zebrons, the Surf Side Four, and a number of others. These groups were the immediate forerunners of the mature, indigenous-based band music of the 1970s and 1980s, and it is thus worth considering a few of them in greater detail.

### The Harare Mambos

Still performing regularly in plush night spots in Harare during the early 1990s, the Harare Mambos is one of the oldest extant guitar bands in Zimbabwe. Under the constant leadership of Green Jangano, the Mambos have had various personnel changes (Zindi 1985: 58) and some shifts in instrumentation over the years.[35] The instrumentation in the early 1960s included lead and rhythm electric guitars, sax, and drums. By 1971 the band included two guitars, bass, sax, drums, and female vocalist Virginia Sillah, Jangano's wife. Lately the group uses two keyboards with bass, drums, guitar, and Sillah on vocals. The Mambos recorded songs in a variety of languages local to Zimbabwe and Malawi, but songs with Shona texts or instrumental pieces were most common.

On a 1963 Central African Film Unit production, *Music Time,* the Harare Mambos played three instrumental numbers indicating their varied repertory. Their opening number was a "twist" with a twelve-bar blues progression and a standard (1950s) rock-and-roll drum part; Jangano played American rock-style lead guitar of that period competently. Their second number was a South African–style jive number, with the sax taking most of the lead; Jangano played one short rock-influenced solo. The third piece was a weak attempt at rumba, with the saxophonist playing straight quarter notes on claves and the drummer doing wonderful patterns on the toms and bongos with sticks. Here, in a nutshell, were the three major foreign-influenced styles played by Zimbabwean guitar bands during the 1960s. As mentioned in chapter 5, the only extant recording of the nationalist-inspired gallop genre that I found was a 1966 recording by the Harare Mambos known as "Mambo Goes South" (RBC #9560A). The "south" referred to is South Africa, and rather than exhibiting any recognizable Zimbabwean musical traits, the recording sounds very much like a mbaqanga piece, especially in the prominent bass line.

The first recording of an indigenous Shona tune by the Harare Mambos that I am aware of is "Manhanga Kutapira," recorded in July 1967 at RBC studios in Mbare (#9948B) and identified on the label as 'Instrumental Traditional Adaptation.' This piece is based on a two-phrase ostinato using the standard southern African progression

I–IV | I–V. The piece is based around a repeated sax-guitar riff (1–3–4–4–4–3–2 | 1–3–5–5–5–3–2) performed in 4/4 meter with a swing feel.

In some Harare Mambos recordings of indigenous songs, like this one and "Chekaukama" (1969, RBC #10223B), the arrangements and performance are so deeply based in the foreign popular styles of the day (rock, rumba, or jive) that one would have to know the original piece to recognize it as an indigenous song.[36] In others, like the shangara dance song "Mazororo Mana" (1970, RBC #10342B), the Mambos closely modeled both the rhythmic feel and their melody on shangara drumming and the original song. On "Mazororo Mana," the drummer actually emphasized patterns that would be typically stamped by the shangara dancers' feet, thus making the reference explicit. As in this recording, by 1970 various bands were incorporating increasingly more indigenous features into their 'traditional adaptations.'

Robert Kauffman's description of popular music trends around 1970 in Harare drew special attention to the Harare Mambos. He characterized them as the best example of a "new Shona band music" which was "a reorchestration of traditional music" (1975: 140). While this is certainly true for some of their repertory, they also continued to record as many versions of rock, jive, rumba, and chacha as of 'traditional adaptations.'

The Harare Mambos continued to play this range of repertory through the early 1980s, although by then they had specifically added the mbira genre. Their early 1980s piece "Mwanasikana" (Teal ZIM 417, 45 rpm) may be one of the first electric-band recordings to incorporate an actual mbira into the ensemble, although recordings of mbira with guitar had already been made by the acoustic guitarist Pamidze Benhura in 1980 ("Zvamunochema" and "Chemtengure," Teal ZIM 4). This trend of playing mbira and guitars together becomes a standard feature among electric bands specializing in indigenous genres after the mid-1980s.

### Other Bands of the
### 1966–1970 Period

A number of other bands performing during this period fit the basic profile described for the Harare Mambos. Prominent groups that recorded for the RBC African Service Radio between 1966 and 1970 include the All Saints Band, the Beatsters, with Naboth Kausio, the Zebrons, and St. Paul's Band from Musami. These groups performed with a basic 1960s rock format of two electric guitars, bass, drums, and

vocals; St. Paul's also used several saxophones. With the exception of
St. Paul's horns, the instrumental sound was very similar among all
these bands. The timbre of the lead guitar was thin and twangy, and the
rhythm guitar sound was dense and somewhat distorted. The overall
effect and level of musicianship was similar to a basic North American
garage band during the 1960s.

Like the Mambos, these groups played rock, South African jive,
kwela, mbaqanga, and Congolese rumba, as well as 'traditional adaptations' of local Shona music. For example, both St. Paul's Band and
the All Saints recorded "Kambiri Kaenda" (1967, #9963B; and 1968,
#10156B, respectively), which is a well-known village song through-
out Mashonaland, used in conjunction with jerusarema.[37] Both of the
guitar-band versions were based on a short, two-phrase harmonic osti-
nato in 4/4 meter—I–IV | I–V, each chord being held for two beats.
When not taking solos, the lead guitarist played single-line guitar ostinatos over the chords played by the rhythm guitarist as accompaniment
for vocals. New to Zimbabwean bands, the performance of a continuous guitar ostinato was probably adopted from Congolese rumba ensembles. Of particular interest in these recordings is that St. Paul's lead
guitarist occasionally used the damped picking style that later becomes
a hallmark feature of "mbira-guitar" playing (see Eyre 1994). This recording (1967) is the earliest example I know of this technique.[38]

The bands slowed the tempo of "Kambiri Kaenda" considerably
from the way the piece would be performed for jerusarema, jit, or in
other village contexts. Both groups sang in leader-chorus responsorial
fashion, as would be done in indigenous performance, and both sang
vocables. In contrast to village style, however, the lead singers in both
bands used a smooth, clear, singing style, and the choruses answered in
a rather bland unison. The overall effect of the vocals is quite unlike the
more varied and richly textured quality of most indigenous singing with
its use of overlapped variations, yodeling, and other vocal techniques.
Both groups sang standard village text lines, repeating two or three
throughout the whole performance: "When I die put my grave on a rock
(×2) / Fame has gone far, oh mother, fame has gone far (×3) / Surrender
oh Shava [Totemic name], Surrender oh Shava (×6) / Shava (×12)."

The Beatsters and the Zebrons also recorded 'traditional adaptations' in rock style. The musical accompaniment and melody of the
Beatsters' "Manhanga Kutapira" (RBC #9953B, 1967) closely resembles "Kambiri Kaenda." The Zebrons' "Ndakadyiwa Zvishoma"
(RBC #10151A, 1968) uses the same 4/4 metric framework, phrase
structure, chord progression, and leader-chorus responsorial organiza-

tion as the other songs just discussed, although against a different melody.

What is striking in the Beatsters' and Zebrons' performances is the rougher throat singing, which is closer to indigenous Shona performance style and contrasts with the vocals of St. Paul's and the All Saints. Of special interest, the Zebrons' lead vocalist actually sings in indigenous *huro* style (high-pitched yodeling technique). Of course, acoustic guitarists had recorded with this vocal style earlier, but huro singing was not to become a common feature in Zimbabwean electric-guitar bands until Mapfumo popularized the style after the mid-1970s. The Zebrons' incorporation of village vocal timbre and technique into their rock-oriented sound strikes me as more revolutionary than the mere adaptation and arrangement of indigenous tunes—something that had been done for some time by "concert" and 'jazz' groups. The use of indigenous vocal style signals a deeper transformation of cosmopolitan rock style and aesthetics.

The leader of the Zebrons, Ronnie Tom, was a former soccer star who had already lived in Harare (Salisbury) for some years before buying instruments and starting the band in November 1965 at age twenty-seven. His interest in "show business" started while still in school, where he played guitar for a group called the City Crackers. Other members of the Zebrons likewise had been living in the city and some, such as Nelson Jero, a former member of the Capital City Dixies coons troupe, had experience in the popular music field.[39] In a 1966 interview with *Parade,* Ronnie Tom stated that his goal was to go professional and "hit the big time." In the same interview he stated that they wanted to compose songs "on the cha cha cha, kwela and a-go-go lines," with no mention of an interest in Shona indigenous styles or sources (*Parade* 1966b: 14). By the time the Zebrons recorded "Ndakadyiwa Zvishoma" in 1968, the idea of incorporating village songs into guitar-band repertory had become commonplace; they simply went one step further by adopting indigenous vocal style.

## Thomas Mapfumo and the Springfields, 1966–1967

A band competition was included as part of the "Miss Rufaro 1966" beauty contest, sponsored by the municipal Liquor Undertaking Department at Stodart Hall in Mbare. First prize was a check for fifty pounds and a contract to play in Mbare's "largest and [most] modern beer hall, Vito Tavern" (*Parade* 1966a: 48). The Beatsters, who had formerly been making the rounds performing at the Highfield Cocktail, the

Highfield Tavern, and "The Stones" beer hall, carried the day and were given full-time work at the Vito by the municipal Liquor Undertaking Department.[40] Having won the contest, they displaced the band that had been under contract to play nightly in the main lounge of the Vito, a group called the Springfields with singer Thomas Mapfumo.

The Springfields was very much in the mold of the other groups of the period already discussed. The band is remarkable only in that it was the training ground for Thomas Mapfumo, who would become one of Zimbabwe's major music stars for the next three decades. Mapfumo's career is central to the next two chapters. Here his early recorded work with the Springfields is discussed in the context of late-1960s guitar bands.

## The Early Career
## of Thomas Mapfumo

Mapfumo was born in 1945 in Marondera (some fifty kilometers southeast of Harare), where he spent his early years with his grandparents. As a child he tended his grandparents' animals and helped in the fields. He began primary school at age nine, and a year later joined his parents, who were parishioners in Mabvuku township outside Harare. Mapfumo attended primary school there for five years and completed his primary education after his parents were transferred to Mbare Township by the church. His father was a co-leader and his mother a chairwoman of their church, and Mapfumo described them as very strict parents (Zindi 1985: 24).[41] After several frustrating attempts to continue his education, he gradually turned to a musical career.

Mapfumo identifies the dance-drumming he heard at all-night gatherings in rural Marondera as his earliest musical influences (e.g., Zindi 1985: 25). He related the following in an interview:

MAPFUMO: When I was a small boy herding cattle, I was very much into traditional music. My grandparents had a big influence on me. They were very much into traditional music; they used to have a lot of gatherings with dancing.

TURINO: Was it mainly ngoma? [drumming]

MAPFUMO: Ngoma and mbira playing. As youths we used to have our own thing, and the elders were inside the house doing something different. We were outside, you see, it's moonlight, and we're singing and dancing in our own way.

TURINO: Is that what would be called jit today?

MAPFUMO: That's sarenda, yes. That is what is being called jit today. (Zim93-46: 6)

The inside/outside the house distinction suggests that the elders were engaged with ceremonial activities (see chapter 1).

After Mapfumo moved to the Harare area to live with his parents in Mabvuku, he came under the influence of various "concert" groups such as The Cool Four, the Capital City Dixies, and De Black Evening Follies (Zindi 1985: 25):

> Many of those groups really had a big influence on me. Because as a youngster I used to attend their concerts and listened to some good singing. Like Dorothy Masuka; I was very young when I used to listen to her, and Moses Mpahlo [of De Black Evening Follies], and Sonny Sondo, and the Capital City Dixies [the 'Coons' troupe]. These were the young generation now, they used to paint their faces. . . . These were some of the groups that had a very very big influence on me. Because I used to say, well, I must be a singer, I want to be a singer. (Zim93-46: 5–6)

The first music Mapfumo attempted to sing was in the style of Little Richard and Elvis Presley. This occurred around 1960 after "concert" groups had already begun performing 1950s-style rock and roll. Mapfumo relates how he went home after these concerts and imitated their singing. He made himself a 'banjo'[42] and began practicing, although he was forbidden to play by his father: "He was very cross with me for learning how to play an instrument which was only associated with beggars and vagabonds in those days" (Zindi 1985: 25).

By the early 1960s, styles like the Mills Brothers, jive, and rock and roll had become localized within the "concert" tradition in Zimbabwe to the extent that Mapfumo's generation could turn to local instead of, or in addition to, foreign models. For this reason such styles are better understood as examples of cosmopolitanism (localized nodes of production for widespread phenomena) rather than simply as cases of westernization or the direct imitation of foreign performers.

Mapfumo sang with a group called The Cosmic Four Dots in the early 1960s after moving to Mbare Township. The "concert" influence is readily apparent in the three RBC recordings the Dots made in 1964. All were vocal quartet numbers sung in Shona and backed by the Springfields guitar band; Mapfumo's voice cannot be distinguished particularly from the other three singers. "Chindunduna Wasara" (RBC #4747B) and "Caroline" (#4759) were South African, jive-influenced, vocal quartet numbers in direct imitation of The Cool Four from Bulawayo. "Bekani Uriwangu" (#4759A) was a stereotypic 1950s rock and roll song but atypically sung by the quartet rather than by a soloist with background vocals, as would have been done by De Black Evening Follies or the Capital City Dixies.

Mapfumo's early involvement with the "concert" tradition is also suggested by the fact that he worked directly with Kenneth Mattaka for six months. According to Mattaka, Mapfumo came to him for training and guidance in 1961, and he even took the Cosmic Four Dots with him on a contract to play for farm workers in a rural area not far from Harare. Mattaka stated that Mapfumo's group was strictly doing "pop" at that time (fieldnotes 4 August 1993).

### Mapfumo with the Springfields: 'Traditional Adaptations'

In 1964 Mapfumo left the Cosmic Four Dots and joined the Springfields as their lead (and only) singer; during this time, his own distinctive voice begins to emerge. In 1966 and 1967 the Springfields, sometimes listed as "The Springfields with Thomas Mapfumo," recorded twenty-two 78-rpm sides for the RBC in Mbare. This is a large number of recordings relative to other groups of this type and time in the RBC collection, and it may indicate the group's prominence and ambitions.

Although in interviews conducted after 1980 Mapfumo usually states that he did not begin concentrating on 'traditional' Shona music until around 1972–73 (e.g., interview with Zindi 1985: 31), the first RBC recording of the Springfields with Thomas Mapfumo was a version of the well-known Shona song "Chemtengure" (#9196B, 1966). The Springfields' recording was labeled 'Shona Traditional Adaptation.' Mapfumo sings the standard Shona lyrics and descending melody in a flat, unornamented style against the two guitars playing strummed or arpeggiated chords with solo guitar interludes on the basic melody. The song was performed in 4/4 time with a feel somewhere between straight-ahead rock and roll and a swing rhythm.[43] The flip side was an instrumental chacha.

Of the remaining eleven pieces recorded by the Springfields in 1966, five were 'traditional adaptations' sung in Shona, there was an instrumental kwela (South African genre), and five were rock and roll (two of these were labeled as "twist"). Thus, about half of their 1966 recordings were 'traditional adaptations.' Mapfumo's rough, head-throat style of singing (but without the high yodeling huro technique), and the Springfield's approach to guitar playing, sometimes with lead-guitar ostinatos over the chording rhythm guitar, resulted in a sound very much like the Beatsters and the Zebrons.

Also like these bands, and the acoustic guitarists before them, the texts of the Springfields' 'traditional adaptations' were largely taken from the original indigenous songs and spoke to issues and problems in the rural areas. For example, the Shona text for "Shungu Dzino-Ndibaya" (#9610) is as follows: "I'm troubled in my heart (×4) / I used to own butcheries, I owned stores, my friends / I had cattle my friends / I had sheep my friends / Today I have nothing, surely I've nothing / What shall I do my friends (×4)?" It is not hard to imagine how a text like this could be reshaped slightly, in the context of the war after 1972, to carry a political message—a practice Mapfumo would later engage in. In 1966, however, this text simply carried a moral about the fall of a rich person in the rural areas—perhaps to be understood in terms of peasant values of distributing rather than amassing personal wealth.

There is only one feature of the Springfield's approach to 'traditional adaptations' that is historically salient. On three recordings ("Kunaka Wakanaka" #9609A; "Shungu DzinoNdibaya" #9610A; retake on side B) the drummer plays constant triple eighth-note divisions on the highhat or snare against the stronger simple duple feel produced by the rest of the band. As a hallmark feature of mature jit and "mbira-guitar" band music after the mid-1970s, and consistent with the *hosho* (shaker) parts of indigenous performance, drummers came to play triple divisions on the highhat within a compound duple framework. The Springfields were the only group that I know that began to do this in the 1966–70 period. Because a simple duple feel remained in the foreground on these three pieces, however, the drummer's triple divisions can only be seen as an incipient step away from the 4/4 jazz-, jive-, and rock-influenced rhythms used for most 'traditional adaptations' at this time.

Nonetheless, this rhythmic feature, along with the Zebrons' introduction of huro singing within an electric-guitar band, St. Paul's intermittent use of the damped guitar technique, and the very use of village songs are all important seeds that ultimately became fundamental components of mature, indigenous-based guitar-band music. The 1966–70 period was thus one of incipient experimentation by various groups simultaneously—belying later claims that any one artist or band created the "mbira-guitar" style. While classical twenty-two key mbira pieces had entered guitar-band repertories by the late 1970s, to my knowledge no electric-guitar bands performed classical mbira pieces during the 1966–70 period.

## Mapfumo the Rock and Roller

Rock and roll was the second largest genre category after 'traditional adaptations' in the Springfields' recorded repertory of 1966. Here, too, there were a variety of approaches. Their instrumental "twists"—"Valley of Lost Souls" (#9611A), and "Sunday Morning" (9611B)—and especially their "instrumental rock" song, "Talking Strings," (#9197B) sound like generic, moderate-tempo, North American "surf-rock" songs of the mid-1960s.[44] On "You Can't Say Goodbye" (#9195A) and "Kiss Me" (#9197A), Mapfumo sings English lyrics in a style that sounds like an imitation of Elvis with classic Little Richard vocal ornaments thrown in.

In telling his own story Thomas Mapfumo has stated that he moved from doing foreign styles and "copyrights" to singing local Shona music and his own songs. In terms of the overall trajectory of his career, this is true, but when comparing the Springfields' recordings of 1966 with those of 1967, the situation is actually the reverse. The group recorded no 'traditional adaptations' in 1967. Instead they did three "Rock" songs, three "Chachas," one "Instrumental Jazz" piece, one "Rumba," one "Instrumental Marabi," and one "Instrumental Kwela." Particularly interesting among these is Mapfumo's performance of a Ray Charles hit "Lonely Avenue" (#9915A). The melody, rhythm, and arrangement are so thoroughly transformed (early 1960s rock and roll arrangement with some "surf-rock" guitar elements) that it can only be linked to the Charles version by the title and text. The last Springfields recordings in the National Archives holdings of the RBC collection were from 1968. These included an "Instrumental Kwela" (#10159B), and a piece called "Springfields Go Latin" (10159A), labeled as "Instrumental Kwela" but sounding like a chacha.

Like his work in the 1966–70 period, Mapfumo's repertory remained stylistically eclectic through the 1990s—incorporating indigenous genres as well as rock, pop, and reggae. During the 1970s, however, the balance of transnational and indigenous styles in his repertory shifts to the point where Zimbabweans began to identify him as the champion of 'traditional' music within the popular music field. Mapfumo came to foster his image as a traditionalist during the 1970s and 1980s for a confluence of reasons.

### Conclusions

Mapfumo and the other electric-band musicians of the 1970s did not create a music or text style, or even fusions, that were fundamentally new. The acoustic guitarists of the 1950s and 1960s were already performing the two genres—jit and classical mbira music—that would later become the most internationally famous types of Zimbabwean guitar-band music. Electric bands would not commonly turn to jit and mbira pieces until after the mid-1970s.

The indigenous songs performed by acoustic guitarists were stylistically close to indigenous performance in terms of rhythm, harmony, vocal style, buzzy timbres, and wealth of genres; the acoustic guitarists were basically performing their own indigenous music on a new instrument. When they adopted South African popular genres like tsaba-tsaba and marabi, they transformed them rhythmically to fit indigenous Zimbabwean sensibilities—jit was the result.

In contrast, the young band musicians of the late 1960s seemed to be more firmly rooted in international styles like rock, rumba, and jive; they approached indigenous Shona music from the outside through processes of experimentation and discovery. Like Mapfumo, other band musicians may have had experiences with rural indigenous music as youngsters, but their own preferences and performance activities began with urban-popular styles like rock. Some of Mapfumo's earliest recordings (1966) were of indigenous Shona songs, but the renditions were stylistically more consistent with cosmopolitan rock.

On the surface it seems that both the early acoustic guitarists and the young band musicians were involved with a similar, syncretic guitar music. They were both 'in the middle,' as Mhlanga put it, but they approached the middle from different artistic and aesthetic positions, and their music was quite different as a result.

Chapter Eight

## Stars of the Seventies: The Rise
## of Indigenous-Based Guitar Bands

Among the 'traditional adaptations' played by guitar bands in the second half of the 1960s, classical, twenty-two-key Zezuru mbira pieces were conspicuously absent, and jit was relatively rare. Yet these genres came to define Zimbabwe's unique contributions to popular music among cosmopolitans at home and abroad in the 1980s. Both genres, previously played by acoustic guitarists, were shaped further by guitar bands in the 1970s. As performed by artists such as Thomas Mapfumo, Zexie Manatsa, Oliver M'tukudzi, and many others, this music became closely linked to nationalism among some sectors of the Zimbabwean population and in international perception during the late 1970s and 1980s (e.g., see Pongweni 1982; Kaemmer 1998).

Political nationalism, however, was only one of several elements that came together to influence the practice, style, and meaning of indigenous-based guitar bands. Musicians' professional aspirations and cosmopolitan discourses about artistic creativity and originality were equally important. My goal here is to closely examine one instance of what is usually considered musical nationalism, and to trace how it actually came about. Conceptual distinctions between explicit political nationalism, national sentiment (vaguer feelings of belonging to a nation), and a more generalized "Africanist sentiment" are central to this task.

Beginning in the 1960–63 period, the nationalist leadership helped create a new type of pride in African culture within certain segments of the black urban population from which guitar-band audiences were drawn. The discourse of 'partnership' during the Federation period had already supported a reevaluation of local arts and African identity among members of the black middle class and cosmopolitan-oriented youth. Finally, a more general Black Pride movement arose after the mid-1960s within cosmopolitan youth culture. This connection to cosmopolitanism is indicated by the local creation of soul music, Afro hair styles, and phrases like "Black is beautiful." Federation reformism, early nationalism, and 1960s youth culture helped shape *Africanist sentiment* that was then sometimes articulated to political nationalism in the 1960s and 1970s.

It was prominently this Africanist shift within guitar-band *audiences,* in conjunction with the artists' professional aspirations to forge a mass audience, that inspired the increased incorporation of indigenous elements within guitar-band performance. The articulation of professional aspirations with a specifically *national* sentiment inspired the move to political lyrics as the war heated up. Here again the artists were largely led by the dispositions of their audiences.

The indigenous-based guitar bands discussed in this chapter represent another explicit case of musical reformism, but with a different agenda: to appeal to the largest possible audience (both 'modern' and 'traditional' people) in order to earn a living from musical performance. This illustrates how musical professionalism, with its need for a mass of consumers, paralleled and in some ways supported the nationalist agenda of incorporating different social groups into the nation.

Nationalism and capitalist enterprises are similar in that they both ultimately depend on mass appeal for success. Reformism became a common technique for both these distinctive commercial and political ends, but the two types of motivations should not be confused. Both articulated well in the Zimbabwean guitar bands during the late 1970s and early 1980s. When fueled jointly by commercial goals and state nationalism, reformist discursive practices take on considerable force. Indeed a syncretic vision of Zimbabwean identity and 'culture' had become fairly generalized by the 1990s (see chapter 1). The events discussed in this chapter represent an important stage in this process.

## Early Electric "Mbira-Guitar" Music and Jit

At the end of *Soul of Mbira* (1978: 244), Paul Berliner notes that "in an interesting recent development in Shona 'jazz bands,' musicians have added to their repertories several traditional mbira pieces, reorchestrated for electric guitars and Western drums." In a footnote to this comment Berliner mentions a version of the mbira piece "Kuzanga," by

M. D. Rhythm Success, released in 1973, and a version of "Taireva," by the Lipopo Jazz Band, released in 1974.[1] In addition, in 1974 "Ngoma Yarira," a piece based on one of the central mbira progressions ("Nyamaropa"/"Karigamombe"), was recorded by the Hallelujah Chicken Run Band, with Thomas Mapfumo and Joshua Hlomayi listed as co-composers.[2] These are the first recordings I have found of classical mbira music played by electric-guitar bands; several groups were experimenting with the same idea simultaneously.

## M. D. Rhythm Success: Jit and "Mbira-Guitar" Music

M. D. Rhythm Success is one of the most innovative and least known Zimbabwean bands recording during the late 1960s and early 1970s.[3] Like the other groups doing 'traditional adaptations' during the second half of the 1960s, M. D. Rhythm Success played a variety of genres, including indigenous music and Congolese-influenced rumbas and chachas (e.g., the chacha, "Shereni;" Gallo GB.3793). Also typical, their instrumentation comprised two electric guitars, bass, traps, and a vocalist. What was novel about this group for the late 1960s and early 1970s was the way they performed indigenous Shona music. Rather than adapting village songs to a rock, jive, or jazz rhythmic-metric feel as the other late-1960s groups did, M. D. Rhythm Success adopted the original feel of the music and other aspects of village performance.

In 1968, they released a jit song called "Sevenza Nhamo Ichanya" (Gallo GB.3739), which had many features that would characterize guitar-band jit through the 1990s; it is the earliest recording of the mature guitar-band jit style that I found. The song has the I–IV–I–V progression typical of guitar-band jit. The song is played in the fast 12/8 meter that is associated with rural jit and became standard for guitar-band versions. The drummer accented beats 1, 4, 7, 10 on the kick drum with a constant triple eighth-note pattern on the highhat. Unlike acoustic-guitar versions and later guitar-band jit (with the bass playing on beats 1 and 7), the bass player here doubled the kick drum accents. This is significant because it avoids the South African–influenced 4/4 feel that is embedded within the typical 12/8 jit structure. That is, this element indicates that M. D. Rhythm Success took village drumming, with its unified 12/8 feel, as the sole model for this piece.

The most innovative feature of this recording was the use of an actual *ngoma* (tall, flat-sounding local drums played here with the hands) prominently foregrounded in the mix. The ngoma player performed an extended solo modeled on village jit drumming, which was

accompanied only by the highhat roles—just as village jit drumming is
accompanied only by hosho. This was a much more direct reference to
indigenous music than most bands exhibited in the late-1960s, and it
would not become common practice to use actual village instruments in
guitar bands until the mid-1980s. The nationalist-affiliated group the
Hurricanes used indigenous drums for their gallop music in 1963 and
was a forerunner of this practice.

M. D. Rhythm Success seems to have produced another innovation
with their recording "Kumntongo" (Gallo GB.3815) in 1973. This was,
as Berliner pointed out, an instrumental version of the mbira standard,
"Kuzanga," and it is the earliest guitar-band version of a classical mbira
piece that I know. The bass line defined the basic four-phrase mbira
ostinato. Rather than playing guitar lines firmly based on melodic parts
drawn from the middle and high mbira keys, the guitarist largely fol-
lowed the harmonic ostinato set up by the bass: G Bm Em | G C Em |
Am C Em | D Bm D. A more independent polyphonic approach to guitar
lines would emerge in bands later. Perhaps owing to the influence of
South African mbaqanga music, all the rage in Zimbabwe after 1968,
the bass guitar was particularly prominent in M. D. Rhythm Success's
recording. This emphasis on the bass remained a feature in much Zimbabwean music throughout the 1970s and only became less prominent
in the 1980s.

M. D. Rhythm Success played this piece in 12/8 meter, and the
drummer played the hosho triple figures on the highhat. Another feature
of the mature "mbira-guitar" style in this recording was the use of the
damped guitar technique. Although it was not used consistently, or even
for the majority of the performance, it was highlighted on the few high,
descending guitar lines that did imitate mbira high-key melodies.

Describing these details in a series does not give the full impact of
just how new and different M. D. Rhythm Success's approach was; one
needs to listen to their recordings against the backdrop of the rock-
oriented 'traditional adaptations' most other groups were producing in
the late 1960s and early 1970s. M. D. Rhythm Success's 1968 and 1973
recordings mark the emergence of the two genres that would become
central through the mid-1990s. Soon after, several other groups, including the Lipopo Jazz Band, began producing records very much in the
same vein.

## Jackson Phiri and Lipopo Jazz
Lipopo Jazz was originally a Congolese rumba band that recruited local
singers such as Jackson Phiri (b. 1940). After the Congolese members

were deported at the end of the 1960s, Phiri took a prominent role in the direction of the group and, because of constant changes in personnel, Lipopo became the training ground for some of the most important guitarists who would later turn to playing mbira music and other village genres.

In the late 1960s and early 1970s, Phiri was working as a full-time musician with Lipopo. They were hired by various municipalities to play in bars and beerhalls such as the Vito Tavern, as well as at private clubs like the Federal Hotel. The professional circuit was a small one, and Phiri describes how most of the major bands of the period played the same places and were constantly sharing ideas and influencing one another (Zim93-40). This explains why certain musical trends, such as playing jit and mbira music, would emerge among various bands almost simultaneously.

In 1974, shortly after the release of M. D. Rhythm Success's single "Kumntongo," the Lipopo Jazz Band recorded "Ndozvireva" (Gallo GB.3868), based on the classical mbira piece "Taireva." Jackson Phiri was listed as composer on the label. I asked Phiri how he got the idea to record this song, and he responded,

> You see, what came to me is this. This song was sung during festivals, say, when they are doing mbira, you know, cultural things, this and that. They used to play ngoma, this and that, singing "Ndozvireva." Now I decided, I must sing it in, I must use the guitars now! I sat down with my musicians, I arranged how we got into it, then we went to record. Instead of recording rumba I decided to record that one. . . . I could just change it like that. To try to change. Instead of playing rumba all the time. Rumba. They also played traditional music in Zaire changing it into guitars. Eh, what about myself? I just decided to, you see, try to change and make it using the guitar. (Zim93-44: 14–15)

Several things emerge from Phiri's response. The main impetus for doing this village song was Phiri's desire to add other types of music to their repertory beyond rumbas. Even when the Congolese (Zairian) band members had been present, Lipopo had constantly been in a process of adding new styles to their repertoire beyond their basic rumba core; indeed, Phiri had originally been brought in to sing rock and roll in English. Phiri's addition of "Ndozvireva" in 1974 was simply a continuation of this trend. Elsewhere in the interview he related how Lipopo also did a variety of other 'traditional' (his term) Shona dance-drumming songs, as well as a piece that originally accompanied Malawian Nyau dancing (Phiri was born in Malawi). These pieces were added to their general repertory, which still contained many rumba, rock, soul, and South African–influenced numbers. As Phiri says, "We liked to mix it up."

Phiri suggested that Congolese (Zairian) musicians' former practice of performing their village music on guitars served as a primary inspiration for his band arrangement of "Ndozvireva." This makes sense, given his involvement with Congolese musicians, and it suggests that adapting indigenous songs for dance-band performance was a common practice in various parts of Africa, as it had been in Zimbabwe from at least the late 1950s on. Phiri also stated that he had been inspired to play mbira music on electric guitars after hearing the music in village ceremonies; later in the interview he mentioned that he had also been influenced to play mbira music by the acoustic guitarist Ngwaru Mapundu. Thus he apparently had multiple models for performing "Ndozvireva" with his band.

The search for musical variety, then, rather than a conscious engagement with nationalism or national sentiment, was the primary impetus for this recording, according to Phiri's hindsight account. Yet later in the interview, when I asked him how audiences responded to their performance of local Shona songs, he did make an immediate connection between the political situation and this music's popularity: "They could jump in! Even in the bush, you know, this song was released during the time of struggle. Yeah, comrades in the bush would dance to it. It was too popular!" (Zim93-40: 17). As we shall see, other artists suggested a similar link between the popularity of indigenous songs and the war.

Phiri did not seem to know M. D. Rhythm Success's earlier recording of an mbira piece; nonetheless, Lipopo's 1974 recording was similar to it in terms of style. They performed the four-phrase mbira ostinato of "Taireva" in 12/8, with the drummer playing the hosho triple patterns on the highhat. The bass guitar is particularly prominent, probably an influence from South African mbaqanga. By doubling pitches or adding passing tones within the ostinato, Lipopo made the bass part somewhat more active than the bass on the M. D. Rhythm Success recording. The lead guitar largely doubles the vocal melody or plays patterns that are roughly modeled on middle- and high-key mbira lines. Unlike M. D. Rhythm Success, Lipopo does not feature the damped guitar technique, and they add vocals. Phiri sings the lead and is answered by a chorus of the other musicians, but no yodeling or other village vocal techniques are present; the text speaks of rural people telling problems to their chief.

In 1975 the Lipopo Jazz Band released another classical mbira song, this time maintaining the original name of the piece, "Dande" (Teal Su 107). Tiney Chikupo is listed as composer on the label and is lead singer. The band maintains the rhythmic-metric feel of mbira music, the highhat playing the hosho part, and the prominent, active bass line, as in their previous recording. Going beyond their first mbira music recording, however, Chikupo adds the prominent use of vocables, *huro* (high yodeling) and *mahon'era* (low, soft vocable singing) vocal techniques as well as ululations of the kind commonly produced by women at village musical events. The damped guitar technique is added on a few high guitar solos, and the lead guitar plays parts based on middle- and high-key mbira lines as well as variations. The third band documented to have adapted classical mbira pieces during 1973–74, and in much the same style, was the Hallelujah Chicken Run Band led by Thomas Mapfumo.

## Thomas Mapfumo: Professional Musician and Traditionalist

With the Springfields, Mapfumo had moved from recording a substantial number of Shona 'traditional adaptations' in 1966 to foreign popular styles (chacha, rock, soul, kwela) in 1967 and 1968. A *Parade* article about Mapfumo, published in 1971, depicts him as an up-and-coming "pop" singer who had "lately emerged as one of the country's top vocalists" (*Parade* 1971a: 9). The *Parade* writer describes Mapfumo's performance at the recently opened Mutanga nightclub in Highfield in the following terms:

> Thomas hip-sways his way through the packed dance floor on to the stage with catcalls from male and female fans who just come into the club to listen to the maestro of pop and a bit of jazz.
> *He has developed a style of his own.* He knows, when playing to an appreciative audience, new gimmicks pay dividends. That is why you will see Thomas hugging the mike and not letting go.
> Amid the screams of joy, Thomas sways backwards, mike still under his arm-pits, and lets out a pulsating timbre which is the envy of many an up and coming artist. (9; my emphasis)

Mapfumo was quoted in this article as saying that he was determined to have a successful career in music, like other young people of that time. He also stated that his primary musical aspiration was to blow tenor saxophone like Stan Getz. He told *Parade*, "I am now concentrating on jazz, because say what you like, 50 years from now, jazz will still be popular when pop is not" (ibid).

## The Quest for Originality

Shortly after this, however, Mapfumo changed directions again and began the search for an original sound; he told me, "You know, something
of my own is what I actually needed" (Zim92-23: 8). Music writers and
critics in Zimbabwe had already begun haranguing local artists for covering foreign music in the 1960s. In his review of a festival of local pop
bands in 1970, a *Parade* music writer complained that "not one group
had its own original tune to render. Come on you band leaders, start
composing music of your own, and when next another Pop Jam Session
is organized, why the cats would possibly double those present [at] the
first Salisbury Pop Extravaganza '70 in an African township" (*Parade*
1970: 29). This demand for originality would continue throughout the
1970s. After judging a local band contest in Harare in 1976, the local
musician N. Todhlana noted that he was impressed by the quality of the
bands and was "mostly impressed with those bands which played their
own music which they composed. For many years, very few African
bands were able to compose their songs. But today, several bands are
able to do so. This to me, is a great step forward" (*Parade* 1977b: 38).
New for Zimbabwe, the emphasis on original compositions and style
became rooted as a facet of cosmopolitan youth culture beginning in the
mid-1960s. It took a decade of experimentation for this value to come
to fruition.

By the early 1970s Mapfumo was concerned with establishing himself with a style that was original, that would have longevity, and that
would attract a wide audience. Like others, he cast about in various directions. After leaving the Springfields, Mapfumo formed a new group
in the early 1970s, the Hallelujah Chicken Run Band. Moving away
from conventional rock, rumba, and South African genres, with the
Chicken Run Band he attempted to create something new to Zimbabwe.
As he told me,

> We were trying to play what we called Afro-rock music. This music
> was a fusion of Shona music and some Western styles. Like, you
> know the music of Osibisa. It was a Nigerian group [actually Ghan-
> aian, formed in London] that used to play Afro-rock who were very
> popular in England. Well, we were trying to take that direction.
> People actually were very excited with the kind of style that we cre-
> ated. But when it came to selling the music, to record sales, that mu-
> sic was not, no people got excited. It was not very popular with the
> rest of our fans; because it didn't sell very well. Well we were record-
> ing some of it, and a lot of it was a flop. Now one record came on top
> because this record was pure traditional—you see where the whole
> thing came about?

We had recorded this other [music] which was a fusion of Western style with our own style and this never got off the ground, but
one song which was pure Zimbabwean traditional—mbira but now
played with guitars—well, people just went for it. They thought it
was the best of them all. So well, by realizing what had happened, I
just thought, well, it was best for us to do the real thing. Like playing
the real Zimbabwean traditional music rather than trying to fuse the
music and come up with something that would sound like, you know,
African, or Western, something that we are going to call "Afro." This
wasn't going to work here! So well, this made me take the direction
that I now am today. (Zim92-23: 8–9)

Mapfumo told me that the record in question was the Teal single
"Ngoma Yarira"/"Murembo."

### "Ngoma Yarira"

In 1974, the same year that Lipopo Jazz Band released "Ndozvireva,"
the Hallelujah Chicken Run Band with Thomas Mapfumo as vocalist
put out an mbira-based piece called "Ngoma Yarira" on the A side, and
a village dance-drumming war song, "Murembo," on side B (Teal Records, Afro Sound AS 105). Although Mapfumo had sung many Shona
'traditional adaptations' with the Springfields, this Teal recording represented a new phase for Mapfumo and the beginning of the style that
he would develop and champion over the next twenty-five years.

"Ngoma Yarira" was derived from one of the most standard Shona
mbira progressions used in classical pieces such as "Karigamombe" and
"Nyamaropa"—G Bm D | G Bm Em | G C Em | Am C Em; in this
recording the four-phrase ostinato is played by the guitar and bass. In
other respects, "Ngoma Yarira" was quite distinct from the mbira-
based recordings of Lipopo Jazz and M. D. Rhythm Success around the
same time. "Ngoma Yarira" opens with Joshua Hlomayi doubling the
notes of a single-line melody in damped guitar style in close imitation of
an mbira. He maintains this technique consistently on melodic lines and
arpeggiated chords throughout the piece, whereas the guitarists in the
other bands only used the damped technique intermittently and never
with the same success of actually creating a close approximation of an
mbira sound. Equally striking as the guitar part, Mapfumo sings consistently in Shona village style, experimenting with the soft mahon'era and
high huro techniques, and vocalizing more on vocables than with actual
text. This was a dramatic departure from his earlier singing.

"Ngoma Yarira" was jointly arranged for the band by Mapfumo
and guitarist Joshua Dube Hlomayi while the Hallelujah Chicken Run
Band was playing on contract for the management of Mangula Mine

(near Mhangura, 125 km north of Harare) during 1973. Both Hlomayi and Mapfumo are given composer credits on the record label. In his interview with Fred Zindi, Mapfumo related that "it was [during] my stint with these guys in Mangula that the idea of singing Shona music came alive. The mineworkers we were playing for were illiterate and could not understand the English songs. The only way out was to sing in a language that they would appreciate and understand" (1985: 31). Judging from Mapfumo's RBC recordings from the late 1960s, he was already singing many songs in Shona. In this remark he seems to be linking Shona texts with indigenous-style music in his mind. His concern with specific audiences is notable. He went on to tell Zindi that "the idea of playing traditional rhythms had always been at the back of my mind, but it wasn't until Mangula that I felt I now had the right ingredients for it because the audiences there were very receptive, and the band members all enjoyed experimenting with this sound" (1985: 32).

Joshua Hlomayi told me that while they were in the rural area around Mangula mine they came in contact with mbira players. He said that one day Mapfumo came to him and asked, "Couldn't we do something like that?" and Joshua began to work out an mbira piece and sound on his guitar. Joshua told a similar story to Banning Eyre: "One day I was just playing the guitar at rehearsal, and I started playing a mbira tune, the one I knew best. Thomas was there, and he said to me, 'I can sing that.' That's where it all began. We started using that staccato playing in our music. When we played that song, everybody at the club went mad" (Eyre 1994: 118–19). Hlomayi's description echoes those of Mapfumo in suggesting that the band was experimenting with different types of music and that the audience's enthusiasm for 'pure traditional' music drew the musicians' attention to this style.

### Early Electric "Mbira-Guitarists"

Although guitarists Jonah Sithole and Leonard Chiyangwa are often credited with creating the electric "mbira-guitar" style, these musicians did not play it with Mapfumo until after the recording of "Ngoma Yarira."[4] It was Hlomayi who first developed the style with Mapfumo at Mangula, although as we have seen, the guitarists with M. D. Rhythm Success and Lipopo Jazz were working along similar lines simultaneously. In his performance on "Ngoma Yarira," Hlomayi was already more advanced toward the mature electric "mbira-guitar" style than his contemporaries, however, in his consistent use of the damped guitar technique, the doubling of notes, and his adherence to mbira-like melodic lines.

Joshua grew up playing acoustic 'country guitar' (his terms) in the Masvingo and Midlands regions. He first played in the style of rural acoustic guitarists such as Sinyoro Jackson Chinemberi—marabi or jit-like songs in two-finger style with chord-based accompaniment. Hlomayi never played mbira and had not previously played mbira music on acoustic guitar, although his father had played njari. Hlomayi told me that when he came up with the guitar part for "Ngoma Yarira," he did not have a specific mbira song in mind and did not know the mbira repertory in any detail. Rather, he had a rather general notion of the sound of mbira music in his mind, and he worked this out on guitar—indeed the progression he came up with is prototypical of many classic pieces.

It might be assumed that the electric "mbira-guitar" style emerged as a kind of natural development among musicians who had grown up with mbira music and knew it well, as had been the case with earlier acoustic guitarists. By his own account this was not true for Hlomayi, and although he continues playing this style in the 1990s, he still does not have a detailed knowledge of the mbira repertory. The late Jonah Sithole, the most acclaimed master of the electric "mbira-guitar" style, also told me that he had not grown up with mbira music and did not know it well. He only began to play it in the mid-1970s after he had moved to the Harare area, where guitar adaptations were beginning to emerge. For Sithole, a major source of contact with mbira music had been the RBC radio broadcasts. As with the performers of 'traditional adaptations' in the late 1960s, the men who came to specialize in the "mbira-guitar" style initially approached it experimentally and as outsiders to the tradition. Once the adaptation of mbira music to electric guitar was established as a style, guitarists typically learned it from other guitarists as a new tradition in its own right.[5]

### Professional Aspirations, Nationalism, and National Sentiment

What generally emerges from Mapfumo's statements to *Parade*, *Zindi*, and me is a portrait of an ambitious young man dedicated, like many of his contemporaries, to building a professional music career—an idea that had firmly entered the realm of the possible by 1970. Between 1966 and 1974 he was actively involved in experimenting with a variety of styles to determine which one would hit with his audiences and make him commercially viable. Mapfumo's interest in jazz was due to the perception that it would give him staying power, a goal he in fact realized with indigenous-based music. His interest in trying the Afro-rock style, which he recognized had worked for Osibisa in London, perhaps indicates another aspect of his ambitions: to make it in the international market, a quest he began in earnest after the early 1980s. Yet jazz did not offer novelty, and Afro-rock did not work well with local audiences where he had to establish his initial base. With Hlomayi's help, and the backing of the Hallelujah Chicken Run Band, Mapfumo came upon the right formula—guitar band performance of 'purely traditional' Shona music—in 1974.

Mapfumo was not particularly dedicated to indigenous music performance himself initially; indeed only three years earlier he had wanted to play like Stan Getz. Moreover, apparently he did not begin specializing in it because of his own conscious feelings of national sentiment or because he was a nationalist. Judging from Mapfumo's own statements, it was his professional aspirations and his quest for originality, in conjunction with the reactions of the record-buying public and nightclub audiences, that first inspired him to specialize in the indigenous Shona style. I also asked Joshua Hlomayi if, when they first started playing mbira music in the Hallelujah Chicken Run Band, he or Mapfumo had thought of it as nationalist or political music. Hlomayi laughed and replied that they had not thought of it in this way; they had simply considered it 'traditional music' and good dance music (fieldnotes 10 June 1991).

In a 1980 interview with Julie Frederikse, Mapfumo gave a slightly different account of how he came to dedicate himself to indigenous Shona music performance. He told her that he was playing with a (unspecified) band that performed primarily "English" songs and that they had only one Shona song:

> After I finished the English songs I could jump into this particular [Shona] tune and start singing. Then all of a sudden I could see people starting clapping this particular tune instead of applauding for the English type. Then I realized that we people of Zimbabwe we were lost . . . we are supposed to do our own music. That gave me courage until . . . I started composing many of them for that time, and I did a hit . . . it stayed on the hit parade for two months. (National Archives tape #ATC 0078)

As in the statements to Zindi and me, Mapfumo once again suggests that he was led to specialize in the performance of indigenous-based music because of audience response and the hit-parade success of this style. This comment to Frederikse, however, adds a new dimension— the realization of "being lost" and the value of doing "our own music"—

suggesting the influence of nationalist discourse. In fact, Mapfumo's choice of words directly mirrors ZANU's cultural policy statements.

The Frederikse interview was conducted in the celebratory moment of 1980 after ZANU was elected to power, and in the context of a project specifically about the links between cultural production, media, and the nationalist war. Here, and increasingly in later interviews with foreign journalists after he enters the worldbeat market (see chapter 9), Mapfumo's nationalist statements may be partially influenced by interviewers' interests and should be understood in relation to the career concerns that he expressed openly to *Parade*, Zindi, and myself.

I am not suggesting that "African sentiment," national sentiment, and nationalism were not involved in Mapfumo's change of direction, but rather that initially their effects were indirectly channeled through the audience and were particularly potent because they intersected with his own professional goals. The crucial point here is that there *had* been a major change in the tastes and desires of the record-buying, nightclub-attending audiences in contrast to the era when the "concert" tradition, with its Mills Brothers and Elvis imitations, was the main draw.

Programs of the Rhodesian state and churches during the Federation, the cosmopolitan hippie and Black Pride Movement of the 1960s, as well as official nationalist party discourse begun during the early 1960s came together and gradually generated national or African sentiment among cosmopolitan-oriented audiences.[6] Such sentiment was probably fortified gradually during the 1970s as the war effort intensified. These shifts in conceptions of identity and taste, in turn, inspired a change in musical style among certain urban-popular musicians seeking to create an original niche and expand their audiences.

This turn to indigenous-based guitar-band music was only one of various simultaneous popular music trajectories during the 1970s—soul, rock, rumba, jazz, country and western, and South African styles were popular and remain so in the 1990s along with rap and other contemporary pop styles. For much of the 1970s indigenous-based electric music was not even a particularly prominent style. Nonetheless, by 1973, a new niche among urban popular music audiences was large enough to inspire musical experiments by M. D. Rhythm Success and Lipopo Jazz, and after 1974 a firm new direction for Thomas Mapfumo.

## Traditionalism and Musical Reformism

By 1975, Mapfumo had cemented his new traditionalist image. As reported by *Parade*, Mapfumo won a 1975 Talent Contest organized by a

Salisbury motel, and "it was not only his voice which wooed the audience of nearly 400, but also his mode of dress which fascinated patrons. Thomas came on the stage, bare from neck to the waist, and wait for it, had on a coloured, long woman's skirt flowing over his lanky legs!" (1975: 5). In fact, Mapfumo is shown in a picture accompanying this article dressed as an indigenous healer with a wooden walking stick (index of authority and age) in one hand and a microphone in the other. The walking stick and microphone are visual images that parallel the reformist character of the music itself. His style and activities represented the epitome of 'modernizing' village music by arranging it for electric instruments, recording it for mass-media diffusion, and performing it in cosmopolitan settings quite distinct from its original contexts, functions, and meanings.

The article continues:

> Another factor in his favour was that he sang winning songs with an appeal to Africans: A traditional tune such as "Torayi Mapadza" (Take your hoes), which is the traditional way of African folk in the TTLs [tribal trust lands] to pick up their hoes and go to the fields to plough in the mornings.
>
> The lesson to be learnt from the contest, from the first round to the finals, is that for a change, our singers and musicians are more and more insisting on playing the kind of music *which has a message to the old and young alike.* Of course, I am not saying that Pop, Soul, and Motown music is dying or is on the way out. Far from it. The message is simply this: A new era is evolving among our musicians, and fans cannot be blamed for saying: And about time too!
>
> Why there is this sudden craze for the traditional music? "It's simple," says Thomas, himself a member of a local band. "Before, we were carried away by Pop, Soul, and Motown. . . . Now we want something different, something that identifies the African with his kind of music. It's just a beginning, mind you, but the future for this kind of music is great!" (*Parade* 1975: 5; my emphasis)

Mapfumo's latter comments signal a conscious recognition of the African, and perhaps national, sentiment that gave rise to his style change in the first place. With his same concern for longevity, and his growing success, he moved into a position to advocate for the chosen style upon which his career depended.

In 1977, *Parade* reported that Mapfumo had again won first prize at a band contest. His name had become synonymous with 'traditional,' music which was beginning to emerge as a market category within the popular music field:

> Nobody in Rhodesia who hears the name Thomas Mapfumo, will fail to associate it with African Traditional music. And recently,

> Thomas Mapfumo, who has climbed and is still climbing the ladder
> of success in traditional music, kept the crowd of more than 3,000
> people on their feet when he sang and pounded the ground to the
> rhythmic beat of drums. (1977b: 43)

The accompanying picture shows him wearing a black robe like the
ones worn by spirit mediums, and again he holds a walking stick in one
hand and the microphone in the other.

Band performance of 'traditional' music remained a minority style,
however, even in 1977 as the height of the war approached, as suggested
by a comment made by one of the contest judges quoted in *Parade*:

> The man [Mapfumo] is really talented, and I wish we had more like
> him in this country. I think most people will agree with me that most
> of our African musicians are concentrating more on the Western type
> of music and ignoring our traditional music. I think this is wrong.
> Because of this, the young generation tends to like Western music
> more than our traditional music. . . . And it is [up to] musicians them-
> selves to start embarking on traditional music. They must follow
> Thomas Mapfumo's example *who now enjoys great support and re-
> spect among Africans of all age groups.* (1977b: 43; my emphasis)

Advocacy of 'traditional' music had been common among middle-class
*Parade* journalists since the late-1950s. As shown in chapter 4, this advocacy was first inspired by the attitudes of 'sophisticated' whites during
the Federation, but later became associated with African cultural nationalism, around 1962.

Both the 1975 and 1977 *Parade* articles also point out that Mapfumo's music succeeded in gaining appeal among both the young and
old. In 1989 Mapfumo made a similar comment to me. I had asked him
why, if he liked mbira music so much, he didn't simply perform with
mbira and hosho rather than guitars, bass, and traps. He replied that
the performance of indigenous music on electric instruments expanded
the appeal of his music. He said that young people who like 'modern'
music are attracted by the electric instruments and that old people in the
rural areas were attracted by his use of 'traditional' music.[7] This is a
particularly clear statement of why a reformist musical style might successfully support a musician's professional aspiration to build a mass
audience. Framed by the discourse of modernity, age and rural/urban
residence are used to stand paradigmatically for contrasting cosmopolitan and indigenous sensibilities. Mapfumo's career goal of appealing to
a wide audience—comprising different social groups—paralleled and
yet remained distinct from the nationalist agenda of incorporating various social groups into "the nation."

## Individual Aptitude
## and Experience

Several groups recorded mbira pieces around 1973–74, and by the end of the 1970s many groups were performing indigenous genres. Mapfumo and his musicians, however, became and remain the leaders in this style because they did it in a particularly convincing way, and they remained dedicated to indigenous-based music over a long period. Like many young artists, Mapfumo experimented with a variety of styles to find a successful niche; unlike many, he found one that worked well with audiences and *that he was particularly good at*. The latter issue should not be undervalued. Perhaps to counter "great person" versions of history, I have had a tendency to stress social and historical conditions in the conjunctural analysis of particular careers and style developments. Yet personal dispositions, investment, physical capabilities, and abilities are certainly important factors within most conjunctures.

Jackson Phiri told me that in the early 1970s he and other musicians had advised Mapfumo to specialize in 'traditional' music, saying, "Leave this English music because your voice can't take you well within English music. He could not sing [it] very well. [Then] he decided to sing traditional music" (Zim93-40: 17). Based on the RBC recordings of the Springfields, and Mapfumo's more recent attempts to sing in transnational pop styles (e.g. on *Chimurenga for Justice*, 1985), I would agree with Phiri's assessment. From his first recorded attempt to sing with mbira music, however, Mapfumo exhibited both the strident vocal quality well suited to huro singing and the potential for a strong, deep mahon'era style that he has continued to develop.

Mapfumo also seemed, and remains, tuned in to the nuances of indigenous Shona music. During my fieldwork in the early 1990s, conservative mbira players such as Mr. Chigamba and Mr. Mhlanga told me that among the different guitar-band musicians that had adapted mbira pieces, Mapfumo and Jonah Sithole were the best. More specifically, they were the ones who "did it correctly." Conservative mbira players frequently criticized the performance of mbira music as done by most bands because they obscured and simplified the music. These same individuals would typically make an exception in regard to Mapfumo and Jonah Sithole. This involved Mapfumo's singing style and choice of lyrics, the bass lines used by his band that were faithful to mbira music, and Sithole's choice of guitar lines which, they felt, accurately rendered mbira parts.

Mapfumo's early experiences with indigenous music at the home of his grandparents may have played a part in his ability "to get it right," but this explanation does not cover Sithole, who only came to indigenous Shona music later in life. Early socialization within a particular soundscape is surely an advantage, but, as in Sithole's case, it is neither a prerequisite nor a guarantee of a particular musical sensibility.

## Mapfumo as Composer and Arranger

In a 1993 interview, Mapfumo emphasized that "Ngoma Yarira" was his own composition: "It was my own tune. Though it was an mbira tune, it was a tune that I just composed" (Zim93-46: 2). I told him that mbira players such as Chris Mhlanga and Chartwell Dutiro associated the song with "Karigamombe." He replied, "Maybe they just thought it was 'Karigamombe,' but this was maybe another 'Karigamombe.' This was my own tune that just came into my head. I just thought, 'This was something good, I have to develop this tune,' and then I thought of the lyrics, the lyrics with a good message" (Zim93-46: 1–2).

### *The Composition Process and Musical Sources*

While Mapfumo is best known for his adaptations of mbira music— "Ngoma Yarira" being the first example—he has also used a variety of other village genres, including agricultural songs (e.g., "Tumira Vana Kuhondo," an early 45-rpm record), war songs ("Nyama Yekugocha," *Chamunorwa* LP, 1989), and dance-drumming genres such as jerusarema ("Muramba Doro" on the *Chamunorwa* LP) and dandanda (e.g., "Tondobayana," *Mr. Music* LP, 1985; "Ndave Kuenda," *Zimbabwe-Mozambique* LP, 1988). Jit songs also form a major portion of his repertoire, and he has recorded and performed other styles, including South African kwela (e.g., "Tombi Wachena," an early 45-rpm record); reggae (e.g. "Ruva Rangu" a 45 from the early 1980s, and "One Man One Woman" on *Chimurenga for Justice*, 1985); and original pieces that defy specific classification. After performing with the Hallelujah Chicken Run Band in the early to mid-1970s, he recorded his first LP, *Hokoyo!* (Watch Out!) with the Acid Band in 1977–78 and then promptly formed the Blacks Unlimited, the name he still uses, although there have been constant personnel changes through the years.

Over the course of his career from 1974 to the 1990s Mapfumo has come up with material for his bands in a variety of ways. Sometimes the band members work together in a collaborative way, with a guitarist or mbira musician supplying a musical structure that is then elaborated and shaped by Mapfumo and others in the group. Chartwell Dutiro, mbira and sax player with Mapfumo between 1986 and 1994, described that he might be playing an mbira piece during a rehearsal or while on a tour bus, and Mapfumo might listen in, begin to sing with it, and ultimately work it up into a new song. He said that he and other musicians supplied the core of new pieces in this way (Dutiro, p.c. October 1990, November 1992). Joshua Hlomayi, who has worked with Mapfumo off and on over the years, related similar stories (fieldnotes 16 March 1993); in fact, "Ngoma Yarira" came about in this way. Mapfumo agreed that "anyone [in the band] with a bright idea can bring it in" (Zim92-23: 16).

Mapfumo and his musicians recombine musical ideas and texts from Shona repertories to create their own versions of well-known pieces; his mbira-based songs often fall into this category. Sometimes, however, one aspect of an indigenous song or mbira piece will be used as the springboard for a new composition, or parts of different songs will be combined in new ways. Dutiro related how the version of "Dangurangu" on the *Chimurenga Masterpiece* LP (1990) was based on a high-part variation he knew of the "typical Dangurangu" (hear the *Soul of Mbira* LP, B-4). The variation, however, became the basis of the entire melody and for new mbira parts which were added; hence the relationship with the classical version "Dangurangu" became clouded (fieldnotes 19 March 1993: 91). For "Chitima Ndikature" (*Chamunorwa*, 1989), Dutiro said he used a kutsinhira (second mbira) part of the classical mbira piece "Nyamaropa" as the kushaura (first part); then he double-tracked the same part a beat behind as the kutsinhira, and triple-tracked a variant of "Karigamombe" as a second kutsinhira part. Dutiro explained how Mapfumo based the song "Hondo" (*Hondo* LP, 1991) on a chipendani (musical bow) song that he had recorded from a television program. Dutiro then added an mbira part which he said was not based on any preexisting mbira piece (fieldnotes 19 March 1993: 92). There are many other such examples. For such songs in the 'traditional' category, Mapfumo may use lyrics largely out of indigenous repertories, a combination of stock and original lyrics, or largely new lyrics.

As another method of coming up with new pieces for the band, Mapfumo sometimes has instructed his musicians to learn pieces directly from recordings of indigenous musicians. One of Mapfumo's most famous songs from the early 1980s, "Pidigori," was learned from an mbira performance on a 45-rpm record by the Chibhora family. Joshua Hlomayi, who was Mapfumo's guitarist at the time, said that Mapfumo had him sit down and learn the song exactly from the mbira recording, also entitled "Pidigori" (fieldnotes 16 March 1993: 84). The vocal melody, text, and accompaniment in the band's rendition is extremely close to the original mbira recording, supporting Hlomayi's recollection of direct imitation. In conversation, Mapfumo also acknowledged the original recording by the Chibhora family.[8]

Early acoustic guitarists were an additional inspiration if not a direct source for Mapfumo's material. For example, Chartwell Dutiro commented that the Mapfumo jit song "Hurukuro" (*Chamunorwa*, 1989) was "the same song" as Ngwaru Mapundu's "Mari Yangu Yapera" (circa 1970, Archives #10394A). Dutiro said Mapundu's guitar line is very much like what they play in the band, although he doubted Mapfumo got the piece directly from Mapundu, since it was a common song. From my comparison of the two recordings, I agree that the musical similarity between them is not exact enough to assume direct imitation; moreover, the two recordings only share one text line in common. Mapfumo, however, told me that Ngwaru Mapundu was one of the people he used to listen to (Zim93-46: 4), and the jit style of the earlier acoustic guitarists seems to have been influential with later electric-guitar bands generally.

In cases like Mapfumo's version of "Kambiri Kaenda" (*Ndangariro*, 1983), it would be difficult to say whether the source was the original indigenous song or the 'traditional adaptation' versions common to bands in the late 1960s such as the All Saints and St. Paul's Band (see chapter 7). In general, however, Mapfumo seems to eschew direct imitation of, or the use of material from, other contemporary guitar bands, given the general emphasis on originality in popular music circles. Finally, Mapfumo has also composed many entirely original songs within the jit and reggae genres as well as songs with a "pop" feel but without any clear genre associations.

Mapfumo told me that when he composes, he typically creates the tune first and then adds the lyrics, "Because, you know, you cannot just write words without a tune. It's the tune that comes first. The tune comes into my head, maybe I can do a little humming on it. And, ah, well, after I'm satisfied that this tune has got right into my head, then I can try to bring in some words, some lyrics" (Mapfumo Zim92-23: 15). Sometimes he works out melodies on guitar, but at other times he simply thinks tunes and then hums them until they are set (Zim92-23: 15). He described the creation process in the following terms:

> I'll do a lot of humming, maybe for some hours. And after a couple
> of hours, this song has disappeared. But you know, it doesn't disappear for good. I'll always expect it to appear some day when I am

just, maybe, moving in the street thinking of something else, and this song just comes up into my mind. I say, "Ah, well, that's the same tune that I was actually humming that day." So, this time when it comes back for the second time, I'm very very careful, you know? I'll have to record the music, to make sure that I have got it on tape. And if I have it on tape I know it's secured. Now I can even go ahead on arranging the music, by listening to the tape, and even add more verses to it, and also some changes, bringing it into a full song.

[Then] I can take it to the place of our practice and play it to the other guys. They will listen to it, and ah well, I will tell them the way to play the chords, everything, the arrangement. And if everything is done, then some other instruments can be added, like brass section. Bring in the brass. So the rhythm section, if it's okay now, then finish with the vocals. When everyone is satisfied that the song is okay, then we can bring in the brass. (Zim92-23: 15-16)

## Local Conceptions of Composition and Originality

Although Mapfumo composes completely original melodies and most or all of the text for many songs, his role as a composer is open to interpretation for pieces heavily based on preexisting pieces and formulas— this is especially at issue for mbira-based pieces. Ignoring his original compositions, various people in Zimbabwe, academics, critics, and indigenous musicians alike, have often suggested that Mapfumo is not a composer, but simply an arranger or performer of indigenous material. The problem here, of course, revolves around how one thinks of composition and the related problem of improvisation. Zimbabweans have different views on these issues.

Echoing other mbira players, Chris Mhlanga feels that there is very little new composition or improvisation within the mbira tradition. Mhlanga thinks of an mbira piece as a bundle of resources (a specific four-phrase cycle, standard bass and melodic lines, standard variations, vocal lines, and some associated text lines) that can be ordered and drawn upon in different ways in each new performance. He conceives of what might be very different performances as being based in the standard material of "the piece" rather than involving new composition or improvisation. Mhlanga noted in another context that each singer might (and should) have his or her own original repertoire of vocal lines that go with a given mbira piece (p.c. February 1995). But since these are largely drawn from the inner patterns of the piece, he did not think of this as improvisation or composition, but rather as a person's individual plucking out of what was already there in the resource bundle of the piece. For people who share Mhlanga's perspective that any performance is more or less a new arrangement or variation of stock resources, Mapfumo is simply a performer of 'traditional' music who, on pieces like "Ngoma Yarira," operates much as other indigenous musicians do.

Other expert mbira players such as Tute Chigamba, however, take a different view. Chigamba composes original mbira pieces which are strongly based on classical pieces. Although he recognizes and talks about the specific model for a given composition, he regards what he does as new creation—to which he applies a new title. This modus operandi resembles Mapfumo's use of preexisting village material, and from this perspective, "Ngoma Yarira" could be considered a new composition.

Zimbabwean academics at the University of Zimbabwe who asserted that Mapfumo was merely an arranger of 'traditional' material in cases like "Ngoma Yarira," were thinking along yet a different set of lines. From their perspective, an original composition must contain substantially new material—similar to copyright criteria in the United States—and hence Mapfumo would not be considered the composer of a piece like "Ngoma Yarira." For the academics who spoke to me, the issue involved cosmopolitan notions of "intellectual property" and the importance of substantial novelty in new art works. When they relegated Mapfumo to the role of *mere* arranger, this was explicitly stated as a criticism. Their position resembled that of the middle-class Africans writing for *Parade* who, throughout the 1970s, pressed local musicians to compose original songs. Within cosmopolitan circles, novelty and originality give prestige to an artist's work, and are important for marketability and the legitimacy of income generation through copyrights within the capitalist music business.

Mhlanga, and others who share his view, would agree with the academics that Mapfumo is not the composer of "Ngoma Yarira," but they express a different attitude about this. This camp's assessment involved the elevated status of "the Tradition," which in their view is basically already complete.[9] How could Mapfumo compose "Ngoma Yarira" when its musical elements were already there in the mbira tradition and the text lines in the common repertories of indigenous performers? Unlike the academics, however, when this group pointed to Mapfumo not as a composer but as a performer of 'traditional' music, they meant it as a compliment; it was indeed a compliment that they accepted his renditions of mbira music in spite of his use of electric instruments.

Although I can only speculate, I believe that Mapfumo's own assertion of himself as the composer of pieces like "Ngoma Yarira" combines indigenous-based modus operandi and positive perceptions of reordering preexisting materials with the prestige attached to originality within cosmopolitan circles. The issue of intellectual property—ownership— also enters in since, after "Ngoma Yarira," co-credited with Hlomayi, Mapfumo claimed full copyright for all subsequent recorded material regardless of the source. He is even listed as composer of the Chibhora's "Pidigori" on the Earthworks international re-release of the song (*Zimbabwe Frontline*, Virgin 1-91001).

The different views on Mapfumo as composer underline the interface of various indigenous and cosmopolitan perspectives as well as commercial pressures. In discussions with me, Mapfumo's own assessment of his role as composer seemed to fuse, or at other times alternate between, these different positions. In contrast to his assertion that he composed "Ngoma Yarira," in one interview he called "Murembo" "pure traditional," and in another he said that he composed the song (Zim93-46: 1). This inconsistency may be due to the fact that he was thinking in general stylistic terms when he called it "pure traditional" and about his specific reordering when he claimed that he composed it. It may simply be due to the ambiguity of what composition implies for people who shift between indigenous and cosmopolitan positions.

## Conceptions of "The Art Work"

In contrast to the indigenous way of reordering the resources of a piece for each new performance, once Mapfumo arrives at a given version of, or composes, a piece, he and his band play it much the same way for many years. Typically in live shows during 1992–93, their performances closely mirrored the previous recordings for all the pieces I was familiar with. This was particularly striking for songs like "Pidigori," which had been recorded over a decade earlier with different guitarists. Thus, while the band's process of reassembling stock resources to construct new pieces resembles the modus operandi of village musicians, they depart from the method of indigenous performance—once a band version is established, it becomes a set item.

New musicians in the Blacks Unlimited learn established parts and play them according to the authoritative "score" of the recording, much as a replacement symphony player would do, although there are spaces for improvised guitar breaks. While in indigenous contexts "a piece" remains a bundle of resources for the constantly unfolding processes of performance, Mapfumo's creative process is directed toward a finished end product which is then reproduced; this attitude was reflected in his own description of composing. His conception of "the art work" thus resembles widely held cosmopolitan attitudes. This represents a fundamental contrast with indigenous Shona conceptions of what music is, yet through his choice of stylistic resources and his discourse about his work, Mapfumo consciously associates himself with Shona lifeways as an explicit alternative to cosmopolitanism.

## Mapfumo: Chimurenga Singer and Song Texts

After 1974, Mapfumo often sang indigenous Shona texts, as he did in 1966 and on his first mbira-based recording, "Ngoma Yarira." Typical of indigenous singing and the acoustic guitarists' performance of indigenous songs, "Ngoma Yarira" contains a good deal of vocable singing and repetition of a single text or vocable line. The lines are organized as a mosaic of formulas rather than as a narrative.

NGOMA YARIRA

Vakomana ngoma yarira     haa
Boys the drum has sounded haa
Yarira          iyerere eya iyo iyo haa
It has sounded iyerere eya iyo iyo haa
Vakomana ngoma yarira     wee
Boys the drum has sounded wee
Iyerere hiyewore eya hiya woye
Vakomana regai ndibaiwe
Boys let me get killed
Iye woye hiye worere iye hoiye (×2)
Nyamutambanemombe wakafa wani
Isn't it that Extravagant-with-cattle [rich person] died?
Iyewo hiye worere iye worere ha (×2)
Kware kwangu ndaishereketa ini
Long ago I used to try out many different things
Iyewo iye worere a iye worere yee (×3)
Hondende hondende hiyewo hiye worere iye worere (×2)
Hiyewo iya ha
Hiye worere eya hiya woiye (×2)
A hiya oh hiya woo
Hiya hiya hiya hiya hiya (×4)

Just as the melody of "Ngoma Yarira" includes variants of stock formulas that are drawn from mbira pieces like "Karigamombe" and "Nyamaropa," variants of text lines of this song such as "Vakomana ngoma yarira" and "regai ndibaiwe" are commonly heard in indigenous performance.

If "Ngoma Yarira" was a turning point in Mapfumo's career musically, the flip side of the 45, "Murembo," was equally important in terms of his work as a singer of political, or chimurenga, songs. In a 1992 interview, Mapfumo remarked that this song "was about the war, yes, when the war broke out. That was the first, ah, chimurenga tune that I sang" (Zim92-23: 9). The first stanza is rendered twice a capella, partially in speechlike style. Then the band enters playing in the rhythm of a dance drumming piece with a strong 3/4 pattern played over a moderate 12/8 frame (chords alternating Bm-A each measure of 12/8). The vocals involve call-and-response singing, and the most unusual aspect of the performance is a Cubanesque legato trumpet solo. As my teacher, Chris Mhlanga, and I listened to this song, he remarked that it was a 'traditional' melody and text to which Mapfumo had added some (unspecified) new words.

### MUREMBO [ELEPHANT'S TUSK]

Here is an elephant's tusks, don't expose it to dry [to the air and
    sun].
When to the hornless cow, owner of tusks.
The result of Muchakata's coming,
Staying with cattle, elephant's tusks
Making a joke of the entanglement of snakes.
In the veldt
The buzz of bees
Elephant's tusk.
A hee iye woiye hoha (×2)
All the children have perished
The war has come
Uuuuuuuu
*[Instrumental interlude]*
All the children are finished
The war has come (×5)
Give me my spear
Today I'll cut you to pieces
I'll savagely cut you with a knife
Just take a look Nhuka [totemic name]
See this old man
Be witness to what I'm going to do
I'll keep on singing
This can't be
*[Instrumental interlude]*
All the children have died
Oha he ohiye
The war has come

Oha he ohiye (×4)
Give me my axe
I'll leave you in pieces
I'll wantonly cut you with a knife
Just have a look Nhuka
See this old man
Witness what I'm going to do.[10]

Speaking of "Murembo," Mapfumo remarked,

> This is my own tune, and when I composed this tune it was during the
> liberation struggle. This is the first chimurenga tune, you know, that
> people went out to buy. When I recorded this music on a single, eh we
> recorded a lot of singles, and out of those singles, this was the only
> single that the people thought was good music. It had a good message.
> And straight away, they received the message loud and clear. And they
> went into the shops to buy it. And the rest of the music that I recorded,
> ah, when I recorded "Murembo," we threw all that music into the
> dustbin because people never liked it. (Zimb93-46: 1)

As with Mapfumo's use of indigenous Shona musical style, his recording
of political lyrics was thus also guided by the desires of his audience. In
this comment he directly and repeatedly connects their desires to record
sales.

Numerous Shona songs like "Murembo" make references to wield-
ing spears and knives, war, and fighting (e.g., "Tondobayana," "Baya
wa baya," "Ndobaiwa," and others; see Berliner 1977: 8).[11] As Robert
Kauffman explains, such songs shifted from being war songs at the end
of the nineteenth century to boxing songs until they were taken up at
political rallies in the 1960s (1970: 313–14). Mapfumo's recording of
this song in 1974 after the Liberation War had begun in earnest took on
a whole new, quite literal meaning.

A number of the pieces that Mapfumo recorded, which later were
called 'chimurenga' songs, used lyrics from indigenous Shona repertories that took on new meaning during the war years. For example,
lines from "Tozvireva Kupiko," such as "Who shall we share our frustrations with?" and "Our country is becoming a desert / there is no rain
here / Our children go unclothed," could be heard from indigenous
singers and the early acoustic guitar players as a general complaint, but
they took on special political meaning during the war. The text from
"Pfumvu Pa Ruzevha" (Hardships in the rural areas) is a similar
example.[12]

Mapfumo said that his early hit with the Acid Band, "Tumira Vana
Kuhondo" (Send their children to war, a 45-rpm record, circa 1977),
was a harvest song. Chris Mhlanga said that it was an old grinding song.

He explained that it had been a complaint about young people being sent out on raids in the precolonial days. Since they were always being sent off to war, there were fewer people to do the grinding, and the work took longer (fieldnotes 15 December 1992: 35). In the context of the mid-1970s, however, the meaning shifted from a complaint against sending children to war to advocating that people join the fight:

TUMIRA VANA KUHONDO

They send their children to war
Hoo oa haa aa
You'll regret
Send their children to war, brother
Send their children to war iyeiye
Send their children to war, sister
Always sending children to war
Children to war
Ho ao
Children to war, mother
Ha aa
Children to war iye
This time you'll regret
They send their children to war father
They send their children to fight
Children to war
Ho aa
Children to war
This time you will regret
Send children to war you will die
Habitually sending children to war.[13]

In 1977–78, Mapfumo recorded his first Gramma Records LP, *Hokoyo!* (Watch Out!), with the Acid Band. The record contained songs on a variety of topics, and some made fairly explicit references to the war. The jit song "Matiregera Mambo" refers to the enemy and the death of old women and men. The mbira-based "Mhandu Musango" says,

My name is you-will-regret [meant as a threat]
My name is Patriot
I'm not afraid of saying it
There are graves scattered about in the forest, Lord
Let the murderers continue to kill, Lord
We die for telling the truth, Lord
This season a jackal will feed on grass
The unusual will happen, Lord
This time the ominous will occur
Kill the enemies in the forests . . .

Alec Pongweni commented that bands singing political music within the country were purposefully ambiguous in contrast to the explicit political content of ZANU's chimurenga songs (1982: ii); this statement has been repeated often (e.g., Chinamhora 1987: 263). In songs like "Mhandu Musango," the ambiguity was not due to a lack of references to war, but rather a failure to specify precisely who the jackals and murderers were. This ambiguity led to the potential for the Rhodesian state, the Patriotic Front, and other political parties to both use and disavow Mapfumo at different times, as in fact happened.

### Mapfumo and Political Nationalism

As is now well known, a number of Mapfumo's records were banned by the government, and he was detained in prison because of his music during the late 1970s (see Frederikse 1982: 109; Zindi 1985: 34). Mapfumo candidly expressed that during that time he was often apprehensive about harsh repercussions for his songs, and yet he continued to record them. This certainly took courage which, by his own statements, was inspired by a desire to support the Liberation War effort as well as by his strong ambition to become a successful singer. Because of the political sentiment among his audience, which he apparently came to share, these two motivations were congruent.

The "indigenous yet cosmopolitan" imagery of his style in conjunction with his broad-based appeal should have made him particularly useful to the African nationalist cause. Mapfumo's music was, in fact, used by various political groups by the end of the 1970s. For example, Mapfumo played for a Muzorewa rally during the Smith-Muzorewa coalition. Here his music and popularity were explicitly harnessed to a nationalist position, albeit an alternative one to the militant Patriotic Front. Mapfumo claims that he was forced to play for Muzorewa under the threat of being sent back to prison; he has repeatedly stated that he was never for Muzorewa (Frederikse 1982: 264; Zindi 1985: 34). Yet his participation in a Muzorewa rally cast lasting suspicion on him in the view of militant nationalists.

More dramatic still, as reported by Frederikse (1982: 265) and widely known in Zimbabwe, Mapfumo records were played on loudspeakers out of Rhodesian helicopters during bombing raids in an attempt to coopt the popular singer and dishearten the guerrillas. Map-

STARS OF THE SEVENTIES

fumo himself can hardly be held accountable, yet several ex-combatants that I spoke with who experienced this—suggesting that it was a common practice—continue to have an ambivalent feeling about Mapfumo. One said that because Mapfumo's lyrics were ambiguous, they could be used by either side, and that he should have been more explicit if he didn't wish to be misused. Coming from men who went into the bush willing to sacrifice everything, such criticism at least seems understandable.

While other Zimbabweans understood Mapfumo's music as supporting the Patriotic Front (Pongweni 1982; Chinamhora 1987: 263), the ZANU leadership expressed ambivalent feelings at best in relation to the popular singer. For example, at the celebration of Zimbabwean independence in April 1980, a number of local indigenous and urban-popular groups performed with Bob Marley as headliner. Mapfumo's band was programmed in a decidedly unprominent position in the wee hours of the morning, which Mapfumo understood as a slight. Yet his music was played on the radio for Independence Day along with Marley's by way of celebration—the disc jockey said, "And now, let's listen to Thomas Mapfumo's *music of Zimbabwe*" (Frederikse 1982: 328; my emphasis).

Regardless of Mapfumo's own feelings and political affiliations, his relation to the victorious nationalist party was complex and is understood in a variety of ways in Zimbabwe. The same can be said for the style of music he has championed. Nonetheless, as Mapfumo and bands like the Bhundu Boys attempted to enter the international worldbeat arena after the mid-1980s, it was precisely nationalist political associations that were used to market the music by Mango Records, the media, and the musicians themselves in England, Europe, and the United States. Politics had, indeed, become a key element of the style abroad because of the desires of cosmopolitan worldbeat fans for musical heroes (see chapter 9).

## Zexie Manatsa and the Green Arrows

Like Thomas Mapfumo, Zexie Manatsa composed and recorded his first song about the war in 1974, and he continued recording political songs throughout the 1970s. Zexie Manatsa's band, the Green Arrows, was one of the most popular and financially successful Zimbabwean groups of the 1970s and early 1980s.

The Green Arrows were formed in 1968 in Bulawayo as an mbaqanga-style band consisting of brothers Zexie Manatsa (lead vocalist, bass, composer), Stanley Manatsa (lead guitar), Kadias Manatsa (rhythm guitar), and Raphael Mboweni (drums). The Manatsas were originally from north central Mashonaland (Guruve), and Zexie started learning music on a homemade banjo before he moved to Bulawayo. In the late 1960s they performed and toured Zimbabwe with the Sakaza Sisters, a South African group with Atalia Dube, Joyce Banda, Philda Tazman, and male singer-dancer Max Mabena (*Parade* 1969b: 10; Manatsa, Zim93-58: 1–3). This ensemble, like the many other 'simanje-manje' groups that took Zimbabwe by storm in the late 1960s, was similar to the Mahotella Queens in style. It included a front line of female singer-dancers and a male "growler" who sang in a low, gravelly voice. The mbaqanga music played by the backup band, in this case the Manatsas, featured stock harmonic ostinatos such as I–V, and I–IV–V–I, and I–IV–I–V in 4/4 meter and moderate tempos. The most influential feature of this style in Zimbabwe was the exceptionally prominent bass line.

While the Green Arrows specialized in mbaqanga, and it remains the prominent influence and favorite music for Zexie Manatsa even in the 1990s, the group has always performed a variety of styles. A review of their Harare performance in 1969 mentions that they performed various shangara (Shona foot-stamping dance) pieces, one of which featured "mbira tunes from guitars" (*Parade* 1969b: 10). No recorded evidence or interviews with Zexie Manatsa indicate that the Green Arrows did classical mbira music this early. Since it was in the context of a shangara song (a type recorded by the Harare Mambos during the same period), the *Parade* writer might have been referring to the damped guitar technique or "mbira-like" lead guitar parts. This evidence, however, points to the fact that the Green Arrows were experimenting along the same lines as other groups doing traditional adaptations at the end of the 1960s.

Leaving Bulawayo, the band resettled permanently in Harare in 1972. In 1974 the band released its first 45-rpm record, "Chipo Chiroowa," which was a major commercial success. By this time, the Green Arrows had moved away from the simanje-manje style dominated by the female choral singing and male "growler." Zexie had taken over the lead singing, and the group had become a more conventional guitar band. As Manatsa told me, "Chipo Chioorwa" was based on South African marabi music and was a light song about marriage. The entire text, repeated many times, is as follows: "Chipo marry so that we may celebrate / Our parents will rejoice / We will have cakes and celebrate." The B side of the record was a fast instrumental piece closely resembling jit in the drum part and overall rhythmic feel but with gestures in the lead guitar and heavy bass line borrowed from South African mbaqanga.

## Political Songs, Eclectic Music

According to Zexie Manatsa and his wife Stella, historian of the group, the band's second recording in 1974 was "Nadji Manawayenda," which was written about the war. It was "about people who go out to fight, those who will not come back" (Zim93-58: 4; recording unavailable). Before the issue of politics had been introduced into the conversation at all, Manatsa led into the topic of composing "Nadji Manawayenda" by saying, "Now, from that time [1974] I was composing the other records just because we Africans, we were fighting so that we should get our country. You see? Now from 'Chipo Chioorwa' the second number was 'Nadji Manawayenda'" (Zim93-58: 3).

He went on to suggest that although the war did not directly affect many people around him in the city during 1974, it was still on everyone's mind, and it was spoken about a great deal by friends, neighbors, and family members (Zim93-58: 5). He explained that as a composer, it was his role to comment on what was going on around him and to reflect the feelings of his peers:

TURINO: The music that you composed about the war during the war years, were you particularly involved with that, or was that just one theme among many?

MANATSA: No, no. I think it was just because if you compose, if you want to be a composer, what you compose or what you do depends, like atmosphere, you see? If it is raining, then you sing about that. Now that time, there was a war so I was speaking some of what was happening, you see? Then in other words, as I am an African, I should sing about war, you see, because we wanted this country to be an African country. We wanted an African government. (Zim93-58: 15)

The Green Arrows recorded a string of hit 45-rpm records in the years between 1974 and 1980, produced by West Nkosi, a South African. These covered a wide range of subjects and musical styles. For example, in 1976 they released "Nowhere Man" (Farayi Farayi FYF 115)—not the Beatles song but an original piece sung in English about a "lonely man"—heavily influenced by British and U.S. rock of the late 1960s. "My Pretty Angel" (Farayi Farayi FYF 120, 1976) and "How Could I Love Someone Else" (side B of FYF 120) were in this same mold. "Ndiyo Nzira Yerudo" (FYF 121, 1977) was a slow, spoken love

song influenced by North American soul, complete with doo-wop vocals. In the same year, however, the Green Arrows released "Musango
Mune Hangaiwa" (FYF130, 1977):

> Dear Lord, we have a request, help us.
> We need rain please,
> But it must not fall in the forests,
> There are some pigeons there
> Birds that have run wild,
> They are dedicated to our ancestral spirits;
> Don't trap them if you see them,
> You get Nehanda's permission first
> The chief guardian spirit of Zimbabwe.
>                     (trans. Pongweni 1982: 140)

Manatsa explained, "What I'm trying to sing, you say, 'Musango Mune
Hangaiwa,' you see, it's like saying the comrades [guerrillas], they are
in the bush. Please don't greet them. Don't do anything to them"
(Zim93-58). This song begins with a request for rain, typical of village
songs, then adds the ambiguous metaphor of guinea-fowls for the guerrillas, and includes the image of Nehanda, a primary nationalist symbol,
as we saw with the ZANU's chimurenga songs. Musically "Musango
Mune Hangaiwa" is an mbaqanga song (moderate 4/4 I–IV–V–V progression, prominent bass, South African–style lead guitar). This is only
one of many examples illustrating that there was no necessary correlation between political texts supporting the guerrillas and the use of
Shona village musical genres.

In 1977, Manatsa composed and recorded "Ndono Baye Bere"
(FYF 130) with the Green Arrows, a political song that was roughly
based on mbira music. This song has the fast 12/8 hosho part played on
the highhat, the bass playing a four-phrase cycle (G Bm D | D Bm D |
Am C Em | D Bm D), Stanley Manatsa playing damped lead-guitar lines
modeled on doubled mbira high parts, and Zexie performing village-
style yodeling and vocable singing. Although the text of "Ndono Baye
Bere" contains lines and images typical of Shona village songs (e.g.,
"Give me my spear," the hyena metaphor), its new political meaning is
quite explicit in the context of 1977:

A

Lead: Give me my spear, please
Chorus: I'm going to kill the hyena
Lead: That has caused havoc
Chorus: Beyond the Manyame River

Lead: My wish is that
Chorus: Ah hiya, I'm going to kill the hyena (×2).
Lead: Hwengoreiye
Chorus: Hiya iya, I'm going to kill the hyena
Lead: Hwengoreiye
Chorus: Hiya iya beyond the Manyame River.
*[Instrumental interlude, then A lines repeated]*

B

Chorus:  Arrive in peace ancestral spirit
         There are children around, Ah aa!
         Do not come with anger, Ah aa!
         Well done great hunter
         You've killed the troublesome rogue
         Which had robbed us of peace in our home.
*[Instrumental interlude, then A lines repeated]*

Zexie mentioned several other songs of 1977, 1978, and 1979 that were, like this one, not actual mbira songs but modeled on mbira music. These include "Ntunusita" (unavailable) and "Madzangara Dzimu" (FYF 134, 1978), a thinly veiled political statement: "Are they the rogues who have robbed us of peace? / Yes they are apparitions, which have robbed us of peace." "Pamusoro Madzai Mayi" (FYF 137, 1778) is an mbira-based song with a mosaic-style text about living in an urban hostel, problems with finding a house, and relations between parents and children; the recording includes local ngoma (drums). Finally, the mbira-based "Baba Kutonga Madzoro" (FYF 145, 1979) instructs chiefs to rule properly because "tomorrow it will be me or my son who will be in charge." Manatsa said this song was a warning to the government, but it also raises issues of intergenerational conflicts and power struggles in the rural areas during the war. Kriger (1992), discusses how the presence of the guerrillas in rural villages and their use of young people as "runners" and informants sometimes provided young people with a base of power against the authority of elders. The ultimate threat was being branded as a "sell-out" by someone attached to the guerrillas—leading to a trial and perhaps execution.

Interspersed with these mbira-based recordings were "Nyoka Yendara" (FYF 136, 1978), a political jit song about killing the ominous *ndara* snake that has crept into the palace of Great Zimbabwe, and other jit songs, one of which, "Mateu 22" (FYF 147), had a Biblical text. They recorded several rumbas (e.g., "Dzamuningwa," FYF 136; "Mawira Mombe Part 2," FYF 147, 1979), and over six sides of mbaqanga.

Manatsa favored an eclectic musical approach for the Green Arrows. He told me that mbaqanga had always been his favorite music but
that

> around me, we are Zimbabweans. If we just play mbaqanga without
> putting that style, mbira, a little mbira in it, you see, the rumba a little
> bit, you see—so that the audience, they will be 500 in a nightclub, or
> in a stadium, 5000, but otherwise, 10 percent or a higher per-
> cent[age] of them, they want rumba style; and then 10 percent of
> them, they want reggae. So you've got to mix those things or they
> wouldn't be happy. . . .
>     I've got to compose a record which, if we have got twelve million
> in Zimbabwe, it should be about eight million or ten million, they
> love that song, they will be the audience. (Zim93-58: 11)

His approach to composing song texts on a variety of themes combined
this concern with audience response and his own vision that composers
should speak to what was going on around them; these two issues were
congruent in his view.

In contrast to Mapfumo, Manatsa noted that he composes the lyrics
first and then creates a suitable tune. Although almost always working
within preexisting styles that he felt would have popular appeal, Manatsa's music is largely original.[14] As he stated above, he composed
songs in mbira style because he felt that part of his audience wanted to
hear that type of music; he himself preferred mbaqanga. While many of
his songs about the war used local Shona genres and features, others did
not; there was no consistent linking of local musical style, for emblematic purposes, with political themes. The same is true for another prominent musician of the late 1970s, Oliver M'tukudzi, who exemplifies a
similar approach to composition and the creation of political songs, but
who stands out in other ways as one of Zimbabwe's most original
artists.

## Oliver M'tukudzi

Oliver M'tukudzi was born on 22 September 1952 in Harare. His
family was of Korekore background from the Mount Darwin district
in northeastern Zimbabwe. M'tukudzi attended secondary school in
Highfield but spent his holidays with his grandparents in Mount Darwin. His father grew up in the Tribal Trust Lands singing in school
choirs, and his parents met through their active participation in choir
competitions. Oliver had also been involved with school choirs, and he
told me that his parents' music "naturally inspired me, but from the

Western world, I had favorite artists like Otis Redding" (Zim93-53: 2). Redding's influence is still apparent in the slow soulful ballads that are a specialty of M'tukudzi.[15]

Younger than Mapfumo and Manatsa, M'tukudzi cites Thomas Mapfumo as an important local influence: "Around 1977 we were all doing copyrights [foreign popular songs], but he [Mapfumo] started creating his own songs in Shona, and I admired him. I said, 'Ah! I think this guy is taking the right direction'" (Zim93-53: 2). For a short time, M'tukudzi's first band, the Wagon Wheels, backed Mapfumo. Although M'tukudzi had composed his first song at age sixteen, it was his close contact with Mapfumo that inspired him to concentrate on his own compositions after 1977.

### The Compositional Process and Musical Style

People in Zimbabwe have difficulty characterizing M'tukudzi's music, although most often it is described as being based in South African mbaqanga (e.g., Zindi 1985: 40). M'tukudzi correctly rejects this assessment. As we have seen, Mapfumo might perform a village song close to the original model, and Manatsa composes his own songs, but typically with strong adherence to a genre's style components. M'tukudzi too sometimes composes within set genres, particularly jit (a term he uses), but often he draws from a variety of sources to create his own idiosyncratic fusions. When I mentioned to him that people have difficulty classifying his music, he answered,

> The reason why is, in my music, I try to fuse a lot into the sound. If you listen to the song "Shanje" [1981] itself, it's jit. But it is also off jit. You can have two, you know, two beats in one song. . . . And I did that as an experimental thing. I never thought that it would work out. Now, if I tell a person "Shanje" is jit, he might not agree with me because his ear is not on the jit side of the song, it is on the other side!
>
> Yeah, I wouldn't blame them for failing to identify my music because it's like that, it's got a lot of fusion in it. I fuse local, different types of music. (Zim93-53: 7)

M'tukudzi emphasized that his music is often strongly based in local Shona music, and he specifically mentioned dandanda, katekwe, jit, and other genres as 'traditional' sources that he uses in composition. But with the exception of a few mbira-based songs and jit, indigenous genres supply elements, not overriding structures, for his music;

hence these resources are not so easily recognized as compared, say, to
Mapfumo's more literal performance of indigenous songs. M'tukudzi
related,

> Yeah, I use a lot of different types of music. I didn't have a particular
> type of music to do. And another thing, I think the difference between
> me and Thomas [Mapfumo] is, I don't do traditional songs. I write
> my own songs, I think of my own tune and my own sound, whereas
> Thomas's songs, most of the songs are traditional songs, songs which
> were done by our ancestors. Songs, I mean mbira songs, you can't
> just search to put them somewhere else, I mean, it has to sound just
> like that [you have to keep them in their original form]. So you are
> limited, you can't maneuver a lot if you are doing traditional songs.
> You have to stick to the mbira, and if you're doing mbira songs, your
> guideline is how the mbira is played, so you have to play it like that.
> (Zim93-53: 5)

Oliver told me that jit is playful music which could therefore be used
more or less loosely to create new songs, but that mbira is the "serious
business" of older people, and that it had to be done correctly. Hence,
he said,

> As an artist, I can't carry on using mbira music only, because it's got
> its own limitations. You can't go beyond that. If you go beyond that
> [you] are not doing it right. I mean, if you try and improve from
> there, you can only add a guitar or something. That's what you find,
> for an example, in Thomas Mapfumo's music. If you listen very care-
> fully to his music, you can't put keyboards to dominate on the song.
> Otherwise you spoil the whole song. You can't do that! Then it won't
> be mbira music. (Zim93-53: 12)

Here M'tukudzi reflects his deep awareness of attitudes about Shona
classical music and 'tradition' among indigenous musicians: it has to be
done correctly. But he very consciously chooses the modernist values of
creative freedom for the artist rather than the indigenous-classicist adherence to a canon. He has thus, in his mature work, set limits on what
sources he will use based on his understanding of these two different
artistic orientations.

Nonetheless, in his early work between 1977 and 1981, M'tukudzi
did record several mbira-based songs, a number of jit-based pieces,
compositions influenced by mbaqanga and rumba, as well as others that
eschew classification. This music was, like all of Manatsa's early recordings, produced by South African West Nkosi. In 1977, with his
first group, the Wagon Wheels, M'tukudzi recorded "Mutavara" (Gallo

company, Kudzanayi label, KDZ 109), a composition with strong rumba elements in the 3 + 3 + 2 rhythmic feel and light guitar work. The B side of the 45 was "Waenda Rosemary," a fast jit song (quick 12/8 meter, I–IV–I–V progression) which, in the guitar and bass parts, closely resembles Mapfumo's piece "Pfumvu Pa Ruzevha" (on *The Chimurenga Singles 1976–1980*, Shanachie Records, Meadowlark 403). In the same year he recorded the jit-based "Ziwere" (KDZ 115) with the Black Spirits, and "Ndiri Bofu," which combines a slow jit feel with strong mbaqanga elements in the bass and guitar parts, bringing jit back to its South African roots. One of his early mbira-based recordings was "Gunguwo" (Kudzanayi [Gallo] KDZ 118, 1978). This piece followed the typical four-phrase, 12/8 structure, although the actual bass progression (A C♯ F♯ | D D F♯ | A C♯ E | E D E) does not correspond to any classical piece that I know; also M'tukudzi did not utilize the damped "mbira-guitar" style.

Already on these early recordings, M'tukudzi's mature vocal and musical style was evident. Even on the mbira-based pieces, he did not use village vocal techniques such as huro (yodeling), mahon'era (soft, low) singing, and extensive use of vocables. Rather he sang (and sings) his songs in a largely unornamented style with his deep, rich, throaty voice, often in call-and-response with female or, more recently, male and female background vocalists.

Contrasting with his later recordings, the instrumentation of these early 45s was guitar-dominated, with M'tukudzi playing lead guitar. By the *Shanji* LP (1981, Kudzanayi BL 304) keyboards (first organ, later synthesizer) became central to his sound, in combination with his own lead guitar playing on electric and sometimes acoustic guitars. Through the 1990s, his band has typically featured two guitarists, keyboards, bass, traps, and between two and four background vocalists-dancers, both male and female. M'tukudzi himself emphasizes the centrality of keyboards as a distinguishing feature of his style.

## Political Music and Song Texts

Like Mapfumo, Manatsa, and many other songwriters during the second half of the 1970s, M'tukudzi wrote many songs about the Liberation War. M'tukudzi told me that during that time,

> You didn't have to think of doing it [writing political songs], because it was the life we were living. You felt it, you are within it, you have to say it. We were all under this pressure of getting liberated. So, music then, we used to sing encouraging songs to the boys in the bush,

and were acting as mediators. The people in the urban areas wanted to put up a message to them, we would put it in a song and send the message over to them, to the boys in the bush. (Zim93-53: 3)

M'tukudzi went on to say that all of his records before independence concerned the war (Zim93-53: 4). This is not literally true. His 1977 jit recording "Waenda Rosemary" was a complaint about a wife who leaves home for a rich man, and "Ndiri Bofu" was an appeal to Jehovah. The text of the jit song "Ziwere" (1977, KDZ 115) again discusses family problems:

LS: Who has eloped with my daughter?
BS: Beware of the snake
LS: Eloping with my daughter in my absence
BS: Beware of the snake
LS: I am going on a rampage
BS: Beware of the snake

As a songwriter and popular performer, M'tukudzi feels he has a responsibility to offer moral guidance and to act as a *sahwira* for the society at large. A *sahwira* is a person—an outsider—who has a special role with another family to observe and try to help or mediate in times of crisis. Very much in the same terms as expressed by Manatsa, M'tukudzi stated that he, as an artist, simply responds to what is going on around him, and then feels moved to comment on it to move things in a positive direction. During the late 1970s the war was uppermost in many peoples' minds, and it was natural for M'tukudzi to write songs about the war and to act, as he said, as mediator between people in the city and the guerrillas.

As with Mapfumo and Manatsa's music, there was no necessary correlation between the use of local Shona musical genres and political lyrics in M'tukudzi's compositions of the 1970s. For example, the rumba-influenced piece "Mutavara" (1977) addresses the war using images found in Shona village repertory:

Start the song, oh Mutavara,
Beat the drum
I am going to die in the forest
Start the song, Mutavara
The kill is only for the dedicated hunter
You better remain behind Marunjeya
I am going to meet my death in the forest.
. . . . . . . . . . . . . . . .
I am going out hunting
*[Backup vocalists]:* Oh mother

I am going to hunt in a thick forest
Oh mother
I am going to hunt all by myself
Oh mother
*[same lines repeated in various order]*.

By contrast, the mbira-styled "Gunguwo" (1978) is a more general statement about differences of wealth in keeping with many village songs:

The crow, oh no
The crow gentlemen, oh women *[vocables]*
The crow ekes out a meager living
Think about it gentlemen
The crow scratches a living from the unyielding land
You have a granary
What is your life like?
Just tell me nephew
Today it is you who is suffering
Just tell me what is your life like?
*[same lines repeated in various order]*

Many of Oliver's songs from the late 1970s simply discussed hardships in general terms. The text of the mbira-related song "Chipatapata" (1978, KDZ 120) is an example.

These your children, Oh God
Are suffering
These your children, My God
Are enduring pain
You know dear God
The cause of their agony
You know dear God
The cause of their suffering

While he considered all of his compositions of the period to be related to the war, the texts were, as he told me, purposefully vague. Such songs are probably best understood as a reflection of the general feeling of the difficult nature of the time rather than as explicit political statements. Regarding the lack of correlation of text content and musical style, M'tukudzi expressed the opinion that it was the text that conveyed meaning about social issues, and musical style was not important in this process.

In his songs composed after independence, M'tukudzi has written texts about Christian religious themes, love, family problems, and a wide range of social problems, including homelessness, street children, ill-treatment of widows, and problems between children and parents and between husbands and wives. He has stared in two locally produced movies (*Jit* and *Neria*), and he still sees his role as a composer and performer in line with the duties of a *sahwira*. He remained one of the most prominent artists in Zimbabwe in the mid-1990s. While he has had a few international releases and has performed in Europe during the late 1980s and 1990s, M'tukudzi has not become a prominent figure in the cosmopolitan worldbeat scene.

### Jonah Sithole

Jonah Sithole was a major performer of "mbira-guitar" music from the late 1970s until his death in the mid-1990s. Along with Thomas Mapfumo, he is the guitar-band musician most highly respected by classical players for his renditions of mbira music. He is largely known for his participation in Mapfumo's bands off and on over the years, but in interviews with me Sithole emphasized his independent career with the bands he has led—the Storm, and Deep Horizone. Sithole's first "mbira-guitar" recording with the Storm, "Sabhuku" (AS 1062), was released during the 1977–78 period just as more bands had begun to turn to this style.

Sithole was born in 1954 (d. 1997) in southeastern Zimbabwe and moved to Bulawayo for secondary school.[16] There, influenced by his brother, he began to play guitar in South African mbaqanga style around 1968. He was attracted to this music because of the South African bands touring the country at the time (Zim92-17: 3). He followed his brother to the town of KweKwe and then to Harare and joined his band, the Delphans, as rhythm guitarist in 1970; the Delphans also played some Zairian-styled rumba. In 1971 he was employed as a bass player for the Lipopo Jazz Band with Jackson Phiri, and then with the Great Sounds as a guitarist, playing rumba in both contexts. He played briefly with Mapfumo in the Black Spirits in 1975 (Zindi 1985: 33; Sithole, Zim92: 17: 6–7). According to Sithole, they were not playing indigenous music, but rather the "Afro-rock" style at the time (see the Mapfumo interview above).

Sithole told me that he didn't begin to specialize in the "mbira-guitar" style until around 1976–77 with The Storm.[17] Growing up in southeastern Zimbabwe and Bulawayo, he had not really come in contact with mbira music until he moved to Harare.

> TURINO: How did you start playing the mbira style? Where did you get the idea, why did you start doing it?

SITHOLE: Well, to be truthful, I got it from the mbira itself, by listening
to records. You know, they would play it on the air, you
see. . . . This is where I got the idea.

TURINO: And what year was that?

SITHOLE: 1977. Yeah with "Sabhuku," that's 1978. (Zim92-17: 9)

Thus, like Joshua Hlomayi and others associated with the "mbira-guitar" style, Sithole did not grow up with Zezuru mbira music; he be-came attracted to it through its diffusion on African Service Radio 2, and was probably influenced by the other bands doing indigenous music during this time.

Sithole stated that when he composes "mbira-guitar" songs, he does not have a particular mbira piece in mind. He starts from a general sound in his head, sometimes discovering later that it might correlate with a particular mbira song. He said that to begin with a particular mbira song as a model would limit creativity (Zim92-17: 14–15). His own compositions with the Storm, and after 1981 with Deep Horizone, usually do not correspond to specific classical mbira pieces. For ex-ample, his original, late-1970s recording of "Sabhuku" was generally related to classical mbira music through the rhythmic feel, the four-phrase 12/8 form, Sithole's consistent use of the damped guitar tech-nique, and some use of Shona yodeling. The harmonic progression, however, has only a skeletal relation to classical mbira music—12/8 ‖: G Bm | Am C | G Am | G :‖.

During the 1980s Sithole played with his own band, Deep Hori-zone, and sometimes played with Mapfumo (e.g., see Eyre 1994: 119). Sithole described Deep Horizone's music as "all mbira. Since we were doing that with Thomas, he was onto this mbira thing, I was already into this mbira thing, so naturally, when I left I just support[ed] that" (Zim92-17: 10). He recorded the first LP of his own compositions with Deep Horizone in 1991 (RTLP 34), the title track being a refined version of his first song "Sabhuku." On the LP, only one song, "Manga Chena," is literally linked to classical mbira music; "Sabhuku" is roughly linked; there is a jit, a rumba-based song, and two pieces that are quite origi-nal.[18] By the time of this recording an actual mbira had been added to all the tracks—following Mapfumo's lead after the mid-1980s. His ap-proach to composition has remained consistent from the late 1970s through the early 1990s. When classical mbira players refer to Sithole as being the guitarist truest to tradition, I believe they are thinking of his work with Mapfumo rather than his own original compositions, which are much less well known. It is also possible that they do not distinguish between Sithole and other guitarists like Hlomayi who have recorded with Mapfumo over the years.

### Susan Mapfumo

Susan Mapfumo (no relation to Thomas), was the most prominent female singer of the late 1970s. She performed jit songs in the style of the Green Arrows (e.g., "Mhesva Mukono," on *Susan and the Fantasy*, 1980, Jongwe Guru JR 523), but she more typically recorded rumba and mbaqanga-style songs with various backup bands. She sang in a strong, clear, alto range without any use of indigenous Shona vocal techniques; her vocal style was closer to cosmopolitan rock conventions than to indigenous singing.

Mapfumo is of particular interest because of the way her lyrics contrast with the political songs of male performers of the 1978–80 period. She was extremely conscious of gender issues and roles in all six pieces I have from this era, and she projects a feminist perspective that grew out of the war itself. Women served in the guerrilla armies, and the political orthodoxy within the socialist Patriotic Front parties emphasized gender-role equality in line with cosmopolitan socialist orthodoxy in places like Russia and China. Her songs were explicitly directed to women and often were about women's problems as well as about the violence of the period.

Unlike her male counterparts, in "Mhesva Mukono" she seems to take a dim view of the fighting. This was not done from a stereotypic female perspective of meekness, or from a mother/sister/wife's position of concern about her men. Rather, she sang from a critical position of moral strength and courage (LS = Mapfumo as lead singer; BV = background vocalists):

LS: Don't hate me for a man
BV: A coward
LS: See
BV: A coward
LS: Don't kill me for a man
BV: A coward
LS: See
BV: A coward
LS: He is a coward
BV: A coward
LS: See
BV: A coward (×3)
LS: Don't kill each other for men
BV: Cowards

LS: See
BV: Who are cowards
LS: Don't kill each other for women
BV: Cowards
LS: See
BV: They're cowards . . .
LS: Don't kill each other
BV: It's cowardly
LS: See
BV: It's cowardly

This last stanza was repeated with variations (e.g., "Don't beat each other") three times. Thus, she turns the usual association of fighting with bravery on its head. Whether this was based in a Christian position I cannot say, but it certainly offers a critical perspective not found in the male guitar-band songs of the time.

In "Gondo Iro" (Susan and the Real Sounds, 1978, JK 511), by contrast, she begins with a mother's perspective but moves to imagery that parallels male political songs, except that women are the protagonists:

Mothers, you have given birth.
Giving birth is painful
The children you bore
Have all died
Girls, boys, old women,
All are dead.
Honestly girls?
There is that bird
Which you all know
This bird is an eagle
This bird alights during the day
At night it doesn't perch
There will be the owners of the home.
So mothers get hold of pestles
Girls get hold of cooking sticks (×2).
Kill that eagle (×3)
Kill it, kill it
It has destroyed the home (×2) . . .

Like other songs about the war released in the country during the late 1970s, this text is certainly open to multiple interpretations, but Susan Mapfumo's attention to women's positions is distinctive.

"Vakomana Vemazuva Ano," (Susan and the Real Sounds, 1978, JK 511) includes fairly direct feminist statements: "Sisters, don't be looked down upon by the boys of nowadays / They don't have money,

not a dollar / Not even pennies / In the Bank / But pride / It's so full /
You girls / Leave them alone." She goes on to sing of Jenny who falls for
rich men, and warns her sisters that they should not be so fooled.

Harsh patriarchal structures remained entrenched in Zimbabwe in
the 1990s, both among blacks and whites. There is a small but active
feminist movement within the country, and gender roles are commonly
debated and discussed in the mass media, in government agencies, and
throughout civil society. Female subservience is often still advocated in
line with the discourse of cultural nationalism—'our traditional culture'—as it has been since at least the late 1950s.[19] Cosmopolitan ideas
about gender equality were strengthened during the war years, and this
struggle continues against a good deal of resistance. The feminist perspectives of Susan Mapfumo certainly deserve closer attention in this
part of Zimbabwean history (see Impey 1992).

## The Rise of "Electric Indigenous Music," 1978–1982

If journals such as *Parade* and *Prize,* and available recordings are any
indication, rumba, British and American rock, African-American soul,
and South African simanje-manje/mbaqanga remained the top popular
musical styles during most of the 1970s in Harare. From 1977 through
the early 1980s, however, a host of bands composed songs loosely based
on indigenous Shona genres and styles. Thus, musicians in ever greater
numbers answered the twin call to compose original material and to
perform "our African music" as expressed earlier by music writers in
*Parade.*

Like Thomas Mapfumo, Manatsa, M'tukudzi, and Sithole, many
bands began to use or combine selected indigenous features in various
ways to create new compositions. These elements included mbira, jit, or
other dance-drumming rhythms; the "mbira" timbre in the damped guitar technique; the four-phrase 12/8 structure of classical mbira music,
or the two-phrase 12/8 structure of many Shona dance-drumming and
makwaya songs; the yodeling vocal technique and extensive use of vocables. Jit-style songs were by far the most common. The same bands
also occasionally performed actual village pieces, or used actual mbira
progressions and melodies, although Mapfumo was the leader in this
practice. Rather than supplanting the other popular styles, indigenous-
based guitar-band music was performed by the same groups along with
other styles, as had been the case since the late 1960s.

Like the prominent artists already discussed, many bands also sang
about the war during the late 1970s; some, like Mapfumo, did so quite

blatantly. And again, there was no strict correlation between the use of local Shona musical resources and political expression in the texts. Thus, in the analysis of musical nationalism and artists' intent, texts and musical style have to be considered separately.

In 1979 Jordan Chataika recorded, "Nguva Yekuchema" (CBC BZ 49), a song based on the classical mbira piece "Karigamombe." Chataika had recorded American-style country and gospel pieces solo on acoustic guitar with African Service radio during the 1960s. In the 1970s he continued primarily in the same vein on electric guitar, and by the late 1970s was recording commercial 45s with his guitar band, the Highway Stars. "Nguva Yekuchema" was one of several mbira-based compositions by Chataika during the late 1970s. The lyrics, addressed to God, concern sorrow, poverty, and the problems of people who have had relatives die far away and were unable to perform last rites. His country song "Tirwireiwo Mwari" (1978, CBC BZ 26), on the other hand, is a much more direct nationalist cry for aid in the Liberation War:

> Surely God fight for us (×2)
> Father I say fight for us for we might perish (×2)
> What you did for others,
> Come and do the same for us
> I say fight for us,
> God, we might perish
> King David cried
> When overwhelmed by wars
> He said God fight for me,
> Father you came to his rescue.
> Daniel cried
> When cast in the den of lions
> He said God fight for me
> Father you rescued him
> Even Samson cried
> When they gouged out his eyes
> When he cried God help me
> Father you came to his rescue
> We are on the lips of a lion
> We are on the lips of a leopard
> Hence I cry fight for us
> For we might perish.
> What you did in Malawi [helped them gain independence]
> Do the same for us in Zimbabwe
> I say Go fight for us
> For we might all perish
> What you did in Maputo [referring to Mozambique's independence]

Come and do likewise here in Zimbabwe
I say fight for us
We might perish

The jit song "Ndopenga," by the Poison Band (1979, WSA29), refers to the ZANU symbols Nehanda and Chaminuka, and says "I will
go to Mutare / Mutoko / Chiredzi [areas of fighting] Let's go out / We
will find the cause." The Soul Saviour's 45, "Chaminuka" (1979, CBS
BZ), uses mbira rhythm and village singing style with a 12/8 I–IV–I–V
progression and rather nondescript melody to implore "Chaminuka /
The children are finished / Father guide us." The Labby Five Band also
addressed Chaminuka and sang "Down with the enemy" in the mbira-
based "Mwoyo Muti" (MBE 20). The Search Brothers released a number of jit-style songs on various topics, including the war, during 1978
and 1979.

The Livestock Company played a blend of jit and mbaqanga very
much in the style of the Green Arrows, although the lead singer specialized in village-style huro (yodeling vocable) singing. Their song
"Mbira" (1979, MDA 054) suggests that by this time the mbira had
begun to take on the status of a cultural-nationalist emblem within
guitar-band circles:

You grandfather [respected elder]
The children are perishing
We are playing mbira
Of the olden days
You boys
Should we perish
We are playing mbira
of the olden days.

Oddly, the musical accompaniment (mbaqanga-influenced jit) in no
way referenced mbira music; even the damped guitar technique was not
used. Evidently the idea of matching the musical accompaniment to text
content did not occur to these musicians. The B side of this single, in the
same musical style but unrelated to the war, was about a first-born child
inheriting wealth.

Trio Camp recorded jit songs very much in the style of the Livestock
Company and the Green Arrows with texts about the general suffering
in the rural areas (e.g., "Nhamo," 1979, MDA 019). During this period
the Okavhango Boys performed pieces that indexed Shona village music, as did Job Mashanda, the New Sounds, the Waynos B. Zenith Band,
and Oliver Samhembere.

The artists that I have listed in this section faded from the scene after the early 1980s; some, such as J. Chataika, have died, and most are forgotten. Nonetheless, these groups attest to the emergence and, for that time, widespread popularity of indigenous-based guitar-band music. As I have been suggesting throughout the book, this emergence represented a culmination of various musical and social trends that began as early as the 1940s and 1950s.

## Musical Nationalism and Popular Music

Paralleling the apex of the war and the honeymoon of independence, the years from 1976 to 1984 were the peak period when national sentiment and political engagement were major defining forces for popular musicians in Zimbabwe. This period differs from the cultural-nationalist movement of 1960–63. The earlier "moment of departure" was top-down, largely orchestrated by the nationalist party. The second period (1976–84) was generated first by audiences and then by the artists themselves, from the ground up, and was perhaps the only truly widespread, populist, cultural-nationalist moment Zimbabwe has known. The honeymoon and ZANU's mandate to achieve a real social revolution faded after the mid-1980s, as discussed in the final chapter.

Musical trends that began as experiments to achieve commercial success became generalized in the second half of the 1970s. Mapfumo's music is a particularly clear demonstration of why reformist musical styles (fusing "the best" of the cosmopolitan and the indigenous) may equally serve a professional musician's aspirations to build a mass audience as well as nationalist agendas to incorporate diverse groups into the nation. On the surface, these two motivational forces may have similar stylistic results; nonetheless, they are not the same thing. Mapfumo's style is a classic example of musical reformism, as he and the *Parade* writers seem to know, and as is generally commented upon whenever he is discussed. That is, his style represents the epitome of 'modernizing' village music by arranging it for electric instruments, recording it for mass-media diffusion, and performing it in cosmopolitan settings quite distinct from its original contexts, functions, and meanings.

Some artists seemed to have shared feelings of national, or at least "Africanist" sentiment with their audiences as a matter of course—the result of living through similar conditions—and they became politically engaged in the same way. This was expressed especially by Manatsa, Sithole, Phiri, and M'tukudzi. Mapfumo seems to have been the one

most clearly awakened to feelings of "Africanist" and national sentiment, and political engagement by his audiences in conjunction with his
professional aspirations.

As was true for ZANU's chimurenga song composers, no simple
congruency existed between the use of indigenous music and nationalist
texts among the guitar bands. It was the lyrics that were connected with
political content. For the artists, indigenous musical features seemed
to be more vaguely associated with national or "Africanist" sentiment,
or simply with good audience response without analyzing the reasons.
I asked Oliver M'tukudzi directly if he felt that musical style could affect
people's feelings about their own identity, or feelings of national sentiment. He replied that it was the song texts, not the music that mattered:
"To the people, anything [in the music] that appeals to them is good to
them, you see. They don't really consider music as something to change
them or whatever. But, ah, the messages in the song, they count. But
music itself, I don't think it has affected or made any change to the
people" (Zim93-53: 15). M'tukudzi's clear separation of the message of
a song text from the musical style vehicle that carries it adds complexities to the consideration of musical nationalism. His attitude about the
lack of importance of musical style for conveying particular messages is
consistent with the lack of strict correlation between political lyrics and
indigenous genres among guitar-band composers. The Livestock Company's song "Mbira" is the most blatant example of lack of concern
with text-music correlation.

From this vantage point, musical style and the content of song texts
have to be kept separate for a more detailed understanding of musical
nationalism in Zimbabwe. Music scholars typically read the reformist
blending of local indigenous and cosmopolitan music elements as musical nationalism. Zimbabwean composers from Chinx to M'tukudzi do
not. As I have suggested, national or "Africanist" sentiment among the
audiences *was* involved in the guitar-band incorporation of indigenous
Shona musical elements, but for most Zimbabwean composers that I
spoke with, this did not translate to explicit connections between political nationalism and musical style.

# Part Five

# Globalization Begins at Home

# Chapter Nine

# Nationalism, Cosmopolitanism, and Popular Music after 1980

With the coming of black majority rule and ZANU-PF's victory at the polls in 1980, Zimbabwe became a symbol to the world of a successful popular revolution and a heroic blow against racism. Idealistic volunteers came to the country to help build a new society, and the victory was celebrated in word and song. For worldbeat audiences, Bob Marley linked the struggle in Zimbabwe to black liberation everywhere. His song "Zimbabwe" on the 1979 *Survival* album proclaimed that "Africans a liberate Zimbabwe" and, more prophetic yet, that "Soon we will find out who is the *real* revolutionary."

In the 1980s Zimbabwean artists such as Thomas Mapfumo and the Bhundu Boys would continue to carry nationalist-revolutionary messages and imagery to the world as they sought international audiences for their music. During the 1980s, indigenous Zimbabwean music and dance were also presented to the world through state-initiated programs and institutions such as the National Dance Company. In both cases Zimbabwean nationalism was represented through local-indigenous arts which became transformed in the very process of making them attractive for cosmopolitan consumption.

This chapter presents an analysis of the ways nationalism and the cosmopolitan dispositions of the leadership shaped the processes of artistic transformation which, through state programs, began to have a wider impact in indigenous communities throughout Zimbabwe after independence. As had been true already in the 1970s, musical professionalism and capitalist market forces worked together in conjunction with nationalist programs to reform participatory indigenous lifeways according to cosmopolitan-capitalist ethics. Globalization begins at home with *this* passive cultural revolution from the base camps of cosmopolitan artists and elites.

## Socialism, Capitalism, and the
## State in the 1980s and 1990s

Consistent with ZANU-PF's position of the 1970s, Robert Mugabe was still articulating his government's commitment to Marxism-Leninism in the late 1980s (Mugabe 1989: 346). During the early part of the decade, the new state seemed committed to a policy of "growth with equity" (MacGarry 1993: 4), consistent with socialist goals, and various efforts were made to enhance the well-being of the poorer segments of the population.

The ZANU-ZAPU Patriotic Front's major populist appeals to win support during the war included promises of land redistribution, and universal education and health care. During the 1980s, the government went into debt to subsidize free health and educational facilities which expanded dramatically (see MacGarry 1993: 7–9). The state also instituted programs to help peasant farmers; they did away with colonial restrictions on the sale of peasant produce, and supplied credit and grain-collection depots (MacGarry 1993: 12). The most important promise made during the war—an equitable redistribution of land—however, was not carried out.[1] Here we begin to grasp the central contradiction between ZANU's stated socialist-populist position and the government's maintenance of capitalist structures, in both the economic and cultural spheres.

From the new government's perspective in 1980, it was imperative to maintain the existing infrastructure and keep existing capital in the country if they were to have an economic base to fund their social programs and to develop the economy, presumably for the benefit of all. In order to stop white flight and the draining of the country's capital reserves, an alliance was formed between the new black political elite and the preexisting white 'settler' elite who still held the lion's share of the country's good agricultural land and capital. This alliance was initiated in 1980 as the Policy of Reconciliation with white Zimbabweans. It was backed by the Lancaster House settlement of 1979 that had brought the new Zimbabwean state into existence with the promises of universal franchise *and* the protection of white economic holdings.[2]

In an about-face from nationalist discourse during the war, but reminiscent of the black elite's rejection of the 'colour bar' in the prenationalist period, the Policy of Reconciliation played down racial distinction as the basis of rights. The policy was more than just rhetoric. Prominent whites were made ministers of agriculture (Dennis Norman) as well as of trade and commerce (David Smith). Ruth Weiss notes that "in 1991 the white members in President Mugabe's government outnumbered ZANU ministers in terms of representation of their constituents." She continues, "The ZANU leader was determined to placate whites and stop them from withdrawing into political isolation" (1994: 66, 67–68). Many high government offices were also filled by people from the black middle class—'African graduates.' These included people involved in the war effort and many others who were going to school inside and outside the country during the war.

While the official Policy of Reconciliation was articulated only in regard to race, Weiss suggests that it was largely a matter of class alliance:

> If reconciliation is defined as establishing peaceful coexistence between two disparate sectors of the population, the black elite and the shrinking number of whites, it was successful. There is no longer any distinction between black and white within the middle classes. Whites still hold and maintain economic power, sharing it with the black elite who hold political sway.
>
> The policy of reconciliation helped to entrench existing economic structures and develop the black bourgeoisie. Thirteen years after independence, the black middle classes have more in common with whites than with lower-income blacks. (1994: xv)

The government's implicit plan was to let white control of the economy naturally wither away with the present generation, thus safeguarding existing economic structures and infrastructure which would be gradually taken over by black Zimbabweans (Herbst 1990: 222). The question remained, which blacks would move ahead? A good amount of evidence suggests that the members of the pre-independence black middle class and their children have benefited most immediately from the maintenance and gradual takeover of existing economic structures and resources. On the crucial question of land redistribution, for example, Davies, Sanders, and Shaw remark that in addition to the Lancaster restrictions,

> the "pragmatists" in Government had also argued that there was a danger of alienating white farmers, who are important both in the production of exports and for food security. The old pattern of land ownership and the existence of a dual land tenure system, part commercial and "white" and part communal (the TTLs [Tribal Trust

Lands]), has thus continued. Moreover, because the new black elite has tended to acquire commercial farms as they went up for sale, land redistribution is likely to be toward rich rather than poor Africans. (1991: 13)

Although perhaps initially formed with the best intentions for the benefit of the majority, the alliance between the new black political elite and the white economic elite firmly entrenched Zimbabwe within the capitalist system and has effectively precluded any alternatives up to the mid-1990s. The watershed of the capitalist trajectory was the adoption in the early 1990s of an Economic Structural Adjustment Program (ESAP) designed by the IMF and World Bank which favored local elites, both white and black, as well as international capital by "liberalizing" the economy and ensuring the continuing flow of aid money. ESAP required substantial belt-tightening in both government and the private sector. Many people lost their jobs, and government health, education, and economic programs such as depots for peasant produce were cut back, creating hardships for the majority of Zimbabweans.

Mugabe himself described ESAP as a means of structuring neocolonial relations in no uncertain terms in his Independence Day speech of 18 April 1993:

> The World Bank and the IMF are the new colonisers. A new revival for the revolutionary transformation of the national economy is now our pressing agenda. We would like to emphasise that the agenda is now economic, not political, and the great Party, ZANU-PF is the vanguard in the struggle for the realisation of the aspirations of our heroic grassroot masses. In this context we condemn in the strongest terms all reactionary manoeuvres by certain racist interests and black stooges to privatise our parastatals and to sell our Government companies without the Party's authority. . . . Isn't it white interests and multinationals riding on the back of the World Bank and IMF who would like to further marginalise blacks in this country? . . . Any parastatals or Government companies that are ever to be sold must be offered to blacks and we make no apologies about this issue. (*The Sunday Mail*, 18 April 1993: 9)

These sentiments are consistent with Mugabe's long-standing socialist-populist stance, and they make sense in a political speech, given the highly unpopular effects of ESAP among the general population. The speech seems somewhat bizarre, however, since Mugabe's ZANU-PF party was in power when the government implemented ESAP. The capitalist liberalization ushered in by ESAP had opened the door to questioning ZANU's authority over government companies, something perhaps not predicted and not to be tolerated. What also seems significant

is the renewed use of the racial divide as the basis for defining rights—
in contrast to the Policy of Reconciliation but consistent with nationalist rhetoric of the 1970s. Puzzling over this speech, I am led to ask,
which blacks in Zimbabwe are in a position to buy parastatals and government companies such as airlines and television stations? One interpretation is that the essentialist invoking of race here and the implied
equation of blackness with the "heroic masses" simply mask an argument that favors the new black elite.

Despite the Mugabe government's stated concern for the advancement of the lower classes, many people in Zimbabwe and outside observers feel that the general population's position has not improved
since independence because of ZANU's political-economic course (e.g.,
Davies, Sanders, and Shaw 1991). Since ESAP and the droughts of the
early 1990s, things have gotten much worse (e.g., MacGarry 1993,
1994a; Weiss 1994). Moreover, the class divisions within the black
population have become wider and more obvious since independence
with the strengthening of the position of the black elite, and this is exacerbated by ESAP (Kanji and Jazdowska 1993).

## The New Black Elite

With racial discrimination outlawed, members of the new black elite
have moved into formerly white middle- and upper-class neighborhoods. They send their children to the best schools, wear expensive
clothes, and drive expensive cars as cosmopolitan elites do everywhere.
Since 1980, blacks have gained upward mobility through government
posts, which expanded to some 12 percent of all wage earners. "The
'blackening' of the public service was part of the process of stratifying
black society. Top black civil servants joined the political and educated
elite, while lower-scale civil servants became part of the black petit
bourgeoisie" (Weiss 1994: 133).

Black Zimbabweans are gradually moving into the professions
(doctors, lawyers, professors, accountants) in greater numbers following the improvement of educational possibilities. 'Black advancement'
in the private industrial sector has been slower than in the public sector,
but is steadily increasing.[3] Most of these black businessmen come from
the ranks of the colonial black middle class. As one successful black
businessman told Ruth Weiss,

> Some businessmen tend to limit themselves, perhaps because they
> think they have to share their prosperity with too many members
> of the extended family. Another thing: you'll find that many of us
> who've made it or are making it have a non-traditional background.

> Usually our fathers were purchase land farmers—you know, good "boys" who'd worked in the public sector and been allowed to buy land in the African Purchase Land area. Or they were traders or transporters. Or chiefs! Then there were the clever ones who got scholarships and studied abroad. (Weiss 1994: 169)

This statement underlines the familial continuity of the black middle class from the colonial to the post-independence period. Since the colonial days, adherence to 'traditional culture' has been seen, realistically, as a hinderance to advancement in the capitalist sector. As this businessman's statement suggests, indigenous patterns of family responsibility and redistribution of wealth were an actual obstacle to the capital accumulation required for success in the capitalist system (e.g., see Fraenkel 1959: 38).

During the colonial period members of the African middle class called for a 'culture bar' to replace the color bar. They emphasized their cultural differences from lower-class Africans based on the degree to which European and American cultural style and ideas had been inculcated, that is, had become localized and thus cosmopolitan. They also often exhibited a real distance from, or lack of familiarity with, 'traditional culture' (chapters 1, 4). The same is true today and is even more pronounced among the younger generations growing up in middle-class households and neighborhoods—the sites and basis of Zimbabwean cosmopolitanism.

Middle-class Africans in my neighborhood in Harare, especially younger people, often knew little about indigenous arts and the cultural activities in nearby 'high-density' townships. Like the *Parade* music writers of the 1950s and 1960s, some of my black neighbors could not identify an mbira on a recording by its sound, or did not know what a chipendani (musical bow) was. These and many other experiences supported Ruth Weiss's contention that "thirteen years after independence, the black middle classes have more in common with whites than with lower-income blacks" (1994: xv)—that is, they had become part of the same cosmopolitan cultural formation. What is less often recognized is that this was also true thirteen years before independence among African cosmopolitans. The main things that changed after 1980 were the size and relative power base of this group.

Members of the black middle class gained leadership positions in the state cultural bureaucracies and, consequently, greater influence over artistic life from their distinct cultural vantage point. Along with the culture industry, the state culture and education bureaucracies are the main agents for diffusing cosmopolitan-capitalist aesthetics and

artistic practices and, along with the schools, are the primary mechanisms for constructing state-directed images of the nation. Because of
nationalist ideology, which defines the nation-state as the ultimate
boundary for culture and identity, and because of essentialist colonial
conceptions of race, however, state officials are projected and perceive
themselves as "insiders" working within "their own culture." It is precisely this misconception, backed by the power of the state, that poses
one of the primary challenges to alternative, indigenous lifeways and
arts in Zimbabwe.

## Culture Bureaucracies
The implementation of state cultural policy regarding the performing
arts falls to two primary institutions: The Ministry of Culture and the
National Arts Council (NAC).[4] High officials in both institutions told
me that as of 1980 their policies and programs directly reflect and are
designed to support government objectives, and those of Mugabe himself, in the cultural-artistic sphere.

These two institutions are separate bodies but are hierarchically related. The NAC is a parastatal organ but is supervised by the Ministry,
and the minister of culture is responsible for appointing the NAC board.
Funds for the NAC are voted in parliament and channeled through the
Ministry of Culture. The NAC does have some independence in setting
its objectives, designing projects, and allocating funds, as well as attempting to raise some of its own funds, but it must stay within guidelines of government objectives. Both institutions have separate organizational structures that pervade the whole country with branches and
workers at the national, provincial, and district levels. Both institutions
independently, and at times cooperatively, organize or subsidize performances and workshops for the performing, visual, and literary arts at
the different structural levels, and they sometimes underwrite international tours.

The National Arts Council, however, largely serves as an umbrella
donor agency and mediator between the Ministry and *registered* arts
institutions and performing groups throughout the country.[5] In the
realms of music and dance, these include the Zimbabwe Union of Musicians, Zimbabwe Ballroom Dancers' Association, the National Ballet,
Choral Society of Zimbabwe, Bulawayo Philharmonic Orchestra, Harare City Orchestra, National Symphony Orchestra, Zimbabwe Music
Industry Association, Harare Association of African Choirs (AAC), and
Harare African Traditional Association, or HATA (National Arts Foundation of Zimbabwe 1985: 9). The disproportionate funding for elite

arts (orchestras, ballroom) is a holdover from the colonial period but clearly sanctioned by the new leadership. The AAC and HATA are umbrella organizations to which township choirs and dance groups like the Murehwa Jerusarema Club belong. The NAC helps fund the major festivals and contests for the members of these two umbrella organizations, including the Neshamwari Festival (chapter 3). In 1985 the NAC had a Z$182,000 grant from the government to support such organizations, its own organizational necessities, and cultural programs (National Arts Foundation of Zimbabwe 1985).

### Portrait of a Ministry
### Cultural Worker

Cultural nationalism stressing indigenous, largely Shona, arts generated many new state programs after 1980. It is interesting, then, that a number of the officials of the NAC and the Ministry of Culture who designed and directed the programs had not been cultural nationalists or personally involved with indigenous arts before independence. Rather, they often came from a middle-class background, a fact that is key to understanding the nature and direction of post-independence cultural programs. The profile of Mr. H is fairly typical of people working in contemporary cultural bureaucracies and is thus worth considering at some length.

Mr. H came from a rural area where indigenous dances were still commonly performed while he was growing up during the colonial period. After he moved to Highfield Township as a young man in 1975, he made a conscious effort to disassociate himself from indigenous lifeways and arts. Once in the capital, he became intensely involved as a ballroom dancer, having internalized, as he put it, "the colonial mentality" that granted higher prestige to such cultural activities (chapter 4). One of the men Mr. H knew through ballroom dancing became a deputy minister in the Education Division; this man induced Mr. H. to leave his accounting job in the private sector soon after independence.

> MR. H: We used to meet at ballroom dancing. So we used to see each other. Now, after independence he was made a deputy minister. So because we knew each other, and he knew I was dancing, I was doing a lot of social work [organizing ballroom dance activities], he said, "Well, do you want to leave the private sector?" And I said, "Oh, will they give me more money in the government?" And he said, "Unfortunately no, but you

will enjoy working for your country. And also [there is] security in government, security job-wise." So he persuaded me,
and I agreed. That's how I joined [the Culture section of the
Ministry] in 1981. . . . In fact I'm one of the founding members
of the culture department in the country. . . .

So after independence, after I joined the Ministry, then the
political order started changing. And also because I had joined
the Culture [Division] I had to be seen to be, eh, Zimbabwean,
promoting Zimbabwean culture. . . . Having been used for so
many years to be doing ballroom dancing, and all the colonial
mentality and so forth, it was not easy to belong to the Culture
Division, and most importantly, promote it.

So then there was a period, in 1980, in 1981, 1983, a period
of change. On my part, well, as an individual, I had to choose
*how I should be a Zimbabwean*. It was very difficult. . . . We
had specialists, a number of specialists or consultants from
Tanzania. Tanzania, ah, from Ghana who came at that time,
you know, to teach to the Zimbabwean Culture Department.
So that, frankly, helped very much.

TURINO: What was their concept?

MR. H: Well, the concept was that we had to change mentally from colonial thinking to Zimbabwean thinking, and from there we
would start to think of ourselves as Zimbabweans and then
start to think of programs. [A government official] suggested to
the Ministry that, in order to get off the ground we need[ed]
experts.

TURINO: They were experts because they had already gone through it in
their county earlier?

MR. H: That's right, yes. So we were taught [about] their experiences,
how they went through it. And, in fact, it really sunk [in], you
know, because we had decided we were going to promote our
culture, we had no out but to be keeping [to?] ourselves and
repeating what those people were saying. And we started to
see, to see things, and then we started organizing seminars for
other cultural workers in the field. (Zim92-29: 2–3)

Mr. H went on to comment that between 1981 and 1985 other 'cultural
consultants' and performing groups came from China, Russia, and the
Eastern Bloc because of the wartime alliances with these governments.
The importance of foreign models for Zimbabwean state cultural nationalism in the post-1980 period is clear from this account.

What I find most poignant is his memory of the personal struggles
of coming to grips with what it meant to be Zimbabwean within the
new social order of the early 1980s. As a young man in the 1970s he

had learned to succeed within urban African middle-class society by taking part in 'sophisticated' cosmopolitan activities such as ballroom dancing. Five years later he had to unlearn all of this and become expert in the very 'Zimbabwean' things he had believed best left behind. This new stance was again based in cosmopolitan thinking and taken from foreign models. The strain of his own personal transformation was due to the same middle-class cultural position that, through social connections, secured his government job and the need to become a nationalist-populist in the first place.

By the time I met Mr. H, he had become quite knowledgeable and enthusiastic about indigenous music and dance. His initial distance from these arts, however, was not uncommon among other people who joined the various government ministries after independence. In fact, one of Mr. H's jobs was to help organize indigenous music and dance performances for state occasions as a way of introducing officials to 'the true Zimbabwean culture.' Apparently this effort was not very successful in inspiring similar personal transformations among other members of the black political elite. Speaking about the early 1990s, for example, he noted,

> The appreciation [of indigenous music and dance] even by the ministers themselves is not there. They, ah, they also needed to go through a period of introduction to the real culture, which we arranged at functions. . . . I have provided entertainment at different places where the President is, where the ministers are, and I have heard their comments, and I have said to myself, most of these comments are out of ignorance! (Zim92-29: 6)

As with cosmopolitan Africans during the colonial period, government officials' distance from indigenous arts is not simply a matter of taste, but often involves a lack of familiarity and knowledge. This is not surprising, given that they had been emerging as a separate cultural group for over sixty years. Difficulties only surface when such individuals claim the right as "cultural insiders" to design programs for and to influence the style and practice of indigenous arts.

## The National Dance Company

The National Dance Company was one of the primary state institutions directly affecting the style of indigenous performing arts in the post-1980 period. The National Dance Company (NDC) was established by the Ministry of Education and Culture in 1981 under the guidance of foreign experts Peggy Harper of Britain and African-American dancer and choreographer Kariamu Welsh-Asante. The official goals of the company were to "revive, *develop,* and promote the traditional dance and music of Zimbabwe" (*Tabex Encyclopedia* 1987: 274; my emphasis). As Mr. H put it, "It was created specifically to promote Zimbabwean, um, *formal* dances and music, and also to be used as a vehicle of communication with other countries to promote mutual understanding" (Zim92-29: 7; my emphasis). As described on a NDC program in 1982 the goals were as follows:

    1. To preserve and exhibit the traditional dances of Zimbabwe
    2. To provide an opportunity for young people to see and perform the traditional dances as taught by the Master Teachers
    3. To develop an appreciation for the aesthetic contributions of Africa to world dance
    4. To serve as an ambassador of culture in international and national arenas
    5. To educate the public to the necessity of discipline and training in order to be able to perform the rigorous traditional dances
    6. To underscore the beauty and energy of the Zimbabwean national expression of the dance aesthetic (Welsh-Asante 1993: 241)

## Cultural Nationalism in the Moment of Arrival

In the nationalist "moments of departure and maneuver," cultural nationalism was designed to fashion images of and to rally people to the new nation and the leading parties. Reformism served both these ends by aiding the creation of forms and practices that were simultaneously indigenous and cosmopolitan, and that would appeal to the largest number of people (both 'modern' and 'traditional').

In the post-1980 "moment of arrival," cultural nationalist activities must continue to serve these functions, but a new priority comes to the fore in which the new nation-state must present and represent itself as a unique and yet 'modern' nation on a par with other nations on the international scene. The National Dance Company's role as "ambassador of culture in the international arena," and the goal of making a contribution to "world dance" indicates this new function. The Ministry of Culture's emphasis on international tours for the NDC and other indigenous performing groups, as described below, was directed toward this end. Because of this new function, nationalist programs concretely connect indigenous performers with international audiences and markets, and thus serve as important conduits between local communities and cosmopolitanism at the levels of values and practice.

## The Organization, Repertory,
## and Activities of the
## National Dance Company

Henry Maposa, an early member of the Ministry of Culture, described
the initial formation of the National Dance Company, which was originally the idea of Eric Mavengere and John Mapondera, two men in the
ministry responsible for performing arts (p.c. December 1992). They
sought a music-dance specialist to manage the company, and a Kwanongoma College graduate, Shesby Matiure, was selected. The Kwanongoma connection is significant for my larger theme of the ways cosmopolitan institutions and individuals link up because of a common
cultural orientation. In this instance, it was felt that foreign experts or
locals with official arts credentials were required to run the NDC—
rather than, say, a steering committee of indigenous dancers. Kwanongoma was the only local institution offering credentials in the realm of
indigenous performing arts, making a Kwanongoma graduate a logical
choice for the job.

Matiure and Maposa joined forces with Harper and Welsh-Asante
to put the company together. They assembled and auditioned a large
number of performers from the Harare area at Stodart Hall in Mbare in
1981. The National Dance Company was formed from audition winners who then held full-time salaried positions in the company. Full-
time professional employment as an indigenous dancer was an innovation in Zimbabwe, and it set a precedent that led to the formation of
other professional dance troupes, especially after the NDC folded in the
early 1990s.

The company originally consisted of 'master performers' of the re-
gionalized shangara (Peter M'Kwesha), mbukumba (Sylvia Mazho),
dhinhe (David Gweshe), muchongoyo (Enos Simango), and jerusarema
(Emmanuel Maseko) dances as well as an mbira player (Thomas Wadharwa) and a choral director (Ernest Shara). The master performers
taught their specific music and dances to each other and some twenty
younger members. The goal was for each teacher and member to learn
all the traditions in as 'authentic' a manner as possible.

Whereas formerly most organized dance groups (e.g., urban-
migrant burial or dance associations) specialized in one or two dances
specific to their own region, the NDC was explicitly pan-regional, that
is, national. With the exception of dhinhe, the company's early repertory consisted of the primary indigenous dances performed in the early
1960s at ZAPU rallies and festivals. This continuity suggests the cre-

ation of a nationalist canon of indigenous Zimbabwean (Shona) music
and dance. As I suggested in chapter 2, however, the selection of dances
was actually based on the fact that nationalist organizers in both instances largely drew on performers and traditions that were readily
available through the dance and burial associations in Harare townships. The African-American choreographer Kariamu Welsh-Asante,
who served as NDC artistic director from 1981 to 1983, specifically
commented that the master teachers came out of existing urban dance
associations (1993: 83). The canon of "rural" indigenous dances thus
comprised those already performed in the city. The absence of an Ndebele component in the company may be due to the Harare-centered auditions as well as, perhaps, ZANU's Shona-centered brand of cultural
nationalism.

An early major production was the staged nationalist dance-drama
"Mbuya Nehanda—The Spirit of Liberation," which was created for
the second anniversary of Zimbabwe's independence in 1982 by Peggy
Harper. More typically, the NDC performed their usual repertory of
dances on stage, television, and for state occasions, and they represented Zimbabwe on various tours abroad. They usually performed at
the airport to welcome foreign and Zimbabwean political dignitaries
and to see them off—thus effectively framing stays in the country with
'national culture.' They also sometimes toured Zimbabwe and performed at regional culture centers and schools. Increasingly after the
mid-1980s, the members of the National Dance Company began to
teach their versions of the dances in schools as part of their full-time
duties. This became an important part of their mission of promoting
indigenous dance, especially among urban school children. It had the
secondary effects of diffusing the company's choreographed versions of
the indigenous dances to a new generation, and of linking the meaning
of the dances to the nation rather than to their original regions.[6]

The company's stage performances were rather standardized (see
Welsh-Asante 1993: 240–49). Their program at the Commonwealth
Arts Festival in Australia was typical of the early years: (1) Mbira
Dance, (2) Shangara, (3) Dhinhe, (4) Mbukumba, and after an intermis-
sion, (5) Choral Selection, (6) "Earth Movers," (7) Mbira Selection,
(8) Muchongoyo, (9) Jerusarema. In addition to Welsh-Asante's arrangements of indigenous dances, the company performed her choreographed pieces such as "Earth Movers"; "The Beginning Again," a piece
set to the music of Quincy Jones; and "Wonder's Suite," described as "a
jazz suite inspired by the music and compositions of Stevie Wonder"

(Welsh-Asante 1993: 254). Thus as in the ZAPU rallies of the early 1960s, indigenous dances were juxtaposed with cosmopolitan popular music and dance forms in NDC performances.

Welsh-Asante's shaping of the NDC programs for stage performance was based on cosmopolitan rather than local aesthetics. In indigenous settings one or two genres might be repeated over and over for a whole night—continual repetition of a single rhythmic feel helps build participation and intensity. During an indigenous ceremony or recreational event, shifts in dynamics and energy might occur in relation to participant fatigue, the coming of dawn, or around occurrences like spirit possession, but they are not planned out in advance. As a product of a presentational rather than a participatory mode of performance, however, the NDC's programs were carefully designed to emphasize continual variation and a purposeful contrast of dynamics (e.g., the softer mbira music versus dance drumming), gradually building toward the loudest and most elaborate dances (muchongoyo and jerusarema) before the finale.

This dynamic shape is familiar within European and North and South American concert conventions. Christopher Small, for example, describes how a typical Western orchestra concert begins with an unstressed item, "an overture, perhaps, or some other relatively lightweight work—followed by a stressed item—a symphony perhaps, or a concerto," with the "heaviest" item being penultimate to a substantial yet lighter conclusion (1987: 23). The conscious use of contrasts and the planning of a program's dynamic shape are important for maintaining interest and entertaining a seated audience; such planning is not necessary, or even possible, in participatory occasions, since each event has its own emergent dynamics.

Welsh-Asante went to Zimbabwe in 1981 on a Fulbright Fellowship. She recounts how she was invited as a foreign expert by Mugabe to

> help form and train a national dance company that would reflect the newly independent nation's ethnic diversity. In addition, the dance company would serve as a cultural ambassador for the country. Commencing in June of 1981, my responsibilities were to identify those dances, dancers, and musicians who were most characteristic of an ethnic group or region and then to shape all concerned for the concert stage. . . .
>
> At the end of my tenure (June 1983) with the now-named National Dance Company of Zimbabwe, I had shaped and structured seven representative dances for the concert stage, taken the company on its first international tour to Australia, set up a syllabus for training the dancers (which included the teaching of the *Mfundalai* dance

technique incorporating Zimbabwean movements), and instituted an examination procedure for auditioning, selecting, and hiring professional dancers and master teachers. (1993: 5–6)

During Welsh-Asante's tenure as artistic director, the troupe was trained in the daily rehearsals using her own Mfundalai technique, which she describes as "based on *universal* African movements and aesthetics" (Welsh-Asante 1993: 257; my emphasis). Thinking in terms of universal African features is part of a cosmopolitan perspective, whereas people grounded in local indigenous practices are more likely to highlight even subtle stylistic differences between neighboring groups. It is significant that Welsh-Asante, a newcomer to Zimbabwe, had a key role in identifying characteristic dancers, musicians, and dances. This parallels Mr. H's description of foreign experts coming to teach the members of the Ministry of Culture how to be Zimbabwean, that is cultural nationalists, in the early 1980s.

Nationalism is a facet of modernist cosmopolitanism and thus it is not unusual that the new government would turn to foreign experts and models to help refine nationalist identities, practices, and forms. The reformist recontextualization of distinctive indigenous forms and practices within a modernist frame is the primary mechanism by which the elements of the twin paradoxes of nationalism are balanced. The National Dance Company and the other Ministry projects discussed below served this end.

## The NDC and
## Modernist Reformism

Rather than incorporating the radically different participatory ethics and aesthetics of indigenous Shona performance and working to "preserve" these facets, Welsh-Asante shaped the company according to cosmopolitan ideas about professional art and dance. The creation of codified, standardized choreographies and programs emphasizes music and dance as finished products rather than as elements in a more flexible process of social interaction. The result was lauded by Deputy Minister of Culture Stephen Chifunyise, who noted that Welsh-Asante had "done a commendable job of organizing and restructuring these traditional dances for the concert stage." In the same article about the company's upcoming trip to Australia Welsh-Asante is quoted as saying, "Most of the members need international exposure, and therefore I hope that the [Commonwealth] festival will provide this exposure, which should improve their art and professionalism" (*Herald,* 10 September 1982). Within the capitalist-cosmopolitan formation, professionalism and international exposure are the acid tests of artistic competence, quality, and value.

These goals, and the state's choice of an African-American artist to realize them, precisely parallel the program of the late 1950s when the Federation government invited an African-American choreographer to teach stagecraft to urban dance associations like the Murehwa Jerusarema Club (chapter 2). This particular Federation program, which resulted in the filming of the Jerusarema group, planted the initial ideas that their dance should be shaped for the stage and that money could be earned through the performance of indigenous dance. Welsh-Asante's role in the National Dance Company, now under the banner of nationalism, is strikingly similar to the earlier colonial project. This case illustrates my general point that cultural nationalism often represents more of a continuity with than a break from earlier colonial cultural projects. The process of reforming indigenous arts for cosmopolitan consumption is the common denominator between the two periods.

From Welsh-Asante's perspective as a professional North American dancer and choreographer, the desire to professionalize the NDC and shape their performance for the concert stage was simply a matter of common sense. For the government officials who wanted a group that could represent the new nation proudly around the world, reforming the dances according to cosmopolitan aesthetics also made perfect sense. The National Dance Company was the result of this sensibility shared by foreign and local cosmopolitans alike.

One member of the company's organizational team, Father Emmanuel Ribiero, however, had a different perspective.[8] A Zimbabwean scholar of indigenous culture, he worked with the company between 1982 and 1990. He told me that his goal had been to have the NDC dance performances remain so true to the local styles that if they presented a dance in its place of origin, the local people would be accepting and would be able to join in (fieldnotes 5 July 1993). Ribiero indicated, however, that the increasing emphasis on stagework, showmanship, and 'artistic development,' as well as the fact that the group was not rooted in a given locale, led to major changes in the dances. He said that this continued to the point where local people began to reject the NDC versions of *their* dances, saying simply, "That's not it," a result reported from other quarters as well.

Mr. Mutasa, the director of the Murehwa Culture House, told me that the National Dance Company performed at the center in 1987 and 1988. He remarked that on both occasions the local people enjoyed the company for its lively character and skill, but focusing on the local dance that they knew best, some complained that "they are lively, but they don't dance jerusarema in the proper way" (fieldnotes 8 July 1993). This sentiment was echoed by the members of the Murehwa Jerusarema Club and Burial Society (e.g., Nyandoro, Zim92-32). The case of jerusarema serves as a good illustration of the effects of reformism for stage presentation.

As described in chapter 2, jerusarema is a recreational dance of a playful nature. Men and women enter the central dance space at will to do standard movements as well as their own choreographic variations and improvisations. Sexual play is sometimes included, along with many other types of acrobatic and humorous movements. The "punch-line" of any section of choreography comes on beat eight of the active section of the dance. Sometimes in private contexts a subtle pelvic thrust is performed by the man, woman, or both—toward the other—as one type of punchline. But the members of the Murehwa Jerusarema Club emphasized that this motion was not proper to do in public settings— especially in front of your in-laws or children.

As they did with their other dances, the National Dance Company regularized the typical jerusarema figures and the order in which people 'went in,' thus eliminating the spontaneous, improvisatory nature which had been the crux of the dance. Significantly, it was the pelvic thrust motion, made more explicit, that became one of the centerpieces of the National Dance Company's standardized jerusarema choreography. The reason for emphasizing this motion is obvious—it never fails to get a strong audience response. By the time of my research in the early 1990s, a dance figure that had begun as an occasional joke had become the most famous and one of the most often repeated movements of the dance when done by professional "folkloric" dance troupes, and even by school children who learned the NDC version. This upset the members of the Murehwa Jerusarema Club and Burial Society, especially its older members like Patrick Nyandoro:

> TURINO: What do you think about the groups that perform all the dances, from every region, like the National Dance Company?
> NYANDORO: They can do it, but they don't do it to detail. That group, they can just pretend to show the people it is like this, but that's not it.
> TURINO: What are some of the differences?
> NYANDORO: The difference is that playing [dancing with] your own group, you know how to do it. Yes. You see, like those who were in the National Dance Company, jerusarema, they

were doing it so very badly, it is not how [people from Mu-
rehwa] play it. They [NDC] just come together [gesturing
the pelvic thrust], that's not it.

TURINO: You mean when the man and woman . . .

NYANDORO: Yes, that's not it. It shows something that is not so good to
the people. You can play there, a woman and a man. We
dance together, but we don't show; you do your styles, and
she does her styles, you finish together. (Zim92-32: 4)

By the mid to late 1980s the NDC had cemented a canon of Zimbabwean 'traditional' dance, had created their own versions of local
dances, and through their public performances and work in the schools,
had begun to diffuse their versions as the model for future performance.
While there is still resistance to the NDC versions among indigenous
dancers, especially of the older generation, it is possible that the styles
set in motion by the NDC and supported by both nationalist and commercial interests, especially tourist venues, will become the standard
as time goes on. As I suggested in the previous chapter, the desire for
mass appeal frequently links the effects of nationalist and commercial
enterprises.

In spite of stated nationalist goals to preserve and celebrate indigenous arts, the use of foreign experts and a Kwanongoma graduate ensured that the National Dance Company would be shaped according to
cosmopolitan values, and indeed, ultimately its main function was to
entertain and to represent Zimbabwe to cosmopolitan audiences both
at home and abroad. The NDC, then, is a prime example of how nationalism functions to make local arts national and, ultimately, cosmopolitan through the process of reformism. This case closely mirrors many
other cultural nationalist projects and processes throughout the world,
a result of the common cosmopolitan basis and orientation of nationalists themselves.

## NDC Splinter Groups

As early as 1985 problems had arisen between the Ministry of Culture
and the National Arts Council over supporting the National Dance
Company. With the cutbacks resulting from ESAP in the early 1990s,
the NDC was disbanded. Already by the mid-1980s some of the NDC
instructors and dancers had formed their own freelance professional
groups, often composed of young 'school leavers' from the townships.
Another original member, Stella Chiweshe, left the company to launch
a successful career in the international worldbeat market as an mbira
player. When the National Dance Company folded in the early 1990s,

other professional groups rose from its ashes, and the earlier freelance groups became more active.

Specializing in muchongoyo, NDC master teacher Enos Simango formed the Chihoo dance troupe with his sons and other young people from Highfield. With her father Mr. T. Chigamba, NDC dancer Irene Chigamba formed the Young Zimbabweans and taught the members the NDC repertory and style. After the NDC folded, a number of the members stayed together and formed Batanai, which also maintained the National Dance Company's style and repertory. Instructor David Gweshe formed Boterekwa Dhinhe Dancers, although by the early 1990s this group, too, did the standard canon of dances. Second generation (non-NDC) members from these groups also sometimes split off to form their own professional dance troupes; thus, by the early 1990s there was a proliferation of professional "folkloric" dance groups based on the National Dance Company model.

These troupes had to compete for National Arts Council funding and for tourist performance engagements to survive. Because of their former government connections, Batanai received some support and referrals; Boterekwa had weekly performances at a famous Shona sculpture outlet in Harare, a major draw for tourists. The Young Zimbabweans and other struggling troupes attempted to organize tours of rural schools and schedule afternoon nightclub engagements in the townships, neither of which turned out to be very lucrative. They sometimes landed foreign tour engagements, but this was not enough to sustain them financially. Tourists in Zimbabwe were the main market; nightclub audiences wanted guitar bands, and in any event, locals could see such dances for free in villages, beerhalls, and other places. The push to professionalize indigenous dances had succeeded, but within the ESAP-influenced economic climate of the 1990s, there was not enough state money or work to go around.

## Government/Rural
## Village Interface

The National Arts Council and the Ministry use funds to influence the cultural and artistic directions of grassroots musicians and dancers both in the rural and urban areas. For those rural people not yet accustomed to thinking about their performing arts as income-generating activities, part of the Ministry's goal was to get them to do so.

The Ministry has cultural workers in rural districts all over the country. These individuals represent "the front line" and primary interface between the government culture bureaucracy and rural villagers' artistic practices. Several of these workers whom I met in the rural northeast had no particular background in cultural work or the arts; the appointments sometimes went to ex-guerrillas or prominent party members. In the realms of music and dance their primary tasks were threefold: (1) to organize formalized performance ensembles in each village; (2) to promote performances in their districts; and (3) to arrange for performances when government officials visited the district. While the third function is straightforward enough, the first two require some comment.

The Ministry push to formalize and bureaucratize village performing ensembles is consistent with the Art Council's insistence that groups be registered. It is a result of the modernist concern with rationalization and control in which formerly ad hoc performance *activities* become definable and identifiable *entities* which can then be managed and utilized for different purposes. I visited six villages in the Murehwa and Uzumba districts where formal ensembles had been established during the mid-1980s, and I heard of various other formalized ensembles in the region—indicating that this government initiative had been successful.

This activity in the Murehwa and neighboring Uzumba districts may have been particularly concentrated because of the existence of the Murehwa Culture House. At independence, the Ministry's Division of Culture set in motion a plan to build a Culture House in every district in the country. Directed by Ministry cultural officers and field staff, these were to be locations where music-dance and theater groups could rehearse and perform, craftsmen could work, government-sponsored workshops could be held, and a craft gallery for tourists would be established. They were also intended to be administrative centers that could organize local cultural activities and supply the central government with artists and regional performing groups.

As the model for the proposed nationwide program, a beautiful stone Culture House complex was built in the town of Murehwa—complete with craft gallery, rehearsal and performance spaces, library, classroom, and administrative offices. The field staff is supposed to facilitate artistic activities in the villages as well as conduct research (and help visiting researchers) to document the local arts and organize events at the Culture House. Because of the expense, however, the program could not be pursued at this scale throughout the country; other regions do have smaller cultural centers housed in one or two rooms in preexisting buildings, but they are not as active and do not receive the financial support for staff and programs that the model in Murehwa does.

## Formalized Rural Dance Groups

The newly formalized village dance ensembles in Murehwa and Uzumba comprised neighbors who formerly danced and played music together in ceremonies and events as a matter of course. That is, music and dance participation was simply a normal, flexible activity in community events, as it often still is. At the urging of the district cultural officer and the Culture House staff, however, in the Murehwa-Uzumba area, village groups began to adopt an official name and uniforms (sometimes based on mission school uniforms), create an organizational hierarchy, including a president, secretary, and treasurer, and formalize memberships (thereby limiting the flexible participation normal to village events). Of particular significance, the groups were also instructed to formalize their performances, that is, identify the dances that they specialized in, and arrange them in stylized form for nonparticipating audiences on stage and in festivals. In one case I know of, this even included a stylized dramatization of spirit possession as part of the dance performance.

The model for these ensembles was not invented in a vacuum by the Ministry in the 1980s. Rather, formalized grassroots urban dance and burial societies had been common in Zimbabwean cities since at least the 1950s (chapter 2). These groups were usually called upon to perform at nationalist functions in the early 1960s, and they took part in the urban dance festivals organized by the municipality. Groups like the Murehwa Jerusarema Club had already been taught to think about stagecraft and the possibility of earning money through dance because of government programs during the Federation period. Formalized music and dance groups were also organized by mining companies in order to control the leisure activities of their workers. Finally, mission-inspired rural and urban self-help organizations also sometimes organized performance groups and activities.

Nonetheless, the idea of organizing formal dance groups was foreign in many villages, and it did not begin happening commonly until after 1980. It was up to the district cultural officers to get people to organize themselves with a name, uniform, bureaucratic structure, and codified repertory. They did this by suggesting that only formal groups would be eligible for financial aid from the Ministry and the Arts Council, and that only formalized groups would be 'called,' and hence paid, for performing locally, in the capital, and—in the most attractive case—abroad.

In several instances, foreign tours were arranged by the government for newly organized, nonprofessional, village groups. The Bikita Chinyambera Dancers performed at Holland Park, in London in 1984. A year later the Mhembere Dandanda Dancers of Murehwa were sent to the same locale to perform in the Ancestral Voices Concerts. The Dandanda dancers performed "Zimbabwean spiritual and ritualistic dances in a programme which included the Inuit Indians of North-Western Canada and Shaman Monks of Northern Korea" (National Arts Foundation 1985: 2). In the same way that worldbeat is defined generally, these different religious traditions from varied parts of the world were grouped together in one concert series primarily on the basis of their noncosmopolitan, 'traditional' status.

The Mhembere people who went to London remembered this trip with pride and excitement. Although they told me that they did not really make much money, it remained a high point for many. The promise of excursions abroad, spread by word of mouth and the media in rural areas, was certainly an important inducement for village groups to organize. That tours abroad happened to people one actually knew, or at least to people in similar circumstances, made them seem like real possibilities, and thus a powerful motivation for following government guidelines.

### State Culture Programs and Professionalism

During the early 1980s the Ministry of Culture instituted a program of busing village dancers from one region to another to teach their local dances so that, ultimately, people in all regions would know a variety of styles—localism would be reduced, and a unified national repertory would be created. This program was discontinued before it could have much effect, but its purpose of diffusing a series of dances to create a shared basis for a national repertory is clear and matches the goals and modus operandi of the National Dance Company. Like the NDC, this program was specifically designed to confront one of the twin paradoxes of nationalism: it celebrated local dance traditions while simultaneously undermining their localness.

During my stay in 1992–93, the Ministry of Culture was organizing workshops for rural groups, teaching them how to further professionalize, organize, and market their dances. Based on the model of the lucrative Shona sculpture business (see Zilberg 1996), the Ministry felt that local performance arts could likewise be better fashioned to become saleable and exportable commodities. The National Arts Council programs were still directed towards helping performing artists professionalize in 1996. Interim National Arts Council Director, Albert Nyathi, put it this way: "Many people do not think of art as a form of

business but now we are trying to encourage that, we are trying to commercialize art. We can't always be saying, "Ah, this is traditional, this is
culture," when people can live from it. We have examples of groups that
have actually survived through art" (Zim96-3: 7). Whatever the artistic
and cultural pros and cons of such an agenda, tourist spots, state functions, and foreign tour possibilities do not provide enough work to
support even the existing professional "folkloric" dance troupes. Thus
although the Ministry's and the NAC's heart may be in the right place—
people certainly need better subsistence possibilities—this move to increase the number of professional musicians and dancers makes little
sense under ESAP and within current economic conditions.

> TURINO: There are so many musicians here, there are so many dancers,
> there is so much talent.
> NYATHI: Yeah, definitely.
> TURINO: There is no question about that. Is there enough money to sup-
> port all those people?
> NYATHI: That's where the difficulty is. However, we are very lucky, of
> course, that we have very willing donors, in the mold of Danish
> Volunteer Service. . . . We have, ah, the Dutch government,
> through its office, its organization called HIVOS. We have,
> um, NOART, the Norwegian organization, we have SIDA, the
> Swedish—these have been very instrumental in the develop-
> ment of culture in Zimbabwe. And the French—Alliance Fran-
> caise. (Zim96-3: 7–8)

By the mid-1990s it was foreign governments and NGOs rather than
the Zimbabwean government or local audience support that provided
one ray of hope. Nyathi also suggested, as I have above, that the promise
of foreign tours was perhaps *the* major impetus for professionalization.
For both guitar bands and dance troupes, he described the situation in
Zimbabwe as "cut-throat competition, and for any mediocre act, ah,
there is no room" (Zim96-3: 8). Nonetheless, the few success stories,
such as those of Thomas Mapfumo and the Bulawayo-based Ndebele
group, Black Umfalosi,[9] continue to inspire people to go professional.
Albert Nyathi explained that

> in Bulawayo, people used to look down on ngoma [indigenous] type
> of music generally. However, a group called Black Umfalosi gave
> back [demonstrated what was possible] to many groups now . . . and
> people have to change: "Ah, so this thing, people can make a living
> out of it. That one now has a house, that one is being overseas.
> Through dance?!" They never used to think that way. *Now, I think
> overseas has had a lot of influence on people locally.* And if you have
> a school leaver who failed at school and is just living there in the

township, and suddenly they see a white friend visiting from overseas, and they see that artist now going down to play mbira or
to dance, then there is a sudden change, *everybody wants to go*.
(Zim96-3: 10; my emphasis)

Gage Averill has coined the phrase, "The Paul Simon Cargo Cult," to
describe local musicians waiting to be discovered and brought into the
transnational market by stars like Simon on projects such as *Graceland*
and *Rhythm of the Saints*. While tongue-in-cheek, the phrase underlines
the ubiquity of the situation I am describing for Zimbabwe.

Federation programs in the 1950s–60s and cosmopolitan youth
culture in the 1960s–70s inspired increasing numbers of Zimbabweans
to reconceptualize music-dance activities as saleable commodities. Nationalist programs of the 1980s strengthened the drive to professionalize and commercialize indigenous music and dance. Thus a desire to
enter the market was created. When the local market proved too weak
to support the army of new professionals, performers had to turn their
attention outward to stronger transnational markets and richer foreign
audiences. This, in turn, had direct effects on musical values, practices,
and style. In a nutshell, cosmopolitan-based ideologies and programs
created increased interest in, and dependence on, local and ultimately
transnational markets. This involvement, in turn, inspired increasing
adoption of cosmopolitan aesthetics and style in order to succeed in the
transnational market. Cosmopolitanism begets more cosmopolitanism,
in this case specifically in its capitalist form. The worldbeat or "world
music" phenomenon is the most recent conjuncture where this is played
out, although in this case the dynamics are organized directly around
transnational markets rather than through state and other local cultural
programs for local audiences.

### Worldbeat

Following on the heels of Paul Simon's phenomenally successful *Graceland* album, it is no accident that Black Umfalosi was one of Zimbabwe's
few successful touring groups. Coming from Zulu-related Ndebele society, they perform a vocal style very close to the *isicathamiya* choral music
of Ladysmith Black Mambazo, the group made internationally famous
by Simon's recording (Meintjes 1990; Erlmann 1996). Simon's album became a worldbeat classic, and in fact helped to define what worldbeat is.

Worldbeat is a marketing label and cosmopolitan genre category for
certain "minority" (e.g., zydeco, Tex-Mex conjunto) and "exotic" or
"Third World" musics that originate outside the mainstream cosmopolitan sphere. Worldbeat is also defined by certain ideological themes

and images, by certain types of production values (or studio sound), and by the very aesthetic choices about what styles might be included and how they should be arranged and presented.[10]

Paul Simon circumscribed worldbeat best when he described why he chose the South African styles he did for the *Graceland* album:

> In the summer of 1984, a friend gave me a cassette of an album called *Gumboots: Accordion Jive Hits,* Volume 2. It sounded vaguely like '50s rock 'n'roll out of the Atlantic Records school of simple three-chord pop hits: Mr. Lee by the Bobettes, Jim Dandy by Laverne Baker. It was very up, very happy music—*familiar and foreign-sounding at the same time.* (*Graceland,* liner notes, 1986; my emphasis)

This aspect of being familiar and yet simultaneously "foreign-sounding" is the key to understanding worldbeat.

The "familiarity" Simon recognized and responded to would, I think, have similar resonances with pop-oriented cosmopolitans the world over. It was the result of South African incorporation of African-American and cosmopolitan musical features and values throughout this century (Erlmann 1990). Within its loops of diffusion, cosmopolitanism often involves feedback of this kind.

Of course worldbeat is defined most importantly by the use of styles that index foreign or exotic difference. Within worldbeat, however, the indices of foreign societies are either selected because they already include aesthetic familiarity within the style, or foreign stylistic differences are tempered by transformations which make them accessible to cosmopolitans. The worldbeat marketing of mbira music involved both these aspects.

Because worldbeat is defined by the fusion of distinctive local elements and cosmopolitan features, it is like all the other modernist-reformist styles discussed in this book. Rather than articulating with specific colonial cultural policies (chapter 3) or nationalist groups (chapters 5–6), however, in worldbeat modernist reformism articulates pragmatically with transnational markets and symbolically with membership in the "global village." That is, it articulates with the capitalist cosmopolitan formation itself.

By the mid-1980s worldbeat provided the major context and market for aspiring Zimbabwean professionals. This has had important effects on Zimbabwean musicians like ex-NDC member Stella Chiweshe, Black Umfalosi, the Bhundu Boys, and touring mbira and karimba players like Ephat Mujuru and Kwanongoma/University of Washington graduate Dumisani Maraire.

More than any other Zimbabwean artist, however, it was Thomas Mapfumo who went after the worldbeat market and achieved relative success.

## Thomas Mapfumo
## and Worldbeat

Inspired by 1960s cosmopolitan youth culture and hopes for international stardom, Mapfumo already seemed to be thinking in terms of foreign markets in the early 1970s. Speaking of his experimental period before he became a traditionalist, Mapfumo told me that they were trying to play "Afro-rock" in the style of a band that was making it in London. Mapfumo discovered that the Afro-rock style did not work with Zimbabwean audiences, and it was at home where he had to build his initial audience. Thus he became a specialist in and the champion of indigenous-based guitar-band music, which articulated with nationalism in complex and sometimes ambiguous ways during the 1970s.

National sentiment began to wane after the early 1980s in Zimbabwe. Many musicians told me that at this point people wanted to forget about the war, and there was growing cynicism about the government. Again in response to audience sentiment, many who had been performing indigenous-based music between 1978 and 1982 began to turn away from this style and from political lyrics. Like others in the early 1980s, Mapfumo experimented with a variety of styles. Unlike many of his colleagues, however, he vigorously returned to indigenous-based music and to nationalist imagery in the mid-1980s. Again he was guided by the desires of his targeted audience, in this case worldbeat fans. His "roots" sound and popular association with the nationalist movement were central to his popularity during this conjuncture.

In November 1984 Mapfumo had a major European tour. He performed with Stella Chiweshe in Hannover. Fred Zindi witnessed his performance in London: "At 10 P.M. the show began. Thomas came on stage decked out in a brand-new sequinned and tight army uniform, his dreadlocks under a woolly red, gold, and green hat, and his hands clenched to his microphone—nervously at first—but he soon gained confidence."

Always conscious of such things, Mapfumo presented London audiences with an image that combined the military index of the "Freedom Fighter," the glitter of the pop star, and the red, gold, and green of rastafarianism. Along with his long dreadlocks,[11] the rasta colors would index one of worldbeat's earliest and most successful styles and stars, reggae artist Bob Marley.

Mapfumo performed "Pidigori" as his opening number at the London show, and then more pop-oriented songs. It may be significant that Mapfumo repeated "Pidigori" for his finale. Based on the Chibhora Family's variant of the classic mbira piece "Nhemamusasa," "Pidigori" contained the strongest indigenous Shona references of all the pieces mentioned by Zindi (1985: 37). At this time, Mapfumo began a new phase of experimenting with visual, verbal, and musical imagery to reach out to a broad international audience.

### The Marley Worldbeat Legacy

Like juju star Sunny Ade earlier, Mapfumo was picked up briefly (1989–91) by Mango, a division of Island Records, in their attempt to find a worldbeat star to replace Bob Marley after his death (Blackwell, in Fox 1986: 320). Island Records was a major force behind the worldbeat phenomenon, and Island's founder, Chris Blackwell, was involved in both discovering and helping to create the worldbeat market niche. In discussing his initial marketing of Bob Marley, Blackwell remarked,

> I felt reggae was the white liberal market. I always hoped that it would sell to black America, but it never did because the music was too ethnic-ish. It wasn't smooth enough. . . . The only people who really related to it were white liberal, college oriented-type people who were interested in it because of its *sociological aspects* as well as its rhythm. But it was really its sociological side that gave it its base. (quoted in Fox 1986: 306; my emphasis)

As with Marley, Mapfumo largely attracted "white liberal, college-oriented" people in the United States, confirming Blackwell's assessment of a major worldbeat market. In a local Champaign, Illinois, radio interview during his 1989 tour, Mapfumo expressed surprise that the great majority of people who came to his shows were white:

> It's been a surprise to me, we have seen a lot of our audience being white and very few black people. I don't know what that means because we are supposed to be seeing our people coming into these gigs. . . . They are Africans; How can they forget their roots? They are not supposed to forget their roots; they are supposed to be with us. When we come here, they are supposed to be the first people who meet us rather than being met by our white friends. Well this disturbs me a lot.

The way race articulates with the worldbeat audience in the United States may be different from other locales (e.g., London, Tokyo). Nonetheless, Blackwell's discovery that worldbeat audiences are primarily composed of a certain sector of cosmopolitans—young, liberal, college types—is probably accurate regardless of locale.

Speaking of the criteria for success within the worldbeat market Blackwell emphasized that "unless that cult grows," as with reggae, "bam! [the music] fades out" (Fox 1986: 321). Cult status depends on what Blackwell called the "sociological side": the ideological themes and images that become part of the style as expressed through musical sound, lyrics, public stance, dress, and spoken discourse.

The sociological side of the Bob Marley worldbeat legacy involves three important streams: liberatory politics, especially as pertaining to the African diaspora; "exotic" spiritualism (e.g., rastafarianism); and a distinctive "roots," yet familiar, musical style indexing a unique [foreign] locality or community.[12] Mapfumo's music and history fit well with all three.

### Politics as Style

Among the three primary worldbeat themes, Mapfumo's connection with politics—Zimbabwean nationalism—was considered his strongest selling point and claim to "cult status" in worldbeat circles. Mango's biographical press release of 1989 emphasized Mapfumo's "political militancy," his political songs of the 1970s, his arrest for activism, and it made the direct connection between his music and Zimbabwe's independence from colonial rule (Mango 1989). In the North American Press, *The Village Voice* said, "The secret of the popularity [Mapfumo] enjoys among world-beat types in America is that he's a heroic figure, not a mere musician" (10 October 1989). *Cash Box* said, "For those interested in the few artists who have used music to effect cultural or political change, the Mapfumo tour is a must-see" (7 October 1989). The *Los Angeles Times* said, "Creating outlaw music that affects the social and political order . . . for Zimbabwe's Thomas Mapfumo, that rock dream was reality . . . his music inspired the independence war" (21 October 1989). Jon Pareles of the *New York Times* said, "Mr. Mapfumo's style has been named 'chimurenga' ('struggle') for its role in the revolution that turned Rhodesia into Zimbabwe" (4 September 1993).

Thus, the nationalist imagery that had articulated in various ways with Mapfumo's rise during the 1970s was explicitly foregrounded in his attempt to enter the worldbeat niche after 1985. Worldbeat fans— white, liberal, college types—wanted a musical hero, and they found one in Thomas Mapfumo. I know I was initially attracted to him for this reason, as were many acquaintances. Scholars, too, still celebrate this facet of the Mapfumo story (e.g., see Lipsitz 1994: 139).

Mapfumo was quite possibly pushed to emphasize a political past in foreign interviews, largely due to the orientation of his foreign interviewers and his awareness of the desires of his worldbeat audience. This was not mere cynical manipulation of the press. In his view he had written songs to support the guerrillas, and so when led by interviewers, he simply emphasized this aspect of his personal history. This often happens with the public presentation of popular performers, who accentuate aspects of their lives according to the desires of their audience (Hennion 1990). In other interviews, however, Mapfumo has emphasized that he is a musician, not a politician (e.g., Zindi 1985: 38). Moreover, in interviews with me he was fairly candid about his own career aspirations as a primary motivation for singing indigenous-based music *and* political texts (see chapter 8). Yet professional goals *and* nationalist-inspired ideas were probably simultaneously involved by the latter part of the 1970s. Both in Zimbabwe during the 1970s and in the worldbeat arena of the 1980s, these two motivations were complimentary—in the first case because of the war; in the second because of liberal idealism.

### Mbira and Images of Exotic Spirituality

Along with politics, the other key component of Mapfumo's international fame was his association with mbira music. This association, in turn, was perfect in relation to the other two primary worldbeat themes—spirituality and a distinctive foreign locality. The mbira's connection with Shona religion came to be known internationally through Paul Berliner's book, as well as through Zimbabwean musicians traveling abroad. Popular publications aimed at worldbeat fans such as *World Music: The Rough Guide* emphasized the mbira's central place in Zimbabwean music and its spiritual associations. Beneath the picture of an mbira in this publication, the caption reads, "Every key a spirit: the mbira." By the late 1980s the connection with Shona spirituality was a "sociological" basis for the international popularity of mbira music generally, and for Mapfumo in particular.

Although not emphasized as much as political activism in Mapfumo's imagery, spiritual connections with the music were recognized. For example, during their 1989 tour of the United States, Mapfumo's mbira player Chartwell Dutiro wore a spirit medium's robe on stage during their Champaign-Urbana performance. Afterwards I asked Chartwell if he was a medium. He responded that he wasn't and that he had worn the robe just for the show. While no one in the band dresses like this when performing in Zimbabwe currently, Mapfumo did sometimes wear costumes that indexed spiritualists during the 1970s (see chapter 8). Shona spirituality is an important aspect for many North American mbira players and fans, especially on the west coast and in the southwest; Mapfumo's very connection with mbira music provided a link with indigenous African spirituality.

### Mapfumo and the
### Mbira Connection

More than any other single component of his style, it was the use of the mbira and mbira music that clearly distinguished Mapfumo's music and linked him to a specific African locality for worldbeat fans. For a variety of reasons, mbira music became Zimbabwe's internationally most famous, recognizable, and popular musical tradition. This led Mapfumo to emphasize the instrument increasingly after the mid-1980s. In fact it was only during Mapfumo's worldbeat phase that mbira really came to the fore in his band, at least in terms of attention and symbolic significance.

More important, I believe that the emergence of the mbira as a major national emblem *in* Zimbabwe and *for* Zimbabwe abroad was actually generated from cosmopolitan world music circles during the 1980s. Mapfumo's international prominence contributed to this shift in meaning, but his increasing emphasis on the mbira during the late 1980s and 1990s was also a dialectical result of international interest in this instrument.

### Mbira-Centric Views
### of Zimbabwean Music

The mbira was not a particularly prominent nationalist emblem in Zimbabwe before the 1980s, nor was mbira music a basis for the majority of songs performed by Mapfumo and other indigenous-based guitar bands during the 1970s. In the nationalist rallies of the early 1960s, ZAPU presented an inclusive range of indigenous and urban popular traditions that indexed a variety of social groups on rather equal footing. The mbira was merely one among other traditions, and more flamboyant dances such as jerusarema and muchongoyo tended to receive more attention in the press. ZANU's chimurenga songs of the 1970s were typically based on hymns, makwaya, jit, and a smattering of indigenous genres; mbira pieces were merely one type within this latter category of sources (see chapters 5 and 6).

During the 1970s Mapfumo and other guitar bands used a wide variety of indigenous and pop genres, as he still does. Numerically, mbira-based pieces were usually in a small minority on Mapfumo's records, and the actual instrument was not permanently included in his band until 1986, after he entered the worldbeat market. On Mapfumo's 1977 *Hokoyo!* LP, only two out of ten pieces were based on classical mbira pieces, and there were only two on his first Mango release, *Corruption* (1989).[13] Jit, other dance-drumming styles, and more pop-oriented pieces made up the rest of both albums; the title track of *Corruption* was a reggae-influenced song atypically sung in English, and of "Hokoyo!" was an 'Afro-rock' number.

Nonetheless, in the international press and in scholarly accounts of Zimbabwean music, musical nationalism, and Mapfumo, mbira is the musical feature most widely recognized and commented upon. For example, in the recent *Garland Encyclopedia of World Music: Africa,* Angela Impey writes,

> A major transition in the popular music of Zimbabwe took place during the war of liberation (1967–1980), when folk songs were used to politicize rural people. These songs, known as *chimurenga* "songs of liberation" were based on ancient melodies and instrumental structures derived from the music of the *mbira dzavadzimu.* In the mid-1970s to appeal to the tastes of urban nightclubs and bars, popular musicians began to adapt *mbira* melodies. (1998: 432)

This statement about chimurenga songs is largely inaccurate if meant to refer to the music generated by the nationalist parties; the statement about urban-popular bands is true but leaves out the fact that mbira songs were only one of a variety of indigenous genres adapted. Thus, although Impey did her dissertation research on women in Zimbabwean popular music and knows that a variety of popular and indigenous musical genres exist there, she foregrounds mbira-based music above all others in this passage. In his overview of indigenous music entitled "Music of the Shona of Zimbabwe" in the same volume, John Kaemmer devotes five pages to lamellophones, mbira prominent among them, and about two pages of text to all "other instrumental and vocal genres" (1998: 745–52). In his 1975 dissertation, however, his description of different genres was more in balance with what one would find in rural Zimbabwe.

International attention was not drawn to the mbira because mbira-based pieces were numerically prominent in indigenous repertories, in Mapfumo's repertory, or in nationalist activities, but because for people unfamiliar with Zimbabwean music, mbira was the style and instrument most easy to recognize and to comment upon. For writers who were familiar with Zimbabwean music such as Impey and Kaemmer, by the 1990s the international popularity of the instrument seems to have gained its own momentum—influencing the emphasis in their writing about Zimbabwe. This same observation applies to my own textbook chapter on Africa in *Excursions in World Music* (1992).

The question is, why did the mbira, originally a localized, special-ist, Zezuru tradition, rise to international prominence above all other Shona lamellophone, dance-drumming, and choral styles? Part of the answer lies in its earlier rise within the country due to Zezuru proxi-mity to Harare, as well as this instrument's fit with local radio (see chap-ters 2, 8; Turino 1998). In terms of its international popularity, the mbira provided a close fit with worldbeat aesthetics: the instrument and its repertory were both locally distinctive and yet musically attractive and accessible (familiar) to cosmopolitan sensibilities.

Distinctiveness and easy identification are essential in the creation of emblems. Zimbabwean drums do not differ much from many other African drums (or even the congas used in Mapfumo's band), but the twenty-two-key mbira is relatively unique to Zimbabwe and thus served well as an index for that country. When played inside a large gourd on stage, the mbira's visual and sonic distinctiveness played a part in draw-ing attention.

One of the most important reasons for the international focus on mbira is that its sound and music are easily accessible and especially attractive for people with cosmopolitan aesthetics. As a player, I find that North Americans and Europeans readily respond with enthusiasm to this music.[14] When I teach large, undergraduate world music classes, mbira tends to be one of the most popular traditions covered relative to the music of other parts of Africa and the world. Undergraduates unfamiliar with non-Western music seem to find the instrument and its music readily attractive, although they often suggest that they would like it even better without the bottlecap buzzers. Colleagues teaching similar courses have reported such generally positive responses from their students as well. Unlike *karnatak* music, Peking Opera, indigenous Aymara *pinkillu* music, and Ewe dance drumming, the mbira, in and of itself, seems to present a balance of accessible qualities and foreign dif-ference, which is so important to success in world music circles.

As suggested in chapter 7, the chord progressions that emerge from guitar arrangements of classical mbira pieces are familiar and particu-larly effective in the context of cosmopolitan popular music conven-tions. The continual shifting between major and minor chords and the ambiguous tonal center help to create a moving, mysterious effect that supports the romantic imagery of foreign places. I believe that these implied harmonic progressions are a key feature that lend a familiarity to mbira music and make it readily attractive and accessible to cosmopolitan listeners.[15] The smooth yet driving continuous flow of the 12/8 rhythm, the cyclical form, and the light timbre of the instrument itself (especially when the bottlecaps are removed) have elements in common with new-age musics which have audience overlap with worldbeat.

In conjunction with the distinctiveness and attractiveness of the instrument, I partially attribute the international focus on the mbira to Paul Berliner's landmark study, *Soul of Mbira*, and the accompanying Nonesuch records. A widely read ethnomusicological classic, this book focused almost exclusively on the twenty-two-key Zezuru mbira. Since it was the only easily available, detailed work on Zimbabwean music, it had a major impact on shaping international perceptions. Although Berliner contextualized the Zezuru mbira in relation to other Shona traditions in his introduction, the amount and quality of attention granted to the Zezuru mbira throughout the rest of the book placed it in the foreground for people not otherwise familiar with Zimbabwean music.[16]

Berliner's work has also served as a primary source for world music textbooks and various secondary accounts of African music. Taken together, this body of literature has helped shape the popular mbira-centered view of Zimbabwean music among world music fans, mass-media music writers, and ethnomusicologists. Throughout this book I have offered examples of the ways ethnomusicologists not only document musical processes and history, but also take part in creating local discourses and history based in cosmopolitan linkages. The international popularity of mbira music is another case in point.

Scholarly attention, however, must be understood as a factor in relation to the nature of the music in question. The other indigenous African traditions that are popular with worldbeat audiences and in world music classes are either made "familiar" by the larger ensemble context (e.g., the hour-glass pressure drum in Nigerian juju), or in themselves balance local distinctiveness with familiarity and attractiveness for cosmopolitans (e.g., South African isicathamiya and mbaqanga; Mande kora, Congolese soukous). Indigenous Ewe drumming has received a great deal of scholarly attention but has not become popular within worldbeat because it lacks sufficient accessibility. In the case of the mbira, cultural distinctiveness, accessibility within cosmopolitan aesthetics, and wide recognition through a particularly attractive scholarly work came together to popularize the instrument internationally.

## Mapfumo, Worldbeat, and
## Aesthetic Transformation

Mapfumo responded to the international interest in the mbira by emphasizing it more in his ensemble as time went on. Consistent with the continual "indigenization" process that has characterized his career, he added a permanent mbira player, Chartwell Dutiro, to his band for the first time in 1986; between 1986 and 1992 the number increased to three mbira players. In stage shows even more than on recordings, the mbira players came to have pride of place—forward and toward the center of the stage—on the pieces for which they were used. On recordings since 1986, even songs not based on mbira music may begin with a short mbira solo.

Between 1977 *(Hokoyo!)* and 1989 *(Corruption),* and in his more recent work, the percentage of classical mbira-based pieces did not necessarily increase on Mapfumo's recordings. For example, on the international release *The Chimurenga Singles, 1976–1980* (1985, Shanachie-Meadow Lark 403), there are no songs based on classical mbira music (four 12/8 phrases), although there are two jit songs ("Kwaendza Mu Zimbabwe" and "Chipatapata"), and several based on two-phrase, 12/8 Shona structures (e.g., "Tozvireva Kupiko" and "Pfumvu Pa Ruzevha"). The international release *Ndangariro* (1983, Earthworks ELP 2005) likewise has no songs based on classical mbira, but indigenous vocal style is prominent on several songs, and there is a piece originally associated with jerusarema that was recorded by guitar bands in the 1960s—"Kambiri Kaenda" (see chapter 7). On *Zimbabwe-Mozambique* (1988, Gramma TML 100) an mbira is featured, but no songs are based on mbira music. On *Chimurenga Masterpiece* (1990, TML 103) one out five pieces is classical mbira ("Dangu Rangu"), and three are jit. On *Hondo* (1991, TML 104) one out of five pieces is mbira-based ("Maiti Kurima"), and three are jit. On a 1994 international release *Vanhu Vatema* (Zimbob TMBU 14), three out of ten pieces were based on classic mbira music, and four were jit.

Against this backdrop, Mapfumo's second Mango release, *Chamunorwa* (1991), is quite distinct: four of the six pieces are mbira-based ("Hwahwa," "Chitima Ndikature," "Chamunorwa," and "Nyama Yekugocha"),[17] one is a jit song ("Hurokuro"), and the remaining piece, "Muramba Doro," is based on jerusarema. In the four mbira-based pieces the instrument is foregrounded in the instrumental introduction. The balance of genres, itself, suggests a conscious emphasis on the mbira for his second attempt with this prominent worldbeat label. Unlike his first Mango recording, this one has no pop-oriented songs, only indigenous-based pieces. The quality of music on *Chamunorwa* is interesting for the way it fits with worldbeat aesthetics generally.

On "Muramba Doro" the reference to jerusarema is heard in the opening ngoma (indigenous drum) part; the highhat part vaguely alludes to jerusarema woodblock patterns. The jerusarema rhythm is subtly maintained throughout the recording but would be easily missed by anyone not familiar with this genre. More prominently, the song has a 4/4 rock-oriented rhythm with snare accents on two and four. The progression is a typical two-phrase Shona type (F Am Dm Dm | F Am C C). On the song Mapfumo emphasizes indigenous-style yodeling *(huro)* and call-and-response singing on vocables with the female chorus. What is striking is the way Mapfumo performs the huro vocal style. Rather than the often penetrating or strident style of indigenous Shona yodeling, Mapfumo softens the vocal quality, doing away with any harsh or strident edges. This juxtaposition of jerusarema and rock rhythm, indigenous-style vocals and form with a softening of the vocal style (like much of his work after 1985), and the recording mix that provides a full, clear, balanced rendering of parts, produces a final effect that is "familiar and foreign-sounding at the same time."

The softening of Mapfumo's yodeling and general vocal style is particularly apparent when comparing the versions of the mbira-based song "Hwahwa" on *Hokoyo!* (1977) and on *Chamunorwa* (1991). Unlike the faster, driving earlier version, which uses only guitars, bass, and traps, the 1991 version begins with a short, delicate introduction played by mbira and sparse hosho. As the band enters, the mbira remains audible in the mix, and the hosho is relatively equal to the echoing highhat part. The overall feel is gentle and flowing. On the earlier version, Mapfumo produced a thinner, more strident vocal timbre for huro singing, in keeping with indigenous style. His voice on the latter recording is smoother, softer, and richer, without any strident edges, although he maintains the use of the distinctive yodeling technique. The mbira itself was transformed in Mapfumo's band in ways that parallel his shift in vocal style.

By the mid-1980s, Mapfumo's British sound engineer, Chris Bolton, had devised a way of putting electric pick-ups on mbira soundboards, which was important for their incorporation. After the mbira had been electrified, Bolton decided to remove the bottlecap buzzers so that the sound would be clearer. This seems to have been Bolton's own aesthetic decision, yet it corresponds with the preferences of people in my world music classes. Recent mbira and karimba recordings aimed at North American audiences, such as the Dumisani Maraire/Ephat Mujuru and Forward Kwenda/Erica Azim (1997) collaborations, likewise feature instruments without buzzers, or with the buzz greatly reduced relative to the instruments preferred in indigenous contexts. It seems as though most people outside Zimbabwe prefer the instrument with no buzzers or with the buzz reduced. By the early 1990s, mbira without buzzers had become the norm for Zimbabwean guitar bands that included the instrument. As is often the case in cosmopolitan encounters with distinctive indigenous traditions, the features of sonic distinction are reduced so as to make the music more accessible "to the world," and this often has ramifications back in the home country.

The instruments used in Mapfumo's band (made by Chris Mhlanga) are tuned in the standard European system so that the pitches match the electric keyboards.[18] Readily apparent on any Mapfumo recording, the light, clear, metallic sound of these mbira (tuned in E, with particularly short, high keys) is quite distinct from the dense, buzzy quality preferred by indigenous players and heard on commercial recordings of such players in Zimbabwe. Similar alterations were made to other African instruments when incorporated into worldbeat. For example, the buzzers typically attached to the Mande kora are also usually removed, and the timbre is made to sound more like an acoustic guitar (bass augmented, higher strings made more resonant) through microphone placement and equalization.

While Mapfumo maintains the characteristic polyphonic textures of indigenous Shona music, he carefully arranges the music so that clarity of parts prevails rather than the dense overlays and spontaneous dynamics and variations of indigenous performance. Similar in process to the National Dance Company's arrangements, Mapfumo has standardized and shaped indigenous Shona music for cosmopolitan consumption at home and abroad.[19]

In an August 1990 interview with *Moto,* a Zimbabwean journal, Mapfumo speaks directly of his relation to indigenous music; he too emphasizes the role of mbira along with other indigenous instruments:

> Chimurenga music [referring to his own music] is the traditional beat of *mbira,* rattles (hosho), and drums played at important gatherings *by our ancestors,* so I would not outrightly agree that I am the founder of the beat, but rather just one who inherited, *improved, and perfected it,* and managed to present it *by modern electrical instruments,* and made it to be liked by more people in these hightec times. *Now I am exporting the beat.* I am very proud of my culture. (*Moto* 1990: 19; my emphasis)

The kernels of this statement sum up Mapfumo's activities as modernist reformer in parallel to so many other cases described in this book:

"by the ancestors," "improved and perfected," "by modern electrical instruments," "now I am exporting the beat." The statement suggests the direct conceptual links between traditionalism, the discourse of modernity, reformism, commodification, and seeking transnational markets.

### Nationalist Discourse and
### Economic Protectionism at Home

Publicity from and about Mapfumo in Zimbabwe during my 1992–93 stay stressed his successes abroad, his joint concerts with foreign stars such as Manu Dibango in Harare, or his own statements about the need for Zimbabweans to turn their attention away from foreign music in support of local artists. Mapfumo has been a vocal advocate for indigenous-based popular music, couched in cultural nationalist terms, ever since he began to specialize in it during the mid-1970s. This emphasis in his 1992–93 interviews was consistent with long-held attitudes.

What was new, however, was the aggressiveness of his attacks on foreign music, and he was particularly critical of the raging popularity of Congolese rumba (kwasa kwasa, soukous). These attacks were sometimes couched in moralist terms reminiscent of the cultural nationalism of the 1970s, which argued that foreign influences were corrupting Zimbabwean youth and culture. In December 1992, for example, Mapfumo is quoted as saying, "This kwasa-kwasa thing must be destroyed. It is corrupting the minds of young people" (in Nyika 1992: 7).

Mapfumo's attacks on foreign music were also related to his realistic assessment of the increasing difficulty of making a living as a musician in Zimbabwe. He stated repeatedly in interviews that "we should be promoted locally by the local promoters here. . . . They are just greedy and therefore are always looking for outsiders" (Mapfumo 1993: 9). As a particularly popular dance music, Congolese rumba represented the most direct competition for Mapfumo's record market share and club engagements—Congolese groups frequently came to Harare. This helps explain why this style received the most pointed attack, rather than rap, reggae, country and western, American top-40, South African music, and all the other popular foreign styles on Zimbabwean radio. This, and Mapfumo's statements about foreign music as an economic threat, suggest that by the mid-1990s cultural-nationalist discourse was again rearticulated to a new professional agenda, this time to a kind of musical economic protectionism at home.

## Troubles in the Global Village

After *Chamunorwa,* Mapfumo was dropped by Mango and by 1995
was having problems with overseas promoters. In the summer of 1996
he took a quick trip to participate in the WOMAD festival in England
with his ensemble greatly reduced to cut costs. The eight musicians who
were selected for the concert included the three mbira players, the bass-
ist, a guitarist, the trap drummer, and a percussionist. The horn players,
keyboardist, his other guitar player, and the accompanying singers and
dancers were left home. Mapfumo's repertory can be roughly divided
into two types of pieces: 'traditional' songs that include mbira; and jit
or more pop-oriented numbers centered around the horns, for which the
mbira are excluded. Mapfumo's choice of instrumentation for the 1996
WOMAD concert clearly suggests a greater emphasis on the mbira and
traditionalist imagery for this central worldbeat event.

Chris Bolton, Mapfumo's associate and sound engineer, told me
that touring with this smaller configuration began in 1992, when Mapfumo played a concert with the Kronos Quartet in San Francisco. They
had also done an "unplugged" concert emphasizing the mbira in London in 1993. Bolton said that Mapfumo liked this smaller sound; it was
more intimate and 'traditional,' with more space for his singing (p.c.
July 1996). This smaller, mbira-centered lineup is also more economi-
cal, and ultimately it provides what worldbeat fans want: mbira-based
roots music. It remains to be seen how the forces of the transnational
market will affect Mapfumo's and other Zimbabwean's future artistic
and career choices, but as of 1996, international interest in the mbira
had inspired Mapfumo to increasingly emphasize and identify with this
particular tradition.

## The New Wave of Indigenous-
## Based Guitar Bands

Following on the heels of Mapfumo's international successes, back in
Zimbabwe there was a new boom of young bands specializing in indigenous-based music after 1988. In fact, between the late 1980s and approximately 1994, the number of indigenous-based guitar bands, now
often quite consciously in the Mapfumo mold, probably equaled or ex-
ceeded the number recording during the high nationalist period of
1978–1982. The success of Chiweshe, the Bhundu Boys, and especially
Thomas Mapfumo in the worldbeat market led more bands to specialize in the indigenous-based electric style.[20]

It is a common phenomenon that international attention to and marketing of particular local styles will give a boost to those styles at home.
Because of international attention, such styles often come to be consid-

ered *the* national or most important local style in postcolonial countries like Zimbabwe. The heightened prominence of mbira-based music, and of the mbira itself in Zimbabwe during the late 1980s is one example. In Harare during the 1988–94 period, not only were increasing numbers of young people showing interest in mbira-based guitar music, the mbira it-self was quite popular with young people, especially but not exclusively, with rural and working-class people. This worldbeat-generated boom created the perception that one could work, and perhaps even tour, as a professional mbira player. For lower-income youth who wanted to play in bands, mbira were more available than guitars. Perhaps also because of the international popularity of mbira, the instrument was beginning to be included in the curricula of elite secondary schools in Harare, where it was studied by white as well as middle-class black students! As I sug-gested in chapter 2, this does not so much represent a "revival" of the mbira as a new phase of flowering and diffusion.[21]

The new wave of young, indigenous-based bands was also tied to the opening of a new, independent record company in Harare in the late 1980s, Record and Tape Productions (RTP), which encouraged bands to record in this style. RTP executives explained to me that they favored this style because they wanted to promote Zimbabwean music. They thus articulated national sentiment as a cause, but they also may have been influenced by Mapfumo's commercial success at home and abroad.

Interviews with young artists in groups like Vadzimba, indicate that they consciously took Mapfumo as their role and style model. Another band, Pio Macheka and the Blackites, imitated Mapfumo down to the dreadlocks, clothing, and dance style on stage. Like all the bands in the new wave, one or more mbira were foregrounded in the instrumenta-tion along with guitars, bass, traps, and keyboards. Those modeled on Mapfumo's Blacks Unlimited, particularly Vadzimba and the Blackites, performed some pieces closely modeled on classical mbira music. Also during this period, new attention was given to veterans of the electric style such as Jonah Sithole and Deep Horizone (also on RTP), and vet-eran mbira players such as Ephat Mujuru, who formed electric bands to take part in this trend.

Other bands of the new wave included the Legal Lions, Traditional Madness, and Zimbabwe Clear Sounds. These groups featured electric mbira prominently and performed some indigenous pieces. They tended to be more experimental, however, and did not adhere to classical mbira music; they would use the mbira on any tune they happened to be play-ing. While I interpreted such experimentation as healthy, my more conservative friends were skeptical. In speaking of the Legal Lions, for example, one of my mbira teachers commented, "They do not know

where they are coming from, and they do not know where they are going," referring to the fact that the band was alluding to indigenous
Shona arts without having any real grounding in them. The same criticism might be leveled at second- and third-generation professional
dance groups descended from the National Dance Company.

### The Summer of 1996

Unfortunately, we will never know where these electric bands might
have gone professionally and stylistically. By my return visit in the summer of 1996 Zimbabwe was in a major economic slump, and this flurry
of activity had already died down. Record company executives told me
that due to a decline in record sales they had to emphasize the big names
such as M'tukudzi, Mapfumo, Leonard Dembo, and Simon Chimbetu,[22]
or foreign artists, and could no longer afford to take chances on newly
formed or little-known local groups. Club owners followed the same
path. Victor Tangweni, marketing specialist for Music Express, noted
that record buyers were conservative during times of limited funds and
would base purchases on past performance, not innovation (Zim96-5:
1). It was primarily the older, established musicians who remained
viable.

During the summer of 1996, Mapfumo's band was going stronger
than ever. With recent major personnel changes, he was playing four
nights a week to large crowds in Harare. As one of the only going concerns in town, he had the pick of a huge range of musicians. To their
disappointment, guitarists Joshua Hlomayi and Jonah Sithole could not
make a living with their own bands because of economic hard times.
Both had returned to play with Mapfumo. Being two of the best, most
experienced, guitarists in the country, they gave a tremendous boost to
the band. The Blacks Unlimited also had some excellent new horn players and backup vocalists. The band was better than I had ever heard it.

As in any depressed market economy, those who have accumulated
capital are best able to stay in business. Mapfumo's long-standing commercial success and his international tours have provided him with the
necessary capital. He is able to record and get engagements because of
his reputation for quality and for maintaining a following. Equally important, he has one of the best sound systems and "band kits" in the
country,[23] not a negligible factor in maintaining quality. The great majority of guitar-band musicians do not own their own instruments. To
perform they have to rent or borrow, or work for a bandleader like
Mapfumo who does own the means of musical production.

With his new lineup and lots of new material, Mapfumo seemed
particularly energized and in touch with his audiences in the summer of

1996. Local fans sang along with him as he moved with them on the dance floor. He was attracting new young followers as well as drawing his old ones. Particularly impressive to me, after working the same clubs for over thirty years, he is still able to periodically renew his enthusiasm and his music and thus maintain his home audience.[24]

Regardless of the various debates, problems, and stories that have surrounded Mapfumo over the years, I believe his Zimbabwean fans keep coming back because they can count on him: he is a great composer/arranger and bandleader who produces great Zimbabwean music. Cutting through all the romantic publicity hype about political pasts and international stardom, even his own, this is perhaps all he ever really wanted or promised.

## Conclusions

Not too long ago in Zimbabwe, full-time professional musicians were a rarity even in the urban-popular music field. In the late 1950s "concert" artists were certainly influenced by cosmopolitan musical styles, but they were amateur-specialists who performed from the more elitist bourgeois ideology of "art for art's sake." By 1996, cosmopolitan-capitalism and Zimbabwean nationalism had created an army of professionals. Competition was "cutthroat," and market forces, substantially directed by transnational organizations like the IMF, had come to be important arbitrators of musical creativity, experimentation, and indeed, survival in the popular music field.

The growing importance of market forces and cosmopolitan aesthetics in Zimbabwean music was not the product of some preconceived, unitary, capitalist plot. Rather, as I have tried to show throughout this book, a series of forces involving colonialism, Federation liberalism, nationalism, 1960s youth culture, and capitalism came together over time to create this conjuncture. I have also tried to show that the articulation of these forces was neither totally arbitrary nor accidental (conjunctural); it was rooted in the common cosmopolitan habitus of the primary actors involved. For such actors, forming a nation-state, creating stageable, saleable versions of indigenous music and dance, and the personal accumulation of capital to compete in the market are all commonsense, taken-for-granted, notions of how the world is and should be.

### Middle-Class Habitus and Passive Revolution of Capital

Throughout this book we have followed the shifting patterns of black elite self-identification, from the emphasis on class distinctions from "the masses" before the late 1950s to the discourse of racial identity and

unity which downplayed class in the nationalist "moment of maneuver," and the return to elite, class-based alliances in the post-1980 period. I do not believe that these were simply cynical moves on the part
of most black nationalists—that is, that when 'partnership' didn't pan
out they turned to nationalism with the requisite need for "African
unity" in a self-serving bid for power as a class. This is how it looks
from hindsight, and certainly in light of the maneuvering of the state in
the post-1980 period (Astrow 1983; Weiss 1994).

Nevertheless, many of the young, self-sacrificing nationalists were
sincere and dedicated to the struggle, for the masses as well as for themselves, during the moment of maneuver. People primarily dedicated to
middle-class comfort and privilege do not knowingly put themselves in
the way of long jail sentences, torture, and death. That the spirit of
self-sacrifice was so strong among the leadership during the period
of struggle and waned so quickly after 1980 among some prominent
leaders points to the power of nationalism as a discourse as well as the
depth of capitalist attitudes and aspirations. Finally, it points to the
complexity of *all* individuals who, at different points in their lives, can
operate according to seemingly contradictory principles.

One of the most poignant cases of this involved Maurice Nyagumbo, a prominent militant nationalist who was imprisoned for over
eleven years for his political activities. In 1989, when he was a government minister, Nyagumbo committed suicide, allegedly out of shame in
connection with the famous "Willowgate" scandal involving government corruption in the motor industry (Weiss 1994: 187). Ruth Weiss
suggests that after independence, "Material values were paramount. Every Zimbabwean yearned for a house, car, and money to spend. Often
the only way to achieve that quickly was to steal" (1994: 185). Perhaps
middle-class material values, inculcated early in life, led some individuals like Nyagumbo to the conclusion that they *deserved* a comfortable
life now that they had come to power, precisely *because* of their years of
self-sacrifice.

Already in 1983 Astrow had, from a straight-line, Marxist-struc-
turalist perspective, offered a harsh critique of the Zimbabwean nationalists and predicted the entrenchment of capitalism and black elite privilege in Zimbabwe. What this type of critique leaves out, however, is the
humanity of the actors involved, and the complexity of their attitudes
and motivations. While we need the large, overarching structuralist
analyses, we also have to look to the human level to try to understand
why and how people can do what they do in relation to given sets of
objective conditions.

The habitus of the leadership and their resulting practices during the 1970s were partially shaped by involvement with nationalism and the struggle itself. Their revolutionary position of the 1970s was not only the product of political pragmatism, or as Astrow would say, cynical opportunism; rather, political events brought about actual changes in nationalists' dispositions in dialectic with the objective conditions of the time. It is true that the leadership's dispositions seemed to shift again rather rapidly after 1980 as class-based agendas returned to replace ZANU's egalitarian socialist vision of the 1970s. This does not mean, however, that ZANU's leaders were not sincere in what they were doing and saying in the heat of the struggle, as the notion of a temporally based, multilayered habitus implies.[25]

Modernist-socialist nationalism, as a discourse and a political practice, appears to have temporarily buried the class-based divisions that were so rife among black Zimbabweans prior to the phase of mass nationalism. But given the cosmopolitan-capitalist underpinnings of their basic dispositions, it is hardly surprising that many of the earlier attitudes (aesthetic as well as materialist) of the black middle-class reemerged after 1980.

## The Peasant Majority
## and the Elite Minority

Outside the cosmopolitan field, indigenous Shona instrumentalists, dancers, and singers are still operating on a different basis and with different conceptions of what music, dance, subsistence, sociability, and spirituality are about (chapter 1). Among Zimbabwe's peasant majority, bira ceremonies and rural beer parties are still more dependent on rain than on the IMF, and the mode of performance is still more dependent on ancestors and local participatory ethics than on the romantic desires of youthful audiences in London or Sidney.

In line with the colonial settlers and missionaries, the post-1980 state has continued to make inroads into these populations to propagate modernist reform—with perhaps the best of intentions. Unlike the former colonials, state-cultural officials and workers claim an insider's right to push reformism—a claim based on nationalist discourse and essentialist conceptions of race and African identity. While genuinely African and Zimbabwean in their own right, cosmopolitan Zimbabweans operate from radically different cultural positions than those of many indigenous peasants and members of the lower classes. Their claim to insider status vis-à-vis "the masses" is thus a complex one, and it presents dangers for the design and institution of indigenous cultural reform, especially when backed by the resources of the state and the capitalist culture industry.

*   *   *

A major purpose of this book has been to clarify the spread and effects of cosmopolitanism in its modernist-capitalist form through the agency of colonialism and nationalism. I have also demonstrated many points of continuity between colonialism, nationalism, and cosmopolitanism, phenomena often thought to be in opposition to each other. I have traced the rise of musical professionalism, initiated during the colonial era and consciously expanded during the post-1980 state-nationalist period. Musical professionalism—the functional and conceptual articulation of music and dance activities with money and markets—was the most direct mechanism for involving musicians with cosmopolitan musical aesthetics and trends; state education and the mass media also played relatively consistent roles in this process across the colonial and nationalist periods.

I have suggested that the twin paradoxes of nationalism required reformist projects that generated a cosmopolitan-indigenous syncretism in the very conceptualization of "the nation" and Zimbabwean art and identity. The requirement of mass appeal in both nationalist projects and capitalist enterprises favored cultural reformism in parallel ways. In Zimbabwe, capitalism and nationalism have become the twin engines for formally and processually similar but motivationally distinct reformist practices and products in the post-1980 period. Ultimately, all of this works to the detriment of distinctive indigenous lifeways in favor of cosmopolitan expansion.

My thrust has been to suggest to cultural administrators, politicians, artists, and audiences that the processes through which modernist-capitalist cosmopolitanism (or any brand of cosmopolitanism) are diffused and naturalized are, in fact, not natural or given. This suggestion makes the conceptualization of alternative government policies and individual practices possible. Cosmopolitanism is not, and does not necessarily have to be, "global"; rather, it is one type of cultural formation among many. This idea, in turn, opens a space for analysis and choice among cosmopolitans with regard to how we will understand the cultural dispositions which are part of us, as well as their impact on people who maintain distinctly different ways of life.

# Notes

## Introduction

1. G. K. Chesterton, *The Napoleon of Notting Hill* (1904; reprint New York: Dover, 1991), 18–19. My thanks to James Lea for bringing this book and passage to my attention.

2. Throughout the text, single quotation marks indicate local Zimbabwean terms or modes of expression. Double quotation marks indicate actual quotations or my bracketing of a term.

3. I use the term *discourse* in the sense of "discursive practice" proposed by Foucault (e.g., 1977: 199). Discourse not only encompasses the terms used and style of utterances, but, more important, the "legitimate" premises of knowledge and ideological bases of those premises. Discourse involves the whole realm of what is thought and believed so as to make certain types of thoughts and utterances possible and other types unlikely or impossible. Thus, the discourse of modernity makes it unlikely to think that *the traditional is modern*, because of the ideological premises elaborated within the discourse about those symbols and their *objects* (entities signified).

4. I would like to thank my colleague Donna Buchanan for this clarification and for so many other helpful comments about this topic.

5. See Herzfeld 1997 for a particularly good (humanizing) discussion of the concept of the *state*.

6. By the mid-twentieth century, the ideology of popular sovereignty had become doxic in the very European countries that were also the imperialist powers. There was thus a contradiction between this aspect of the nationalist discourse of the mother countries and the project of colonialism. Anticolonialist, nationalist leaderships emerged from the elite-colonized class that had resulted from colonial education. The local elite learned the ideas of nationalism and popular sovereignty from their colonial masters and then turned those same ideas against them. The bid for legitimacy based on doxic principles of popular sovereignty often has been important for winning international as well as local-liberal support for independence struggles.

7. It may be significant that in the United States, at least, subordinate groups' self-identification in ethnic terms typically accompanies integrative or client-patron movements vis-à-vis the state, whereas more radical movements such as the Black Panthers or AIM typically frame themselves in national terms—on a par with and in competition with the nation-state. Current multicultural programs may be a continuing attempt to ethnicize the swelling populations of culturally distinct groups in the United States and thus diffuse possible threats—simultaneously celebrating difference and incorporating it: "our ethnics."

8. Other racial categories besides blacks and whites included coloreds (people of mixed heritage), and Asians.

9. The theoretical and descriptive utility of the rural/urban cultural dichotomy must be understood in historically and geographically specific terms. While the two types of places are rarely completely sealed off from each other within contemporary states, the degree of interchange and influence between them can be quite varied. For example, rural and urban differences were quite pronounced in my case study of Conimeños in the southern Peruvian highlands and in Lima because of distances and the cultural chauvinism of the rural people involved (Turino 1993). This is not so much the case for people in the Mantaro Valley of Central Peru (Romero 1990), and—as I will suggest for Zimbabwe, and as Erlmann (1990) has argued for South Africa—the rural/urban dichotomy is particularly problematic in these countries.

10. "According to the 1969 Census Report the number of African domestic servants living in the European areas of Salisbury exceeds the number of Europeans in those areas" (Davis 1975: 301). Michael West reports that "most domestic servants, who, throughout the colonial period, constituted one of the largest category of workers, lived on their employers' premises" (1990: 151).

11. Michael West states that the township's population in 1930 was 3,488 (1990: 138). In 1972 the population of Mbare was estimated at just under 34,000, of which just over two-thirds were single men accommodated in four large hostels. Houses for married persons are of six types, ranging from two-room flats to six-room, semidetached houses for which rentals are based according to income, from a minimum of $5 [Zim] up to a maximum of $18.50 per month. For people in a higher income bracket, home-ownership schemes were started in 1963 with either freehold or 99-year leasehold tenure (Davies 1975: 296). Writing of the earlier decades of the century, however, West notes that "in contrast to other urban centers, there were very few private dwellings in Salisbury's municipal African township [Mbare]" (1990: 145); rather, the City Council built and owned the dwellings.

12. Through sociological research regarding relative socioeconomic levels of inhabitants, Mbare hostels and township were categorized as low, Mufakose township as medium, and Kambuzuma township as high (Gwata and Reader 1977: 2). Marimba Park, while not included in this study, must be considered higher still.

## Chapter One

1. References such as "Zim96-1: 4" indicate interview transcriptions; they show the year when the interview was conducted (e.g., 96), then a dash and a number indicating the interview tape and transcript number (1), and the page number of the transcript following the colon.

2. A number of people distinguished between dances done 'inside the house' and 'outside the house' to indicate a genre's or activity's relation to spirit possession. This distinction does not exactly translate as "sacred" and "secular," since 'outside the house' dances and activities can be performed within

the overall context of a religious ceremony and therefore are not thought of as distinctly secular. The inside/outside distinction is better thought of as indicating intensity and instrumentality in relation to spirit possession. These concepts were related to me in English.

3. I do not have good statistics on the size of the African middle class and elite, but they are a small minority in relation to rural agriculturalists and the working and lower classes.

4. The Division of Culture has been resituated in various ministries of the central government several times since 1980; Chifunyise is head of the Cultural Division of the central government.

5. Mabelreign was formerly a white, working-class suburb which was almost entirely vacated by white Rhodesians and resettled by medium-income Africans during the 1980s.

6. Simultaneous group participation might be distinguished from "sequential participatory events" such as the singing at Albanian weddings described by Sugarman (1997).

7. The Murehwa Jerusarema Club and Burial Society, of which I became a member, had such a song that we would sing in the wee hours of the morning.

8. "Ground" and "elaboration" parts are my terminology.

9. The emphasis on new composition and originality is by no means specific to modernist-capitalist ethos. The same value is held among indigenous Aymara musicians in Conima, Peru, although in this case originality functions to mark distinct identities and competence among different local communities, rather than having to do with market forces.

10. Peirce developed three trichotomies of concepts to cover the different aspects of a given sign: Trichotomy I *(qualisign, sinsign, legisign)* involves the nature of the sign itself; Trichotomy II *(icon, index, symbol)* involves the basis of the relationship between the sign and its *object* (idea or entity signified); and Trichotomy III involves the way the sign is interpreted as representing its object—as a sign of a possible object *(rheme)*, as a sign actually affected by its object *(dicent)*, and as a sign based on elaborated linguistic premises *(argument)*. Every sign combines one or more components from the three trichotomies (e.g., dicent-indexical-legisign), although a sign may be identified according to the features most salient for a given analysis (simply index, or dicent-index).

11. "Body language" can be used to deceive about inner feelings, and a weathervane may be stuck and thus inaccurate. If, when interpreting a sign, we take these things into consideration, the signs are operating as rhemes—only signs of possible objects. Usually, however, signs like body language are habitually interpreted as dicents, and we react directly to them as true; often they are not even in our focal awareness.

12. Although widespread, participatory traditions in historically unrelated places like Peru and Zimbabwe are similar in various ways because of common goals, but they operate in isolation from each other and hence are not cosmopolitan in the sense I am developing.

**Chapter Two**

1. This group, which I joined in 1992, has changed names several times: from the Murehwa Jerusarema Club to Murehwa No. 1 Jerusarema Club in the early 1960s when another club was formed (No. 2). After 1987 they became the Murehwa Jerusarema Club and Burial Society because they split with No. 1 and formed a Burial Society. For convenience I will refer to them as the Murehwa Jerusarema Club, or simply the Murehwa Club, unless I need to differentiate them from other Murehwa jerusarema groups in some way.

2. In a survey of eighty-seven inhabitants of Highfield township, Stopforth found that 65.5 percent said they would eventually return to live in the rural home permanently, 31 percent said they would not, and 3.5 percent said they were unsure (1972: 72). I assume that the number of people planning to return home permanently in the more transient Mbare hostels and township would be higher, and it would be lower in the higher-class Kambuzuma and Marimba Park areas.

3. Unlike all the Shona dances I know, *nyau* is a masked dance, originally with esoteric meaning and functions.

4. These included the Murehwa No.1 Jerusarema Club, the original name for the group I joined; Jerusarema No. 2, recorded in 1963; Uzumba Jerusarema No. 1 Club; and Uzumba Jerusarema No. 2 Club, recorded in 1970.

5. Older Shona ngororombe players in Uzumba told me that this style had been learned from people from Mozambique during the previous generation in the rural northeast; that is, the style had not been diffused to the northeast from Mbare.

6. *Ngoma* is the generic word for drum. There are various types in Zimbabwe, but the tall, single-headed drums used for ngororombe are particularly common. These drums are carved from a single tree trunk which is hollowed out. Three cutaways are carved at the bottom to make "feet" on which the drums stand. They are usually played in two-pitched pairs with the hands.

7. *Guva*, or grave, ceremonies are held by a family approximately one year after a death to commemorate the deceased and decorate the grave. I was told that the *guva* marks the period after which the deceased, if he or she chooses to come back through a medium, may do so. Guvas may involve spirit possession inside the house, but the dancing and music outside does not have this function.

8. Some of the music recorded by the Rhodesian Broadcasting Corporation in the early 1960s and labeled as "shangara" was in simple duple meter. Genre designations for these recordings were usually supplied by the performers.

9. My teacher, Chris Mhlanga, emphasized that "dzaVadzimu" was not commonly used as a qualifier for denoting mbira among people he knew; the instrument was just called mbira. This fits my general experience among musicians but not necessarily among nonspecialists. Kaemmer writes that "The Zezuru refer to them simply as *mbira*, but to differentiate them from other types they say *mbira huru* (great mbira) or *mbira chaidzo* (true mbira; 1975: 85). In his paper written in 1932 Hugh Tracey sometimes used the term *mbira*

generically, and sometimes to refer specifically to the Zezuru mbira. The Traceys and Berliner worked with people who used the names "mbira dza-Vadzimu" or "dzaMidzimu." I cannot account for these differences in terminology except to say that various "schools" of players and people from different regions and times seem to have different terminology. Context of speaking and levels of musical knowledge also may play a part.

10. Kauffman often referred to the karimba as an mbira (generic designation) in his writing (e.g., 1970).

11. It is possible, for instance, that Africans did not want to show a white man instruments associated with religious ritual, but this, too, is only speculation.

12. Some people (e.g., Patrick Nyandoro) played mbira in the Murehwa area in the 1930s and 1940s, although njari was the majority tradition. To my knowledge there were no njari players in the region during the time of my research in the early 1990s.

13. The audio archivist, Beatrice Mareyaya, graciously let me scan the entire catalogue on computer, but could only print out a partial list for me due to economic constraints. The figures I have are roughly representative but are not comprehensive. My counts for traditions I was particularly interested in, however (jerusarema, mbira, shangara, mbukumba, muchongoyo, acoustic guitarists, among others), are close to being comprehensive for the collection as it existed in 1993. Unfortunately it is often not possible to identify the type of lamellophone from designations in the catalogue. The term *mbira* was sometimes used generically to refer to all types; for example, the famous karimba player J. Tapera was listed as mbira, as was the well-known njari player Simon Mashoko. They were thus not distinguished from Zezuru-mbira players in the collection such as Bandambira and Hakurotwi Mude. In other cases, specific designations such as njari were included.

14. He went into radio work after leaving a post as an agricultural extension assistant, a position based on a higher level of education and indicating higher class standing. The radio typically hired middle-class Africans as announcers.

15. This is apparent from documentation in the National Archive RBC collection.

16. The fact that the term *shangara* was used for a rather loosely defined, catch-all genre category also helps explain why so many recordings might have been labeled this way.

17. As I suggest elsewhere (1998), the African programmers at Radio 2 seem to have felt that lamellophone music provided a better fit with the radio format relative to many indigenous dance-drumming traditions, which depended on dance choreography for much of their interest.

18. A standard story explaining the name *jerusarema* is that the dance was discouraged by missionaries; the name jerusarema (Jerusalem) was adopted to imply a Christian connection and thus legitimate the dance. The name *mbende* "fieldmouse," may refer to the male "swimming motion" (moving through the grass) that is standard for the dance.

19. Ndubiwa (1974) reports that by 1973, 248 burial societies had registered in Bulawayo, and he estimated that perhaps an equal number in that city had not registered. Figures for Harare around that time, according to Hall, seemed to be much less. Hall's survey in the mid-1980s turned up 134 burial societies in the Harare area, but as he notes, "this study is likely to be an underestimate, and a definite count may have to wait until registration of societies is compulsory" (1987: 51).

20. Not specific to Zimbabwe, burial societies exist in other African countries, their formation originally accompanying labor migration (e.g., see Dandala and Moraka 1990).

21. During the hard economic times of the early 1990s, some burial societies have started cooperative economic development projects such as the raising of chickens for sale, generating jobs and income for members (Mukanganwa 1993: 6; *Herald,* 21 February 1993).

22. For example, Murehwa Jerusarema and Burial Society has approximately thirty-six members, but only eighteen or twenty perform jerusarema regularly (Zim92-32: 1). The Tete No. 3 Mwatidzi Makhanga Ngororombe Society has over one hundred burial society members, and although Ngororombe is in the name, the music ensemble only has thirteen players (fieldnotes, 11 October 1992).

23. Both Nyandoro and Kambiriri remembered that this event occurred in 1959, but neither could remember the name of the African-American dancer involved nor knew who had sponsored the program. I searched for references to this program in the National Archives of Zimbabwe but was unsuccessful in finding any mention of it. Once back in the United States I asked the USIS if they had supported such a visit, but to no avail. I also communicated with Katherine Dunham, a well known African-American dancer who had worked in a similar capacity in other parts of Africa around that time; she had no information about the Zimbabwe project.

24. These films are now housed at the National Archives of Zimbabwe and are generously made available for viewing and copying.

25. Jocho is an informal social dance akin to jiti (see Kaemmer 1975: 108); jiti is discussed at length in chapter 7.

26. It is interesting that twenty years after the fact, Nyandoro remembers this performance as lasting three minutes. Given the usual long duration of indigenous music-dance performances in participatory occasions, the twenty minutes captured on film must have seemed extremely short.

27. Uzumba has become part of a new district, but it was formerly included within the Murehwa district.

### Chapter Three
1. Mr. Mbofana worked with African Radio Service for many years and is currently the head of Radio 2 at Mbare Studios. I am grateful to him for his openness with information and for making recordings in the radio's archives available to me.

2. Although 'African' broadcasting was formally transferred from the

FBC in Lusaka to the (S)RBC in Harare on 1 January 1964, some items for use in Lusaka were produced in Zimbabwe before this. Items formerly housed in the Mbare studios date from 1957.

3. There were some commercial records from the 1960s in the collection produced elsewhere, especially South Africa. Commercial recordings (45s and LPs) become the norm in the RBC collection after the mid-1970s when commercial recording in Zimbabwe expanded.

4. Dr. John T. Carrington wrote in 1954, "I am engaged on preparing a syllabus for our school in music. We have to follow the programme laid down by the State for primary schools, and so it must inevitably be European in approach. But your example in Ngoma has made me very unsatisfied with anything that is not African, and I am trying hard to get our teachers to build up songs in true African manner" (1954: 83); see also Hyslop 1955.

5. Referring to the success of McHarg's approach in the 1960s, Robert Kauffman writes, "The music syllabus was prepared by a musician who attempted to introduce African music as well as European music into the curriculum. The African music outline is of necessity more nebulous than that for European music; so, consequently, many teachers ignore the African music and attempt to teach a reading knowledge of European music in staff notation" (1970: 197).

6. Kwanongoma translates roughly as "Place of Music." *Ngoma* really translates as "drum" or as "ceremony," but in the context of this school's name it was often translated as "music"; there is no single Shona gloss for the word *music*.

7. In 1977 Gwata counted fifteen beerhalls in Mbare, five in Mufakose township, and three in Kambuzuma township (Gwata and Reader 1977:33).

8. Middle-class patrons prefer drinking in the hotels and nightclubs established after the Liquor Act was amended in 1957 (Gwata and Reader 1977: 18).

9. At my request, Mr. Reason Muskwe interviewed Mr. J. Mangani, the current secretary of the Harare African Traditional [Music and Dance] Association, who has this information on file.

10. Panpipe festivals in Lima, Peru, organized by a middle-class group had a similar effect of inspiring the creation of more panpipe ensembles among urban migrants (Turino 1993).

11. A parallel national competition for choral groups grew up as an off-shoot of the original festival.

12. Independent African churches emerged earlier, some of which had already integrated African forms of music and dance into their forms of group worship.

### Chapter Four

1. In many Latin American countries, for example, concepts of race are intimately and complexly affected by class standing and cultural style. In the Andean region indigenous people are sometimes constructed in racial terms, but because physical differences between native Andeans, mestizos, and

criollos (Euro-Andeans) may not be pronounced, class and cultural style often play a stronger role in social definitions than physical aspects. In the United States and Southern Africa, skin color and geographical heritage (i.e., African versus European) are central to racial constructs. Similarly, for the Nazis, physical distinctions could not be relied upon; thus religion and cultural style were central to their racial constructs of Jews.

2. Bourdieu's notion of the interplay between different types of capital involves processes where, for example, educational capital (attending Harvard) can be used to establish social capital (connections with the industrial elite in the United States), which in turn can be used to get a good corporate job leading to economic capital accumulation. Conversely, economic capital can be exchanged for educational and social capital and may be used in the attempt to enhance cultural capital.

3. Working-class Zimbabweans sometimes refer to the speakers of this elite African accent as "the nose brigade," a comment on the maneristic round head tones that partly distinguish the style, and perhaps a comment on "noses being in the air," which is certainly the meaning if not the intent of the phrase.

4. *African Parade,* later simply *Parade,* is a monthly magazine published in Salisbury and directed specifically to an African readership, and most specifically a middle-class readership. Sometimes following the magazine's title were the words, "The only magazine in Southern Africa edited and printed by Africans for Africans" (e.g., on the cover of vol. 7, no. 1, 1959). To my knowledge, all the writers for the journal were black Zimbabweans. I surveyed the journal from its first volume through the 1970s. By studying the advertisements, letters to the editor, editorials, and articles, we can learn much about the political and cultural positions and concerns of urban middle-class Africans in the townships during this period. My survey of *Parade* is one of the major sources for the material presented in this chapter.

5. As Coplan notes in *In Township Tonight!* (1985), middle-class black music in South Africa was likewise influenced by African-American models.

6. Coplan (1985), mentions the term *makwaya* for South Africa, although it is not clear if the term refers to the same style, significance, and development as in Zimbabwe. Veit Erlmann (p.c. 1998) comments that in South Africa, school singing and makwaya are virtually identical stylistically.

7. As with images of the United States, South Africa was, and is, considered a cosmopolitan center for cultural sophistication among Zimbabweans. As will be seen, South African styles and performers have long been influential in Zimbabwean urban popular music. Urban South African performers themselves were heavily influenced by North American (minstrelsy and vaudeville), and especially African-American musical styles such as ragtime and jazz early in this century. The reader should consult David Coplan's *In Township Tonight!* (1985) and Veit Erlmann's *African Stars* (1991) and *Nightsong* (1996) for good background on black urban South African Music and its connections to North American sources.

8. In contrast to missionary schools, which taught liberal education, government schools often concentrated on technical skills in keeping with the

government's view of the roles Africans should take within the society (see Moyana 1989: 38–42).

9. Mattaka's daughter, Bertha Mattaka Msora, indicated that her father occasionally composed songs and that he translated a few American popular songs into Shona or put altered Shona texts to the American tunes (Makwenda 1992a). She, however, was referring to the 1950s, whereas when stating that they did few songs in Shona, Mattaka was referring to the earlier 1930s–1940s period.

10. As but one example in the contemporary United States, for a band to be recognized as a real entity, it is almost requisite for them to produce a CD. Most local bands know that they will not make much, or any, money on these projects. The production of such CDs has as much to do with a validation or "reality" function as with other goals—economic, creative, archival, being discovered, and so on. European and American music history is constructed on the basis of material traces such as scores, written documents and, in this century, recordings. This basis of cosmopolitan conceptions of history (different from, say, indigenous West African modes of keeping history in processual oral-aural memory) augments the "reality function" of objectified forms.

11. A number of "concert" and jazz performers cited the Mills Brothers as a prominent influence in Zimbabwean township music.

12. Manhattan Brothers records were regularly reviewed in *African Parade* in the mid-1950s, as were Zimbabwean artists such as De Black Evening Follies and August Musarurwa. Since this column, "Record Parade," only reviewed records produced by Gallo (of South Africa), I assume that this company sponsored the column.

13. Watching this film in class one day, a Brazilian graduate student, Adriana Fernandez, immediately made the Miranda connection before I had the opportunity to suggest it.

14. This type of performance was documented on films housed in the National Archives of Zimbabwe.

15. Commercial 'hillbilly' groups like the Skillet Lickers sometimes prefaced their musical performances on recordings with comic dialogues depicting stereotypes of rural whites—the same social group from which the performers had emerged.

16. The City Quads were the first township group in Salisbury to record a long-playing record: "Music from an African Township," on the Polydor label (circa 1960). According to Sam Matamba, one of the pieces on the record, "Lizofika nini llanga" (When will the day of freedom come?), was banned by the government. It was a slow, jazz number in the same Mills Brothers vein. Significantly, Matamba associated the message of the song to American spirituals, one of the early sources of the "concert" tradition. The piece was "a prayer song, shall I say, a Negro Spiritual." He said it was banned since "it sounded political, because at that time the struggle was on ... it was a spiritual of the African people saying, 'When will the day of freedom come?'" (Makwenda 1992a). This is an early example of a political song within the formerly conservative "concert" tradition.

17. Beginning as the Epworth Theatrical Stars in the mid-1940s, this

group consisted of Andrew Nesbitt, Peter Kanyowa, Gilbert Chimbalanga, Herbert Simemeza, and later, John Mate and Douglas Maruba (Chinamhora 1987: 260) as well as other instrumental accompanists. The Strutters' style differed from the other "concert" groups discussed in that piano was used primarily to accompany the vocal quintet (although guitar and percussion were sometimes added). Unlike the swing feel of other groups, the Strutters used rather square rhythms and a four-part homophonic approach. Sounding like a church group, their sound was generally more conservative than the other ensembles discussed, as was their repertory. Pieces recorded by African Service Radio between 1960 and 1962 included hymns in English ("De Church of God" #818B), popular songs like "Tommy the Piper's Son" (#944B), and rather unjazzy jive numbers ("Barberton," #2799A; "Baby Can Jive" #2799B)—no Elvis or Little Richard here. Like the Follies and other groups, however, they were influenced by the Mills Brothers, and when a vocal solo was taken, as in their song "Kudzidza Kwakanaka" (Education is good), the background vocalists sang vocables imitating a horn accompaniment—complete with gestures representing trumpet playing, as indicated by a film clip.

18. Masuka has a recently released CD on Mango Records, "Dorothy Masuka—Pata Pata" (Mango 162 539 911-2).

19. Isabel Wong has traced the incorporation of the Cuban clave pattern and 3 + 3 + 2 bass line in Chinese popular music through a French connection.

20. Speaking in Joyce Makwenda's 1992 film *Zimbabwe Township Music,* Sam Matambo of the City Quads states that they used to charge six pense or a shilling or two, and that ten shillings was the highest ticket price they ever charged.

21. Mattaka reported that whites attended their performances on several special occasions, but most whites needed special passes to enter the townships and so were not part of their usual audience.

22. In the Zimbabwean context, the term *jazz* often refers very loosely to cosmopolitan-based instrumental dance music rather than to music that would be conceptualized in the Americas and Europe as jazz. When used in this way, the term appears in single quotation marks.

23. Lawrence Vambe states that there were several large African bands ("consisting of saxophones, violins, drums, and other instruments") that played for ballroom dancing in the early 1930s (1976: 213). Since these predate the Police Band, it cannot be understood as the only source for the training of African dance band musicians.

24. Sources differ on the location in Zimbabwe where and the date when Musarurwa was born. Chinamhora says he was born in Gweru in 1922; an article in *African Parade,* (1955a: 6) states that he was born on 1 August 1921 in Chinoyi. There are also different spellings of his name. On South African record labels and in Coplan (1985: 154) it is spelled "Musururgwa" or "Masarurgwa," whereas Zimbabwean sources typically spell the name "Musarurwa" (e.g., *African Parade* 1955a: 6; Chinamhora 1987: 262; Makwenda 1990: 93, 1992e; Vambe 1976: 213).

25. While banjos were used in the late 1940s and early 1950s, guitars replaced banjos on his later Gallo recordings with the Sweet Rhythm Band.

26. My thanks to Hayes McCauley for bringing this record to my attention.

27. In interviews with older Zimbabwean musicians I found that the terms *tsaba-tsaba* and *jive* were sometimes used interchangeably.

28. Some examples are "1960 Drought" and "Kwamusha Patha" (Gallo GB. 3058); and "Kwela Zulu" and "Rhythm Boys Patha Patha" (GB. 3057), housed in the National Archives of Zimbabwe.

29. During the Federation years several dance bands or jazz bands performed in Harare and other cities like Bulawayo and Mutare (Umtali), including the Broadway Quartet led by S. Tutani (still an active jazz performer today), the Sweet Havana Band, and the Umtali Jazz Revellers, who recorded for Gallo.

30. Dumisani Maraire has made this song famous among Zimbabwe music fans in the United States through his recordings of the piece on karimba— *Mbira Music of Rhodesia*, Seattle: University of Washington Press; *Chaminuka*, Music of the World C-208.

31. Dorothy Masuka is an exception, but her case is different because she lived outside Zimbabwe.

32. Musicians of the 1970s generation like Oliver M'tukudzi and others have stated that their musical activities met with resistance from their parents because music was associated with marginal lifestyles and was not thought of as lucrative. This was especially true in Christian and middle-class families.

33. Although Mr. H spoke to me without concern about ramifications from this part of his story, I prefer to use a pseudonym.

34. The festival included De Black Evening Follies, the Melodians, Peter Sibanda and the Hilltones, and the Shangani (muchongoyo) dancers.

### Chapter Five

1. Chikerema was born at Kutama mission and studied at St. Francis College, but did not complete his studies because he became caught up in nationalist activities.

2. In Zimbabwe, Shona and Ndebele were used within the nationalist movements, but English served as the common denominator, and the colonial language could hardly serve to distinguish or emotionally unify the new nation.

3. The old saying, "Photographs don't lie," is based on the indexical-dicent relationship between the lens and the subject of the photo. Although we all know that photographs can lie, we still commonly react to them based on the "reality potential" of indexical-dicent relations.

4. According to Bhebe (1989: 103), by the time the NDP was banned it had "50,000 members, and it had active branches in every town, in most of the Native Purchase Areas and rural townships."

5. A statement about a revival of the mbira was made by Andrew Tracey in the same year (1963), suggesting that the idea of a nationalist cultural renaissance or revival was becoming widespread at that time (see chapter 2).

6. Once when I asked an acquaintance, a long-time Mbare resident from Murehwa, if he had been involved in nationalist politics in the early 1960s, he responded, "Oh yes, I had my fur hat and everything!"

### Chapter Six

1. Although ZAPU's army, ZIPRA, was also involved in contacting the peasants, they tended to be less dependent on local support than ZANLA, according to various sources (e.g., see Frederikse 1982: 232); mass mobilization was less central to ZIPRA strategy.

2. In her book *None But Ourselves,* Julie Frederikse (1982) provides a wealth of information about the battle for "the hearts and minds" of the Zimbabwean people, that is, the propaganda campaigns waged both by the Smith Regime and the nationalist parties during the 1970s.

3. Chinx was born Dick Chingaira Makoni on 27 September 1955; his family was from Rusape in eastern Zimbabwe. Chinx was his military name during the war years, and he is still known by this name.

4. For concise yet detailed accounts of the political and military histories of this period, see Canaan Banana, ed., *Tenacity and Turmoil* (1989).

5. *Parade* remained pro-Muzorewa and basically hostile to the Patriotic Front through the November 1979 issue.

6. In the same interview this man contended that Mugabe won the elections because people were tired of war, and many felt that if ZANU-PF did not win the elections, they would return to the bush and continue fighting. Again, I do not know how many people felt this way during 1979 and 1980. I offer this interpretation as one of several alternatives to the more typical view of Mugabe as a universally accepted hero among the Shona majority.

7. For example, I surveyed available copies of ZANU's publication *Zimbabwe News,* published outside the country. I found that it was not until around volume 10, in 1978, that articles on cultural issues became common. I mentioned these findings to Charles Ndhlovu, ZANU director of information since 1977, who was in charge of the "Voice of Zimbabwe" radio programming and the *Zimbabwe News.* He responded that "it depended, but that war and political issues, and the president's speeches took precedence" (fieldnotes 25 November 1992).

8. Lan (1985: 7) notes that the government was equally aware of the potential political power of the mediums and made a major attempt to form alliances with them.

9. Depending on the author, Nehanda is spelled with either a lowercase or capital h: NeHanda, or Nehanda.

10. Another version is that Nehanda stated that her children would one day liberate the country (Martin and Johnson 1981: 75).

11. In contemporary Shona, *murenga* means "supreme being," "warlike spirit," "rebellion," "cattle plague," and "good hunting dog;" *chi* is a nounclass prefix.

12. This LP was a ZANU publication out of Maputo; it had no record number, and was reissued by Teal Records in Zimbabwe with no number.

ZANU Choir's LP is not dated, but one of the texts on the record speaks of a liberated Mozambique, indicating that it was issued somewhere between 1975, when Mozambique became independent, and 1979.

13. As discussed in chapter 4, makwaya (choir) is a syncretic vocal tradition that combines local chorus singing styles with church and school singing traditions; thus it is not always easy to distinguish between makwaya and hymn-based performance, since makwaya, too, may be hymn-based, especially in terms of the melodies sung. For the present discussion, I call pieces makwaya if they are in a balanced, call-and-response form with the chorus primarily singing in unison or with occasional fourths and fifths. Hymn-based songs are those with homophonic texture and triadic harmony, although a song leader may sing short phrases, in lining-out fashion, before he or she joins the homophonic texture.

14. *Majukwa* is a spiritual dance of the Karanga people of south central Zimbabwe. The genre is customarily accompanied by a simple drum part, beating out a straight triple meter ($\flat = 80$), and a kudu horn used as a drone. The descending melody comprises a two-phrase ostinato (four bars each); quintal harmony is sung by the chorus.

15. As has happened elsewhere (e.g., Peru), cosmopolitan socialism was linked to local social life in ZANU cultural discourse by the argument that Shona villagers had always had collective, cooperative economic relations, and hence they had been socialists all along.

16. It is striking how much attention and money are invested in airports in cash-poor countries as well as in rich ones. They are the symbolic as well as actual gateways to the cosmopolitan world.

17. Technically speaking, repeated text lines, identical but for one paradigmatic substitution, are iconically related; that is, the lines are brought together in the mind because of overall resemblance. The items paradigmatically substituted are thus also iconically related. When ZANU is substituted for "nation," the implicit suggestion made through the poetic context is that "ZANU is like nation."

18. The four recorded examples of the ZAPU Choir's chimurenga songs that I have contrast greatly in this regard.

### Chapter Seven

1. The 1970s bands that had horns (saxophones, trumpets, trombones) and electric organs might or might not have used them on mbira-based pieces.

2. There may be some variation in the patterns of chord duration, depending on the song.

3. Following Berliner (1978), I use the term *mosaic* to refer to texts in which relatively independent lines or verses (without any obvious thematic or narrative relationships) are juxtaposed; an overall coherence of feeling or imagery may emerge from skillful juxtapositions.

4. Artists of the late 1970s who performed indigenous-style Shona pieces included Mapfumo, Jonah Sithole and Storm, Oliver M'tukudzi, the Green Arrows, the Livestock Company, the Search Brothers, Jordan Chataika and

the Highway Stars, Blues Revolution, the Poison Band, Soul Savior, the Labby Five Band, Oliver Samhemere and the Elbows, Trio Camp, and the New Sounds, among others. I have reviewed commercial 45-rpm records by these groups which remain in the National Archives and the ZBC Archives.

5. The terms *jit* or *jiti* are disliked by some artists, Mapfumo among them. Mapfumo argues that these labels should be rejected because they are not indigenous to Zimbabwe. Moreover, terminology for this basic style has shifted over time, and some individuals and regional groups use alternative names. With these caveats in mind, I continue to use the term *jit* because it is presently the most commonly understood name for the genre in question.

6. Solomon Linda's classic recording of "Mbube" can be heard on *Mbube Roots* (Rounder Records 5025). Spokes Mashiyane, a saxophonist particularly influential in Zimbabwe, can be heard on Gallo GB 3332 and Gallo GB 3128.

7. I have pieced together the following history of jit based on over twenty interviews on the topic among both rural and urban musicians, and on recorded examples from the National Archives of Zimbabwe recorded between the late 1950s and the early 1970s.

8. The Bhundu Boys entitled a piece "Jit Jive" on their *True Jit* LP (Jit 1, circa mid-1980s). Oddly, this piece did not have the musical characteristics that became standard for guitar-band jit.

9. This comment is complicated by the fact that he might have been relating tsaba-tsaba to Zimbabwean performers like August Musarurwa as much as to South African bands. As discussed in chapter 4, Musarurwa's tsaba-tsaba often used the I–IV–I–V progression in 4/4 meter with quick tempos ranging from $\flat = 144$ to $\flat = 186$.

10. The instruments mentioned by Chinamhora were widely diffused among black South Africans (see Coplan 1985). Some sense of this music is provided in historical recordings of the zitherists, harmonica, and concertina players made by Hugh Tracey in South Africa on *Siya Hamba* (Original Music OMA 111).

11. Because of such images, successful performers like Thomas Mapfumo and Oliver M'tukudzi were discouraged by their parents from playing guitar as teenagers.

12. From photographs and a few extant examples, it appears that the manufactured ("store-bought") banjos used in Zimbabwe were of the British variety consisting of a small skin head mounted within a wooden sound-box with a back (a bit like a larger version of Appalachian "mountain" banjos). In contrast to the standard American five-string variety, on British banjos the fifth, drone, string runs from the peghead through a hollow canal under the fretboard to the place where it emerges at the fifth fret. In Zimbabwe, boys also make their own banjos and guitars out of oil-tins, drums, and other materials.

13. The count of seventy-five acoustic guitarists comes from a printout of the RBC 78s collection in the National Archives of Zimbabwe. The great majority of these players sang in Shona. I could not obtain a full printout of the

RBC collection, so this count is probably incomplete even for the guitarists who recorded for the RBC. In contrast to the large number of guitarists, I was only able to find recordings of four Zimbabwean accordionists for the same period. Harmonica and banjo appeared on a few recordings; I found no zither recordings.

14. His progressions were, like most, centered on I, IV, and V chords, but the changes did not necessarily follow set cyclical patterns common in much southern African guitar music (e.g., I–IV–I–V), or patterns common to U.S. country music.

15. "Ndakamirira Nguva," by the guitar-vocal duet Clement Jumira and Amon Pikaita, was recorded by the African Radio Service in Zimbabwe in 1960 (RBC #805). To help its broadcasters, RBC put genre designations on the labels of most of their 78s. This piece, like the great majority of acoustic guitar recordings, is listed as "topical song." The Shona text of "Ndakamirira Nguva" is unusual within this guitar tradition in that it speaks of romantic love in a very un-Zimbabwean way for that time: "I waited for a long time / If you thought you would love me / I feel sorry for you. When I'm far away I give all my heart / to the one who genuinely loves me." This theme and manner of expression itself seems to be drawn from cosmopolitan popular music.

16. Tshawe's "Whisper Your Mother's Name" was recorded by the African Radio Service in Zimbabwe in 1960 and is listed by RBC as "Cowboy" on the label. The piece included guitar and harmonica accompaniment and Rodgers-style strumming and yodeling. The overall vocal style is a close imitation of Jimmie Rodgers. The English title and text are worth noting because recordings with English lyrics were rather rare in this acoustic guitar tradition.

17. Such harmonically static, riff-based music is not common in Zimbabwe. African-American music using this approach was recorded in the United States in the 1920s (e.g., Peg Leg Howell) and after (e.g., Bo Diddley in the 1950s, and Fred McDowell), but it was hardly a majority or widely diffused style. Given Kainga's rather original approach to guitar playing, this may be a case of parallel invention.

18. My thanks to Mark Perry for suggesting the phrase "African common practice guitar style," to refer to this rather widespread, generic African approach to acoustic guitar playing.

19. Mwenda's recording "Mama na Mwana" on Tracey's African Guitar 1 anthology (Kaleidophone KMA 6, side 1, selection 2), sounds very much like the playing of Hadebe, Sibanda and other Zimbabweans.

20. The bottleneck technique was not used commonly by guitarists for non-indigenous-based music although there are some exceptions. John White, for example, plays slide on country and gospel tunes.

21. The practice of imitating musical bow music on the guitar was a more widespread tradition in South Africa, and Shaangan connections with the south may explain Cubai's innovation for Zimbabwe.

22. I spoke with only four early acoustic guitarists, and with the children of two others about their parents' careers. These interviews gave a good sense of the broader acoustic guitar tradition. Joyce Makwenda has provided

additional insights, interviewing several guitarists that I did not meet (1992a, 1992d). I also interviewed many people who had contact with and information about this tradition, such as Mr. Mbofana of Radio 2, and other rural and urban musicians, such as Reason Muskwe and Kenneth Mattaka.

23. In several articles, Robert Kauffman (1975, 1980) makes the case that Zimbabwean acoustic guitarists "indigenized" the instrument by adapting it to Shona conceptions and principles of performance. While this is not particularly true for the Jimmie Rodgers imitators, Kauffman at least raises the idea that the guitar could be conceptualized in a variety of ways in Zimbabwe.

24. Mapfumo's song "Tozvireva Kupiko" ("Whom Shall We Share Our Frustrations With?") can be heard on the compilation "The Chimurenga Singles 1976–1980" (Meadowlark Records 403).

25. While there are still a number of itinerant acoustic guitarists (and even one or two accordionists) playing the beerhalls in the 1990s, especially in the Midlands Province and in the townships of major cities, this tradition began to decline sharply because of competition with electric-guitar bands in the mid-1970s (Chinemberi Zim93-72: 11). Chinemberi also attributed the decline in popularity to the war, because guitarists could not move freely between their rural homes and 'town' to record. When he returned to Harare in 1979, the people at Teal Records told him, "Ah, we don't want one-man band, we want people who will be in a group" (Chinemberi Zim93-72: 11). Indeed, this music was no longer being recorded, and it received virtually no air play on the radio in the 1990s—quite a contrast with the 1960s, when it was a prominent style.

26. See Erlmann 1996: 83–85, and Coplan 1985. Examples of this style can be heard on *Phezulu Eqhudeni: The Mahotella Queens, Mahlathini and Other Great Stars* (Carthage CGLP 4415), and on *Zulu Jive* (Earthworks ELP 2002).

27. Lipopo Jazz Band recordings from the mid-1960s are available in the RBC 78s collection in the National Archive (e.g., nos. 9530, 9531, 9532, 9533, sides A and B, from 1966). For Zairian examples of the style, hear *The Sound of Kinshasa* (Original Music OMA 102) and the reissue of early Franco recordings *Franco et Le T.P. O.K. Jazz: The Original 1956 Recordings of O.K. Jazz* (RetroAfric RETRO 02).

28. Such events took place in and around Harare as well as in other major cities like Mutare.

29. This information comes from the files on these companies in the government Companies Register in Harare.

30. This statement was made in a public lecture at the University of Zimbabwe in the spring of 1993.

31. Without taking a formal count, over the course of my fieldwork I met several hundred unemployed or extremely underemployed musicians and dancers in Harare who were waiting for their big break.

32. Chigamba made this comment to me in the context of explaining why his own new mbira compositions could not be performed frequently in ceremonies; see chapter 1.

33. I never found mention of Rocky in the media again, and he was not a known performer by the time of my research.

34. The City Slicker's 1961 version of "Chemtengure" was simply labeled "Instrumental Waltz." The Springfields' 1966 version of the same song was labeled 'Traditional Adaptation.'

35. Fred Zindi states that the band, led by Green Jangano under this name, has been in existence since 1957 (1985: 58). An article in *Prize* magazine based on an interview with Jangano states that the band was founded in 1961 (*Prize* 1974: 9). In a later statement (1988: 9), Jangano says that the band was formed in the 1960s. In 1974, the members were Clancy Mbirimi (guitar, bass), Basil Kumpeu (sax), William Kashiri (drums, vocal), Paul Sillah (guitar), Green Jangano (guitar, vocals), and Virginia Sillah, later Virginia Jangano (vocal). In 1988, the lineup included Green, Virginia, and their son, along with W. Kashiri, C. Mbirimi, and N. Kanengoni.

36. Since I did not know the local repertory extensively enough to identify such connections with the original, indigenous songs, I made a point of listening to the archives recordings with knowledgeable musicians in Harare, and I attempted to get various people's opinions on genre and piece identification when possible. Sometimes links with the original songs were based only on relationships in the texts. Usually, however, relationships were recognized because of melody as well as text; the rhythm of the melody and the metric-rhythmic feel of the accompaniment were the aspects most commonly changed.

37. For example, the Murehwa Jerusarema Players made an RBC recording of this piece in jerusarema style in the early 1960s (#4215).

38. In Banning Eyre's article on the Zimbabwean "mbira-guitar" style, I am quoted as saying that a 1973 recording by M. D. Rhythm Success was the first example of the damped guitar technique that I was aware of (1994: 118). Subsequently, I discovered it in the St. Paul's recording, although the technique was used much more consistently in the 1973 recording. I do not know of earlier acoustic guitarists using the damped technique; one reason would certainly be the softer volume produced with damped strings, and the acoustic guitarists' need to play loudly in noisy places like beerhalls, streets, and trains.

39. The other members of the Zebrons included James Diamond, Silas Kayirosi, Silas Zhanje, and Herbert Chiponda.

40. During the 1960s, the increasing number of clubs and beerhalls created more full-time work for the best bands—making young musicians' aspirations for a professional career not totally unrealistic.

41. Fred Zindi's book *Roots Rocking in Zimbabwe* contains a long interview with Thomas Mapfumo in which he tells his own life story. My own piecing together of Mapfumo's history comes from comparing a variety of sources; the Zindi interview is certainly important.

42. The term *banjo* was sometimes used as a synonym for the homemade guitars constructed with a cooking-oil can for the soundbox and a rough-hewn wooden neck, the type of instrument many Zimbabweans still learn on.

43. I have heard "Chemtengure" performed as a karimba (lamellophone)

piece in 12/8 meter, in 4/4 time in makwaya singing, and as a waltz by the City Slickers. The song seems to lend itself to a variety of metric-rhythmic treatments.

44. "Talking Strings," for example, sounds like a combination of the Ventures' "Walk Don't Run" and "Wipe Out," with an occasional Chuck Berry lick added for flavor.

### Chapter Eight

1. I would like to thank Paul Berliner for making these recordings available to me. Both were issued by Gallo Records and are dated on the label.

2. This 45-rpm record was issued by Teal Records on the "Afro Sound" label (AS 105). The label has no date, but Immanuel Vori, sales manager for Gramma Records (formerly Teal), confirmed this date by consulting the company's files on the dates of releases.

3. I found no references to this band in the popular press of the era, nor were their recordings part of the RBC holdings in the National Archives during the time of my research. I questioned many Zimbabwean friends and musicians about this group during 1992–93 and in the summer of 1996, but no one remembered them. Thus, I did not interview members of this band, and my only information comes from their recordings.

4. Hlomayi left this band soon after recording "Ngoma Yarira," although he returned to play lead guitar for Mapfumo at different times (e.g., on the single "Pidigori" circa 1980; on the LPs *Ndangariro*, 1983, and *Mabasa*, 1984). Hlomayi was back with Mapfumo between 1993 and 1996 (see Eyre 1994:119, chapter 9).

5. Before joining the Hallelujah Chicken Run Band, Hlomayi had played with Jackson Phiri in the Lipopo Jazz Band, as had Elijsha Josum, the Chicken Run Band's other guitarist. Jonah Sithole began his career as a lead guitarist with Phiri in Lipopo Jazz (Zindi 1985: 39). Phiri had also played with Charles Makokowe, one of the most enduring members of Thomas Mapfumo's bands. I am not suggesting that Lipopo was necessarily the incubator for the electric "mbira-guitar" style but only pointing to the close association of major musicians who experimented with it early on.

6. I only have descriptive data on the demographics of this audience, but can assume that its members were predominantly young and middle-aged urban dwellers, and substantially of the middle and upper working classes, with enough money to buy records and attend nightclubs (as opposed to beerhalls).

7. This comment is paraphrased from a conversation, but Mapfumo himself used the terms *modern* and *traditional,* and described the split in audience according to age and rural/urban residence.

8. "Pidigori" can be heard on *Zimbabwe Frontline* (Earthworks/Virgin 1-91001) and on *Thomas Mapfumo: The Singles Collection, 1977–1986* (Zimbob ZIM-7).

9. Once when discussing the genesis of mbira music with Mr. Mhlanga, I argued that someone had to have composed or improvised mbira music sometime for the present mbira repertory with its multitude of variants to exist. I suggested further that this process was probably ongoing (I was thinking of

Chigamba). He conceded that my position was logical but was uncomfortable with it nonetheless because it conflicted with his emphasis on the stability of the mbira tradition.

10. This is a direct, literal translation of this stanza. The translator, Francis, was unable to clarify the meaning further and found it difficult to translate into English. He notes that "the emphasis of the first stanza lies more on the ability to speak fast and articulate the words," as if in a word game. The second half is performed in a speechlike style.

11. For example, in the famous song "Baya wa baya" this first line refers to a stabbing motion with the arm, using a spear or knife. Another common line in the song "Nyama Yekugocha" translates literally, "It's now meat for roasting," but it is sometimes interpreted as "total victory over the enemy."

12. These songs and the text translations are available on *Thomas Mapfumo: The Chimurenga Singles 1976–1980* (Meadowlark Records 403). Acoustic guitarist Marko Takaingofa recorded the song "Chaminingwa" with the RBC in 1961 (Archives #1841) with similar lyrics: "All my kinsmen died / Who'll I play with / Who'll I share my troubles with." The dandanda dance drumming song "Pasi Pane Mhanda" from Mhembere Murehwa is a similar complaint: "There are problems on the earth / problems problems / There is suffering in this world / . . . / Hoo poverty / There is suffering in this world."

13. The transcription and translation of this text by my translator differs substantially from Pongweni's (1982: 134–35). I cannot explain the difference, since both were working from the same recording, but listening to the recording with both transcriptions in front of me, I stand by Francis's more accurate transcription and literal translation.

14. As noted, his mbira-based music was not based on classical pieces, but used only the general stylistic characteristics (the 12/8 feel, a four-phrase cycle, timbral features in the voice, and damped guitar) to create a new piece.

15. M'tukudzi's slow ballads especially resemble pieces like Redding's version of Sam Cooke's "A Change Is Gonna Come," in their passionate spirit rather than in terms of actual musical or vocal style.

16. This date given by Sithole in interview (Zim92-17: 1) differs from the 1 November 1952 birth date in Zindi (1985: 38).

17. Sithole sometimes had trouble remembering the exact year of certain occurrences, such as the year of his first 45-rpm record, "Sabhuku," which he used as a memory guide to the time he began playing mbira music on the guitar. This date should be taken as approximate.

18. Music from this and a second LP issued by RTP (Record and Tape Production) in Harare are available on *Jonah Sithole-Sabhuku* (Zimbob, Zim-4, P.O. Box 2421 Champaign, IL 61825).

19. This was a common theme for debate in articles and letters to the editor in *Parade* during the 1950s and 1960s.

### Chapter Nine

1. Of an estimated 400,000 families who could not expect to live off the land in communal areas in 1977, only 52,000 families had been resettled between 1980 and 1987 (MacGarry 1993: 10).

2. By 1979 the war between Rhodesian forces and the ZANU-ZAPU Patriotic Front guerrillas was at a stalemate. Neither side was able to claim a clear victory, but the guerrillas and international sentiment were effective enough to force the Smith regime to the negotiating table at the Lancaster House in London. Given the ZANU-ZAPU Patriotic Front's relatively weak bargaining position at the end of 1979, they accepted many conditions of the Lancaster House negotiations which did not seem consistent with ZANU's wartime social project. Among the agreements of the new constitution, guaranteed for ten years, was the stipulation that any takeover of commercial farmland by government be on a "willing buyer, willing seller" basis. Because these conditions were honored, the many white farmers stayed on (Weiss 1994). The constitution also safeguarded white businesses and property.

3. The black-to-white ratio in upper management was 10 percent to 90 percent in 1986, 37 to 63 percent in 1989, and 38 to 62 percent in 1991. Confederation of Zimbabwe Industries figures for middle management were higher: 65:35 in 1989 and 68:32 in 1991, and junior management levels were higher still, 71:29 in 1986, 78:22 in 1989, and 92:8 in 1991, (Weiss 1994: 166).

4. "Culture" is actually the domain of the Culture Division, which has shifted between different ministries such as Education and Youth, Sports, and Culture, over time. The Culture Division is headed by a deputy minister of culture. For the sake of clarity and brevity, I simply refer to this bureaucracy as the Ministry of Culture, and to its head as the minister of culture.

5. Before independence the National Arts Foundation (renamed the National Arts Council) acted as a donor agency for white-settler arts organizations, with a few exceptions (National Arts foundation of Zimbabwe 1985: 9). The only exception in the area of music and dance included $200 for the Harare Association of African Choirs in 1979.

6. The school dance festival and performances that I witnessed in the early 1990s indicates that this process had been quite effective. The repertory and style of the dances done by school groups were modeled on the NDC versions, and this was especially pronounced in the case of jerusarema, as described below.

7. The emblems and discourses used to distinguish individual nation-states vary historically and in terms of the region. For example, initially after independence in the nineteenth century, Latin American nationalisms were unabashedly elite movements without the need for populist imagery and appeals. Populist nationalisms and the employment of "folk" emblems did not become common until the early decades of the twentieth century, a shift that accompanied programs for 'modernization' in various Latin American countries (e.g., Peru, Brazil). Italian nationalism during the facist period did not use "folk" imagery as much as former high-culture achievements. By the mid-twentieth century, however, the pattern described for Zimbabwe had become common throughout much of the postcolonial world.

8. Ribiero has had training in folkloristics and ethnomusicology at Indiana University.

9. Black Umfalosi is an Ndebele choir-dance group that performs in the style of *mbube* or *isicathamiya*. They have toured internationally and have had some success locally.

10. The incorporation of "exotic" musics or musical elements into the cosmopolitan sphere has a long history. The various "Latin" music and dance crazes in the United States throughout this century, Louis Armstrong's version of Skokiaan, and Lieber and Stoller's use of Brazilian *baião* rhythm in the Drifters' music are well-known examples. It is the ideological discourse and themes surrounding worldbeat that help differentiate it as a specific, although certainly related, phenomenon. From this point of view, the Beatles use of the sitar, with its connection to "exotic spirituality," is perhaps an early forerunner to worldbeat.

11. Some commentators have observed that Mapfumo's long dreadlocks are in imitation of Marley and other reggae musicians. Mapfumo has, correctly, responded that dreadlocks are also indigenous to Zimbabwe, especially among indigenous spiritualists. In my experience, the two styles of dreads differ in that Zimbabweans tend to keep them much shorter.

12. Like the South African styles chosen by Simon for the *Graceland* album, reggae historically had strong stylistic roots in North American popular music—especially African-American R&B and soul—which accounts for the familiarity of the sound. Also like the South African township music, reggae included its own distinctive features (especially rhythm, verbal accent, and text themes) that indexed a specific, foreign, locality.

13. On *Hokoyo!* the mbira-based pieces were "Hwahwa" and "Mhandu Musango"; on *Corruption,* they were "Moyo Wangu" and "Muchadura."

14. Not so with my Aymara friends in Conima, Peru. I played karimba for people while I was there, and few showed the slightest interest in the instrument; if anything they were scornful of it.

15. The major and minor thirds distinguishing chords are often not realized in mbira performance as they are in guitar renditions of mbira music. Yet even when not explicitly stated as minor, the root and fifth of a iii or iv chord might be translated as minor by listeners socialized with tonal music. Even if this is not true for mbira renditions, the harmonic movement is still tonally ambiguous with regard to a single tonic or final.

16. The dissertations by Robert Kauffman and John Kaemmer, and the work of Hugh and Andrew Tracey provided a much broader picture of Zimbabwean music, but these sources were little known except to specialists. Berliner opens his book with an overview of Zimbabwean music, but his goal was to discuss the mbira. Thus, although it is not the fault of the author, this overview is short and easy to forget.

17. "Nyama Yekugocha," or "Baya wa Baya," is not specific to the classical mbira repertory; it is a war song performed with dandanda drumming as well as in other formats. It is commonly performed by mbira players with four phrases, although its rhythm does not easily fit the typical 12/8 metric structure, as with Mapfumo's rendition here.

18. Mbira tunings in indigenous contexts can be quite idiosyncratic, and they typically vary from standard Western tuning (see Berliner 1978).

19. While some aspects of his stage show may differ when at home and abroad, the musical sound stays basically identical in both contexts.

20. Mapfumo's prominence as a model is partially based on the fact that while he frequently tours outside the country, he remains based in Harare, whereas Chiweshe and the Bhundu Boys are based in Germany and England, respectively—out of sight and out of mind. Mapfumo is seen to be constantly coming and going, and his travels receive more attention in the press at home.

21. Even with this new boost, Zimbabweans outside cosmopolitan circles are not nearly as mbira-centric in their views of indigenous music as foreigners are, whereas because of international attention, mbira may be the main indigenous tradition that Zimbabwean cosmopolitans are aware of.

22. Leonard Dembo and Simon Chimbetu were among the best-selling Zimbabwean recording artists during the first half of the 1990s. According to Victor Tangweni, marketing specialist of Music Express, Zimbabwe's largest retail record chain, these musicians outsold Mapfumo, who was approximately number three. Dembo and Chimbetu perform a style of music that is considered the Zimbabwean version of Congolese rumba, a relatively apt description.

23. The phrase "band kit" refers to a complete set of instruments.

24. Bob Diener, who distributes Zimbabwean music internationally (Zimbob productions) and has worked closely with Mapfumo for a number of years, told me that he has witnessed several cycles of a waxing and waning of creative energy on Mapfumo's part. He interpreted my description of Mapfumo in the summer of 1996 as fitting into this pattern.

25. Although less dramatic, as an analogy closer to home, consider all those radical SDS members of the late 1960s in the United States who went on to become "establishment" bankers, college professors, and business executives.

# References and Bibliography

*African Parade/Parade* (cited by this title when no author listed). 1954. "Entertainment in the Early Thirties, by an Old Timer." *African Parade* November, 14; continued December, 20.

———. 1955a. "Skoky Skokiaan." *African Parade* March, 6–7.

———. 1955b. "It's the Best Band in the Land." *African Parade* July, 6–7.

———. 1958. "The Coons in Harare." *African Parade* November, 14–16.

———. 1959a. "It's All Showbusiness, by Mr. Music." *African Parade* January 14.

———. 1959b. "The All African Music Festival, by Mr. Music." *African Parade* February, 22.

———. 1960. "My Grandpa's Music," in the column "This Music Business—From Charlie." *African Parade* January, 27.

———. 1963a. "Teen-Time in the Townships! by Showbiz Reporter." *African Parade* February, 15–17.

———. 1963b. "Zimbabwe Festival of African Culture." *African Parade* July, 8–9.

———. 1963c. "Detainees Return Home." African Parade March 14–15.

———. 1964. "Lipopo Jazz Band." *Parade* October, 54–57.

———. 1965. "Hit-Parade Simon [Mashoko]: Now His Son's at It Too!" *Parade* May, 17.

———. 1966a. "Miss Rufaro." *Parade* July, 48.

———. 1966b. "Goalposts and Footlights!" *Parade* August, 14.

———. 1969a. "A Festival of African Music, Dance, and Song." *Parade* January, 32.

———. 1969b. "Simanje-Manje Is Here to Stay!" *Parade* May, 10–11.

———. 1970. "Pop Music Extravaganza Was Big Success!" *Parade* November, 28–29.

———. 1971a. "Portrait of an Emerging Vocalist, " *Parade* February, 9.

———. 1971b. "Pop Bands Compete in Charity Festival." *Parade* May, 34.

———. 1975. "Thomas Mapfumo Wins 1975 Talent Contest." *Parade* August, 5.

———. 1977a. "S. A. Dancers Sweep the Floor!" *Parade* May, 8.

———. 1977b. "Mapfumo Wins First Prize." *Parade* December, 43.

Anderson, Amanda. 1998. "Cosmopolitanism, Universalism, and the Divided Legacies of Modernity." In *Cosmopolitics: Thinking and Feeling Beyond the Nation,* ed. Pheng Cheah and Bruce Robbins. Minneapolis: University of Minnesota Press.

Anderson, Benedict. 1991. *Imagined Communities: Reflections on the Origin and Spread of Nationalism.* London: Verso.

Appadurai, Arjun. 1990. "Disjuncture and Difference in the Global Cultural Economy." *Public Culture* 2 (2): 1–24.

———. 1993. "Patriotism and Its Futures." *Public Culture* 5: 411–29.

———. 1996. "The Globalized Production of Locality." In *Modernity at Large: Cultural Dimensions of Globalization.* Minneapolis: University of Minnesota Press.

Appiah, Kwame Anthony. 1998. "Cosmopolitan Patriots." In *Cosmopolitics: Thinking and Feeling Beyond the Nation,* ed. Pheng Cheah and Bruce Robbins. Minneapolis: University of Minnesota Press.

Araujo, Sammuel. 1992. "Acoustic Labor in the Timing of Everyday Life: A Critical Contribution to the History of Samba in Rio de Janeiro." Ph.D. diss. University of Illinois at Urbana-Champaign.

Astrow, Andre. 1983. *Zimbabwe: A Revolution That Lost Its Way?* London: Zed Books.

Austerlitz, Paul. 1997. *Merengue: Dominican Music and Dominican Identity.* Philadelphia: Temple University Press.

Averill, Gage. 1997. *A Day for the Hunter, A Day for the Prey: Popular Music and Power in Haiti.* Chicago: University of Chicago Press.

Axelsson, Olof E. 1973. "Historical Notes on Neo-African Church Music." *Zambezia* 3 (1): 89–100.

———. 1981. "The Development of African Church Music in Zimbabwe." In *Papers Presented at the Second Symposium on Ethnomusicology,* ed. Andrew Tracey. Grahamstown: International Library of African Music.

Banana, Canaan S. 1989. *Turmoil and Tenacity: Zimbabwe, 1890–1990.* Harare: The College Press.

Barthes, Roland. 1977. "Musica Practica." In *Image, Music, Text.* New York: Noonday.

Bender, Wolfgang. 1991. *Sweet Mother: Modern African Music.* Chicago: University of Chicago Press.

Berliner, Paul. 1977. "Political Sentiment in Shona Song and Oral Literature." *Essays in Arts and Sciences* 6 (1): 1–29. University of New Haven: Symposium, "American Ethnomusicology."

———. 1978. *The Soul of Mbira: Music and Traditions of the Shona People of Zimbabwe.* Berkeley: University of California Press.

———. 1980. "John Kunaka, Mbira Maker." *African Arts* 14 (1): 61–68, 88.

Bhabha, Homi. 1992. "The World and the Home." *Social Text* 31–32: 141–53.

Bhebe, Ngwabi. 1989. "The Nationalist Struggle, 1957–1962." In *Turmoil and Tenacity: Zimbabwe, 1890–1990,* ed. Canaan S. Banana. Harare: The College Press, 50–114.

Bohlman, Philip V. 1988. *The Study of Folk Music in the Modern World.* Bloomington: Indiana University Press.

Bourdieu, Pierre. 1977. *Outline of a Theory of Practice.* Cambridge: Cambridge University Press.

Bourdillon, Michael. 1987. *The Shona People.* Gweru: Mambo Press.

Brand, C. M. 1976. "Race and Politics in Rhodesian Trade Unions." *African Perspectives* 1: 55–80.

Brennan, Timothy. 1997. *At Home in the World: Cosmopolitanism Now.* ✓
    Cambridge: Harvard University Press.
Broughton, Simon, et al., eds. 1994. *World Music: The Rough Guide.* London: Penguin Books.
Brown, Ernest. 1994. "The Guitar and the *Mbira:* Resilience, Assimilation,
    and Pan-Africanism in Zimbabwean Music." *The World of Music* 36 (2):
    73–117.
Buchanan, Donna. 1995. "Metaphors of Power, Metaphors of Truth: The
    Politics of Music Professionalism in Bulgarian Folk Orchestras." *Ethnomusicology* 39 (3): 381–416.
Capwell, Charles. 1976. "Sourindo Mohun Tagore and the National Anthem
    Project." *Ethnomusicology* 31 (3): 407–30.
———. 1991. "Marginality and Musicology in Nineteenth-Century Calcutta:
    The Case of Sourindro Mohun Tagore." In *Comparative Musicology and
    Anthropology of Music: Essays on the History of Ethnomusicology,* ed.
    Bruno Nettl and Philip V. Bohlman. Chicago: University of Chicago Press.
Carrington, John T. 1954. "Letter to the Editor." *African Music Society Journal* 1 (1): 83.
Carroll, Father K. 1954. "Letter to the Editor." *African Music Society Journal*
    1 (1): 81.
Census. 1992. *Census 1992: Zimbabwe Preliminary Report.* Harare: Central
    Statistical Office.
Chambati, Ariston M. 1989. "National Unity—ANC." In *Turmoil and Tenacity: Zimbabwe, 1890–1990,* ed. Canaan S. Banana. Harare: The College Press.
Chatterjee, Partha. 1986. *Nationalist Thought and the Colonial World.* Minneapolis: University of Minnesota Press.
———. 1993. *The Nation and Its Fragments: Colonial and Post-Colonial
    Histories.* Princeton: Princeton University Press.
Cheah, Pheng. 1998. "The Cosmopolitical—Today." In *Cosmopolitics:
    Thinking and Feeling Beyond the Nation,* ed. Pheng Cheah and Bruce
    Robbins. Minneapolis: University of Minnesota Press.
Cheater, Angela. 1984. *Idioms of Accumulation: Rural Development and
    Class Formation among Freeholders in Zimbabwe.* Gweru: Mambo
    Press.
Chifunyise, Steven J. 1987. "Cultural Festivals and Competitions." Unpublished paper presented to the meeting with provincial officers and center
    heads, 28 January; held in the National Archives of Zimbabwe.
Chinamhora, Brian. 1987. "African Popular Music." In *Tabex Encyclopedia
    Zimbabwe,* ed. Katherine Sayce. Harare: Quest Publishing, 261–63.
Chopyak, James D. 1987. "The Role of Music in Mass Media, Public Education, and the Formation of a Malaysian National Culture." *Ethnomusicology* 31 (3): 431–54.
Clifford, James. 1992. "Traveling Cultures." In *Cultural Studies,* ed. Lawrence
    Grossberg, Cary Nelson, and Paula Treichler. New York: Routledge.
Collins, E. J. 1972. "Highlife: A Study in Syncretic Neofolk Music." Unpublished paper.

————. 1976. "Ghanaian Highlife." *African Arts* 10 (1): 62–68.

————. 1985. *African Pop Roots.* London: Foulsham Publications.

Comaroff, Jean, and John Comaroff, eds. 1993. *Modernity and Its Malcontents: Ritual and Power in Postcolonial Africa.* Chicago: University of Chicago Press.

Coplan, David. 1978. "Go to My Town, Cape Coast! The Social History of Ghanaian Highlife." In *Eight Urban Musical Cultures,* ed. Bruno Nettl. Urbana: University of Illinois Press.

————. 1982. "The Urbanization of African Music: Some Theoretical Observations." *Popular Music* 2: 113–29.

————. 1985. *In Township Tonight! South Africa's Black City Music and Theatre.* London: Longman.

Cormack, I. R. N. 1983. *Towards Self-Reliance: Urban Social Development in Zimbabwe.* Gweru: Mambo Press.

Csikszentmihalyi, Mihaly, and Isabella Selega Csikszentmihalyi. 1988. *Optimal Experience: Psychological Studies in Flow Consciousness.* Cambridge: Cambridge University Press.

*Daily News.* 1963a. "Take This Axe." *Daily News,* 30 July, 1.

————. 1963b. "Nkomo Is Back in a Fighting Mood: Streets Lined." *Daily News,* 30 July, 1.

————. 1963c. "Keep Up the Traditional Dances." *Daily News,* 30 July, 1.

Dandala, H. M., and K. Moraka. 1990. *Masingcwabisane A re Bolokaneng: A Book on the Burial Societies.* Johannesburg and Cape Town: Skotaville Publishers.

Daniel, Valentine E. 1984. *Fluid Signs: Being a Person the Tamil Way.* Berkeley: University of California Press.

Davies, Dorothy Keyworth. 1975. *Race Relations in Rhodesia: A Survey for 1972–73.* London: Rex Collings.

Davies, Robert, David Sanders, and Timothy Shaw. 1991. *Liberalisation for Development: Zimbabwe's Adjustment without the Fund.* Innocenti Occasional Papers, no. 16. Florence: Unicef.

Díaz, Edgardo. 1996. "Puerto Rican Affirmation and Denial of Musical Nationalism: The Cases of Campos Parsi and Aponte Ledée." *Latin American Music Review* 17 (1): 1–20.

*Drum.* 1992. *Zimbabwe: The Search for Common Ground, Our National Pride from the Pages of Drum.* Lanseria, S.A.: Bailey's African Archives Publication.

Ellingson, Ter. 1992. "Notation." In *Ethnomusicology: An Introduction,* ed. Helen Myers. New York: W. W. Norton.

Erlmann, Veit. 1990. "Migration and Performance: Zulu Migrant Workers' *Isicathamiya* Performance in South Africa, 1890–1950." *Ethnomusicology* 34 (2): 199–220.

————. 1991. *African Stars: Studies in Black South African Performance.* Chicago: University of Chicago Press.

————. 1993. "The Politics and Aesthetics of Transnational Musics." *The World of Music* 35 (2): 3–15.

———. 1996. *Nightsong: Performance, Power, and Practice in South Africa.* Chicago: University of Chicago Press.

Eyre, Banning. 1994. "Zimbabwe Roots Guitar." *Guitar Player* 28 (12): 117–24.

Fabian, Johannes. 1983. *Time and the Other: How Anthropology Makes Its Object.* New York: Columbia University Press.

Featherstone, Michel. 1990. *Global Culture: Nationalism, Globalization, and Modernity.* London: Sage Publications.

Feld, Steven. 1988. "Aesthetics as Iconicity of Style, or 'Lift-Up-Over-Sounding': Getting Into the Kaluli Groove." *Yearbook for Traditional Music* 20: 74–113.

Finnegan, Ruth. 1989. *Hidden Musicians: Music Making in an English Town.* Cambridge: Cambridge University Press.

Foucault, Michel. 1977. *Language, Counter-Memory, Practice: Selected Essays and Interviews.* Ithaca, NY: Cornell University Press.

Fox, Ted. 1986. *In the Groove: The People Behind the Music.* New York: St. Martin's Press.

Fraenkel, Peter. 1959. *Wayaleshi.* London: Weidenfeld and Nicolson.

Frederikse, Julie. 1982. *None But Ourselves: Masses vs. Media in the Making of Zimbabwe.* Harmondsworth, Middlesex, England: Penguin Books.

Frith, Simon. 1989. *World Music, Politics, and Social Change.* Manchester: Manchester University Press.

Fry, Peter. 1976. *Spirits of Protest: Spirit-Mediums and the Articulation of Consensus among the Zezuru of Southern Rhodesia (Zimbabwe).* Cambridge: Cambridge University Press.

Gellner, Ernest. 1983. *Nations and Nationalism.* Oxford: Basil Blackwell.

Gilroy, Paul. 1987. *"There Ain't No Black in the Union Jack": The Cultural Politics of Race and Nation.* Chicago: University of Chicago Press.

Godwin, Peter, and Ian Hancock. 1993. *"Rhodesians Never Die": The Impact of War and Political Change on White Rhodesia, c. 1970–1980.* Oxford: Oxford University Press.

Gramsci, Antonio. 1971. *Selections from the Prison Notebooks of Antonio Gramsci.* Trans. and ed. Q. Hoare and G. Norwell Smith. New York: International Publishers.

———. 1988. *An Antonio Gramsci Reader: Selected Writings, 1916–1935.* Ed. David Forgacs. New York: Schocken Books.

Guilbault, Jocelyne. 1993a. *Zouk: World Music in the West Indies.* Chicago: University of Chicago Press.

———. 1993b. "On Redefining the 'Local' through World Music." *The World of Music* 35 (2): 33–47.

Guvi, Tinos. 1964. "Why Did They Kill Sonny Sondo?" *Parade,* July, 26–28).

Gwata, M. F., and D. H. Reader. 1977. "Rhodesian African Cultural and Leisure Needs." Unpublished paper, Department of Sociology, University of Rhodesia, commissioned by the National Arts Foundation of Rhodesia.

Hall, Edward. 1977. *Beyond Culture.* Garden City: Anchor Press.

Hall, N. 1987. "Self-Reliance in Practice: A Study of Burial Societies in Harare, Zimbabwe." *Journal of Social Development in Africa* 2: 49–71.

Hall, Stuart. 1991. "The Local and the Global: Globalization and Ethnicity."
In *Globalization and the World System*, ed. Anthony B. King. Bingham-
ton, NY: State University of New York Press.

Hampton, Barbara. 1980. "A Revised Analytical Approach to Musical Processes in Urban Africa." *African Urban Studies* 6: 1–16.

Hennion, Antoine. 1990. "The Production of Success: An Antimusicology of
the Pop Song." In *On Record: Rock, Pop, and the Written Word*, ed.
Simon Frith and Andrew Goodwin. New York: Pantheon Books.

Herbst, Jeffrey. 1990. *State Politics in Zimbabwe*. Harare: University of
Zimbabwe.

Herzfeld, Michael. 1997. *Cultural Intimacy: Social Poetics in the Nation-
State*. New York: Routledge.

Hobsbawm, Eric J. 1990. *Nations and Nationalism Since 1780: Programme,
Myth, Reality*. Cambridge: Cambridge University Press.

Holderness, Hardwicke. 1985. *Lost Chance: Southern Rhodesia, 1945–58*.
Harare: Zimbabwe Publishing House.

Hyslop, Graham H. 1955. "Brief Report of a Music Course Conducted at
Siriba for the Nyanza Musical Society." *African Music Society Journal*
1 (2): 58–59.

Impey, Angela Marguerite. 1992. "They Want Us with Salt and Onions:
Women in the Zimbabwean Music Industry." Ph.D. diss. Indiana
University.

———. 1998. "Popular Music in Africa." In *The Garland Encyclopedia of
World Music: Africa*, ed. Ruth Stone. New York: Garland Publishing.

Jameson, Fredric. 1991. *Postmodernism or, the Cultural Logic of Late Capitalism*. Durham, NC: Duke University Press.

Jangano, Green. 1988. "Jangano Talks about Music and Culture." *Zimbabwe
News* 19 (11): 9–10.

Jones, A. M. 1948. "Hymns for the Africans." *African Music Society Newsletter* 1 (3): 8.

Jones, Claire. 1992. *Making Music: Musical Instruments in Zimbabwe Past
and Present*. Harare: Academic Books.

Kaemmer, John E. 1975. "The Dynamics of a Changing Music System in Rural Rhodesia." Ph.D. diss. Indiana University.

———. 1977. "Changing Music in Contemporary Africa." In *Africa*, ed.
Phyllis M. Martin and Patrick O'Meara. Bloomington: Indiana University Press.

———. 1989. "Social Power and Musical Change among the Shona." *Ethnomusicology* 33 (1): 31–46.

———. 1998. "Music of the Shona of Zimbabwe." In *The Garland Encyclopedia of World Music: Africa*, ed. Ruth Stone. New York: Garland
Publishing.

Kameat, Biz. 1966a. "Showbiz Reborn?" *Parade* May, 11.

———. 1966b. "Showbiz." *Parade* September, 40.

Kanji, Nazneen, and Niki Jazdowska. 1993. "Structural Adjustment and Women in Zimbabwe." *Review of African Political Economy* 56: 11–26.

Kanyangarara, Maclay. 1978. "Class Struggle in Zimbabwe." *Zimbabwe News* 10 (3): 13–15.

Kauffman, Robert. 1970. "Multi-Part Relationships in the Shona Music of Rhodesia." Ph.D. diss. University of California at Los Angeles.

———. 1975. "Shona Urban Music: A Process which Maintains Traditional Values." In *Urban Man in Southern Africa*, ed. Clive Kileff and Wade C. Pendleton. Gweru: Mambo Press.

———. 1980. "Tradition and Innovation in the Urban Music of Zimbabwe." *African Urban Studies* 6: 41–48.

Keil, Charles. 1985. "People's Music Comparatively: Style and Stereotype, Class and Hegemony." *Dialectical Anthropology* 10: 119–30.

———. 1987. "Participatory Discrepancies and the Power of Music." *Cultural Anthropology* 2 (3): 275–83.

Kileff, Clive, and Peggy Kileff, eds. 1970. *Shona Customs*. Gweru: Mambo Press.

Kinloch, G. C. 1975. "Changing Intergroup Attitudes of Whites as Defined by the Press: The Process of Colonial Adaptation." *Zambezia* 4 (1): 105–17.

Knight, Virginia Curtin. 1992. "Zimbabwe: The Politics of Economic Reform." *Current History: A World Affairs Journal* (Africa): 219–23.

Kriger, Norma. 1991. "Popular Struggles in Zimbabwe's War of National Liberation." In *Cultural Struggle and Development in Southern Africa*, ed. Preben Kaarsholm. Harare: Bobab Books, 125–48.

———. 1992. *Zimbabwe's Guerrilla War: Peasant Voices*. Cambridge: Cambridge University Press.

Kubik, Gerhard. 1964. "Generic Names for the Mbira: A Contribution to Hugh Tracey's Article, 'A Case for the Name Mbira.'" *African Music* 3 (3): 25–36.

———. 1981. "Neo-traditional Popular Music in East Africa since 1945." *Popular Music* 1: 83–104.

———. 1985. "African Tone-Systems—A Reassessment." *Yearbook for Traditional Music* 17: 31–63.

Kumalo, M. E. 1959. "City Tribal Dancing Display." *African Parade* February, 14–15.

Lan, David. 1985. *Guns and Rain: Guerrillas and Spirit Mediums in Zimbabwe*. London: James Currey.

Lane, Martha S. B. 1993. "'The Blood That Made the Body Go': The Role of Song, Poetry, and Drama in Zimbabwe's War of Liberation, 1966–1980." Ph.D. diss. Northwestern University.

Lipsitz, George. 1994. *Dangerous Crossroads: Popular Music, Postmodernism, and the Poetics of Place*. London: Verso.

Locke, David. 1996. "Africa/Ewe, Mande, Dagbamba, Shona, BaAka." In *Worlds of Music*, ed. Jeff Todd Titon. 3rd ed. New York: Schirmer Books.

Lomax, Alan. 1968. *Folk Song Style and Culture*. Washington, DC: American Association for the Advancement of Science.

Louw, J. K. 1956. "The Use of African Music in the Church." *African Music Society Journal* 1 (3): 43–44.

———. 1958. "African Music in Christian Worship." *African Music Society Journal* 2 (1): 51–53.

Lury, Canon. 1956. "Music in East African Churches." *African Music Society Journal* 1 (3): 34–36.

MacGarry, Brian. 1993. *Growth? Without Equity? The Zimbabwe Economy and the Economic Structural Adjustment Programme.* Gweru: Mambo Press.

———. 1994a. *Double Damage: Rural People and Economic Structural Adjustment in a Time of Drought.* Gweru: Mambo Press.

———. 1994b. *Land for Which People?* Gweru: Mambo Press.

Makwenda, Joyce. 1990. "Research and Recent Traditions: Zimbabwe Contemporary Music of the 1940s to the 1960s." *AVA Conference Proceedings,* 91–101.

———. 1992a. *Zimbabwe Township Music: 1930s to 1960s.* A film produced for the Zimbabwe Broadcast Corporation (ZBC).

———. 1992b. "Singing without Guitars." *Sunday Mail* October 25, 15.

———. 1992c. "Showman Who Set Concert-goers on Fire." *Sunday Mail* July 19.

———. 1992d. "Dancer, Guitarist of the 50s." *Sunday Mail* October 18.

———. 1992e. "Skokiaan Still Popular." *Sunday Times* June 21.

Manuel, Peter. 1985. "Formal Structure in Popular Music as a Reflection of Socio-Economic Change." *International Review of the Aesthetics and Sociology of Music* 16 (2): 163–80.

———. 1987. "Marxism, Nationalism, and Popular Music in Revolutionary Cuba." *Popular Music* 6 (2): 161–78.

———. 1994. "Puerto Rican Music and Cultural Identity: Creative Appropriation of Cuban Sources from the Danza to Salsa." *Ethnomusicology* 38 (2): 249–80.

Manungo, K. D. 1991. "The Peasantry in Zimbabwe: A Vehicle for Change." In *Cultural Struggle and Development in Southern Africa,* ed. Preben Kaarsholm. Harare: Bobab Books, 115–24.

Mapfumo, Thomas. 1993. "Promoting Zimbabwean Culture through Chimurenga Music (Interview with Thomas Mapfumo)." *Southern Africa Political and Economic Monthly* 6 (3–4): 9–10.

Maraire, Dumisani Abraham. 1990. "The Position of Music in Shona 'Mudzimu' (Ancestral Spirit) Possession." Ph.D. diss. University of Washington.

Marothy, Janos. 1974. *Music and the Bourgeois, Music and the Proletarian.* Trans. Eva Rona. Budapest: Akademiai Kiado.

Martin, David, and Phyllis Johnson. 1981. *The Struggle for Zimbabwe: The Chimurenga War.* New York: Monthly Review Press.

McAllester, David. 1979. "The Astonished Ethno-Muse." *Ethnomusicology* 23 (2): 179–89.

McCall, John. 1998. "The Representation of African Music in Early Documents." In *The Garland Encyclopedia of World Music: Africa,* ed. Ruth Stone. New York: Garland Publishers.

McHarg, James. 1958. "African Music in Rhodesian Native Education." *African Music Society Journal* 2 (1): 46–50.

Meintjes, Louise. 1990. "Paul Simon's Graceland, South Africa, and the Mediation of Musical Meaning." *Ethnomusicology* 34: 57–75.

Merriam, Alan. 1955. "The Use of Music in the Study of a Problem of Acculturation." *American Anthropologist* 57: 28–34.

———. 1959. "African Music." In *Continuity and Change in African Cultures,* ed. William R. Bascom and Melville J. Herskovits, 49–86. Chicago: University of Chicago Press.

———. 1964. *The Anthropology of Music.* Evanston, IL: Northwestern University Press.

MEP. 1990. *Mashonaland East Province Comparative Tables: District Population Indicators and Information for Development Planning.* Harare: Central Statistical Office.

Mnyanda, B. J. 1954. *In Search of Truth: A Commentary on Certain Aspects of Southern Rhodesia's Native Policy.* Bombay: Hind Kitabs.

*Moto.* 1990. "Hurukuro with Thomas Mapfumo." August, 19.

Moyana, Henry V. 1984. *The Political Economy of Land in Zimbabwe.* Gweru: Mambo Press.

Moyana, Toby Tafirenyika. 1989. *Education, Liberation, and the Creative Act.* Harare: Zimbabwe Publishing House.

Mpofu, Lazarus. 1978. "Pan-African Symposium: Zimbabwe Culture and the Liberation Struggle." *Zimbabwe News* 10 (3): 13–15.

Mugabe, Robert. 1989. "The Unity Accord: Its Promise for the Future." In *Turmoil and Tenacity: Zimbabwe, 1890–1990,* ed. Canaan S. Banana, 336–60. Harara: The College Press.

Mukanganwa, Tendai. 1993. "Burial Societies Come in Handy for Poor People." *Herald* 28 July, 6.

Mukuna, Kazadiwa. 1980. "The Origin of Zairean Modern Music: A Socioeconomic Aspect." *African Urban Studies* 6: 31–39.

Mushwe, M. 1962. "African Traditional Music Is a Reflection of African Personality." *African Parade* June, 60–62.

National Arts Foundation of Zimbabwe. 1985. *Annual Report.* National Archives of Zimbabwe.

Ndubiwa, M. M. 1974. *Bulawayo Municipal African Township.* Bulawayo: Housing and Amenities Department. Occasional Paper no. 2.

Nelson, Harold D. 1983. *Zimbabwe: A Country Study.* Washington, DC: U.S. Government Printing Office.

Nelson, Kristina. 1985. *The Art of Reciting the Qur'an.* Austin: University of Texas Press.

Nettl, Bruno. 1953. "Stylistic Change in Folk Music." *Southern Folklore Quarterly* 17: 216–20.

———. 1978. "Some Aspects of the History of World Music in the Twentieth Century: Questions, Problems, and Concepts." *Ethnomusicology* 22 (1): 123–36.

———. 1985. *Western Impact on World Music: Change, Adaptation, and Survival.* New York: Schirmer Books.

Nketia, J. H. Kwabena. 1998. "The Scholarly Study of African Music: A Historical Review." In *The Garland Encyclopedia of World Music: Africa,* ed. Ruth Stone. New York: Garland Publishers.

Noll, William. 1991. "Music Institutions and National Consciousness among Polish and Ukrainian Peasants." In *Ethnomusicology and Modern Music History,* ed. Stephen Blum, Philip V. Bohlman, and Daniel M. Neuman. Urbana: University of Illinois Press.

"Notes and News." 1965. "Kwanongoma College of the Rhodesian Academy of Music." *African Music Society Journal* 3 (4): 80.

Nyangoni, Christopher, and Gideon Nyandoro. 1979. *Zimbabwe Independence Movements: Select Documents.* London: Rex Collings.

Nyagumbo, Maurice. 1980. *With the People: An Autobiography from the Zimbabwe Struggle.* London: Allison & Busby.

Nyika, Tambayi. 1992. "Music Giant Thunders: Kwasa Kwasa Business Must Stop." *Chronicle* 25 December, 7.

Pacini Hernandez, Deborah. 1993. "A View from the South: Spanish Caribbean Perspectives on World Beat." *The World of Music* 35 (2): 48–69.

———. 1995. *Bachata: A Social History of a Dominican Popular Music.* Philadelphia: Temple University Press.

Parrinder, E. G. 1956. "Music in West African Churches." *African Music Society Journal* 1 (3): 37–38.

Patel, D. H., and R. J. Adams. 1981. *Chirambahuyo: A Case Study in Low-Income Housing.* Gweru: Mambo Press.

Peirce, Charles Sanders. 1955. *Philosophical Writings of Peirce.* Ed. Justus Buchler. New York: Dover.

———. 1998. *The Essential Peirce: Selected Philosophical Writings of Peirce.* Vol. 2. Ed. Nathan Houser. Bloomington: Indiana University Press.

Peña, Manuel. 1985. *Texas-Mexican Conjunto: History of a Working-Class Music.* Austin: University of Texas Press.

Pongweni, Alec J. C. 1982. *Songs That Won the Liberation War.* Harare: The College Press.

*Prize.* 1974. "The Mambos." *Prize Magazine* February, 9

———. 1976. "Soul & Blues Union." *Prize Magazine* June, 6.

RBC (Rhodesian Broadcasting Corporation).

n.d. *Broadcasting in the Seventies.* Harare: RBC/Government Printer.

Ranger, Terence. 1982. "The Death of Chaminuka: Spirit Mediums, Nationalism, and the Guerilla War in Zimbabwe." *African Affairs* 81 (324): 349–69.

———. 1984. "Religions and Rural Protests in Makoni District, Zimbabwe, 1900–80." In *Religion and Rural Revolt,* ed. Janos M. Bak and Gerhard Benecke. Dover, NH: Manchester University Press.

———. 1985. *Peasant Consciousness and Guerrilla War in Zimbabwe: A Comparative Study.* London: James Currey; Berkeley: University of California Press.

Rhodes, Willard. 1958. "Letter to the Editor." *African Music Society Journal* 1 (1): 82–84.

Robbins, Bruce. 1992. "Comparative Cosmopolitanism." *Social Text* 31 (2): 169–186.

Robbin, James. 1990. "Making Popular Music in Cuba: A Study of the Cuban Institutions of Musical Production and the Musical Life of Santiago de Cuba." Ph.D diss. University of Illinois.

Roberts, John Storm. 1972. *Black Music of Two Worlds.* New York: Schocken Books.

Romero, Raul. 1990. "Musical Change and Cultural Resistance in the Central Andes." *Latin American Music Review* 11 (1): 1–35.

Rosaldo, Renato. 1989. *Culture and Truth: The Remaking of Social Analysis.* Boston: Beacon Press.

Rusike, A. B. C. 1960. "Capital City Dixies." *African Parade* August, 38–39, 60.

Rycroft, David. 1977. "Evidence of Stylistic Continuity in Zulu Town Music." In *Essays for a Humanist: An Offering to Klaus Wachsman.* New York: Town House Press, 216–60.

Sayce, Katherine, ed. 1987. *Tabex Encyclopedia Zimbabwe.* Harare: Quest Publishing.

Seton-Watson, Hugh. 1977. *Nations and States: An Enquiry into the Origins of Nations and the Politics of Nationalism.* Boulder, CO: Westview Press.

Shaffer, Jacqueline. 1956. "Experiments in Indigenous Church Music among the Batetela." *African Music Society Journal* 1 (3): 39–42.

Shamuyarira, Nathan. 1965. *Crisis in Rhodesia,* London: Andre Deutsch.

———. 1978. "Education as an Instrument for Social Transformation in Zimbabwe." *Zimbabwe News* 10 (2): 61–64.

Shamuyarira, Wilson. 1960. "Preserve and Improve on Our African Tribal Music." *African Parade* February, 22–24, 78.

Sithole, Ndabaningi. 1968. *African Nationalism.* 2d ed. London: Oxford University Press.

Slobin, Mark. 1992. "Micromusics of the West: A Comparative Approach." *Ethnomusicology* 36 (1): 1–88.

Small, Christopher. 1987. "Performance as Ritual: Sketch for an Enquiry into the True Nature of a Symphony concert." In *Lost in Music: Culture, Style, and the Musical Event,* ed. Avnon Levine White, 6–32. New York: Routledge and Kegan Paul.

Smith, Anthony. 1971. *Theories of Nationalism.* London: Camelot Press.

Smith, David, and Colin Simpson. 1981. *Mugabe.* London: Sphere Books.

Sparshott, Francis. 1994. "Music and Feeling." *Journal of Aesthetics and Art Criticism* 52 (1): 23–36.

Stapleton, Chris, and Chris May. 1987. *African All-Stars: The Pop Music of a Continent.* London: Quartet Books.

Stopforth, P. 1971. *Survey of Highfield African Township*. Department of So-
ciology, University of Rhodesia. Occasional Paper no. 6.
———. 1972. *Two Aspects of Social Change: Highfield African Township,
Salisbury*. Department of Sociology, University of Rhodesia. Occasional
Paper no. 7.
Sugarman, Jane. 1997. *Engendering Song: Singing and Subjectivity at Prespa
Albanian Weddings*. Chicago: University of Chicago Press.
*Sunday Mail*. 1993. "The Cradle of African Nationalism Today." *Sunday Mail*
(Harare) 4 April, 9.
Supiya, Stephen T. 1962. "ZAPU Endeavours to Blend the Old and the New."
*African Parade* May, 8, 53, 58.
SYZ. 1989. *Statistical Yearbook of Zimbabwe*. Harare: Central Statistical
Office.
Tololyan, Khachig. 1996. "Rethinking Diaspora(s): Stateless Power in the
Transnational Moment." *Diaspora* 5 (1): 3–36.
Tracey, Andrew. 1963. "Three Tunes for 'Mbira Dza Vadzimu.'" *African Mu-
sic* 3 (2): 23–26.
———. 1969. "The Tuning of Mbira Reeds." *African Music* 4 (3): 96–100.
———. 1970. "The Matepe Mbira Music of Rhodesia." *African Music* 4 (4):
37–61.
———. 1972. "The Original African Mbira?" *African Music* 5 (2): 85–104.
———. 1973. "The Family of the Mbira: The Evidence of the Tuning Plans."
*Zambezia* 3 (1): 1–10.
Tracey, Hugh. 1961. "A Case for the Name Mbira." *African Music* 2 (4): 17–
25.
———. 1969 [1932]. "The Mbira Class of African Instruments in Rhodesia."
*African Music* 4 (3): 78–95.
Turino, Thomas. 1984. "The Urban-Mestizo Charango Tradition in Southern Peru: A Statement of Shifting Identity." *Ethnomusicology* 28 (2):
253–70.
———. 1988. "The Music of Andean Migrants in Lima, Peru: Demographics,
Social Power, and Style." *Latin American Music Review* 9 (2): 127–49.
———. 1992 [1997]. "The Music of Sub-Saharan Africa." In *Excursions in
World Music*, edited by Bruno Nettl et al., 161–90. Upper Saddle River,
NJ: Prentice Hall.
———. 1993. *Moving Away from Silence: Music of the Peruvian Altiplano
and the Experience of Urban Migration*. Chicago: University of Chicago
Press.
———. 1996. "From Essentialism to the Essential: Pragmatics and Meaning
of Puneño Sikuri Performance in Lima." In *Cosmología y Música en los
Andes*, ed. Max Peter Baumann. Vervuert: Iberoamericana.
———. 1998. "The Mbira, Worldbeat, and the International Imagination,"
*World of Music* 40 (2): 85–106.
———. 1999. "Signs of Imagination, Identity, and Experience: A Peircian Semiotic Theory for Music." *Ethnomusicology* 43 (2): 221–55.
Utete, C. Munhamu Botsio. 1978. *The Road to Zimbabwe: The Political*

*Economy of Settler Colonialism, National Liberation, and Foreign Intervention.* Montclair, NJ: University Press of America.

Vambe, Lawrence. 1976. *From Rhodesia to Zimbabwe.* Pittsburgh: University of Pittsburgh Press.

Verdery, Katherine. 1991. *National Ideology under Socialism: Identity and Cultural Politics in Ceausescu's Romania.* Berkeley: University of California Press.

Wald, Elijah. 1992. "African Guitar Pioneer." *Acoustic Guitar* May/June.

Ware, Naomi. 1978. "Popular Music and African Identity in Freetown, Sierra Leone." In *Eight Urban Musical Cultures,* ed. Bruno Nettl. Urbana: University of Illinois Press.

Waterman, Christopher. 1982. "'I'm a Leader, Not a Boss': Social Identity and Popular Music in Ibadan, Nigeria." *Ethnomusicology* 26 (1): 59–72.

———. 1990a. "Our Tradition Is a Very Modern Tradition: Popular Music and the Construction of Pan-Yoruba Identity." *Ethnomusicology* 34 (3): 367–80.

———. 1990b. *Juju: A Social History and Ethnography of an African Popular Music.* Chicago: University of Chicago Press.

Weber, Max. 1958. *The Protestant Ethic and the Spirit of Capitalism.* New York: Charles Scribner's Sons.

Weiss, Ruth. 1994. *Zimbabwe and the New Elite.* London: British Academic Press.

Welsh-Asante, Kariamu. 1993. "Zimbabwean Dance: An Aesthetic Analysis of the Jerusarema and Muchongoyo Dances." Ph.D. diss. New York University.

West, Michael. 1990. "African Middle Class Formation in Colonial Zimbabwe, 1890–1965." Ph.D. diss. Harvard University.

Williamson, Leslie. 1963. "Kwanongomo [*sic*] College, Bulawayo." *African Music Society Journal* 3 (2): 48–49.

———. 1964. "The Kwanongoma College of African Music, June Newsletter." *African Music Society Journal* 3 (3): 117–18.

Witmer, Robert. 1987. "'Local' and 'Foreign': The Popular Music Culture of Kingston, Jamaica, before Ska, Rock Steady, and Reggae." *Latin American Music Review* 8 (1): 1–25.

Wong, Isabel K. F. 1984. "*Geming Gequ:* Songs for the Education of the Masses." In *Popular Chinese Literature and Performing Arts in the People's Republic of China, 1949–1979,* ed. Bonnie S. MacDougall. Berkeley: University of California Press.

Zilberg, Jonathan Leslie. 1996. "Zimbabwean Stone Sculpture: The Invention of a Shona Tradition." Ph.D. diss. University of Illinois at Urbana-Champaign.

Zindi, Fred. 1985. *Roots Rocking in Zimbabwe.* Gweru: Mambo Press.

———. 1993. "Thomas Mapfumo: A Cultural Ambassador?" *Southern Africa* 6 (3): 11–12.

# Discography

Banda, Robson. 1995. *Greatest Hits,* CD, Zimbob ZIM-5.

Berliner, Paul. n.d. *The Soul of Mbira,* LP, Nonesuch H-72054.

———. 1977. *Shona Mbira Music,* LP, Nonesuch H-72077.

The Bhundu Boys. 1989. *Pamberi!* LP, Mango MLPS9858.

Chibadura, John. 1989. *The Essential John Chibadura,* LP, CSA Records, CSLP 5002.

Chimombe, James. 1996. *The Best of James Chimombe,* CD, Zimbob ZIM-6.

Kwenda, Forward, and Erica Azim. 1997. *Svikiro—Meditations from an Mbira Master,* CD, Shanachie 64095.

Mapfumo, Thomas, and the Acid Band n.d. *Hokoyo!* LP, Gramma ZASLP 5000.

Mapfumo, Thomas, and the Blacks Unlimited. 1980. *Gwindingwi Rine Shumba,* LP, Gramma ZASLP 5002.

———. 1983. *Ndangariro,* LP, Gramma/Earthworks ELP 2005.

———. 1984. *Mabasa,* LP, Gramma ZASLP 5004.

———. 1985a. *Mr. Music,* LP, Gramma ZASLP.

———. 1985b. *Chimurenga for Justice,* LP, Chimurenga Music Rough 91.

———. 1985c. *The Chimurenga Singles 1976–1980,* LP, Meadowlark 403; compilation of previously released single recordings.

———. 1988a. *Zimbabwe-Mozambique,* LP, Chimurenga Music TML 100.

———. 1988b. *Varomba Kuvaromba,* LP, Chimurenga Music TML 101, re-released as *Corruption,* 1989, Mango MLPS 9848.

———. 1989. *Chamunorwa,* LP, Chimurenga Music TML 102; re-released 1991, Mango MLPS 9848.

———. 1990. *Chimurenga Masterpiece,* LP, Chimurenga Music TML 103.

———. 1990. *Shumba,* Earthworks international re-release of earlier material.

———. 1991. *Hondo,* LP, Chimurenga Music, TML 104. Re-released with two extra songs on *Hondo,* CD, Zimbob ZIM-1 (1993).

———. 1993. *Chimurenga International,* LP, Chimurenga Music TML 105.

———. 1995. *Vanhu Vatema,* CD, Zimbob ZIM-2.

———. 1996. *Singles Collection,* CD, Zimbob ZIM-7.

Maraire, Dumisani Abraham. 1971. *The African Mbira: Music of the Shona People of Rhodesia,* LP, Nonesuch H-72043.

———. 1989. *Chaminuka,* LP, Music of the World, CDC 208.

Marimba Ava Murehwa. 1997. *Mazuna Ano,* CD, Zimbob ZIM-8.

M'tukudzi, Oliver. 1988. *Sugar Pie,* LP, CSA Records CSLP 5001.

———. 1990. *Psss Psss Hallo!,* LP, CSA Records CSLP 5005.

Ngane Khamba. n.d. *Zulu Traditionnel,* LP, Celluloid 66838-1.

The Real Sounds. 1987. *Wende Zako,* LP, Rounder 5029.

Roberts, John Storm. n.d. *The Sound of Kinshasha: Guitar Classics from Zaire,* LP, Original Music OMA 102.

Simon, Paul. 1986. *Graceland,* LP, Warner Brothers 25447-1.

Sithole, Jonah. 1995. *Sabhuku.* Zimbob ZIM-4.

Tracey, Hugh. 1972. *Musical Instruments 6: Guitars 1,* LP, Kaleidophone KMA 6, from the *Music of Africa* series.

———. 1989. *Siya Hamba! 1950s South African Country and Small Town Sounds,* LP, Original Music OMA 111, compiled and produced by John Storm Roberts.

ZANU (Zimbabwe African National Union). n.d. *Chimurenga Songs: Music of the Revolutionary People's War in Zimbabwe,* LP, Teal Records, no catalogue number.

Various artists. 1991. *Jit!* cassette, Earthworks 3-1023-4, features songs from the movie *Jit!* plus other material.o

———. 1984. *Phezulu Eqhudeni (On Eqhudini Mountain),* LP, Carthage CGLP 4415, with Mahotella Queens, Mahlathini, and others.

———. 1987. *Take Cover! Zimbabwe Hits,* LP, Shanachie 43045.

———. 1994. *Vibrant Zimbabwe,* CD, Zimbob ZIM-3.

———. 1983. *Viva Zimbabwe! A Compilation of Contemporary Dance Music from Zimbabwe,* LP, Earthworks ELP 2001.

———. 1983. *Zulu Jive (Umbaqanga): Urban and Rural Beats from South Africa,* LP, Earthworks ELP 2002.

# Index

Abraham, Donald, 201
Acid Band, The, 278, 286–87
Ade, Sunny, 337
African/European dichotomy, 32
African National Congress (ANC), 170, 193–94
*African Parade,* 102, 196; and middle-class modernist cosmopolitanism, 148–56; and ethnomusicology, 152–53
African Service Radio (Radio 2), 77, 79, 121
African Welfare Society (AWS), 110–11, 145, 147–48
All-African Music Festival, 150
All Saints Band, 252–55, 280
ancestral spirits, 35–41, 200
Anderson, Benedict, 13, 164–66, 173–74, 180, 198, 212–13
Antonio Morel y su Orquesta, 141
Appadurai, Arjun, 12–13, 46
Appiah, Kwame Anthony, 18
Armstrong, Louis, 141
Arnaz, Desi, 132
Astrow, Andre, 352–53
Averill, Gage, 334
Axelsson, Olof E., 113–16, 151, 156
Azim, Erica, 345

ballroom dancing, 146–48
Banana, Canaan, 22, 165
Banda, Joyce, 290
Bandambira, 79
Bantu Actors, The, 126–28, 130, 133, 136, 144–45
*Bantu Mirror,* 102, 148
Barthes, Roland, 47
Batanai, 329
Beatles, The, 247–50, 291
Beatsters, The, 252–55, 258
Belafonte, Harry, 152
Bender, Wolfgang, 34

Benhura, Pamidze, 225, 230, 238, 241, 253
Berliner, Paul, 33–34, 37, 47, 51, 53, 74–76, 201, 263, 265, 339, 343
Berry, Chuck, 250
Bhebe, Ngwabi, 161, 173
Bhundu Boys, The, 4, 5, 223–24, 227, 232, 289, 311, 335, 348
Bikita Chinyambera Dancers, The, 331
*bira* ceremonies, 36, 45, 47, 51
black elite, new, 315–17
Black Power, 34
Black Spirits, The, 297, 300
Blacks Unlimited, The, 223, 225, 278, 283, 349–50
Black Umfalosi, 333–35
Blackwell, Chris, 337–38
Bledisloe Commission, 95
Bolton, Chris, 345, 348
Bomba, Baboth, 236
Boterekwa Dhinhe Dancers, 329
Bourdieu, Pierre, 121, 362
Boykie (leader of Soul and Blues Union), 248
British South African Police Band, 140
Bulawayo Municipal Housing and Amenities Department, 110
Bulawayo Philharmonic Orchestra, 317
burial societies, 84–85

Capital City Dixies, The, 135, 255, 257
Central African Broadcasting Service (CABS), 97–99, 102, 117
Chambati, Ariston M., 194
Chaminuka, 201–2, 211–14, 306; and the medium, Pasipamira, 201
Charles, Ray, 247, 260
Chataika, Jordan, 236, 243–44, 305
Chatterjee, Partha, 13, 162, 164–65
Chavunduka, Gordon, 165
Cheater, Angela, 26
Chibhora family, 279–80, 283, 337

Chifunyise, Stephen, 43–44, 46, 108, 325
Chigamba, Henry, 41–42
Chigamba, Irene, 329
Chigamba, Tute, 17, 35–42, 44, 54, 79, 237, 277, 282, 329
Chihoo Dance Troupe, 329
Chikerema, James, 30, 165, 168–69, 185–86, 188
Chikupo, Tiney, 268
*chimanjemanje,* definition of, 231
Chimbetu, Simon, 350
*chimurenga,* definition of, 200, 205, 223, 224
chimurenga songs, 22, 191, 199, 205–6; and Christian hymns, 202–3, 208–9; and group participation, 209; and musical nationalism, 218; style of, 207; texts of, 210–11, 213–15
Chinamano, Josiah, 165
Chinamhora, Brian, 233–34, 245
Chinamhora, Nyamasoka, 184
Chinemberi, Sinoyoro Jackson, 229, 233–35, 240, 272
*chinungu,* definition of, 183, 231
Chinx, Comrade, 17, 192–93, 203, 206–11, 214–15, 218, 223, 308
*chinyambera,* definition of, 147
*chipendani,* definition of, 45, 238
Chitepo, Herbert, 30, 165, 202, 211
Chiweshe, Stella, 4, 5, 223–24, 226, 329, 335–36, 348
Chiyangwa, Leonard, 271
Choral Society of Zimbabwe, 317
City Crackers, The, 255
City Quads, The, 134, 144
City Slickers, The, 140, 143–44, 146, 183
class, 21, 119, 120; in colonial Zimbabwe, 121; definition of, 121; musical literacy as mark of, 128–30; as primary variable in shaping tendencies, 44. *See also* middle-class
Clifford, James, 9, 18
Clutton-Brock, Guy, 96, 168–69
Cold Storage Band (Bulawayo Street Rhythms Band), The, 141
College of Music in Harare, 77
colonialism, 4, 8, 20, 31; and mission education, 12
"common-practice" guitar style, 236–37

"concert" style of performance, 125–26; contrasted with indigenous, 137–38; decline of, 138–39
Congolese rumba, 244–46, 265–66
Cool Four, The, 134, 178, 257
Coons Carnival, 135
Coplan, David, 19, 124, 142–43
Cosmic Four Dots, The, 257–58
cosmopolitanism, 4, 7–9, 12, 16–17, 354; and alliances, 12; and alternative lifeways to, 19; and concert conventions, 136; and elitism, 10, 11; and individualism, 10, 11; modernist-capitalist form of, 10; particular formations of, 10
Cripps, Arthur Shearly, 201
Csikszentmihalyi, Isabella, 52
Csikszentmihalyi, Mihaly, 52
Cubai, James, 239
Cuban influence on cosmopolitan pop, 131–32, 135
cultural bureaucracies, 317–18
cultural nationalism, 16–17, 21, 170–73, 177–79, 182, 185, 321; and acoustic guitarists, 240; and anticolonialism, 195; decline of, 186–88; definition of, 14, 162; and party discourse, 195; and religion, 199; and traditional/modern dichotomy, 180
cultural reformism, definition of, 107, 108, 110
cultural syndicate, 150
'culture brokers,' and cosmopolitanism, 101–2
culture houses, 22

*dagga,* definition of, 247
Dambaza, Lovemore, 236
*dandanda,* 41, 63; description of, 71–72
Davies, Robert, 313
De Black Evening Follies, 83, 130–33, 136, 140, 150, 178, 191, 246, 257; and cosmopolitanism, 135; and indigenous dances, 134; and *jerusarema,* 139
Deep Horizone, 300–301, 349
Delphans, The, 300
Dembo, Leonard, 350
*dhinhe,* 63; description of, 71–72
Dibango, Manu, 347

"discrepant" cosmopolitanism, 18
Domboshawa (Rhodesia's first government school), 127
Dube, Atalia, 290
Dube, Christine, 130
Dube, Soche, 237
Dutiro, Chartwell, 144, 278–79, 339, 344
Dylan, Bob, 250

Economic Structural Adjustment Program (ESAP), 23, 314–15, 328–29, 333
Epworth Theatrical Strutters, 134
Erlmann, Veit, 20
Eyre, Banning, 271

Federation, 21, 94; and cosmopolitanism, 117–18; history of, 94–98; and modernism, 117–18; performances during, 93; and policy encouraging African music in schools, 104
Federation Broadcasting Corporation (FBC), 97–98, 117
Feld, Steven, 48
'First Chimurenga,' 20, 200–212, 217
Fitzgerald, Ella, 134
Foucault, Michel, 154
Fraenkel, Peter, 99–101
Frederikse, Julie, 204–5, 273–74, 288
Fry, Peter, 76, 200

Gabellah, Elliot, 165
*Gallop* (dance), 183–84
Gelfand, Michael, 201
Gellner, Ernest, 13, 164–65, 180, 198
gender issues, 81–82, 302–4, 327–28
Getz, Stan, 268, 273
Gilbert, Bernard, 77
Glazer, Tom, 141
globalization, 3, 6, 7, 19
Golden City Dixies, The, 152
Golden Rhythm Crooners, The, 134
Gotora, Samuel, 130
Great Sounds, The, 300
Green Arrows, The, 189, 227, 289–93, 302, 306
Green Jangano, 251–52

*guva,* 69, 80–81, 90, 209, 358; definition of, 51
Guvi, Tinos, 138
Gwata, M. F., 111–12
Gweshe, David, 322, 329

Hadebe, Josaya, 236–38
Hallelujah Chicken Run Band, The, 264, 268–70, 273, 278
Harare African Traditional Association (HATA), 317–18
Harare Association of African Choirs (AAC), 317–18
Harare City Orchestra, 317
Harare Hot Shots, The, 134, 140, 143–44
Harare Mambos, The, 183–84, 225, 251, 254, 290; history of, 252–53
Harper, Peggy, 320, 323
Hernandez, Deborah Pacini, 12
Herzfeld, Michael, 13, 24, 180, 216
high-fidelity music, 47–48; definition of, 49
Highlife (instrumental dance band), 140
Highway Stars, The, 305
Hilltones, The, 151
Hlomayi, Joshua, 264, 270–73, 279–80, 283, 301–2, 350
Holderness, Hardwicke, 96, 117
Holly, Buddy, 250
Hornbostel, Eric von, 114–15
*hosho,* definition of, 53, 71–72, 80, 83, 259
Huggins, Godfrey, 95
*huro,* definition of, 226, 241, 255, 268, 345
Hurricanes, The, 182–84, 265

Impey, Angela, 341
Independence Day Celebration, 90, 93
indigenization, definition of, 46, 117; and ethnomusicology, 114
indigenous: aesthetics, 20, 46; beliefs, 41; culture, discourse of decline of, 33–34, 99–101; defined, 18; economics, 26; ethics, 20; faith, 42; missionary oppression of, 113–14; music and dance, 63; music and dance during the Federation, 86;

indigenous (*continued*)
    and party discourse, 196; preserva-
    tion of during the Federation, 97,
    103, 108; style, contrasted with
    "concert" style, 137–38
indigenous-based acoustic guitar music,
    238–39
indigenous/Western dichotomy, 32
Ink Spots, The, 131
'inside/outside the house' activities, 37,
    51, 71–72, 80, 209, 256, 356
intensive, definition of, 54
interlocking, definition of, 54, 55
International Monetary Fund (IMF), 23,
    314, 353
*isicathamiya* (type of choral music), 334
itinerant guitarists, 233; song texts of,
    241–45; style of, 234–37


Jabvurayi, Rocky Costain, 250–51
Jeron, Nelson, 255
*jerusarema*, 37, 63, 79–82, 84–85, 133,
    136, 327–28, 359
*jit*, 4, 263–64; guitar-band style, 227–
    29; history of, 227–33
*jiti*, 230
Johnson, Phyllis, 199, 201
Johnston, Johnny, and the Johnston
    Brothers, 141
Jones, A. M., 115–16
Jones, Quincy, 323
Jumira, Clement, 236
Junod, H. A., 114


Kaemmer, John, 74, 76, 115–16, 218,
    231, 341
Kagubi (spirit), 200
Kainga, Jeremiah, 136, 235
Kambiriri, Nicholas, 66, 85–86, 88, 93
Kameat, Biz, 131, 139, 250
Kanda Bongo Man, 245
Kassim, Elisha, 130
Kauffman, Robert, 46, 66, 72, 74, 97,
    115–16, 240, 253, 286
Kausio, Naboth, 253
Keil, Charles, 48
Kittermaster, Michael, 98–99, 102, 113,
    117
Kotsore Dancers, 178

Kriger, Norma, 293
Kronos Quartet, 348
*kudeketara* technique, 241
Kumalo, M. E., 149–51
*kumusha* (home), 64
*kushaura*, definition of, 54, 73
*kutsinhira*, definition of, 54, 73
Kwanongoma College of Music, 105–7,
    108–10, 116, 136, 322, 328, 361;
    and cosmopolitan values, 109; eth-
    nomusicology program at, 106
*kwasa kwasa*, definition of, 245
Kwenda, Forward, 345


*labola*, definition of, 81
Ladysmith Black Mambazo, 335
Lancaster House settlement, 22, 312–13
Land Apportionment Act, 20, 25, 27,
    161, 170
Land Husbandry Act, 161
Legal Lions, The, 349
Lenherr, Joseph, 115
Lever Brothers, The, 145
Lewanika, Peter, 236
Liberation War, 12, 192–95
Lipopo Jazz Band, 245–47, 264–65,
    267, 268, 270–71, 274, 300
Liquor Act, 29, 111, 146
Little Richard, 132, 257, 260
Livestock Company, The, 306, 308
Lobengula (King of the Ndebele), 201
local, 3; definition of, 17–18


Mabena, Max, 290
*magandanga*, definition of, 192
Magomere, Fidelis, 237
*mahon'era*, definition of, 226, 241, 268
Mahotella Queens, The, 245, 290
Makeba, Miriam, 134
*makwaya*, 125, 367
Makwenda, Joyce, 130, 249
Malianga, Morton, 165
Maluwa, Mr., 66, 72–74
Manatsa, Kadias, 290
Manatsa, Stanley, 290, 292
Manatsa, Stella, 291
Manatsa, Zexie, 17, 262, 289–95, 297–
    98, 304, 307
Mangwende, Munhywapayi, 177–78

Manhattan Brothers, The, 131, 134–35

*manja*, 80

Manungu, K. D., 205

Maoist military principles, 22, 192, 199, 210, 214

Mao Tse Tung, 215

Mapfumo, Noah, 41

Mapfumo, Susan, 302–4

Mapfumo, Thomas, 4, 5, 12, 17, 73, 126, 139, 144, 184, 189, 205–6, 223–25, 227, 229, 243–44, 249, 251–52, 255, 261–62, 268, 271–75, 277, 294–98, 300–302, 304, 307, 311, 333, 349–51; association of with the mbira, 339–40; attacks on foreign music, 347; on attracting a mass audience, 276; chimurenga song texts, 284–89; compositional process, 278–81; concept of "the art work," 283–89; early career of, 256–60; European tour, 336; imprisonment of, 288; originality, 269–70, 282–83; and 'traditional adaptations,' 258–60; and worldbeat, 336–42, 344–46

Mapondera, John, 322

Maposa, Henry, 322

Mapundu, Ngwaru, 230, 238–39, 241–42, 267, 280

Maraire, Dumisani, 106, 335, 345

Marley, Bob, 289, 311, 336–38

Martin, David, 199, 201

Masekela, Hugh, 134

Maseko, Emmanuel, 91, 322

Mashanda, Job, 306

Mashiyane, Spokes, 228

Mashoko, Simon, 153

Masuka, Dorothy, 134, 135, 150–51, 257

Matambo, Sam, 134, 144

Matiure, Shesby, 322

Mattaka, Kenneth, 17, 84, 111, 126–31, 134, 136–37, 144–45, 147, 154–55, 229, 233, 235, 257–58

Mattaka Family, The, 145

Matutu, Colin, 204

Mavengere, Eric, 322

Mazho, Sylvia, 322

Mazura, Benedict, 140

*mbaquanga*, 244

mbira, 3, 63; definition of, 73; and discourse of revival, 75–77; law of, 37; on radio, 77, 79

mbira-guitar music, 4, 225–26; electric, 263–64, 271–72

Mbirimi, Jona, 140

Mbofana, Mr., 77–78, 229

Mboweni, Raphael, 290

*mbukumba*, 63, description of, 71

Mbukumba Dancers, 178–79

McAllester, David, 20

McHarg, James, 104–6, 117

M. D. Rhythm Success, 232, 264–67, 270–71, 274

Merriam, Alan, 152

*Mfundalai* dance technique, 324–25

Mhembere Dandanda Dancers, 332

Mhlanga, Chris, 17, 32, 35–36, 38–42, 44–46, 53, 58, 79, 237, 239, 261, 277–78, 281–82, 285–86, 346

Mhungu, Jacob, 132, 229, 235, 238, 240

Michel, Samora, 215

middle-class: aesthetics, 44; and cosmopolitanism, 42–43, 119, 157; economics, 44; and mission-school education, 122; and modernist capitalism, 155, 351–53; and music as means for articulating distinction, 123; political organizations, 167; relation of to indigenous practices, 45

Mills Brothers, The, 4, 77, 130–35, 138–39, 257, 274

Milton Brothers, The, 136

Ministry of Culture, 23, 44, 317–18, 320, 322, 325, 328, 331; and professionalism, 332–33; and village ensembles, 329–30

Miranda, Carmen, 4, 132

missionaries: and oppression of indigenous activities, 113–14; and ethnomusicology, 115–16; and universalism, 114

M'kwesha, Peter, 322

Mnyanda, B. J., 122, 123

modernism, 6–7, 12, 354

modernist-reformism, 17, 108, 110; definition of, 16; at Kwanongoma College of Music, 106; and musical literacy, 107

Mpahlo, Moses, 130–33, 257

Mpofu, Lazarus, 195

Mpofu, Paul, 227
M'tukudzi, Oliver, 17, 184, 189, 227, 249, 262, 294, 299–300, 304, 307–8, 350; compositional process, 295–96; political song texts, 297–98
Mtunyane, Steve, 134
Muchena, Mondrek, 17, 36, 231
*muchongoyo,* 37, 63, 178; description of, 70
Muchongoyo Dancers, 185
Mude, Hakurotwi, 78–79
Mudendi, Joseph, 246
Mugabe, Davies, 181
Mugabe, Robert, 14, 21–23, 30, 77, 164–65, 169, 170–74, 177, 186, 194, 211–12, 312–15, 317, 324
*mujibas,* definition of, 192
Mujuru, Ephat, 335, 345, 349
Mujuru, Muchatera, 201–2
Mukotsanjera, Titus, 134
Munangatire, Herbert, 150
Murehwa Culture House, 326, 330–31
Murehwa Jerusarema Club, 17, 66, 81–82, 93–94, 102, 109, 185, 191, 206, 318, 326, 331; and Burial Society, 30, 64, 327; history of, 85–92
Musango, Davis, 144
Musarurwa, August, 140–43, 146
*musha,* 42, 64, 212; definition of, 24–25
Mushanga, Paul, 168
Mushwe, M., 153
musical literacy: as mark of class, 128–30; emphasis on notation, 129
musical nationalism, 4, 217; definition of, 13, 190–91; and popular music, 307–8
Muskwe, Reason, 90–91, 93, 112, 230–31
Mutasa, Mr., 326
Muzorewa, Abel, 22, 165, 194–95, 288
Mwenda, Jean Bosco, 236–37
Mzingeli, Charles, 65


nation, definition of, 13
National Archives of Zimbabwe, 68
National Arts Council, 317–18, 328–29, 331–33
National Ballet, 317
National Dance Company (NDC), 5, 15, 22–23, 63, 72, 82, 91, 110, 311,

320, 332, 346, 350; and cosmopolitan aesthetics, 324–25; and cultural nationalism, 326; history of, 321–29; and *jerusarema,* 327–28; lack of participatory ethic, 325; splintering and decline of, 328–29
National Democratic Party (NDP), 21, 169–73, 177, 187, 189
nationalism, 4, 12, 22, 163; and class, 168–69; confused with national sentiment, 14; and cosmopolitanism, 15, 164–67; and cultural analysis, 14; and cultural renaissance, 181; definition of, 13, 162; and mission schools, 165–66; and modernism, 163–64; as political movement, 14; and professionalism, 272–74
nationalist participation and rallies, 88–89; renaissance, 34
national sentiment, 13, 14, 263, 272–74
National Symphony Orchestra, 317
Native Affairs Department, 161
Native Locations Ordinance, 28
Natives (Urban Areas) Act, 26
Natonga, George, 232
Ndoro, Joyce, 130, 132–33, 178
Negro Brothers, The, 132
Nehanda, Mbuya (spirit), 200–202, 211–12, 214, 292, 306; and the medium, Charwe, 200
Nemapore, Reverend E. T. J., 122
Neshamwari Traditional Song and Dance Festival, 112–13, 138, 318
New Sounds, The, 306
*ngoma,* definition of, 69, 80, 133, 264, 358
*ngororombe,* 53; description of, 69–70
Nico Carstens en sy Orkes, 141
*njari,* 63
Nkala, Enos, 30
Nkhata, Alick, 99–102
Nkomo, John, 238, 241, 243
Nkomo, Joshua, 15, 30, 165, 169–70, 177, 184–86, 194
Nkosi, West, 291, 296
Nkrumah, Kwane, 171; and the Youth League, 172
nongovernmental organizations (NGOs), 9, 11, 333

Norman, Dennis, 313
Nyagumbo, Maurice, 165, 168, 352
Nyamhondera, Bothwell, 232
Nyamundande, Renny, 130
Nyandoro, George, 30, 165, 168, 185, 202
Nyandoro, Patrick, 66–67, 71, 85–86, 88–91, 93, 112, 230–31, 327–28
Nyathi, Albert, 332–33
Nyerere, 215

Okavhango Boys, The, 306
originality, conceptions of, 281–83
Osibisa, 273

Pareles, Jon, 338
Parirenyatwa, Dr. S. T., 178
participatory: ethics, 47, 52–54, 219; events, 50–51; music *(see main entry)*; performance, semiotics of, 56–58; style, 54–56, 59
participatory music, 47, 48; and cosmopolitanism, 58
Patriotic Front (PF), 10, 193–94, 289. *See also* ZAPU
Peirce, Charles Sanders, 14, 56–57, 129, 174, 357
People's Caretaker Council (PCC), 169, 187. *See also* ZAPU
Phiri, Jackson, 17, 184, 189, 229, 245–46, 265–67, 277, 300, 307
Pikaita, Amon, 236
Poison Band, The, 306
Police Band, The, 141, 143, 145–46, 234
Policy of Reconciliation, 23, 312–13, 315
Pongweni, Alec, 213, 288
presentational music, 47–48; definition of, 49
Presley, Elvis, 4, 132, 257, 260, 274
Prison Band, The, 140
professional, definition of, 52
professionalism, 4, 5, 88, 145–46, 334, 354; and national sentiment, 263, 272–74
Pro Machecka and the Blackties, 349
*pungwes,* 22, 204–5; definition of, 203

race, 119–20; as subject for analysis, 120
'racial partnership,' 21, 94–96, 104, 106, 117, 151, 161, 167, 170, 194, 262, 352–53
Ranger, Terence, 199, 201
Reader, D. H., 111
Redding, Otis, 295
regionalism, 91–92
religious orientation, 35. *See also* ancestral spirits
Rhodes, Cecil, 21, 121
Rhodesian Academy of Music, 105
Rhodesian Bantu Voters' Association, 167
Rhodesian Broadcasting Corporation (RBC), 68, 77, 97–98, 103, 116–17
Rhodesian Front Party, 161
Ribiero, Father Emmanuel, 326
Ritter, Tex, 238, 240
Rodgers, Jimmie, 4, 235–36
Roskilly, Steve, 232
rural/urban dichotomy, 25, 32, 38; and modernism, 24

*sahwira,* definition of, 298, 300
Saidi, William, 136
Sakaza Sisters, 290
Salisbury African Ballroom Dancing Association, 148
Salisbury City Council, 111–12
Salisbury City Youth League, 165, 168, 170, 202
Samhembere, Oliver, 306
Sanders, David, 313
Search Brothers, The, 306
'Second Chimurenga,' 200, 211–12, 217
semiotics, 14, 56–58, 129; and nation-building, 173–74; nonpropositional semiotic potentials, 174–77, 179
*serenda,* definition of, 230
Seton-Watson, Hugh, 13, 167
Shamuyarira, Nathan, 33, 96, 166, 168–73, 185, 202, 219
Shamuyarira, Wilson, 152
*shangara,* 63; description of, 70–71
Shangara Dancers, 178
Shara, Ernest, 322
Shaw, Timothy, 313
Sibanda, George, 236–38

sign, definition of, 56
Silunkika, George, 165
Sillah, Virginia, 252
Simango, Enos, 322, 329
Simon, Paul, 334–35
Simpson, Colin, 171
Sinoia (Chinoyi), Battle of, 187, 191
Sithole, Jonah, 79, 271–72, 277–78,
    300–302, 304, 307, 349–50; and
    compositional process, 301
Sithole, Ndabaningi, 163–67, 169–70,
    180, 197
Small, Christopher, 324
Smith, Anthony, 163–65, 180, 198
Smith, David, 171, 313
Smith, Ian, 21–22, 138, 161, 194, 199
"snowballing" (semantic effect), 175–76
socialism: and nationalist discourse,
    197–98
socialization, 8–9
Sondo, Sonny, 130–31, 134, 138, 144–
    45, 257
soukous, definition of, 245
Soul and Blues Union, 248
Soul Saviour, 306
Southern Rhodesia African National
    Congress, 169
specialist, definition of, 52
specialization, 51–53
spirits. See ancestral spirits
Springfields, The, 251, 255–60, 269,
    277
Stopforth, P., 170
Storm, The, 300
St. Paul's Band, 252–55, 280
studio music, 47–48; definition of, 49
Supiya, Stephen, 177–79
Surf Side Four, The, 252
syncretism, 38–40, 46, 189

Takaingofa, Marko, 230, 238, 241–42
Takawira, Leopold, 165, 169, 211–12
Tangweni, Victor, 350
Taruvinga, Richard, 86
Tazman, Philda, 290
Tendayi, Israel, 236
Timba, Elias, 236
Todd, Garfield, 96
Todhlanga, N., 269

Tom, Ronnie, 255
Tongogara, Josiah, 192
Tracey, Andrew, 74–78
Tracey, Hugh, 73–76, 99–102, 116,
    196, 236
Traditional Madness, 349
traditional/modern dichotomy, 32, 154–
    55, 180
tribal fantasy, definition of, 18
Trio Camp, 306
tsaba-tsaba (tsava-tsava), 140, 142–43
Tshawe, Phinias, 236
Tungamirai, Josiah, 200–201
Tutani, Simangliso, 132
twin paradoxes of nationalism, 15–16,
    198–99, 215–17, 325, 354

Unilateral Declaration of Independence
    (UDI), 21, 138–39
Unity Accord, 15, 22
urban-pop: and middle-class conceptions
    of 'modern' and 'progressive,' 119–
    24

Vadzimba, 349
Vambe, Douglas, 86
Vambe, Lawrence, 28, 29, 66–67, 72–
    74, 111, 140, 142, 146, 202
Verdery, Katherine, 10
village dance groups, formalization of,
    331–32
Vintiware, Ali, 243

Wadharwa, Thomas, 322
Wagon Wheels, The, 295–96
Waterman, Christopher, 68
Waynos B. Zenith Band, 306
Weiss, Ruth, 313, 315–16, 352
Welensky, Roy, 94
Welsh-Asante, Kariamu, 70, 321–26
Weman, Dr. H., 115
West, Michael, 29, 110, 122, 147, 167
White, John, 236
Whitehead, Edgar, 94
Williamson, Eric, 135
Williamson, Leslie, 105, 106, 108–10,
    113, 151, 196

Wonder, Stevie, 323
World Bank, 23, 314
worldbeat, 4, 12, 17, 334–49

Young Zimbabweans, The, 329
youth culture, 246–51, 263; and incor-
    poration of indigenous materials,
    251; and originality, 250–51
Youth Wing, The, 172

*zango,* definition of, 133
Zebrons, The, 252, 253, 254, 255, 258
Zeppelin, Comrade, 204, 205
Zimbabwe African National Liberation
    Army (ZANLA), 21–22, 191, 192–
    93, 199, 202, 204–5, 210, 219; and
    ancestral spirits, 200
Zimbabwe African National Union
    (ZANU), 22, 33, 90, 169, 187,
    192–96, 198–99, 202–3, 205–7,
    210–11, 213, 215, 217–19, 274,
    289, 306–8, 312–13, 315, 323,
    340, 353; Chimurenga songs of,
    191; and modernist idea of cultural
    loss, 197

Zimbabwe African National Union–
    Patriotic Front (ZANU-PF), 14–15,
    21–23, 30, 169, 188, 213, 288,
    311–12, 314
Zimbabwe African People's Union
    (ZAPU), 15, 21–22, 33, 89–90,
    165, 169, 177, 183, 185–87, 189,
    191, 193–97, 203, 205–6, 218,
    322, 324, 340; celebration of found-
    ing, 177–78; rallies, 93, 179
Zimbabwean Clear Sounds, 349
Zimbabwe Ballroom Dancers' Associa-
    tion, 317
Zimbabwe Festival of African Culture,
    180, 186
Zimbabwe Institute, 33
Zimbabwe Music Industry Association,
    317
Zimbabwe People's Revolutionary Army
    (ZIPRA), 22, 204
Zimbabwe Traditional and Cultural
    Club, 180–82, 185
Zimbabwe Union of Musicians, 317
Zimonte, John, 236
Zindi, Fred, 32, 34, 97, 271–74, 336–37
Zvobogo, Edson, 165, 210